Proscription by Degrees

In this book, Kenneth Morgan provides the most comprehensive account of the abolition of the slave trade to the United States since W. E. B. Du Bois's 1896 *The Suppression of the African Slave Trade to the United States of America, 1638–1870*. Utilising a wider range of resources and exploring the economic, social, moral and political considerations, Morgan creates a multi-layered account that explains why abolition was a protracted affair that proceeded by degrees over nearly half a century. He appraises the role of abolitionist individuals, groups and societies in bringing abolition to the forefront of public discussion across North America, and the decisive role of the US Constitution and the Constitutional Convention that eventually led to proscription in 1808, which made abolition constitutionally possible.

Kenneth Morgan is Professor of History at Brunel University of London. He is the author of *Slavery and the British Empire: From Africa to America* and *A Short History of Transatlantic Slavery*.

Proscription by Degrees

The Abolition of the Slave Trade to the United States

KENNETH MORGAN
Brunel University of London

Shaftesbury Road, Cambridge CB2 8EA, United Kingdom

One Liberty Plaza, 20th Floor, New York, NY 10006, USA

477 Williamstown Road, Port Melbourne, VIC 3207, Australia

314–321, 3rd Floor, Plot 3, Splendor Forum, Jasola District Centre,
New Delhi – 110025, India

103 Penang Road, #05-06/07, Visioncrest Commercial, Singapore 238467

Cambridge University Press is part of Cambridge University Press & Assessment,
a department of the University of Cambridge.

We share the University's mission to contribute to society through the pursuit of
education, learning and research at the highest international levels of excellence.

www.cambridge.org
Information on this title: www.cambridge.org/9781009597944
DOI: 10.1017/9781009597913

© Kenneth Morgan 2025

This publication is in copyright. Subject to statutory exception and to the provisions
of relevant collective licensing agreements, no reproduction of any part may take
place without the written permission of Cambridge University Press & Assessment.

When citing this work, please include a reference to the DOI 10.1017/9781009597913

First published 2025

A catalogue record for this publication is available from the British Library

Library of Congress Cataloging-in-Publication Data
NAMES: Morgan, Kenneth, 1953- author.
TITLE: Proscription by degrees : the abolition of the slave trade to the United States /
Kenneth Morgan.
DESCRIPTION: Cambridge ; New York, NY : Cambridge University Press, 2025. |
Includes bibliographical references and index.
IDENTIFIERS: LCCN 2024061436 (print) | LCCN 2024061437 (ebook) |
ISBN 9781009597944 (hardback) | ISBN 9781009597920 (paperback) |
ISBN 9781009597913 (epub)
SUBJECTS: LCSH: Slave trade–United States–History. | Slavery–United States–History. |
Antislavery movements–United States–History. | United States–Race relations–History.
CLASSIFICATION: LCC E441 .J763 2025 (print) | LCC E441 (ebook) | DDC 381/.440973–dc23/
eng/20250220
LC record available at https://lccn.loc.gov/2024061436
LC ebook record available at https://lccn.loc.gov/2024061437

ISBN 978-1-009-59794-4 Hardback
ISBN 978-1-009-59792-0 Paperback

Cambridge University Press & Assessment has no responsibility for the persistence
or accuracy of URLs for external or third-party internet websites referred to in this
publication and does not guarantee that any content on such websites is, or will
remain, accurate or appropriate.

For EU product safety concerns, contact us at Calle de José Abascal, 56, 1°, 28003
Madrid, Spain, or email eugpsr@cambridge.org.

To the memory of three friends:
Richard S. Dunn, Duncan J. MacLeod, Trevor Burnard
Historians of slavery and abolition

Contents

List of Tables		*page* ix
Preface		xi
List of Abbreviations		xv
	Introduction	1
1	Colonial Restrictions on the Slave Trade, 1700–1774	14
2	The Slave Trade and Revolutionary North America, 1774–1787	51
3	The US Constitution, the Debates over Ratification and the Slave Trade, 1787–1788	92
4	Opposition to the Slave Trade in the Early National Period, 1789–1802	136
5	Final Controversies over the US Slave Trade, 1803–1807	189
	Epilogue	227
Bibliography		239
Index		273

Tables

1.1	Duties on slave imports to Pennsylvania, 1700–1773	*page* 30
1.2	Duties on slave imports to Maryland, 1695–1771	33
1.3	Duties on slave imports to Virginia, 1699–1776	37
1.4	Duties on slave imports to South Carolina, 1703–1764	45

Preface

This book arises out of a long research and teaching commitment to slavery, the slave trade and abolition in the Atlantic world. Its seed corn lay in an invitation to prepare an address for a conference of the College of Charleston's Carolina Lowcountry and Atlantic World programme to commemorate the bicentenary of the abolition of the slave trade to the United States in 2008. That paper was published as 'Proscription by Degrees: The Ending of the African Slave Trade to the United States' in David. T. Gleeson and Simon Lewis, eds., *Ambiguous Anniversary: The Bicentennial of the International Slave Trade Bans* (University of South Carolina Press, 2012). When preparing that chapter, I soon became aware that a vast amount of primary research material has survived on the topic and that this had never been thoroughly researched and interpreted. This book is an attempt to rectify that omission by analysing the abolition of the slave trade to the United States as an incremental process that largely proceeded step by step on an individual colony or state basis before a Constitutional clause enabled it to be dismantled throughout the American nation.

The only book-length study of my topic is W. E. B. Du Bois's *The Suppression of the African Slave Trade to the United States of America, 1638–1870* (1896). Though it is still cited, it is clearly out of date and needs to be replaced with a modern, comprehensive study. Many historians have devoted scholarly articles and book chapters on specific episodes relating to the abolition of the slave trade to the United States, and the study of Quaker involvement in the eighteenth-century antislavery movement has attracted insightful biographies and thematic accounts in recent years. But no one has produced an overarching history of the proscription of the African slave to the United States by drawing upon legislative debates, the texts of relevant laws in individual colonies and states, the personal papers of politicians and extensive newspaper coverage. My study draws upon these and other sources and contextualises them in relation to a large secondary literature to provide a chronological and thematic analysis of the topic under consideration.

My research for this project was immeasurably helped by the award of three fellowships (in 2010, 2012 and 2022) at the Robert H. Smith Center for International Jefferson Studies at Monticello and the University of Virginia. I owe thanks to Andrew Jackson O'Shaughnessy who oversaw these visiting appointments while he was the Saunders Director of the Center. While based in Charlottesville, working on the project, I was considerably aided by access to the facilities of the Jefferson Library at the Center and by the impressively large scholarly resources of the Alderman Library at the University of Virginia. In addition to the libraries and archives listed in my bibliography, I also undertook research on this book at the British Library and Cambridge University Library. Brunel University of London librarians helped me to order some obscure printed items through inter-library loan. I would like to thank the staff at the various libraries and archives I visited to carry out research for this book, especially the staff at the South Caroliniana Library for pulling out the stops to assist me when I was on a tight schedule to complete my work there. The availability of high-quality scholarly editions of many presidential and constitutional materials was a boon to the research as were the ready supply of printed materials in the Internet Archive and on online platforms.

Sean M. Kelley offered a constructive critique of my draft manuscript from an expert perspective as he had just published the most detailed monograph on slave trading merchants operating out of US ports. He also guided me carefully through some knotty problems that arose from data in the Transatlantic Slave Trade Database (www.slavevoyages.org). Nicholas P. Wood aided me in the early stages of the project by providing some helpful references.

Three deceased historians also influenced my thinking on the abolition of the US slave trade. One was Duncan J. MacLeod of St Catharine's College, Oxford, who, long ago when I was a fledging graduate student at New College, Oxford, introduced me to the political history of the American Revolution and early Republic. Duncan, a scholar of slavery, race and the American Revolution, encouraged my studies in my early academic career. Another was Richard S. Dunn, who published extensively on transatlantic slavery and abolitionism. Richard was my mentor when I held a Fulbright-Hays scholarship at the University of Pennsylvania in the late 1970s. He was instrumental in setting up my fellowship at the McNeil Center for Early American Studies in Philadelphia in its initial year, and took a continuing and cordial interest in my subsequent career. The third was Trevor Burnard, a friend and former colleague who passed away recently while still in post as Wilberforce Professor of Slavery and Emancipation at the University of Hull. Trevor commented in detail on this manuscript and gave me sterling support on this and other academic projects. A version of Chapter 3 was previously published as 'Slavery and the Debate over Ratification of the United States Constitution', *Slavery & Abolition*, 22/3 (2001):40–65.

Abbreviations

CO	Colonial Office
Donnan, ed., *Documents*	Elizabeth Donnan, ed., *Documents Illustrative of the History of the Slave Trade to America*, 4 vols. (Washington, DC: Carnegie Institution of Washington, 1930–5)
HS	Historical Society
HSP	Historical Society of Pennsylvania
JecH	*Journal of Economic History*
JSH	*Journal of Southern History*
LCP	Library Company of Philadelphia
NYPL	New York Public Library
PMHB	*Pennsylvania Magazine of History and Biography*
RIHS	Rhode Island Historical Society, Providence
SCDAH	South Carolina Department of Archives and History, Columbia
SCHM	*South Carolina Historical Magazine*
SCL	South Caroliniana Library, Columbia
TNA	The National Archives, Kew
VMHB	*Virginia Magazine of History and Biography*
WMQ	*William and Mary Quarterly*, 3rd series

Introduction

Over the course of the eighteenth and nineteenth centuries, the transatlantic slave trade delivered millions of Africans to American markets but also encountered serious attempts to dismantle what contemporaries called the 'Guinea traffic', all of which were eventually successful. One by one, different nations – Britain, Denmark, the United States, Spain, Portugal, France, the Netherlands, Brazil – abolished their slave trades for various reasons. The demolition of the slave trade mainly occurred in the first half of the nineteenth century by the same governments who had created it.[1] Moral and humanitarian criticism of what has been described as 'the cruellest commerce' was one significant component in the motivation to eradicate the slave trade.[2] But there were always other factors lying behind anti-slave trade sentiment, including economics, political decisions and pragmatic considerations, all of which combined with humanitarian abolitionism, in varying proportions in different countries, to bring about slave trade abolition. Thus one major theme in analysing the ending of various slave trades is the variety of methods deployed in each nation, none of which directly duplicated one another and not all of which were based on sustained humanitarian campaigning.[3] Another major theme in the history of slave trade abolition was that in most cases – Denmark being an exception, as it was ended by royal decree – a long

---

[1] Christopher Leslie Brown, 'Abolition of the Atlantic Slave Trade' in Gad Heuman and Trevor Burnard, eds., *The Routledge History of Slavery* (Abingdon, 2011), 281.
[2] Colin A. Palmer, Maggie Steber and Jerry Pinkney, 'The Cruelest Commerce: African Slave Trade', *National Geographic*, 182/3 (1992), 62–91.
[3] For the interplay of various factors in abolishing different slave trades, see Kenneth Morgan, *A Short History of Transatlantic Slavery* (London, 2016), 115–39.

period of years was necessary to generate favourable political conditions under which abolition could proceed. Proscribing the transatlantic slave trade in any country was never an easy matter: Too many vested interests were at stake and too many arguments and counter-arguments were put forward in discussions and debates on the topic for abolition of the slave trade to proceed rapidly.

This book takes account of these broad themes to investigate the abolition of the transatlantic slave trade in one country, the United States, which was a significant recipient of slaves for over a century and a half, first as a set of British colonies and later as an independent nation. The United States ended slave importation by congressional action in a law that came into effect on 1 January 1808. The passage to this outcome was a long and somewhat erratic affair, with plenty of individual colony and state proscriptions preceding it over several decades. The entire process has only attracted one monograph, written well over a century ago by a celebrated author. The author and the book in question is W.E. B. Du Bois's *The Suppression of the African Slave-Trade to the United States of America, 1638–1870*, published as the first volume in the Harvard Historical Studies in 1896. This was a revision of a Harvard University PhD dissertation, awarded the year before – the first North American doctorate on the slave trade.[4] Drawing upon records such as colonial, state and national statutes, congressional documents, reports of abolition societies and personal narratives, Du Bois divided his book into seven chapters dealing with restrictions on slave imports to the British North American colonies and the United States before 1808 and four chapters examining the international slave trade in relation to the United States between 1808 and 1870. The book is mainly a factual narrative, and it is still cited today by scholars as I do myself in the pages here.

Since Du Bois published his pioneering book, many new sources have become available to historians on the abolition of the slave trade to the United States. Numerous scholars have used some of these materials to publish their findings on one or another aspect of the subject, but there has been no monograph on proscribing slave imports into the United States, and its colonial antecedents, since Du Bois wrote on the topic. This book is an attempt to provide such a fully comprehensive study, which is based on sources used by Du Bois but which ranges much more widely to cover important material, in both printed and manuscript form, that was

---

[4] Stephen D. Behrendt, 'The Transatlantic Slave Trade' in Robert L. Paquette and Mark M. Smith, eds., *The Oxford Handbook of Slavery in the Americas* (New York, 2010), 255.

unavailable to him. Thus, my study includes material drawn from the personal papers of Americans who played an instrumental role in the moves towards abolition of slave importations; the proceedings of various legislative bodies; petitions and memorials; extensive newspaper coverage; and the material left in abolitionist archives. These primary sources enrich the study of the subject and enable a historian to explore it in more depth than Du Bois was able to do with the materials at his disposal. My time frame, however, differs from that of Du Bois. As mentioned here, he covered material dealing with more than two centuries between 1638 and 1870. My study, by contrast, confines itself to the period from c.1700 to the congressional edict abolishing the slave trade into the United States in 1808. Most of the evidence falls within the period from c.1750 to 1808, when the subject of slave trade abolition was regularly discussed in North America. For the period thereafter, Leonardo Marques's *The United States and the Transatlantic Slave Trade to the Americas, 1776–1867* (2016) has already analysed the relevant material in detail.[5]

The online Trans-Atlantic Slave Trade Database, which is now the standard accepted source on quantitative data dealing with the subject, records 389,000 Africans arriving in North America.[6] The great majority of these captives disembarked directly from Africa rather than from the Caribbean.[7] Most of these slaves ended up as plantation workers cultivating staple crops in colonies and states from Maryland southwards, though some enslaved people were also imported in the northern colonies. The numerical and regional distribution of slave arrivals in North

---

[5] See also Don E. Fehrenbacher with Ward M. McAfee, *The Slaveholding Republic: The United States Government's Relations to Slavery* (New York, 2001) and Ernest Obadele-Starks, *Freebooters and Smugglers: The Foreign Slave Trade to the United States after 1808* (Fayetteville, AR, 2007).

[6] www.slavevoyages.org. The main contributors to this impressive database, currently hosted by Rice University, are David Eltis, Stephen D. Behrendt, David Richardson and Manolo Garcia Florentino. See also David Eltis, 'The U.S. Transatlantic Slave Trade, 1644–1867: An Assessment', *Civil War History*, LIV/4 (2008), 350, and David Eltis and David Richardson, 'A New Assessment of the Transatlantic Slave Trade' in David Eltis and David Richardson, eds., *Extending the Frontiers: Essays on the New Transatlantic Slave Trade Database* (New Haven, CT, 2008), 48. For a brief description of the Trans-Atlantic Slave Trade Database and other databases dealing with the delivery of Africans to North America, see David Hackett Fischer, *African Founders: How Enslaved People expanded American Ideals* (New York, 2022), 4–7.

[7] Data to support this generalisation are included throughout Gregory E. O'Malley, *Final Passages: The Inter-Colonial Slave Trade of British America, 1619–1807* (Chapel Hill, NC, 2014).

America varied over time. Some 72 per cent of the influx of Africans to North America came before 1776. All the imported Africans to the Chesapeake (or Upper South) had arrived by then along with 98 per cent of the slaves taken by the northern colonies. The Lower South (mainly South Carolina and Georgia) was the region that took the highest number of captives. Thus 55 per cent of the Africans coming to the British North American colonies entered via Charleston, South Carolina and (to a much lesser extent) Savannah, Georgia. Another third came to the Chesapeake, primarily to the five river systems of Virginia rather than Maryland. Before 1776, the great majority of slaves were carried by British ships leaving the ports of London, Bristol and Liverpool.[8]

Slave imports to North America, as the above paragraph suggests, were heavily concentrated in the Chesapeake and South Carolina. Between 1701 and 1807, South Carolina and Georgia (mostly Charleston) accounted for 209,430 slave disembarkations, the Chesapeake (mostly Virginia) 115,480, the northern states 24,128, and the Gulf states (mostly New Orleans) 16,130. In the narrower period of 1781–1810 South Carolina imported 56,270 imputed slaves, of which 47,404 arrived between 1801 and 1810. These figures are for direct arrivals from Africa. In addition, Africans were taken to North America in an intra-American slave trade after they had been first landed in the Caribbean. The numbers in this branch of the slave trade were much smaller. Between 1701 and 1825 in the intra-American slave trade, 38,171 imputed slaves disembarked in North America, including 18,506 in South Carolina.[9]

During the American revolutionary war, North American slave imports fell markedly, but they revived after the peace treaty of 1783. US merchants now assumed greater importance in the slave trade. Most of them were based in Newport, Rhode Island, New York, Boston and Charleston.[10] They took slaves to different Caribbean islands as well as importing them to the North American mainland. After 1776, US merchants brought in 61 per cent of all slave arrivals coming directly from Africa whereas the share had been only 8 per cent before 1776.

---

[8] Data in this paragraph are taken from www.slavevoyages.org. Throughout the book I have used imputed data from this database: these are projected figures that take account of gaps in the data on individual voyages.
[9] Calculated from www.slave.voyages.org.
[10] Information on these merchants and their activities is found throughout Sean M. Kelley, *American Slavers: Merchants, Mariners, and the Transatlantic Commerce in Captives, 1644–1865* (New Haven, CT, 2023).

Interestingly, this demonstrates a large increase in the North American participation in the slave trade at a time when the colonies were declaring independence from Britain and trumpeting the values of liberty and equality. Only in the final phase of the slave trade to the United States, when South Carolina reopened the traffic between 1803 and 1807, did British firms recapture a portion of their former market share.[11]

Captives brought to the North American colonies and the United States came from seven major regions in West Africa strung along about 2,000 miles of coast – Senegambia, Sierra Leone, the Windward Coast, the Gold Coast, the Bight of Benin, the Bight of Biafra and West-Central

[11] All these proportions are based on data in www.slavevoyages.org summarised in Eltis, 'The U.S. Transatlantic Slave Trade', 356–60, 365–6. For an earlier examination of the slave trade to the North American colonies, see Steven Deyle, '"By Farr the Most Profitable Trade": Slave Trading in British Colonial North America', *Slavery & Abolition*, 10/2 (1989), 107–25. A long bibliography of studies exists for the slave trade into individual North American colonies, including Jeanne Chase, 'New York Slave Trade, 1698–1741', *Histoire & Mesure*, 18/1–2 (2003), 95–112; Darold D. Wax, 'Black Immigrants: The Slave Trade in Colonial Maryland', *Maryland Historical Magazine*, 73/1 (1978), 3–45; Susan Alice Westbury, 'Colonial Virginia and the Atlantic Slave Trade' (University of Illinois, Urbana-Champaign, PhD dissertation, 1981); Susan Westbury, 'The Slaves of Colonial Virginia: Where They Came from', *WMQ*, 3rd series, 42/2 (1985), 228–37; Douglas B. Chambers, 'The Transatlantic Slave Trade to Virginia in Comparative Historical Perspective, 1698-1778' in John Saillant, ed., *Afro-Virginian History and Culture* (New York, 1999), 3–28; Lorena S. Walsh, 'The Chesapeake Slave Trade: Regional Patterns, African Origins, and Some Implications', *WMQ*, 3rd series, 58/1 (2001), 139–70; Darold D. Wax, '"New Negroes Are Always in Demand": The Slave Trade in Eighteenth-Century Georgia', *Georgia Historical Quarterly*, 68/2 (1984), 193–220; Daniel C. Littlefield, *Rice and Slaves: Ethnicity and the Slave Trade in Colonial South Carolina* (Baton Rouge, LA, 1981); Daniel C. Littlefield, 'Charleston and Internal Slave Redistribution', *SCHM*, 87/2 (1986), 93–105; Daniel C. Littlefield, 'The Slave Trade to Colonial South Carolina: A Profile', *SCHM*, 91/2 (1990), 68–99; David Richardson, 'The British Slave Trade to Colonial South Carolina', *Slavery & Abolition*, 12/3 (1991), 125–72; W. Robert Higgins, 'Charleston: Terminus and Entrepôt of the Colonial Slave Trade' in Martin L. Kilson and Robert I. Rotberg, eds., *The African Diaspora: Interpretive Essays* (Cambridge, MA, 1976); W. Robert Higgins, 'Charlestown Merchants and Factors Dealing in the External Negro Trade, 1735–1775', *SCHM*, 65/4 (1964), 205–17; Philip D. Morgan, *Slave Counterpoint: Black Culture in the Eighteenth-Century Chesapeake and Lowcountry* (Chapel Hill, NC, 1998), 58–79; and Gregory E. O'Malley, 'Slavery's Converging Ground: Charleston's Slave Trade as the Black Heart of the Lowcountry', *WMQ*, 3rd series, 74/2 (2017), 271–302. For the US slave trade after 1776, see Leonardo Marques, *The United States and the Transatlantic Slave Trade to the Americas, 1776–1867* (New Haven, CT, 2016). North America's participation in the slave trade is fully discussed in Kelley, *American Slavers*. See also Melissa A. Maestri, 'The Atlantic Web of Bondage: Comparing the Slave Trades of New York City and Charleston, South Carolina' (University of Delaware PhD dissertation, 2015). Slaves were also imported into North America from the Caribbean but in far smaller numbers than those arriving directly from Africa: see O'Malley, *Final Passages*.

Africa. Every major North American region imported slaves from diverse west African areas.[12] Some regions were preferred more than others in supplying slaves for the North American market. The most favoured region was Upper Guinea (comprising Senegambia, Sierra Leone and the Windward Coast), which provided 40 per cent of the arrivals in North America. This was significantly higher than the 10 per cent of captives taken from Upper Guinea in the entire transatlantic slave trade to all destinations. By contrast, very few slaves arrived in North America from the Bight of Benin compared with its contribution to the transatlantic slave trade as a whole. Different regions of North America had different levels of connections with specific African regions. Thus, colonies and states north of the Chesapeake took one third of their slaves from Upper Guinea whereas 35 per cent of the captives entering Virginia and Maryland emanated from the Bight of Biafra.[13]

The North American regional distribution of newly imported slaves changed over time. The northern colonies were never major importers of Africans because they lacked plantations and their associated staple crops that accounted for most slave labour. However, slaves were imported on a modest scale north of Maryland and utilised in small groups at ironworks, on farms and as domestic servants.[14] Within the northern colonies, New England imported far fewer slaves than the middle colonies. The delivery of saltwater Africans to New England comprised 9.3 slaves per 1,000 residents in the period 1700–20 but minus 6.5 slaves per 1,000 residents by 1760–80.[15] In the middle colonies, the ratios were 66.7 slaves per 1,000 residents between 1700 and 1720 but only 1.6 slaves per 1,000 residents between 1760 and 1780.[16] Philadelphia and New York merchants were mainly responsible for this branch of slave importation.[17]

---

[12] Fischer, *African Founders*, 11.
[13] Eltis, 'The U.S. Transatlantic Slave Trade', 357–8. For further breakdown of the African coastal origins of Virginia and South Carolina Africans, 1710s–1770s, see Morgan, *Slave Counterpoint*, 63.
[14] Ira Berlin, *Many Thousands Gone: The First Two Centuries of Slavery in North America* (Cambridge, MA, 1998), 109–94.
[15] 'Saltwater' is a term used by historians to denote Africans sold or forced into the transatlantic slave trade.
[16] Duncan J. MacLeod, 'Toward Caste' in Ira Berlin and Ronald Hoffman, eds., *Slavery and Freedom in the Age of the American Revolution* (Charlottesville, VA, 1983), 218.
[17] See three articles by Darold D. Wax: 'Quaker Merchants and the Slave Trade in Colonial Pennsylvania', *PMHB*, 86/2 (1962), 143–59; 'Negro Imports into Pennsylvania, 1720–1766', *Pennsylvania History*, 32/3 (1965), 254–87; and 'Africans on the Delaware: The Pennsylvania Slave Trade, 1759–1765', *Pennsylvania History*, 50/1

Slave deliveries to the middle and northern states never recovered from the low levels of the American revolutionary war era, and were virtually non-existent after 1780.[18]

Throughout the southern colonies and states, slavery was essential to operate plantations producing staple crops and the slave trade was a much more important phenomenon than in the northern colonies and states. Slave imports south of Pennsylvania were closely tied to export earnings from staple crops. Virginia was an early importer of significant numbers of slaves for its tobacco plantations. In the mid-1730s, the Virginian planter William Byrd thought the influx of Africans was extensive enough to instil the notion that 'this Colony will some time or other be confirmed by the name of New Guinea'.[19] This never occurred, however, because Virginia's slave trade levelled off in the 1730s when a transition from a naturally declining to an increasing slave population began in that region. The slave trade to Virginia then started to decline from about 1740 onwards, with sufficient native-born fertile women sustaining natural increase in the colony's black population. Maryland had less tobacco-growing acreage and less piedmont or backcountry land suitable for tobacco growing than Virginia. Accordingly, its demand for African labour was lower than in the Old Dominion. The transition from tobacco to grain in the Chesapeake economy by the time of the American revolutionary war reduced demand for slaves as work outside the tobacco sector could be undertaken by white men and women.[20] As a result of these factors, an importation of 170.6 slaves per 1,000 of population in the Upper South between 1740 and 1760 declined to 72.2 per 1,000 in the subsequent twenty years.[21]

By contrast, in South Carolina, which had a plantation system mainly comprising rice growing in swampy coastal areas along with indigo cultivation from the 1740s, the unbalanced sex ratio of African imports, much favouring men over women, along with diseases found in

---

(1983), 38–49; and James G. Lydon, 'New York and the Slave Trade, 1700–1774', *WMQ*, 3rd series, 35/2 (1978), 375–94.

[18] Fewer than 400 Africans were imported to states north of the Mason-Dixon line after 1776. See the data in www.slavevoyages.org.

[19] Col. William Byrd to the Earl of Egmont, 12 July 1736, in Donnan, ed., *Documents*, IV, 131.

[20] Allan Kulikoff, 'A "Prolifick" People: Black Population Growth in the Chesapeake Colonies, 1700-1790', *Southern Studies*, 16 (1977), 391-428; Ibid, *Tobacco and Slaves: The Development of Southern Cultures in the Chesapeake, 1680–1800* (Chapel Hill, NC, 1986), 5–6, 64, 71.

[21] MacLeod, 'Toward Caste', 218.

lowcountry areas, hard physical labour and heavy mortality, meant that the slave population decreased naturally before 1750. In the generation before 1776, South Carolina's slave population and reproductive levels remained low, even when a surplus of births over deaths was achieved. These demographic problems meant that the delivery of slaves to South Carolina was a thriving affair for most of the half century leading up to the American Revolution. The numbers dipped in the 1740s after increased import duties were introduced to stem the fear of slave revolt after the Stono rebellion of 1739 – the most significant slave uprising in North America before the War of Independence – but the flow of slaves increased in the late 1740s. Charleston, in the mid-eighteenth century, became the focal point of entry for Africans entering the Lower South region.[22]

A further fall in slave imports came with the non-importation regulations of the late 1760s, implemented as a counterblast to British commercial policies towards the North American colonies. Despite these fluctuations, South Carolina easily imported more Africans than its neighbours to the north and south, North Carolina and Georgia.[23] South Carolina's planters became the most wealthy occupational group in North America in the late colonial period when the 'opulence' of the Palmetto colony was noted.[24] Between 1740 and 1760, the Lower South had 263.7 slave importations per 1,000 residents; this fell to 178.5 per 1,000 over the next twenty years.[25] The revival of rice cultivation after the end of the American revolutionary war and the rapid emergence of long staple cotton production from the early 1790s boosted the demand for slave labour in the Lower South. Not all of this could be met by natural increase, and consequently, as Ira Berlin noted, 'African slave traders found a welcome reception in Charleston and Savannah'.[26]

North American slave traders were also active in the slave trade. Their significance in the Guinea traffic increased during the eighteenth century.

---

[22] Charleston as a slave trading port has attracted many studies. The main publications are listed in n. 11 here.
[23] Richardson, 'The British Slave Trade to Colonial South Carolina'; Daniel C. Littlefield, 'The Slave Trade to Colonial South Carolina: A Profile' *SCHM*, 91/2 (1990), 68–99; Russell R. Menard, 'Slave Demography in the Lowcountry, 1670–1740: From Frontier Society to Plantation Regime', *SCHM*, 101/3 (2000), 190–213; Morgan, *Slave Counterpoint*, 59–62, 79–95.
[24] David Ramsay, *The History of South Carolina, from its First Settlement in 1670 to the Year 1808*, (Charleston, SC, 1858), 123.
[25] MacLeod, 'Toward Caste', 218.   [26] Berlin, *Many Thousands Gone*, 308.

The slaves carried by vessels leaving North American ports increased from 10,000 in the early 1740s to 30,000 in the mid-1760s.[27] There was then a precipitous fall over the next fifteen years, but the number rose again from 9,000 in the early 1780s to 55,000 by 1808, when the US slave trade was abolished. In the last four-year period of the trade, between 1804 and 1808, the number of Africans taken by slave ships setting out from US ports reached a peak and there are no signs that it would have diminished suddenly if abolition had not occurred.[28] Many North American merchants found a niche market to trade rum from New England distilleries for slaves in the Gambia, the Sierra Leone estuary and along the Gold Coast.[29] By 1776–1800 over three-quarters of the captives taken on voyages starting from US ports came from Sierra Leone and the Gold Coast. Between 1800 and 1810 Senegambia, Sierra Leone, the Gold Coast and West Central Africa provided three-quarters of the slaves taken in such ships.[30]

US slave ships took the majority of their slave cargoes to the Caribbean and Spanish America rather than to mainland North America. Apart from slaves delivered to the United States, notably South Carolina, most captives were delivered to non-Anglophone destinations such as the Dutch Americas, the Danish West Indies, Cuba, Puerto Rico and the Rio de la Plata rather than to the British Caribbean. A final dimension of the slave trade involving the United States occurred between 1821 and 1867 when 85,114 slaves arrived in the Americas using the US flag as a symbol of convenience for at least part of their voyage. A caveat is in order, however, because most of the vessels in these voyages were not American owned.[31]

Several themes run throughout the book. First, attention is paid to the role of abolitionism in securing the various state proscriptions of the slave trade and the eventual congressional prohibition of the trade in 1808. Abolitionist writings, speeches and networks are considered in each

---

[27] www.slavevoyages.org. For statistics on ships leaving Boston and Newport on slaving voyages between 1753 and 1774, see David Richardson, 'Slavery, Trade, and Economic Growth in Eighteenth-Century New England' in Barbara L. Solow, ed., *Slavery and the Rise of the Atlantic System* (Cambridge, 1991), 254.

[28] For estimates per decade of slaves carried by ships from the North American colonies and the United States, see Eltis and Richardson, 'A New Assessment of the Transatlantic Slave Trade', 32–3.

[29] For a demand-side explanation of this commerce, see Sean M. Kelley, 'American Rum, African Consumers, and the Transatlantic Slave Trade', *African Economic History*, 46/2 (2018), 1–29.

[30] Eltis, 'The U.S. Transatlantic Slave Trade', 363–8. [31] Ibid., 370–1.

chapter. Their contribution to the ending of the slave trade is weighed up against economic, pragmatic and political decision-making. The extent to which abolitionists established viable networks to influence state legislatures and the federal government is also evaluated. Second, the role of South Carolina as the colony and state most resistant to supporting measures to proscribe the slave trade is explained in relation to the political decisions made by its colonial and state legislatures and the attitudes and interventions of its delegates to Congress from 1789 onwards. South Carolina's economy was dominated by slave-produced rice production and exports and its society was based on an uncomfortable dichotomy between a wealthy planter elite that held political control and thousands of slaves with no political rights, who formed a black majority in the colony and state. These factors made it difficult for abolitionist ideas to make an impact in South Carolina, for planters' livelihoods were centred on slave labour.

A third theme in the book is to show that various mechanisms were followed by different colonies and states to end the slave trade: there was no single route to abolition. In some cases, a law was passed; in others, the abolition of the slave trade was written into state constitutions. In still other cases, laws were passed dealing with gradual slave emancipation and it was implied that a legal ending to slavery would also include prohibiting the slave trade. These different ways of handling the slave trade at state level will be explained. A fourth theme comprises the complex role of the new Federal Congress in relation to slave trade abolition after it began proceedings in 1789. Restrained from acting over the slave trade before 1808 by a clause in the US Constitution, Congress nevertheless played an important role in discussing the slave trade and limiting the despatch of US slave trading ships to foreign ports. Under Thomas Jefferson's presidency (1801–9), Congress came to the fore in debates over the slave trade as the date when it could act on this subject began to approach. The congressional vote in 1807 in favour of closing the slave trade was vital for proscription of the Guinea traffic to take place.

The book is divided into five chapters. Each covers a chronological period of varying extent, but the issues dealt with are thematically analysed or presented as part of a multi-layered narrative. The structure allows for the abolition of the slave trade to the United States to be covered as a sequence of actions and decisions over time, thereby facilitating the process as a matter of proscription by degrees on a step-by-step basis. Thus, the structure and content of the chapters reflect the incremental stages through which ending the slave trade was achieved. In each period covered by the chapters, many ideas and attitudes expressed on the slave trade were replicated but with significant alterations as unexpected events and changes in political institutions affected consideration of the subject. New scrutiny was also added to the evaluation of the operation of the slave trade over time. The book analyses why it was not until 1808 that a federal proscription of slave imports into the United States could occur but also why the ban on the US slave trade was then ushered in quickly, almost in one fell swoop.

The first two chapters analyse restrictions of the slave trade before the Constitutional Convention of 1787 and also the actions that were set aside or blocked by legislatures and British institutions. Chapter 1 shows that it was common for individual colonies to restrict the level of slave imports by raising import duties on slaves – effectively local taxes – from the first decade of the eighteenth century through to the imperial crisis of the mid-1770s. Some colonies, such as Virginia and South Carolina, were particularly active in raising such duties but many other British North American colonies also did so. The monies raised were used for various purposes ranging from improvements to infrastructure to support for white immigration. But the British Crown, Privy Council and Board of Trade had the constitutional right to veto laws dealing with import duties on slaves, and they frequently exercised this prerogative.

Chapter 2 shows that there was considerable progress achieved in banning the slave trade to some states between the introduction of the Coercive Acts in 1774 – four laws intended to punish Massachusetts for the Boston Tea Party – and the convening of the Constitutional Convention. Virginia, Maryland, Pennsylvania and Massachusetts all prohibited slave imports within a few years of one another in this period. Attempts were made to proscribe slave imports to North America under the two Continental Congresses, but these lacked the political authority to enforce this measure. The same was true of the Confederation governments. Quakers were among the anti-slave trade groups raising concerns about the immorality of the slave trade in the 1770s and 1780s, but they had insufficient influence across the new American nation to secure their goals. South Carolina's legislature was involved in continuing debates and disagreements over the slave trade between 1783 and 1787, and it became crystal clear that the Palmetto state's politicians were unwilling to surrender their political control over decisions about whether to open and close Charleston as the main receiving port for enslaved Africans in the state.

Chapter 3 focuses closely on the years 1787–8 when the subject of the slave trade became a matter of discussion and debate at the Constitutional Convention in Philadelphia and during the ratification process in a number of states. The chapter considers the diverse views about the slave trade expressed in these forums and why the subject was so acrimonious. Consideration of the slave trade raised fundamental issues about regional differences between the northern and southern states, the allocation of political responsibility for this matter between the new federal government and the states, the weighing up of economic versus moral aspects of the topic, and the relationship of slavery and the slave trade to the political trajectory of the new nation. In the end, the political debates of 1787–8 incorporated the slave trade as a potential issue to be decided by Congress at federal level. At the time, of course, no federal authority existed to deal with this matter. A clause was inserted in the Constitution (Article 1, Section 9) that expressly forbade any congressional action over the slave trade for twenty-one years, backed up by another section (Article 5) that disallowed any repeal of that clause. The Constitutional Convention and the state ratification debates were the first time that the slave trade had been debated by political delegates from most of the states – first behind closed doors during the Convention and then in public as part of the ratification process. The detailed opposing views expressed indicated that the matter of what to do about the slave trade still needed many further debates before it was settled.

Chapter 4 examines the early years of federal government in the United States from the convening of the First Federal Congress in 1789 until Jefferson's Louisiana Purchase in 1803 persuaded South Carolina to reopen its slave trade to supply additional slaves to western territories. The initial focus on the slave trade in this period witnessed the presentation of several Quaker petitions to Congress on the subject and the ensuing debates over the slave trade in the House of Representatives. These were divisive discussions, with the Lower South representatives standing firmly behind the constitutional protection for the slave trade until 1808. The leading American statesman James Madison, in particular, wanted to avoid controversy over the slave trade just when Congress was finding its feet on important national political issues. The decision to place those petitions on the table of the House meant that their contents were acknowledged but they were not taken up further at this juncture. Abolitionists turned, from 1791 onwards, first to pressing for more regulation of the participation of US citizens in the foreign slave trade, and also for organising abolition societies in different North American cities under the leadership of the Pennsylvania Society for the Abolition of Slavery. Two congressional acts, in 1794 and 1800, tightened regulations about the participation of US citizens in the slave trade, bringing in penalties for those flouting the new rules; but difficulties occurred in enforcing these laws. South Carolina, the state objecting most to any national proscription of the slave trade, continued laws to keep its own slave trade closed throughout the whole period between 1789 and 1803. It was able to do so because of constitutional protection but the decision for repeated closures was not unanimously supported at state level.

The final phase of the struggle to proscribe the US slave trade is covered in Chapter 5, which concentrates on the complicated means through which South Carolina reopened its slave trade and the action taken by Congress to prohibit the slave trade at national level at the first available opportunity. South Carolina's state politicians were divided about whether to reopen the slave trade to the state in 1803 but they did so, after some narrow votes in the state legislature, to take advantage of sending new enslaved Africans to the territories carved out of the Louisiana Purchase. Annual debates in South Carolina in 1804, 1805 and 1806, with slim majorities for maintaining an open slave trade, reflected opposing views on the course of action to proceed. At the federal level, Thomas Jefferson's presidential message of December 1806, exhorting Congress to proscribe the slave trade at the earliest opportunity was heeded and both houses of Congress prepared legislation to this effect in 1807. In the debates over the proposed laws, much more attention was paid to the mechanics of the legislation and to the penalties for breaking the law than to the morality of the slave trade. From 1 January 1808, slave importations to the United States were forbidden by law in the first important congressional intervention over anything connected to slavery in the nineteenth century. This was possible because the slave trade had been cordoned off from slavery in the Constitution, which meant that it could be prohibited without any tampering with slavery itself. This was a necessity in 1808, when there was no prospect of slave emancipation happening either soon or at all.

I

Colonial Restrictions on the Slave Trade, 1700–1774

Before the thirteen North American colonies first came together in 1774 to challenge Britain over taxation, representation and their membership of the British Empire, individual colonies handled slave importation: no coordination between them existed. The delivery of Africans to the mainland colonies expanded significantly in the period 1700–75. Estimated totals of Africans arriving on the North American mainland rose from 9,800 in 1676–1700 to 37,400 in 1701–25 to 96,800 in 1726–50 and to 116,900 in 1751–75.[1] The southern colonies, which had plantation economies based on slave labour, imported far more Africans than the northern colonies, where smaller numbers of slaves were required for non-plantation work. The racial composition of different regions reflected this difference. Thus, the white population of New England was 90,700 in 1700 and 665,700 in 1770 whereas black people totalled 1,700 in 1700 and 15,400 in 1770. In the middle colonies, the total number of white people was 49,900 in 1700 and 521,000 in 1770: the black population amounted to 3,700 in 1700 and 34,900 in 1770. The total number of white people in the Chesapeake colonies was 85,200 in 1700 and 398,200 in 1770, while the black population totalled 12,900 in 1700 and 251,400 in 1770. There were 13,600 white people in the Lower South in 1700 and 189,400 in 1770 compared with 2,900 black people in 1700 and 155,400 in 1770.[2]

---

[1] James Horn and Philip D. Morgan, 'Settlers and Slaves: European and African Migrations to Early Modern British America' in Elizabeth Mancke and Carole Shammas, eds., *The Creation of the British Atlantic World* (Baltimore, MD, 2005), 24.

[2] John J. McCusker and Russell R. Menard, *The Economy of British America, 1607–1789* (Chapel Hill, NC, 1985), 103, 136, 172, 203. The tables in this book use 'blacks' as a label; nearly all of them would have been enslaved people.

Despite these regional disparities in slave populations, most of the thirteen colonies enacted some form of restriction on slave imports during the eighteenth century. There was no flourishing, organised abolitionist movement to which North American critics of the slave trade could subscribe before the American revolutionary era, but individual colonies could, and sometimes did, take measures to limit slave importation. One cannot argue that the colonies were unanimous in an anti-slave trade stance before 1776; such a position took many decades to evolve and coalesce. Moreover, mixed motives were apparent in various attempts to proscribe British slave imports at the colony level by law. Not all actions taken drew impetus from a sense of the immorality of the transatlantic slave traffic, though some did; others were connected with broader social, economic and political matters.

This chapter mainly concentrates on the methods of restricting slave imports implemented by North American colonies between 1700 and 1774. The end date marks the point where the colonies first acted together over the slave trade in the First Continental Congress. The main mechanism used to restrict slave imports consisted of import duties levied by colonial assemblies on Africans entering particular colonies. The discussion below indicates that such duties were regularly implemented. They became an important component of local public policy. The analysis will show that, in most cases, import duties were not associated with abolitionist concerns, but with regulating the flow of enslaved Africans into particular colonies. The chapter is bookended by an account of the slow emergence of antislavery and the role of the Quakers, the main group who attacked the slave trade before the American War of Independence, and by evidence that newspapers were starting to publicise condemnation of the slave trade in the final years of colonial North America.

THE SLOW EMERGENCE OF ANTISLAVERY AND THE ROLE OF THE QUAKERS

In both Britain and her American colonies, an antislavery movement based on legal, philosophical and religious objections to the enslavement of Africans, and influenced by Christian benevolence and notions of liberty, was only beginning to emerge step-by-step in the quarter century before the American War of Independence. At the turn of the eighteenth century, the judge, businessman and printer Samuel Sewall equated the slave trade with the stealing of people that broke up families; it could not be supported by either moral or biblical arguments.[3] The Quaker abolitionist schoolteacher Anthony Benezet reported that uneasiness at importing slaves had spread to ports north of Maryland by the end of the Seven Years' War and that this was partly the result of Quaker testimony against 'this iniquitous practice'.[4] In Massachusetts, popular antislavery sentiment had gained some traction by the late 1730s and early 1740s.[5]

In Connecticut, religious leaders Ebenezer Baldwin and Jonathan Edwards, Jr argued by the 1770s against the enslavement and importation of Africans in relation to increasing arguments by North American colonists stressing the rhetoric of liberty.[6] In late 1773, the views of Edwards and Baldwin were echoed in an article in the *Connecticut Journal* which attacked the immorality of slave importation, noting that it was surprising that 'while we in the American colonies, have been so jealous of our own liberties, and so cautious to guard against every encroachment upon them from our mother country; we have been so inattentive to our own conduct in enslaving the Negroes, or at least in joining in the trade whereby they are enslaved'.[7] In 1773, Ezra Stiles and Samuel Hopkins, congregational ministers in Rhode Island, also railed against the iniquity of the slave trade and indicated their willingness to

---

[3] Among many discussions of the growth of antislavery sentiment in mid-eighteenth century Britain and North America are Roger Anstey, *The Atlantic Slave Trade and British Abolition 1760–1810* (London, 1975) and David Brion Davis, *The Problem of Slavery in Western Culture* (New York, 1966), 291–445. For early North American condemnations of the slave trade, see two pamphlets by Samuel Sewall: *The Selling of Joseph: A Memorial* (Boston, 1700), the first antislavery tract published in New England, and *The Athenian Oracle*, 2nd ed. (Boston, 1705). These publications are contextualised in Sidney Kaplan, '"The Selling of Joseph": Samuel Sewall and the Iniquity of Slavery' in Allan D. Austin, ed., *American Studies in Black and White* (Amherst, MA, 1991), 3–18; Mark A. Peterson, 'The Selling of Joseph: Bostonians, Antislavery, and the Protestant International, 1689–1733', *Massachusetts Historical Review*, 4 (2002), 1–22; and Molly Oshatz, *Slavery and Sin: The Fight against Slavery and the Rise of Liberal Protestantism* (New York, 2011), 18–19.

[4] New York HS, Benezet to Granville Sharp, 20 May 1773, Copies of letters to Granville Sharp.

[5] Kenneth P. Minkema, 'Jonathan Edwards on Slavery and the Slave Trade', *WMQ*, 3rd series, 54/4 (1997), 823–34; Oshatz, *Slavery and Sin*, 20.

[6] Christopher P. Sawula, '"The Hidden Springs of Prejudice and Oppression": Slavery and Abolitionism in Connecticut' (Boston College B.A. thesis, 2008), 45.

[7] 'Some Observations upon the Slavery of Negroes', *Connecticut Journal*, October–December 1773, in Roger Bruns, ed., *Am I Not a Man and a Brother? The Antislavery Crusade of Revolutionary America, 1688–1788* (New York, 1977), 294.

testify against its inhumanity and cruelty.[8] Other publications dealing with the moral iniquity of the slave trade were occasionally published in North America in the 1760s and 1770s.[9]

However, up to at least the time of the American revolutionary war, it was more common for slavery and the slave trade to be accepted as normal features of life in the colonies rather than singled out as morally unacceptable anomalies. Thus a New England writer in 1795, cast his mind back half a century to recollect that 'it was a very rare thing to hear the trade reprobated' and that any religious scruples about slave importation 'were confined to the most liberal thinkers'.[10] In 1819, former president John Adams recalled that in colonial Massachusetts sixty or so years earlier slave owning was not frowned upon and 'the best men in my vicinity – thought it not inconsistent with their characters'.[11]

In the period 1700–74, the Religious Society of Friends or Quakers was, by some margin, the main Christian religious body to condemn the slave trade but even it was, as Jean Soderlund succinctly put it, 'a divided spirit' on the moral issues related to slavery and the slave trade.[12] Participation in the slave trade was an affront to Quaker rejection of violence and stolen goods, for all Africans were wrenched from their home environments by force against their will. Quakerism in Colonial North America was centred on Pennsylvania and New Jersey. George Keith, who was disowned by the Quakers for arguing that the movement's leaders were worldly sinners, argued in 1693 that the slave trade violated scriptural prescriptions against stealing people. John Hepburn, a New Jersey tailor, also made biblical criticisms of the slave trade in 1715.[13] The Philadelphia Yearly Meeting of the Religious Society of Friends, which represented the highest level of decision-making among North American Quakers, had advised against slave imports in 1696 but this had little effect.[14] Philadelphia had numerous Quaker merchants who participated

---

[8] Samuel Hopkins and Ezra Stiles, 'To the Public', 31 August 1773, ibid., 292.
[9] For example, [Nathaniel Appleton], *Considerations on Slavery. In a Letter to a Friend* (Boston, 1767) and James Swan, *A Dissuasion to Great Britain and the Colonies, from the Slave Trade to Africa* (Boston, 1772).
[10] Samuel Dexter to Dr. Belknap, 23 Feb. 1795, in Charles Deane, ed., *Letters and Documents Relating to Slavery in Massachusetts* (Cambridge, MA, 1877), 384.
[11] John Adams to Robert J. Evans, 8 June 1819, in Gordon S. Wood, ed., *John Adams: Writings from the New Nation, 1784–1826* (New York, 2016), 647–8.
[12] Jean R. Soderlund, *Quakers and Slavery: A Divided Spirit* (Princeton, NJ, 1985).
[13] Oshatz, *Slavery and Sin*, 21.
[14] Gary B. Nash and Jean R. Soderlund, *Freedom by Degrees: Emancipation in Pennsylvania and Its Aftermath* (New York, 1991), 44; Nicholas P. Wood and Jean

in the slave trade and Quaker slaveholders were commonly found in Pennsylvania. By the 1730s, Quakers comprised one third of slave masters in Philadelphia.[15] By 1767, 15 per cent of Philadelphia's households owned slaves and Quakers owned the majority of these captives.[16]

Quakers in Pennsylvania and New Jersey wrestled with the ethical issues associated with slavery and the slave trade, shifting their positions regularly. In 1688, the Friends' Meeting in Germantown, on the outskirts of Philadelphia, issued a strong written condemnation of slavery and the slave trade; but this was not followed up by action.[17] The Chester Monthly Meeting, in southeastern Pennsylvania, petitioned the Philadelphia Yearly Meeting in 1711, 1715 and 1716 to ban slave importation to Pennsylvania, but failed to receive support. It was probably the first monthly meeting in the Delaware Valley to make such a request. By 1743, the buying and selling of enslaved people had become a social embarrassment in the Delaware Valley. In 1755, the Philadelphia Yearly Meeting instructed monthly meetings to discipline any Friend who imported slaves. Three years later, it made the buying, keeping and selling of slaves a responsibility of all Quaker meetings. These orders were put into practice and monthly meetings informed buyers of slaves that the Society disapproved. This marked an end to official toleration of slave trading in Philadelphia and its vicinity.[18] Some early abolitionists thought the Quakers should be more bold and more rapid in their condemnation of slavery and the slave trade, notably the eccentric agitator Benjamin Lay, who denounced slaveholding at the 1738 Philadelphia Yearly Meeting, but progress was relatively slow.[19] It is important to note, in this context, that Quakers were sluggish in liaising with other Christian groups to promote an anti-slave trade stance.[20]

R. Soderlund, '"To Friends and All Whom It May Concerne": William Southeby's Rediscovered 1696 Antislavery Protest', *PMHB*, 141/2 (2017), 185.

[15] Nash and Soderlund, *Freedom by Degrees*, 10–11, 26; Darold D. Wax, 'Quaker Merchants and the Slave Trade in Colonial Pennsylvania', *PMHB*, 86/2 (1962), 143–59.

[16] Beverly C. Tomek, *Slavery and Abolition in Pennsylvania* (Philadelphia, 2021), 9.

[17] Ira V. Brown, 'Pennsylvania's Antislavery Pioneers, 1688–1776', *Pennsylvania History*, 55/2 (1988), 61.

[18] Ibid., 65; Nash and Soderlund, *Freedom by Degrees*, 45, 46, 48, 54, 70, 89; Jack D. Marietta, *The Reformation of American Quakerism, 1748–1783* (Philadelphia, 1984), 114–16.

[19] Marcus Rediker, *The Fearless Benjamin Lay: The Quaker Dwarf Who Became the First Revolutionary Abolitionist* (Boston, 2017), 92.

[20] Stanley Harrold, *American Abolitionism: Its Direct Political Impact from Colonial Times into Reconstruction* (Charlottesville, VA, 2019), 18.

Disapproval of slavery and the slave trade by Quakers was sincere, but the growth of abolitionism among Friends by 1770 was hesitant. To some extent, this resulted from the fact that membership rules of the Society of Friends made it difficult to view the enslaved as spiritual equals. African Americans were not admitted into Quaker societies despite the Friends' reputation for tolerance. It was not until 1774 that Philadelphia Quakers banned slave ownership as incompatible with their Christian principles.[21] Disownment from the Philadelphia Yearly Meeting would follow except in cases where Friends had purchased slaves to manumit them.[22] In the following year, Philadelphia Quakers formed the first known antislavery society in North America – 'the Society for the Relief of Free Negroes, unlawfully held in Bondage'.[23]

In the quarter century before American independence a number of prominent Quakers, including the merchant, tailor and preacher John Woolman and Anthony Benezet, had produced texts with antislavery views that influenced the growth of abolitionist thinking in Britain and North America. They concentrated on an appeal to conscience, feeling and intellect and influenced one another in their ideas on abolitionism.[24] Woolman visited Newport, Rhode Island in 1760, where the great number of slaves and vessels fitted out for the slave trade made a deep impression on him.[25] Through publications such as *Some Considerations on the Keeping of Negroes* (1753) and many visits to Friends, Woolman personally persuaded many Quakers to free their slaves.[26] Benezet, more than any other single individual, transformed the inward-looking self-purification of Friends into a broader emphasis on how society at large

---

[21] Davis, *The Problem of Slavery in Western Culture*, 305; Sydney V. James, *A People among Peoples: Quaker Benevolence in Eighteenth-Century America* (Cambridge, MA, 1963), 138; Gary B. Nash, *Warner Mifflin: Unflinching Quaker Abolitionist* (Philadelphia, 2017), 41.

[22] Richard Bauman, *For the Reputation of Truth: Politics, Religion, and Conflict among the Pennsylvania Quakers 1750–1800* (Baltimore, 1971), 196.

[23] Edward Raymond Turner, 'The First Abolition Society in the United States', *PMHB*, 36/1 (1912), 94; Gordon S. Wood, *Power and Liberty: Constitutionalism in the American Revolution* (New York, 2021), 100.

[24] Maurice Jackson, 'Anthony Benezet and the Dream of Freedom: Then and Now' in Marie-Jeanne Rossignol and Bertram Van Ruymbeke, eds., *The Atlantic World of Anthony Benezet (1713–1784): From French Reformation to North American Quaker Antislavery Activism* (Leiden, 2016), xi.

[25] *The Journal of John Woolman. With an Introduction by John G. Whittier*, 8th ed. (Boston, 1884), 178.

[26] Thomas P. Slaughter, *The Beautiful Soul of John Woolman, Apostle of Abolition* (New York, 2008), 390.

perceived the slave trade. Unlike Woolman, he participated in transatlantic antislavery correspondence.[27] His writings sought to reach a wide Atlantic audience, including non-Quakers. The influence of the Society of Friends on attitudes towards slavery and the slave trade spread beyond these individuals to other commentators proffering rhetorical arguments that condemned slavery.[28] In 1754, the pious Benezet, a member of Philadelphia Meeting for Sufferings, laid before the monthly, quarterly and yearly meetings of Friends in Philadelphia the first epistle proposing that slave importation was against their rules. This had the effect, in the words of J. William Frost, of making 'legitimate for the first time an open debate among Friends about slavery'.[29]

In the 1760s Benezet published important critiques of gathering slaves in Africa in *A Short Account of Africa* and *A Caution and Warning to Great Britain*.[30] By the mid-1770s, Benezet had circulated his pamphlets and books, and those of other anti-slave trade advocates, among a web of North American and transatlantic contacts.[31] He was instrumental in the compilation of a petition challenging the inequity of the slave trade that was signed by 200 people 'of most weight' in Philadelphia and presented to Pennsylvania's government in 1773.[32] The circulation of these

---

[27] Jon R. Kershner, *John Woolman and the Government of Christ: A Colonial Quaker's Vision for the British Atlantic World* (Oxford, 2018), 161. On Benezet's career, see Nancy Hornick, 'Anthony Benezet: Eighteenth-Century Social Critic, Educator, and Abolitionist' (University of Maryland PhD dissertation, 1975).

[28] Brycchan Carey, *From Peace to Freedom: Quaker Rhetoric and the Birth of American Antislavery, 1657–1761* (New Haven, CT, 2012); Christopher Leslie Brown, 'Abolition of the Atlantic Slave Trade' in Gad Heuman and Trevor Burnard, eds., *The Routledge History of Slavery* (Abingdon, 2011), 284; Christopher Leslie Brown, *Moral Capital: Foundations of British Abolitionism* (Chapel Hill, NC, 2006), 396–7.

[29] J. William Frost, 'Anthony Benezet: The Emergence of a Weighty Friend', *Quaker History*, 103/2 (2014), 10–11. The authorship of the epistle has yet to be determined.

[30] Ibid., 12. For consideration of Benezet's writings on Africa, see Jonathan D. Sassi, 'Africans in the Quaker Image: Anthony Benezet, African Travel Narratives, and Revolutionary-Era Anti-slavery', *Journal of Early Modern History*, 10/1–2 (2006), 95–130.

[31] Jonathan D. Sassi, 'With a Little Help from the Friends: The Quaker and Tactical Contexts of Anthony Benezet's Abolitionist Publishing', *PMHB*, 135/1 (2011), 33–71. For examples of letters to sympathetic contacts, see Henry E. Huntington Library, San Marino, California, Anthony Benezet to Robert Pleasants, 14 Mar. 1762, Pleasants Family Papers (1745–1898), R. A. Brock Collection, box 12; Haverford College, Quaker Collection, Benezet to George Dillwyn, Apr. 1767, and to Samuel Fothergill, 24 Oct. 1771, Anthony Benezet Correspondence, and Benezet to Samuel Allinson, 7 July 1774, Allinson Papers, box 4, folder 5.

[32] Huntington Library, Petition to the Representatives of the Province of Pennsylvania sent by Benezet to Robert Pleasants, 1773, Pleasants Papers, Brock Collection, box 12.

materials helped to promote a challenge to the slave trade. Moreover, Benezet wrote about the immorality of the Guinea traffic in eloquent prose. He developed a rhetorical style that appealed to both the minds and emotions of his readers, emphasising the crucial role of individual moral sense in forging an anti-slave trade posture.[33]

Benezet drew attention to the greed of slave buyers and noted that 'without Purchasers, there would be no Trade; and consequently every Purchaser as he encourages the Trade, becomes partaker in the Guilt of it'.[34] This was included in the first antislavery publication addressed to a general non-Quaker audience to receive the official approval of the Philadelphia Yearly Meeting's Overseers of the Poor.[35] Other pamphlets concerning the moral degradation of the slave trade were circulated by the Philadelphia Yearly Meeting. One example was *An Epistle of Caution and Advice Concerning the Buying and Keeping of Slaves*, which described buying Africans as man-stealing and as failing to observe the Christian injunction of treating others as one would treat oneself.[36] No doubt many Quakers read and discussed this pamphlet, but it was not until after the American revolutionary war that meetings required Friends to free all their slaves.[37]

However, the impact of anti-slave trade attitudes on slave importations to North America was relatively limited before 1776. Quaker condemnation of slavery and the slave trade was largely confined to members in the northern colonies; those living below the Mason-Dixon line found it harder to break the connection with slavery. Before the mid-1750s, the interest of many Southern Quakers in slavery made it difficult for

---

[33] Brycchan Carey, 'Anthony Benezet, Antislavery Rhetoric, and the Age of Sensibility', *Quaker Studies*, 21/2 (2016), 141–58; Kirsten Sword, 'Remembering Dinah Nevil: Strategic Deceptions in Eighteenth-Century Antislavery', *Journal of American History*, 97/2 (2010), 324. See also Maurice Jackson, 'The Social and Intellectual Origins of Anthony Benezet's Antislavery Radicalism', *Pennsylvania History*, LXVI, special supplemental issue (1999), 86–112.

[34] Anthony Benezet, *Observations on the inslaving, importing and purchasing of Negroes with some advice thereon extracted from the Yearly Meeting epistle of London for the present year also some remarks on the absolute necessity of self-denial, renouncing the world, and true charity for all such as sincerely desire to be our blessed Saviour's disciples* (Germantown, PA, 1759), 3-4.

[35] Peter Stamatov, *The Origins of Global Humanitarianism: Religion, Empires, and Advocacy* (New York, 2013), 115.

[36] *An Epistle of Caution and Advice Concerning the Buying and Keeping of Slaves* (Philadelphia, 1754).

[37] J. William Frost, 'Quaker Antislavery: From Dissidence to Sense of the Meeting', *Quaker History*, 101/1 (2012), 30.

antislavery sentiment to progress in southern colonies. Many Southern Friends owned slaves and justified slavery on Biblical grounds. However, in the 1760s and 1770s, reformers argued that ending slavery would purify Quakers and curb worldliness. Though getting rid of slavery would not occur for decades, in 1758, the Philadelphia Yearly Meeting decided to remove slaveholders from positions of power in the Society of Friends. In 1776, it agreed to disown any member who owned a slave. Northern Virginia Friends, who came with its orbit, followed this instruction in subsequent years.[38]

One Southern Quaker who heeded the admonitions of Benezet against the slave trade was Robert Pleasants, who privately referred to the traffic in slaves being 'so detestable a trade'.[39] Pleasants, a slaveowner and tobacco merchant from Henrico County, Virginia, served as clerk of the Quarterly Meeting of Virginia in 1750 and 1757. Inspired by Benezet, he manumitted his slaves when that became possible in Virginia through a state law passed in 1782.[40] Pleasants frequently wrote critically about the slave trade, and his views on the subject are further discussed later in the chapter.

NORTH AMERICAN RESTRICTIONS ON THE SLAVE TRADE

Given that the Quakers, who were at the forefront of abolitionism, found it took several decades between c.1730 and c.1760 to influence their own community to stop importing slaves, it is unsurprising that antislavery ideas in themselves were not a major factor in stemming the flow of slaves from Africa to the North American colonies. However, there were means of restricting the slave trade in the colonial period in other ways. This chapter discusses the main types of proscription pursued in colonial laws. As each colony operated independently, an examination of limitations enacted to stem the stream of slave imports can only proceed on a colony-by-colony basis. In each case, different patterns emerged: there was no linear form of Whiggish progression from accepting all slave imports to banning them. However, the varied reasons why colonies attempted to

---

[38] A. Glenn Crothers, *Quakers Living in the Lion's Mouth: The Society of Friends in Northern Virginia, 1730–1865* (Gainesville, FL, 2012), 42–3.

[39] Swem Library, College of William and Mary, undated letter by Robert Pleasants [but 1773] to an unknown recipient, Robert Pleasants letterbook (1771–81), fol. 110.

[40] William Fernandez Hardin, 'Robert Pleasants (1723–1801)', *Encyclopedia Virginia* (https://encyclopediavirginia.org).

restrict slave imports between 1700 and 1774 illuminate contemporary attitudes towards trafficking in slaves, indicating the parameters put in place to limit or curtail slave importation before antislavery ideas had a widespread influence on this matter.

The only way in which the slave trade to the North American colonies could be ended before the American Revolution was by British legislation and that was out of the question at a time when an abolitionist movement in Britain still had to be formed to exert pressure on Parliament. But a degree of curtailment was available to individual colonies either through import duties on incoming slave shipments or nonimportation agreements that covered not just goods but enslaved people. Colonial self-determination rather than antislavery opinion underpinned such proscription. Individual colonies exercised their right to control slave imports in relation to their social structure and economic needs.[41] This was put into practice through laws passed by individual colonial legislatures. All British North American colonies apart from New Hampshire, Connecticut, Delaware and North Carolina implemented slave import duties at various times between 1700 and 1774.[42] Constitutionally, however, British institutions controlled such levies because colonial laws could be vetoed by the monarch or the Privy Council. The general position of the Privy Council before the American War of Independence was to allow import duties by individual colonies to be enacted if they were designed to generate income for local government but to reject duties intended to curtail the sale of imported Africans.[43] Instructions authorised by the British Parliament were despatched to colonies when they considered implementing import duties on slaves as taxation measures. In these missives, it was made clear to colonial governors that parliamentary assent would be withheld in such circumstances.[44]

---

[41] Philip D. Morgan, 'Ending the Slave Trade: A Caribbean and Atlantic Context' in Derek R. Peterson, ed., *Abolition and Imperialism in Britain, Africa, and the Atlantic* (Athens, OH, 2010), 102.

[42] Kenneth Morgan, 'Proscription by Degrees: The Ending of the African Slave Trade to the United States' in David T. Gleeson and Simon Lewis, eds., *Ambiguous Anniversary: The Bicentennial of the International Slave Trade Bans* (Columbia, SC, 2012), 4. Slave import duties were also implemented in British Caribbean colonies such as Jamaica and Barbados.

[43] Brown, *Moral Capital*, 144.

[44] Lorenzo Johnston Greene, *The Negro in Colonial New England 1620–1776* (New York, 1942), 56–7.

NEW ENGLAND RESTRICTIONS ON THE SLAVE TRADE

Opposition to slave importation emerged sporadically in New England in the period 1700–74 even though relatively small numbers of Africans were disembarked in that region. Massachusetts was the main colony in New England to implement laws imposing duties on slave imports, and it did so for diverse reasons. In 1700, colonists lobbied the provincial legislature to impose a 40 shillings tax per head on imported slaves. A response to this request only occurred five years later when the assembly passed a law restricting inter-racial sexual relations to which was added an import duty of £4 per imported slave in an attempt to increase white emigration to the colony and restrict slave arrivals. This levy was reaffirmed in later laws passed by the Massachusetts legislature in 1728 and 1739.[45] The act of 1728, stating that many evasions had taken place, was intended to secure the collection of the duty by instigating a penalty of £100 for ship masters who tried to falsify bringing Africans to the colony.[46] But this was not always enforced. Petitions were presented to the Massachusetts House of Representatives to seek redress for the import duties on Africans, and these were sometimes successful.[47]

In 1764, the Massachusetts House of Representatives considered a bill to restrict slave importations, but it was not acted upon after it had received careful scrutiny and amendment.[48] In 1766 and the following year, the Boston Town Meeting stated that such a bill should be reintroduced.[49] In 1767, another bill to prevent slave importation into Massachusetts was introduced in the legislature. It was read three times on 17 and 18 March but dropped after the council made many amendments but disagreed with the assembly over the proposed legislation. Thus, both houses failed to support the bill.[50] This was because it aimed

---

[45] *Acts and Resolves, Public and Private, of the Massachusetts Bay Colony*, 21 vols. (Boston, 1869–1919), I, 578–9, 634, II, 517–18, 981–2; James J. Allegro, '"Increasing and Strengthening the Country": Law, Politics, and the Antislavery Movement in Early Eighteenth-Century Massachusetts Bay', *The New England Quarterly*, 75/1 (2002), 6.
[46] 'Act for Laying a Duty on Negroes Imported, 1728' in Donnan, ed., *Documents*, III, 35.
[47] Greene, *The Negro in Colonial New England*, 54–5.
[48] Minutes, 6 Jan. and 2 Feb. 1764, in *Journals of the House of Representatives of Massachusetts. Volume 40. 1763–1764* (Boston, 1970), 170, 263.
[49] Boston Town Meeting Vote for Representatives, 6 and 27 May 1766, 16 Mar. 1767, in *A Report of the Record Commissioners of the City of Boston Containing the Boston Town Records, 1758–1769* (Boston, 1886), 16, 183, 200.
[50] W. E. B. Du Bois, *The Suppression of the African Slave-Trade to the United States of America* (Cambridge, MA, 1896), 30; Samuel Dexter to Jeremy Belknap, 23 Feb. 1795, in

to put an end to slave imports as well as slavery in Massachusetts. This proved a premature attempt to proceed quickly on both issues. It was reported that the royal governor, Francis Bernard, considered the levies on slave imports too high and was not minded to support the bill.[51] A letter to the *Boston Gazette* of 30 March 1767 regretted that the bill had miscarried for the present and took the opportunity to hope that 'this very desirable act' would be revived as the traffic in slaves was based on 'Perfidy, Avarice and Barbarity'.

This situation changed fairly rapidly, for in 1771, the General Court of Massachusetts approved a bill to stop slave importation after a proposal was received from a representative of the town of Hadley.[52] This was vetoed, however, by Governor Thomas Hutchinson, who had three concerns about the proposed law. One was that taxing slaves should not be equated with import duties on goods. Another was that the bill's sponsors included what Hutchinson regarded as an unsubstantiated claim that slavery was unlawful. The third reservation was that slave importation to Massachusetts was unnecessary because the demand for Africans in the colony was too small to require a new law. In 1773, a slave importation bill passed the Council, but it was carried over to the following year.[53] In the same year, town meetings in Salem, Sandwich, Medford and Leicester called for an end to slave imports.[54] Thus, for example, on 19 May 1773, the Leicester town meeting requested that the Massachusetts assembly should use their influence to stop the slave trade by the colony's inhabitants either by laying a heavy duty on every slave imported into the province or by passing a law that every African brought

---

Deane, ed., *Letters and Documents*, 385; Mary Stoughton Locke, *Anti-slavery in America: From the Introduction of African Slaves to the Prohibition of the Slave Trade (1619–1808)* (Boston, 1901), 69.

[51] Minutes, 13 Mar. 1767, in *Journals of the House of Representatives of Massachusetts. Volume 43. Part 2* (Boston, 1974), 387; Samuel Dexter to Jeremy Belknap, 23 Feb. 1795, in Deane, ed., *Letters and Documents*, 385.

[52] Minutes, 19 Apr. 1771, in *Journal of the House of Representatives of Massachusetts. Volume 47. 1770–1771* (Boston, 1978), 197.

[53] Minutes, 28 Jan., 2 Feb., 5 Mar. 1773, in *Journal of the House of Representatives of Massachusetts. Volume 49. 1772–1773* (Boston, 1980), 95, 204–5, 287; Robert G. Parkinson, *Thirteen Clocks: How Race United the Colonies and Made the Declaration of Independence* (Chapel Hill, NC, 2021), 54.

[54] Christian M. McBurney, 'The First Efforts to Limit the African Slave Trade Arise in the American Revolution: Part 1 of 3, The New England Colonies', n.p., available at https://allthingsliberty.com; Locke, *Anti-slavery in America*, 69; Sandwich Town Meeting Resolution, 18 May 1773, in Frederick Freeman, *The History of Cape Cod. The Annals of the Thirteen Towns of Barnstable County*, 2 vols. (Boston, 1862), II, 114–15.

to Massachusetts should be declared a free man or woman as soon as they entered its jurisdiction.[55]

In 1774, another bill to prohibit slave imports into Massachusetts was passed easily by both legislative houses, with a suggested an £80 fine for each slave imported. Governor Hutchinson refused to sign it and the assembly was dissolved before it could be enacted. The governor's action appeared to support British measures against the colony in the aftermath of the Coercive Acts of 1774.[56] Hutchinson's successor, General Thomas Gage, also refused to sign a slave non-importation bill on the grounds that he had not received authorisation from Britain.[57]

Rhode Island was another New England colony that periodically introduced statutes to limit slave importations, but before the American revolutionary era they were lukewarm measures. A Rhode Island act of 1708 laid a duty of £3 per head on slave imports but it was poorly enforced. Many traders in Newport, a significant port sending out slaving vessels, hid slaves to avoid paying the impost. In 1715, a further act removed any import duty on Africans entering Rhode Island. The incomplete state of the surviving records of the colony render it difficult to state with certainty whether that act remained in use, or was replaced by another measure, but it was not until the 1770s that further legislation on imported slaves was enacted.[58]

In 1770, a bill drawn up by the Rhode Island Assembly to prohibit slave importation was rejected. Local Quakers urged the colony's assembly to take action against the slave trade, however, and in 1774 an act to this effect was passed that emphasised how the slave traffic contradicted natural rights ideology.[59] The preamble to the law emphasised Americans' search for liberty and encouraged Rhode Islanders to be

---

[55] Emory Washburn, *Historical Sketches of the Town of Leicester, Massachusetts, during the First Century from its Settlement* (Boston, 1860), 443.

[56] Allegro, 'Increasing and Strengthening the country', 20–1; George H. Moore, *Notes on the History of Slavery in Massachusetts* (New York, 1866), 130–40; Bernard Bailyn, *The Ordeal of Thomas Hutchinson* (Cambridge, MA, 1974), 378.

[57] Moore, *Notes on the History of Slavery*, 142–3.

[58] Du Bois, *The Suppression of the African Slave-Trade*, 34–5; John Russell Bartlett, ed., *Records of the Colony of Rhode Island and Providence Plantations, in New England*, 10 vols. (Providence, RI, 1856–65), IV, 34.

[59] Mack Thompson, *Moses Brown: Reluctant Reformer* (Chapel Hill, NC, 1962), 81; Arthur Zilversmit, *The First Emancipation: The Abolition of Slavery in the North* (Chicago, IL, 1967), 106; William Read Staples, *Annals of the Town of Providence: From its First Settlement to the Organization of City Government in June, 1832* (Providence, RI, 1843), 236.

willing to extend personal liberty to others, in this context meaning Africans.[60] This was echoed by a pronouncement from the city of Providence that slavery and the slave trade in Rhode Island should cease on the grounds of liberty and natural rights.[61] These were some of the first public statements linking the elimination of the slave trade to rhetorical arguments in favour of political freedom in North America.

The Rhode Island slave trade act of 1774 was influenced by the revolutionary rhetoric associated with personal liberty in the struggle against Britain for control of North America. Under its terms, any African brought to Rhode Island would immediately be freed and able to enjoy the rights of private property as any other free person. Africans brought across the Atlantic in a Rhode Island vessel that were not sold after the ship arrived in the West Indies and then brought to the colony were exempt from the ruling and the owners of the slave had to give a bond of £100 to the general treasurer of the colony within ten days after arrival. Each slave falling under this resolution had then to be removed from the colony within a year. Those importing slaves clandestinely into the colony were to be fined £100 for each African imported.[62]

Connecticut was the only other New England colony to enact legislation against the slave trade before the War of Independence, but it took no action before 1774, when two Congregational clergymen, Jonathan Edwards, Jr and Levi Hart, wrote and preached about the immorality of the slave trade. Their views influenced the Connecticut Assembly to end slave importation.[63] Thus after 5 December 1774, Connecticut would not import or purchase any more slaves and the slave trade would be wholly discontinued. Connecticut's colonists breaking this law could be fined £100.[64] These sentiments were applauded at a legal meeting of the town of Danbury on 12 December 1774.[65] However, the cessation of the slave trade to Connecticut, a very minor part of the overall traffic in Africans, was probably more influenced by the effects of the slave trade on the

---

[60] Resolution, 1774 session, in Bartlett, ed., *Records of the Colony of Rhode Island and Providence Plantations*, VII, 251.
[61] Du Bois, *The Suppression of the African Slave-Trade*, 35–6.
[62] Bartlett, ed., *Records of the Colony of Rhode Island and Providence Plantations*, VII, 251–2.
[63] Morgan, 'Proscription by Degrees', 5.
[64] 'Association &c.', *Connecticut Journal*, 25 Nov. 1774; *The New-London Gazette*, 2 Dec. 1774.
[65] 'At a Legal Meeting of the Inhabitants of the Town of Danbury', *Connecticut Journal*, 12 Dec. 1774.

white population than by antislavery ideas. Thus, the statute passed claimed that 'the increase of slaves in this Colony is injurious to the poor and inconvenient'. All constables and grand jurors were enjoined to deal with such cases.[66] Actions against slave importations in colonial New England were therefore patchy. They appear mainly to have been brought in as revenue measures rather than as a serious attempt to limit slave imports.[67]

RESTRICTIONS ON THE SLAVE TRADE IN THE MIDDLE COLONIES

New York and New Jersey enacted several laws against slave importation, but they were sporadic measures. In 1709, a duty of £3 was laid on slaves not brought to New York directly from Africa, which was aimed at captives first taken to the West Indies. An act of 1716 raised the duty on all slave imports to £1 12½ shillings. This was increased to 40 shillings per slave in 1728 but, after objections from Bristol merchants as being prejudicial to their interests, it was disallowed in 1735. The 40 shillings duty was restored in 1753 and renewed annually down to 1774. No restrictions were placed on New Yorkers taking slaves to other colonies.[68] In the early 1770s, Quakers sent a petition to the New York legislature in favour of a slave import duty.[69] In 1773, the New York Assembly approved a high import duty of £20 per slave but the royal governor and upper council refused to accept this level.[70]

The first New Jersey statute dealing with the slave trade was passed in 1713; it laid down an import duty of £10 in currency. As with early-

---

[66] Charles J. Hoadly, ed., *The Public Records of the Colony of Connecticut, from October, 1772, to April, 1775, inclusive*, 15 vols. (Hartford, CT, 1887), IV, 329.
[67] Greene, *The Negro in Colonial New England*, 55–6.
[68] Du Bois, *The Suppression of the African Slave-Trade*, 18–19; *Acts of Assembly, Passed in the Province of New-York, from 1691, to 1718* (London, 1719), 224; E. B. O'Callaghan, ed., John Romeyn Brodhead, *Documents Relative to the Colonial History of the State of New York; Procured in Holland, England, and France*, 11 vols. (Albany, 1853–87), VI, 32–4, 37–8.
[69] Robert G. Parkinson, '"Manifest Signs of Passion": The First Federal Congress, Antislavery, and Legacies of the Revolutionary War' in John Craig Hammond and Matthew Mason, eds., *Contesting Slavery: The Politics of Slavery and Freedom in the New American Nation* (Charlottesville, VA, 2011), 53.
[70] Zilversmit, *The First Emancipation*, 91; Anthony Benezet to Robert Pleasants, 8 Apr. 1773, in George S. Brookes, *Friend Anthony Benezet* (Philadelphia, 1937), 300; Anthony Benezet to Moses Brown, 5 Sept. 1774, in J. William Frost, ed., *The Quaker Origins of Antislavery* (Norwood, PA, 1980), 190.

eighteenth century Massachusetts, the measure was intended to boost the immigration of white servants. In 1744, the Provincial Council of New Jersey rejected a bill to stop slave imports to the colony. It argued that a new influx of slaves would help the colony adjust to the loss of workers to privateering in wartime and high labourers' wages. In 1762, Josiah Hardy, the governor of New Jersey, complained that slaves were being landed in the colony because traders wished to avoid paying duties on slave imports levied in New York and Pennsylvania.[71] New Jersey's government responded to this claim in the same year when, in response to two petitions, duties were imposed that cited 'hardship' and an excess of slaves as contributing to the levy. The decision of 1762 was not presented by the Board of Trade to the king, but the Board disclaimed any opposition to the suggested duties.[72] However, in that year the Board of Trade instructed the royal governor of New Jersey to veto a bill on slave trade imports.[73]

An act of 1769 noted that it was the intention to settle foreigners in New Jersey, which meant the slave trade should be discouraged. Accordingly, that act established a £15 duty on the first purchasers of slaves. The preamble to this statute stated that neighbouring colonies had benefited from similar legislation that had settled foreigners successfully as industrious workers. It was hoped that New Jersey would follow suit. In 1773, the New Jersey Assembly received several petitions from the counties of Salem, Essex and Somerset requesting an end to slave importations, but these were not followed up. A further measure to stop slave imports in 1774 was dismissed by New Jersey's Council.[74]

Pennsylvania's first act dealing with slave import duties, passed in 1700, instigated a differential duty based on the age of the enslaved (see Table 1.1). The duty was 20 shillings for those aged over sixteen (i.e. adults) and 6 shillings for Africans under sixteen years old. The rate for adult slaves doubled in 1706 and then increased significantly six years later. In 1711, slave importation into Pennsylvania was prohibited but this was overruled by the Privy Council which claimed that the colony's

---

[71] Josiah Hardy to the Board of Trade, 20 Jan. 1762, in Donnan, ed., *Documents*, III, 456.
[72] Du Bois, *The Suppression of the African Slave-Trade*, 24–5; Henry Scofield Cooley, *A Study of Slavery in New Jersey* (Baltimore, 1896), 15–16; James C. Connolly, 'Slavery in Colonial New Jersey and the Causes Operating against Its Extension', *Proceedings of the New Jersey Historical Society*, XIV (1929), 189, 191.
[73] Josiah Hardy to the Board of Trade, 20 Jan. 1762, in Donnan, ed., *Documents*, III, 456.
[74] Cooley, *A Study of Slavery in New Jersey*, 17; Haverford College, Quaker Collection, Anthony Benezet to Robert Pleasants, 7 May 1774, Anthony Benezet correspondence.

TABLE 1.1 *Duties on slave imports to Pennsylvania, 1700–1773*

1700	20 shillings for slaves above 16 years
	6 shillings for slaves under 16 years
1706	40 shillings for adult slaves
1712	£20 on all slaves
1715–25	£5 per slave
1726	£10 per slave
1729	£2 per slave
1761	£10 per slave
1773	£20 per slave

Source: Darold D. Wax, 'Negro Import Duties in Colonial Pennsylvania', *Pennsylvania Magazine of History and Biography*, 97/1 (1973), 22–44; W. E. B. Du Bois, *The Suppression of the African Slave-Trade to the United States of America, 1638–1870* (Cambridge, MA, 1896), 23.

assembly had overreached its authority.[75] The measures implemented before 1712 were intended to increase Pennsylvania's revenue but the duty act of that year, raising the levy to £20 per slave, was influenced by petitions from concerned Pennsylvanians wanting to prohibit the slave trade. The Coromantee uprising in New York City in 1712 had struck fear into Pennsylvania's slaveholders. The slave import duty increase of that year cited slave plots and insurrections as a contributory factor.[76]

A series of acts reduced the duty on slaves imported to Pennsylvania to £5 between 1715 and 1729. The levy was decreased to £2 per imported slave in 1729, but this lapsed two years later.[77] It was not until 1761 that the import duty was increased, to £10 per slave, and then doubled from 1773, which served as a deterrent to slave imports. Negative attitudes towards the slave trade were then increasing, especially among Quakers. In drafting the 1761 law, the Pennsylvania Assembly considered a remonstrance by citizens of Philadelphia against the slave trade and rebuffed demands by some merchants that the legislation should be delayed. Pennsylvania's legislators were concerned about smuggling of slaves into the colony and the evasion of duties, but strenuous efforts by collectors to

---

[75] Slaughter, *The Beautiful Soul of John Woolman*, 200.
[76] Vincent Brown, *Tacky's Revolt: The Story of an Atlantic Slave War* (Cambridge, MA, 2020), 228.
[77] Gary B. Nash, *The Urban Crucible: Social Change, Political Consciousness, and the Origins of the American Revolution* (Cambridge, MA, 1979), 109.

check for these problems were not made until after the 1761 act.[78] Import duties on slaves and the spread of anti-slave trade ideas by the Quakers and their associates influenced attitudes towards trafficking in slaves, for it was reported from Philadelphia in 1767 that refraining from importing Africans was 'now a rule pretty well obs[erve]d here'.[79]

A serious moral argument against slave imports to Pennsylvania emerged towards the end of the colonial era. In 1773, the Society of Friends gathered sufficient support to petition the colony's assembly to end the slave trade. 'We your petitioners', they wrote, 'most earnestly beseech you to take this matter, which we apprehend to be of the utmost consequence, to the Welfare and safety of the British Colonies, under your most serious consideration and to use your utmost endeavours with the other Colonies, in making such representations to the King as to you may appear most effectual towards putting a stop to this mighty evil'.[80] The petition was signed by 200 people, including three Anglican clergymen, five Presbyterian preachers and two Baptist ministers in Philadelphia. If time had allowed, Benezet was confident that several thousand names could have been appended to the petition.[81]

The physician Dr Benjamin Rush, who had international connections among antislavery advocates, published a widely circulated pamphlet entitled *An Address to the Inhabitants of the British Settlements in America, upon Slave-Keeping* supporting the petition's views, aiming to show the iniquity of the slave trade.[82] The publication was written at Benezet's suggestion, and a copy sent to Benjamin Franklin.[83] Rush attributed the passing of Pennsylvania's increased slave import duty to the influence of his publication.[84] Benezet lay behind this strategy of

---

[78] Darold D. Wax, 'Negro Import Duties in Colonial Pennsylvania', *PMHB*, 97/1 (1973), 22–44; Nash and Soderlund, *Freedom by Degrees*, 71; 'Petition of the Merchants of Philadelphia, 1761' in Donnan, ed., *Documents*, III, 453–4.
[79] HSP, Samuel Pleasants to Edward Stabler, 7 May 1767, box 14, folder 35, Cox-Parrish-Wharton Papers.
[80] New York HS, Anthony Benezet to Granville Sharp, 18 Feb. 1773, Copies of letters to Granville Sharp.
[81] Ibid.; Micah Alpaugh, *Friends of Freedom: The Rise of Social Movements in the Age of Atlantic Revolutions* (Cambridge, 2021), 181.
[82] [Benjamin Rush], *An Address to the Inhabitants of the British Settlements in America, upon Slave-Keeping* (Philadelphia, 1773).
[83] Rush to Franklin, 1 May 1773, in L. H. Butterfield, ed., *Letters of Benjamin Rush*, 2 vols. (Princeton, NJ, 1951), I, 79.
[84] Duncan J. MacLeod, *Slavery, Race and the American Revolution* (Cambridge, 1974), 35.

presenting the petition and pamphlet simultaneously to add weight to the anti-slave trade argument.[85] Rush quickly published a revised version of his pamphlet after its arguments had been attacked by Richard Nesbit of St Kitts.[86]

Rush forwarded a copy of his pamphlet to the British abolitionist, Granville Sharp, noting that rising anti-slave trade sentiment had begun to appear in Pennsylvania in clerical circles as public testimony to the 'violation of the laws of nature and Christianity'. Rush credited Benezet with promoting opposition to slavery and the slave trade in that province, stating that three-quarters of the colony and the city of Philadelphia now stood against it. Rush also arranged for his pamphlet to be displayed at the Pennsylvania coffee house, London, on the basis that wider circulation of his ideas about the slave trade would help to stir up opposition to its continuation both in Britain and North America.[87]

The Pennsylvania Assembly considered the petition, agreed with the proposal and appointed a short time for its second reading. They then judged it was too premature to comply with the petition and decided instead to prepare a bill to make the import duty on slaves entering Pennsylvania perpetual at £20 per head, which was double the existing rate. Benezet thought the increase in duty would amount to 'a tacit prohibition of the trade'.[88] He criticised this handling of the petition as amounting to nothing in practice 'as the number imported in this province is so small that the Officer tells me, more are sent off than are brought in'.[89] In London, the Lords of Trade disallowed Pennsylvania's attempt to restrict the slave trade further at a time when Britain was still encouraging the slave trade.[90]

---

[85] Sword, 'Remembering Dinah Nevil', 328; Jonathan D. Sassi, 'Anthony Benezet as Intermediary between the Transatlantic and Provincial: New Jersey's Antislavery Campaign on the Eve of the American Revolution' in Rossignol and Van Ruymbeke, eds., *The Atlantic World of Anthony Benezet*, 133.

[86] George W. Corner, ed., *The Autobiography of Benjamin Rush. His 'Travels through Life' together with His Commonplace Book for 1789–1813* (Princeton, NJ, 1948), 83.

[87] Rush to Sharp, 1 May 1773, in Butterfield, ed., *Letters of Benjamin Rush*, I, 81.

[88] LCP, Benezet to Sharp, 29 Mar. 1773 (quotation), Granville Sharp received letterbook. See also Haverford College, Quaker Collection, Benezet to Robert Pleasants, 8 Apr. 1773, Anthony Benezet correspondence. The text of the act is printed in Samuel Hazard et al., eds., *Pennsylvania Archives*, 16 vols. (Harrisburg, PA, 1831–53), VIII, 695–6.

[89] New York HS, Benezet to Sharp, 18 Feb. 1773, Copies of letters to Granville Sharp.

[90] William Renwick Riddell, 'Pre-revolutionary Pennsylvania and the Slave Trade', *PMHB*, 52/1 (1928), 18.

TABLE 1.2 *Duties on slave imports to Maryland, 1695–1771*

1695	10 shillings per slave
1704	20 shillings per slave
1715	20 shillings
1716	20 shillings and £4 currency per slave
1717	20 shillings and 20 shillings currency per slave
1754	50 shillings per slave
1756	40 shillings per slave
1763	£4 per slave
1771	£9 per slave

Source: W.E.B. Du Bois, *The Suppression of the African Slave-Trade to the United States of America, 1638–1870* (Cambridge, MA, 1896), 14–15, 210; Clayton Colman Hall, ed., *Archives of Maryland. Proceedings and Acts of the General Assembly of Maryland. May 1717–April 1720. Volume XXXIII* (Baltimore, 1913), 109–11.

THE CHESAPEAKE COLONIES AND SLAVE TRADE RESTRICTION

Maryland, which had a relatively small slave trade, introduced various import duties on slaves (summarised in Table 1.2). The levy was increased modestly over time, though it went up steeply from £4 to £9 per slave in 1771.[91] Maryland had a number of idiosyncrasies in its laws specifying slave import duties. Thus, an act of 1717 brought in an additional 20 shillings currency duty for each slave imported to establish a fund to support education in the colony.[92] Various regulations were implemented in Maryland to assist those based in the colony who imported slaves. Before 1720, for example, those who owned vessels in Maryland were allowed to import slaves free of duty. In 1721, an act was passed allowing Marylanders to avoid the import duty if they were bringing in Africans who would not be put up for sale.[93] An act of 1735 exempted those from paying the duty whose slaves died or who exported the slaves out of Maryland.[94] No abolitionist influence is apparent in any of these measures. In the 1760s, attacks on slave importation emanated particularly

---

[91] Du Bois, *The Suppression of the African Slave-Trade*, 14–15.
[92] *Proceedings and Acts of the General Assembly of Maryland, 1717–April, 1720*, part of *Archives of Maryland*, 72 vols. (Baltimore, 1883–1972), XXXIII, 109.
[93] *Proceedings and Acts of the General Assembly of Maryland, October 1720–October 1723*, ibid., XXXIV, 268–70.
[94] 'An Act for Laying a Duty on Slaves, 1735' in Donnan, ed., *Documents*, IV, 25.

from promoters of the then-flourishing convict trade to Maryland who wanted to increase the demand for transported felons in the colony.[95]

Moves to curtail the slave trade were evident particularly in the largest southern colony, Virginia, which had a sizeable slave population. These developments produced more commentary and debate than similar measures in the northern colonies. In 1699, 1710, 1723, 1728, 1767 and 1769, the Virginia House of Burgesses voted for laws in favour of slave import duties. On the two latter occasions, it voted to double the duty from 10 to 20 per cent, but the Privy Council vetoed the proposal.[96] The first law passed in 1699 was intended to raise revenue to rebuild the state house, which had been burned down the previous year. The act was renewed in 1701 with an additional clause allowing importers to claim back three-quarters of the duty if they exported the slaves within six weeks of entry into Virginia.[97] The increase in the import duty from 20 shillings to £5 in 1710, which lasted until 1718, provided funds for Virginia's assembly to fund public projects and act as a brake on the number of Africans imported.[98] This was the preferred method of raising revenue for infrastructure rather than imposing an unpopular poll tax.[99] The slave import duty between 1710 and 1718 was also used for paying off Virginia's debts and maintaining public credit.[100]

By the 1720s, Virginia's tobacco economy was in the throes of economic depression and, to counter the problem, the burgesses attempted in 1723 to raise the slave import duty to 40 shillings to curb the introduction of Africans to the colony when they were not specifically needed to increase tobacco production. Many slaveholders in Virginia opposed the levy and English merchants also objected to the proposal, arguing that it was a burden on them and destructive of the slave trade. The act was repealed in the following year by royal proclamation. Another attempt in

---

[95] MacLeod, *Slavery, Race and the American Revolution*, 31.
[96] Virginia statutes laying down duties on imported slaves are summarised in Donnan, ed., *Documents*, IV, 66, 102–3, 122–3, 127–31, 133–5, 137–42, 144, 150–6, 158–9.
[97] 'Act for Laying a Duty on Slaves, 1699' ibid., IV, 66.
[98] Robert McColley, *Slavery and Jeffersonian Virginia*, 2nd ed. (Champaign-Urbana, IL, 1974), 123.
[99] Leonidas Dodson, *Alexander Spotswood, Governor of Colonial Virginia, 1710–1722* (Philadelphia, 1932), 59.
[100] Alexander Spotswood to the Board of Trade, 27 Jan. 1715, in R. A. Brock, ed., *The Official Letters of Alexander Spotswood, Lieutenant-Governor of the Colony of Virginia, 1710–1722*, 2 vols. (Richmond, VA, 1882–5), II, 97.

1728 to raise slave import duties in Virginia to 40 shillings per head was rejected in Britain for similar reasons.[101]

Further legislation concerning slave import taxes was passed in future years. The measure of 1732 stipulated that the buyer should pay the duty on an *ad valorem* basis, which meant that the duty took account of slave sale prices. It was intended that the monies raised would contribute towards necessary expenses of the Virginia government.[102] This duty was intended to continue for four years but it remained in place until 1770.[103] Further laws passed in Virginia in 1736 and 1738 fine-tuned the administration for collecting the duties.[104] An additional duty of £5 per cent between 1740 and 1744 contributed towards defence costs and the enlistment of troops for a war against Spain.[105] In 1752, this rate was revived by an act placing this duty on the buyer.[106] Two years later, an act of 1754 doubled the duty to be paid by the purchaser.[107]

An additional *ad valorem* duty in 1755 helped to defray military costs against the French in the early stages of the Seven Years' War. The assembly added an additional duty of 10 per cent in 1757 for the same purpose. These levies appear to have influenced the decline in Africans imported to Virginia, which amounted to only sixty slaves between 1756 and 1759. Low tobacco prices discouraged slave importation to Virginia in the mid-1760s.[108] It has been argued that 'the high Virginia

---

[101] McColley, *Slavery and Jeffersonian Virginia*, 124; Benjamin J. Hillman, ed., *Executive Journals of the Council of Colonial Virginia. Volume VI (June 20, 1754–May 3, 1775)* (Richmond, VA, 1966), 149. For objections by British merchants to the attempts to raise slave import duties in 1723 and 1728, see TNA, CO 5/1319, fol. 140, Memorial from several Bristol merchants trading to Africa in relation to the Virginia act laying a duty on liquor and slaves, 1723, and CO 5/1321, Orders in Council relating to a petition of several merchants and an act for taxing slave imports, 26 Sept. 1728. See also TNA, CO 5/1321, Francis Fane's report upon the duty placed on importing slaves to Virginia, 10 Dec. 1728. Material on the early import duties on slaves entering Virginia can be found in Elizabeth I. Suttell, 'The British Slave Trade to Virginia, 1698-1728' (College of William and Mary M.A. dissertation, 1965), available at https://scholarworks.wm.edu.

[102] Hillman, ed., *Executive Journals*, VI, 149; 'Act for Laying a Duty on Slaves, 1732' in Donnan, ed., *Documents*, IV, 127-31.

[103] TNA, CO 5/1349, William Nelson, 'Observations on the several Acts of Assembly imposing duties on slaves', 27 Mar. 1771, fol. 84r.

[104] 'Act for Laying a Duty on Slaves, 1736' and 'Act for Laying a Duty on Slaves, 1738' in Donnan, ed., *Documents*, IV, 133-5, 137-9.

[105] McColley, *Slavery and Jeffersonian Virginia*, 125.

[106] TNA, CO 5/1396, An Act for reviving the duty upon slaves to be paid by the buyer, 27 Feb. 1752.

[107] 'Act for Laying a Duty on Slaves, 1754' in Donnan, ed., *Documents*, IV, 140-1.

[108] McColley, *Slavery and Jeffersonian Virginia*, 115, 125-6.

duty after 1755 inhibited the legal importation of slaves for sale'.[109] There is some contemporary support for this view: A Virginia merchant trading on James River in 1770 thought the duty amounted almost to a prohibition.[110]

Further adjustments to slave import duties in Virginia occurred at intervals during the 1760s and early 1770s. After protracted attempts to alter the law, the duty was reduced in 1761 to a 10 per cent *ad valorem* rate.[111] This was implemented after considerable division among the burgesses between those who wanted slave trade restriction in order to encourage free labour to migrate to Virginia and those who believed the economic prospects of small planters would benefit from enslaved imports.[112] Supporters of the move for restriction mainly came from tidewater planters who already owned enough slaves and who, by limiting new imports, would benefit from higher slave sale prices.[113] In 1767, the House of Burgesses prepared a bill for increasing the import duty on slaves but, after objections were raised by the Board of Trade and the Privy Council, it never came into effect.[114] Similarly, an attempt in 1769 by the House of Burgesses to increase the duty on imported slaves by 20 per cent was rejected by the Privy Council.[115]

Though the slave import duty was increased in the late 1760s, it reverted to 10 per cent *ad valorem* in 1772 with an additional levy of £5 on slaves imported from other colonies.[116] Half of the main duty was

---

[109] Donald M. Sweig, 'The Importation of African Slaves to the Potomac River, 1732–1772', *WMQ*, 3rd series, 42/4 (1985), 519.

[110] Alderman Library, University of Virginia, Harry Piper to Dixon & Littledale, 16 Dec. 1770, Harry Piper letterbook (1767–76).

[111] 'Act for Laying a Duty on Slaves, 1755', 'Act for Laying a Duty on Slaves, 1759' and 'Act Repealing a Duty on Slaves, 1761' in Donnan, ed., *Documents*, IV, 141–2, 144, 146–7.

[112] McColley, *Slavery and Jeffersonian Virginia*, 127. These opposing interests were explained in Francis Fauquier to the Board of Trade, 2 June 1760, in George Henkle Reese, ed., *The Official Papers of Francis Fauquier, Lieutenant Governor of Virginia, 1758–1768*, Virginia Historical Society Documents, 3 vols. (Charlottesville, VA, 1980–3), I, 372.

[113] MacLeod, *Slavery, Race and the American Revolution*, 31.

[114] McColley, *Slavery and Jeffersonian Virginia*, 128–9.

[115] Woody Holton, *Liberty is Sweet: The Hidden History of the American Revolution* (New York, 2021), 144.

[116] 'Act for Laying a Duty on Slaves, 1772' in Donnan, ed., *Documents*, IV, 158–9; TNA, CO 5/1404, An Act for continuing and amending several acts for laying duties upon slaves imported, 11 Apr. 1772. For a complaint by Liverpool and Lancaster merchants about the additional levy, see TNA, CO 5/1332, Petition of slave traders concerning a tax on slaves imported into Virginia, June 1770.

TABLE 1.3 *Duties on slave imports to Virginia, 1699–1776*

1699–1710	20 shillings per head
1710–18	£5 per head
1718–32	No import duty
1732–39	5% ad valorem duty
1740–51	10% ad valorem duty
1752	5% on the sale price of imported slaves
1754	10% ad valorem duty
1755–60	20% ad valorem duty
1761–7	10% ad valorem duty
1766	5% on slaves imported from other colonies
1767–71	20% ad valorem duty
1772	10% on slave imports from Africa and £5 on slaves imported from other colonies

Source: Darold D. Wax, 'Negro Import Duties in Colonial Virginia: A Study in British Commercial Policy and Local Public Policy', *Virginia Magazine of History and Biography*, 79/1 (1971), 31–2; Richard K. MacMaster, 'Arthur Lee's "Address on Slavery": An Aspect of Virginia's Struggle to end the Slave Trade', *Virginia Magazine of History and Biography*, 89/2 (1972), 143.

applied to the costs of government.[117] It is probable that significant levels of evasion impeded the collection of many of these levies because colonists waited for Africans to be delivered on ships via the River Potomac to Maryland or crossed over into North Carolina to purchase slaves there in order to avoid Virginia's slave import duties.[118]

Table 1.3 summarises the duties levied on imported slaves in Virginia. The only period in the first three-quarters of the eighteenth century where no such duties were imposed was between 1718 and 1732. By 1760, there is some evidence that wealthier planters, who had sufficient slaves, wanted to maintain the 20 per cent *ad valorem* duty whereas impecunious planters, who needed saltwater Africans, would have preferred the duty to be reduced to 10 per cent.[119] Table 1.3 shows that the less wealthy planters prevailed. As indicated above, the British government disallowed Virginia statutes dealing with slave imports in 1723 and 1728, both of which proposed an import duty of 40 shillings per slave, but then did not

---

[117] TNA, CO 5/1349, Nelson, 'Observations on the Several Acts of Assembly', fol. 84v.
[118] Hillman, ed., *Executive Journals*, VI, 150.
[119] Library of Virginia, Richmond, William Allason to Halliday & Dunbar, 19 Aug. 1760, William Allason letterbook (1757–70), Allason Papers.

interfere for another thirty-five years.[120] However, the Privy Council vetoed Virginia laws of 1767 and 1769 doubling the slave import duty and rejected the Assembly's petition to abolish the slave trade.[121]

The Virginians' actions raised revenue to defend their citizens but also limited slave importations. The grounds for implementing import duties were not always made explicit, but mixed motives were apparent. On some occasions, Virginians introduced such duties through fear of slave insurrections, to prevent the accumulation of debts from purchasing slaves, and to pay for financing the Seven Years' War. On other occasions, duties were imposed from the desire to restrict slave imports to increase the value of slaves already living in Virginia.[122] One Virginia governor, worried about slave insurrections in the colony, thought additional levies on imported slaves would lessen their increase.[123] Virginia had numerous indebted tobacco plantations on the eve of the War of Independence coupled with significant demographic growth among existing slave communities. The transition from tobacco to grain in the Chesapeake economy in the revolutionary era meant that fewer imported Africans were needed for field labour, because cultivation of grain products did not require a plantation workforce.[124] Raising import duties on Africans arriving in the colony seemed the solution to these economic problems. These various considerations 'far outweighed any humanitarian impulse to end the traffic'.[125]

In the Virginia Assembly's debate on slave import duties in 1759, Richard Henry Lee argued that importing more Africans would deter Virginia from attracting skilled European immigrants needed for a diversifying regional economy.[126] This theme was frequently aired over the next fifteen years. Influenced by antislavery ideas and the effects of slavery on white people, Arthur Lee, in his 'Address on Slavery' (*Rind's Virginia*

---

[120] Darold D. Wax, 'Negro Import Duties in Colonial Virginia: A Study in British Commercial Policy and Local Public Policy,' *VMHB*, 79/1 (1971), 40, 43. For numerous objections to the proposed import duty discussed in 1723 and 1728, see Donnan, ed., *Documents*, IV, 104–17, 122–7.
[121] Woody Holton, *Forced Founders: Indians, Debtors, Slaves, and the Making of the American Revolution in Virginia* (Chapel Hill, NC, 1999), 71.
[122] Wax, 'Negro Import Duties in Colonial Virginia', 29–44; Alexander Spotswood to the Council of Trade, 6 Mar. 1710/11 in Brock, ed., *The Official Letters of Alexander Spotswood*, I, 52–3.
[123] Brown, *Tacky's Revolt*, 228.   [124] Holton, *Forced Founders*, 66–7, 71.
[125] Wax, 'Negro Import Duties in Colonial Virginia', 43.
[126] Bruce A. Ragsdale, *A Planter's Republic: The Search for Economic Independence in Revolutionary Virginia* (Madison, WI, 1996), 120.

Gazette, 19 March 1767) attempted to persuade the House of Burgesses to end the slave trade to the colony.[127] He argued that 'to people the American Colonies was no excuse for the slave trade. Great Britain and America would alike profit from the increase of free settlers and the abolition of the slave trade'.[128]

Lee's sentiments were echoed by the planter George Mason, who argued that Virginia should pay more attention to importing white labourers rather than slaves.[129] Mason reported in April 1769 that the Virginia non-importation association would not import any more slaves until government acts harming trade were repealed.[130] A month later the Virginia non-importation resolutions stated that the colony would not import any slaves after 1 November 1769 until Britain repealed parliamentary acts dealing with trade.[131] A contributor to the *Virginia Gazette* in 1771 also urged the end of slave imports to the Old Dominion to discourage 'a Practice which must forever prevent our Country from flourishing as the northern Colonies have done'.[132]

These ideas were never implemented in legislation, but further efforts were made to restrict slave imports to Virginia. Not all were successful. Thus, the Board of Trade informed the king that a Virginia act of November 1769 laid an additional duty of 15 per cent on the purchase price of each slave imported to the colony. This was to be paid by the purchaser, and it came on top of all other duties applied to slave importations then in force. Amounting to a duty of 20 per cent on imported Africans, it was 'intended to operate as an intire prohibition to the importation of Slaves into Virginia'. However, the Privy Council advised the king that the act should be disallowed because it could diminish the level of Anglo–Virginian trade.[133]

---

[127] Oliver Perry Chitwood, *Richard Henry Lee, Statesman of the Revolution* (Morgantown, WV, 1967), 18–19.
[128] Richard K. MacMaster, 'Arthur Lee's "Address on Slavery": An Aspect of Virginia's Struggle to end the Slave Trade, 1765–1774', *VMHB*, 80/2 (1972), 146.
[129] George Mason to George William Fairfax and George Washington, 23 Dec. 1765, in Robert A. Rutland, ed., *The Papers of George Mason, 1725–1792*, 3 vols. (Chapel Hill, NC, 1970), I, 61–2.
[130] 'The Nonimportation Association as Corrected by Mason', Apr. 1769, ibid., I, 105. This was a response to the new taxes levied by the Townshend Acts of 1767 and 1768.
[131] Virginia Non-importation resolutions, 17 May 1769, in Julian P. Boyd, ed., *The Papers of Thomas Jefferson. Volume 1. 1760–1776* (Princeton, NJ, 1950), 27–31.
[132] 'Associator Humanus', *Virginia Gazette* (Purdie & Dixon), 18 July 1771.
[133] John C. Van Horne, ed., *The Correspondence of William Nelson as Acting Governor of Virginia 1770–1771* (Charlottesville, VA, 1976), 77, 79 (quotation), 82.

By the early 1770s, various high-profile Virginia planters called for an end to slave imports to the colony. They seemingly recognised that a continuance of the slave trade would affect the colony's economic potential. The slave population in the Old Dominion was now growing steadily and it made no financial sense to continue to import saltwater Africans.[134] In 1772, Thomas Jefferson and all other members of the Virginia House of Burgesses voted to ask George III to abolish the entire British transatlantic slave trade, which was described as 'a trade of great inhumanity'. Benjamin Franklin credited Benezet's pamphlets and antislavery petitions with influencing the Virginia House of Burgesses to submit this petition to the monarch. No action followed.[135] A committee of Virginia's burgesses argued that considerations of humanity needed to be taken into account to restrict slave imports to Virginia; that eliminating the traffic would improve the security of the colony; and that ending the slave trade would lead to the introduction of free white migrants to benefit the colony.[136] The Board of Trade considered that the act of 1772 to raise slave duties would harm British commerce with the colony; it therefore recommended that it should be disallowed.[137] George III refused his assent to an act passed by Virginia's House of Burgesses to lay this additional duty on slaves imported to Virginia.[138]

Further attacks on the slave trade emanated from Virginia. Attempts by the Virginia Assembly to increase slave import duties were frustrated.[139] At a June 1774 meeting of Prince George County freeholders, it was argued that 'the African trade is injurious to this colony, obstructs the population of it by freemen, prevents manufacturers and other useful

---

[134] Ragsdale, *A Planter's Republic*, 111–12; Parkinson, *Thirteen Clocks*, 55.
[135] Holton, *Forced Founders*, 66; John Pendleton Kennedy and Henry Read McIlwaine, eds., *Journals of the House of Burgesses of Virginia, 1770–1772* (Richmond, VA, 1906), 283–4 (quotation); Maurice Jackson, 'Anthony Benezet and the Dream of Freedom: Then and Now' in Rossignol and Van Ruymbeke, eds., *The Atlantic World of Anthony Benezet*, xiv. In 1773, the London Quaker David Barclay led a visitation to the Board of Trade to support Virginia's attempt to levy a tax on imported slaves: see David Brion Davis, *The Problem of Slavery in the Age of Revolution, 1770–1823* (Ithaca, NY, 1975), 231.
[136] McColley, *Slavery and Jeffersonian Virginia*, 133–4; Kennedy and McIlwaine, eds., *Journals of the House of Burgesses, 1770–1772*, 256–7, 283–4.
[137] McColley, *Slavery and Jeffersonian Virginia*, 134.
[138] Haverford College, Quaker Collection, Anthony Benezet to Moses Brown, 28 Dec. 1773, Anthony Benezet correspondence; Benezet to Moses Brown, 5 Sept. 1774, in Frost, ed., *The Quaker Origins of Antislavery*, 189.
[139] Swem Library, College of William and Mary, Robert Pleasants to Anthony Benezet, 22 Feb. 1774, Robert Pleasants letterbook (1771–81).

emigrants from Europe from settling among us, and occasions an annual increase of the balance of trade against this colony'.[140] The Fairfax County Resolves of July 1774, written by Mason and approved with George Washington presiding, announced a stop to slave importation and asked for an end to 'such a wicked cruel and unnatural trade'.[141] Mason argued that free labour would lead to a more productive use of land in Virginia than the continuing use of slave workers. Various county committees in Virginia also called for an end to slave imports to encourage skilled, free labourers to settle in the colony instead.[142] George Washington took the resolutions to Williamsburg in August 1774 and to Philadelphia to present them to delegates of the First Continental Congress, who had convened to coordinate opposition to British imperial policies.[143]

Virginia planters sometimes condemned the slave trade while wanting to retain slaves as an essential part of their livelihood. Patrick Henry, who referred to the slave trade as 'an abominable practice' but wanted to remain master of his slaves, was a prominent example. He thought a time would come when the 'lamentable evil' of the slave trade would be abolished, but the moment had not yet arrived.[144] Nevertheless, on receiving a copy of Benezet's book opposing the slave trade, he informed its author that he would honour the Quakers for opposing slavery.[145]

Tidewater planters, in particular, opposed the slave trade at this juncture, for they had sufficient slaves already and did not want to see new supplies depress prices.[146] Many Virginia politicians nevertheless condemned the slave trade. On 18 July 1774, the freeholders and inhabitants of Fairfax County called for an end to the African slave trade, in the context of continuing political disputes with Britain: 'Resolved, That it is

---

[140] MacMaster, 'Arthur Lee's "Address on Slavery"', 152. For a similar view emanating from Culpeper County, see Robert L. Scribner, ed., *Revolutionary Virginia. The Road to Independence. Volume 1. Forming Thunderclouds and the First Convention, 1763–1774* (Charlottesville, VA, 1975), 119.

[141] Quoted in Eva Sheppard Wolf, *Race and Liberty in the New Nation: Emancipation in Virginia from the Revolution to Nat Turner's Rebellion* (Baton Rouge, LA, 2006), 23. See also Crothers, *Quakers in the Lion's Mouth*, 45–6, and Alpaugh, *Friends of Freedom*, 184.

[142] McColley, *Slavery and Jeffersonian Virginia*, 121.

[143] David L. Ammerman, *In the Common Cause: American Response to the Coercive Acts of 1774* (Charlottesville, VA, 1974), 86.

[144] Patrick Henry to a correspondent, 18 Jan. 1773, in William Wirt Henry, ed., *Patrick Henry: Life, Correspondence, and Speeches*, 3 vols. (New York, 1891), I, 152–3.

[145] Haverford College, Quaker Collection, Patrick Henry to Robert Pleasants, 18 Jan. 1773, Anthony Benezet correspondence.

[146] Sheppard, *Race and Liberty in the New Nation*, 24.

the Opinion of this meeting, that during our present difficulties and distress, no Slaves ought to be imported into any of the British Colonies on this Continent. And we take this Opportunity of declaring our most earnest wishes, to see an Entire stop forever put to such a Wicked, Cruel & unnatural trade.'[147] Members of the Convention declared that they would neither import nor purchase slaves after 1 November from Africa, the West Indies or anywhere else.[148] By that time the supply of slaves to Virginia had ended and the colony had a self-sustaining slave population.[149]

Calls for ending the slave trade in Virginia before American independence were occasionally influenced by humanitarian concerns but were more frequently the result of political economy and arguments for free labour and economic independence.[150] In Virginia's non-importation agreements of 1774, which challenged British policies towards her North American colonies, opposition to the slave trade was expressed for various reasons. These included the dangers of the slave trade to virtue, the deterrence slave imports gave to the development of manufactures and trade, and the barrier to white immigration occurring from a continued influx of Africans. The inhumanity of the slave trade was also emphasised in the non-importation agreements of 1774, but not as the major reason for curtailing slave imports.[151]

RESTRICTIONS ON THE SLAVE TRADE IN THE CAROLINAS

North Carolina imported few slaves directly from Africa. Opposition to the slave trade in this colony nevertheless emerged in the years immediately prior to American independence. On 8 August 1774, the freeholders of Rowan County singled out the slave trade as 'injurious to this colony' because it was alleged to obstruct manufacturing and to lessen immigration from Europe. Three weeks later the Provincial Congress declared that 'we will not import any slave or slaves imported or brought into this

---

[147] *Virginia Gazette* (Rind), 11 Aug. 1774; General Meeting of the Freeholders & Inhabitants of the County of Fairfax, at the Court House in the Town of Alexandria, 18 July 1774, in Scribner, ed., *Revolutionary Virginia* (quotation), 131.

[148] Virginia Convention Resolutions, 1 Aug. 1774, in Peter Force, ed., *American Archives*, 4th series (Washington, DC, 1853), I, 686–7.

[149] Justin Roberts, 'The Development of Slavery in the British Americas' in Ignacio Gallup Diaz, ed., *The World of Colonial America: An Atlantic Handbook* (New York, 2017), 130; Haverford College, Quaker Collection, Anthony Benezet to Samuel Allinson, 23 Oct. 1774, Allinson Papers, box 4, folder 5.

[150] McColley, *Slavery and Jeffersonian Virginia*, 122.

[151] MacLeod, *Slavery, Race and the American Revolution*, 32.

province by others from any part of the world after the first day of November next'.[152] Thereafter a safety committee at Wilmington investigated individual infringements of this resolve and made arrangements for those found in breach of them to reship slaves to the place whence they came as soon as possible.[153] These developments indicate that W. E. B. Du Bois was incorrect in stating that 'there is no evidence of any effort to restrict or in any way regulate' the slave trade to North Carolina in the colonial period.[154]

South Carolina's public policy on slave imports also indicates changes through specific legislation designed to curb the entry of enslaved Africans into the colony. Raising the level of slave import duties occurred when the colony was worried about the possible dangers to public order thought likely to occur through having a black majority in the population already by the first decade of the eighteenth century – the only North American colony where this was the case.[155] The modest slave import duties implemented in statutes of 1703, 1714 and 1716 were raised significantly to an additional duty of £40 per slave in 1717 to limit the extension of slavery in the colony. Thus, the act of 1714, which imposed a duty of £2 currency on every imported African aged over twelve, referred to South Carolina's safety being compromised by the slow growth of the white population.[156]

A 1719 South Carolina statute brought in a duty to £10 for each slave imported from Africa and £30 per head for those arriving from other colonies. In 1722, the duty for the latter was increased to £50 per head.[157] Apprehensions over slave rebelliousness in the aftermath of the Stono

---

[152] Donnan, ed., *Documents*, IV, 237 (quotations); North Carolina Convention Resolutions, 24 Aug. 1774, in Force, ed., *American Archives*, I, 735.

[153] Extracts from the proceedings of the safety committee at Wilmington in Donnan, ed., *Documents*, IV, 237–9; William Laurence Saunders, ed., *The Colonial Records of North Carolina*, 29 vols. (Raleigh, NC, 1886), IX, 1,098–9, 1,113, 1,149–51, 1,168, 1,170–1.

[154] Du Bois, *The Suppression of the African Slave-Trade*, 12.

[155] Peter H. Wood, *Black Majority: Negroes in South Carolina from 1670 through the Stono Rebellion* (New York, 1974), 36. For a detailed study of South Carolina's policies on slave imports, see W. Robert Higgins, 'The South Carolina Negro Duty Law' (University of South Carolina M.A. thesis, 1967).

[156] 'Act for Governing Negroes, 1714' in Donnan, ed., *Documents*, IV, 257; Edward McCrady, *The History of South Carolina under the Royal Government 1719–1776* (New York, 1901), 48.

[157] McCrady, *The History of South Carolina*, 48; Paul Finkelman, 'Regulating the African Slave Trade', *Civil War History*, LIV/4 (2008), 380. Complaints about this level of duty were made by London and Bristol merchants, who considered it exorbitant: see 'Concerning Duties on Slaves, 1730–1732' and 'Concerning a Duty on Slaves, 1734' in Donnan, ed., *Documents*, IV, 274–5, 281–9.

rebellion in 1739 produced a different tax policy whereby duties on imported slaves were raised to a high level for three years between 1741 and 1744, amounting effectively to a temporary ban: no Africans were imported into South Carolina in 1741, 1742 and 1743.[158] The 1741 law was introduced because of the 'very dangerous consequence to the peace and safety' of South Carolina from the 'barbarous and savage disposition' of Africans.[159] For the first fifteen months after it was introduced, South Carolinians had to pay the £10 duty per slave imported to the colony; then, for three years a tax of £100 per adult slave imported from Africa would be imposed. The tax was sufficiently high to deter slave imports; it amounted to a prohibition.[160] Between 1741 and 1744, South Carolina had the highest import duties on slaves in the North American colonies. After the act for the prohibition of slaves expired on 5 July 1744, Charleston merchants had to produce a certificate specifying that any 'new negroes' had been brought directly from Africa or importers had to pay an extraordinary duty of £50 per head, the common duty being £10 currency per head for men and women and £5 per head for boys and girls.[161]

However, it was probably the continuing warfare of the 1740s rather than the lingering effect of import duties on captives that led to no slave ships arriving in Charleston between 1745 and 1749. This suited the needs of the South Carolina Assembly, which had become concerned about the Africanisation of the colony's population. In 1751, South Carolina passed an act to use three-fifths of the slave import duty collected to help settle Protestant immigrants in the colony.[162] During the 1750s, South Carolina used duties collected on slave imports for several diverse purposes: to encourage shipbuilding, to repair infrastructure, and to establish new parishes.[163]

---

[158] Finkelman, 'Regulating the African Slave Trade', 381; David Richardson, 'The British Slave Trade to Colonial South Carolina,' *Slavery & Abolition*, 12/3 (1991), 171.

[159] Thomas Cooper, ed., *Statutes at Large of South Carolina* (Columbia, SC, 1836), section for 1740.

[160] Paul Finkelman, 'The American Suppression of the African Slave Trade: Lessons on Legal Change, Social Policy, and Legislation', *Akron Law Review*, 42/2 (2009), 435; Edward B. Rugemer, *Slave Law and the Politics of Resistance in the Early Atlantic World* (Cambridge, MA, 2018), 114.

[161] Robert Pringle to Edward Pare, 5 May 1744, in Walter B. Edgar, ed., *The Letterbook of Robert Pringle, 1737–1745*, 2 vols. (Columbia, SC, 1972), II, 684.

[162] Robert M. Weir, *Colonial South Carolina: A History* (Columbia, SC, 1997), 208.

[163] TNA, CO 5/420, South Carolina Acts passed 11 May 1754.

TABLE 1.4 *Duties on slave imports to South Carolina, 1703–1764*

1703	10 shillings per slave
1714	£2 per slave
1716	£3 per slave
1717	Additional duty of £40 per slave
1719	£10 per slave
1741–4	£10 per slave for fifteen months and then £100 per slave
1751	£10 per slave
1764	Additional duty of £100 per slave

Source: W. E. B. Du Bois, *The Suppression of the African Slave-Trade to the United States of America, 1638–1870* (Cambridge, MA, 1896), 9; Thomas Cooper, ed., *Statutes at Large of South Carolina* (Columbia, SC, 1836), section 1 for 1740. The table omits levies on slaves who entered South Carolina from other American colonies.

In 1760, South Carolina's Assembly banned the slave trade because of fears of a growing African presence in the colony's population, but royal authorities disallowed the measure. The prevailing sentiment against Africans continued, however, and in 1764 another statute levied an additional tax of £100 current money per slave for three years from 1 January 1766. This was chargeable and collected by the public treasurer because the increasing number of African-born slaves 'may prove of the most dangerous consequence'.[164] Merchant bankruptcies and mounting debts in the colony were additional factors influencing the passing of this law.[165] As with the 1741 law, the implementation of the 1764 statute was delayed, this time by just over sixteen months.[166] A firm of Charleston factors considered that the new duties would result in South Carolina's backcountry settlers bringing in slaves from Georgia.[167]

---

[164] Thomas Cooper and David James McCord, eds., *The Statutes at Large of South Carolina: Acts 1753–1786* (Columbia, SC, 1838), IV, 187–8 (quotation); Finkelman, 'Regulating the African Slave Trade', 381. For commentary on the law by a leading Charleston merchant, see Henry Laurens to John Knight, 24 Aug. 1764, in George C. Rogers, Jr, David R. Chesnutt, Peggy J. Clark, Walter B. Edgar, eds., *The Papers of Henry Laurens. Volume 4. September 1, 1763–August 31, 1765* (Columbia, SC, 1968), 381-3.
[165] Weir, *Colonial South Carolina*, 165; Richardson, 'The British Slave Trade to South Carolina', 131.
[166] Finkelman, 'The American Suppression of the African Slave Trade', 431.
[167] Library of Congress, Robertson, Jamieson & Co. to Neil Jamieson, 5 Apr. 1765, Neil Jamieson Papers.

Heavy duties on slave imports continued in the mid-1760s, which witnessed the implementation of the 1764 statute, enacted to assuage planter indebtedness. These were effective, for only 3,354 captives were landed at Charleston between 1766 and 1768 on five transatlantic slavers and eleven intra-American slavers.[168] A motion to continue the slave duty for one year beyond 1 January 1769 was defeated in the House of Representatives on 27 January 1768.[169] Thus the duties on slave imports into South Carolina ended on 31 December 1768.[170] A Non-Importation Agreement of 1769, signed by 142 merchants and importers at Charleston, noted that South Carolina would not import any further Africans after 1 January 1770.[171] A second Non-Importation Agreement, involving a boycott of slave imports, came into effect on 1 December 1774.[172] These were partially effective: 25,736 captives were imported into Charleston between 1770 and 1775.[173] In all of the restrictive measures, South Carolina relied upon tax collectors to enforce policies rather than broadening the case for slave trade restriction to cover moral issues: those were avoided possibly because too many South Carolinians wanted to preserve slavery in their colony.[174]

Georgia, the last of the thirteen British American colonies to be created, had a distinctive position in relation to slavery and the slave trade. James Oglethorpe, the founder of the colony, wanted to settle Georgia with poor English migrants and to avoid slavery altogether. In 1734, his trustees received an agreement from the British Parliament that no slave imports into the colony would occur.[175] Without slave labour, however, the productive capacity of Georgia languished and so in 1749 the colonists, after complaining about the situation for several years, persuaded the trustees and the British authorities to open a limited importation of slaves, laying an import duty on new arrivals from Africa.

---

[168] www.slavevoyages.org
[169] SCDAH, House of Representatives Journal, 37 part 2, 27 Jan. 1768, fol. 518; Henry Laurens to John Moultrie, 28 Jan. 1768, in George C. Rogers, Jr and David R. Chesnutt, eds., *The Papers of Henry Laurens. Volume 5: September 1, 1765–July 31, 1768* (Columbia, SC, 1976), 571.
[170] Henry Laurens to Thomas & Richard Millerson & Co., 25 May 1768, in Rogers et al., eds., *The Papers of Henry Laurens. Volume 5*, 697.
[171] 'Non-importation Agreement, 1769' in Donnan, ed., *Documents*, IV, 433; McCrady, *The History of South Carolina*, 380.
[172] 'Non-Importation Agreement, 1774' in Donnan, ed., *Documents*, IV, 470.
[173] www.slavevoyages.org
[174] Finkelman, 'The American Suppression of the African Slave Trade,' 436.
[175] Brown, *Moral Capital*, 83.

Slaves were brought into Georgia after 1749, but is not known whether the import duty was enforced and collected.[176] However, in 1761, Georgia instigated a policy for taxing seasoned slaves aged over ten years at a per capita rate of £10 in order to prevent the dumping of unwanted slaves from other colonies.[177]

NORTH AMERICAN ATTACKS ON THE SLAVE TRADE IN THE LATE COLONIAL ERA

Towards the end of the colonial era, an opportunity to criticise slave importations arose with the non-importation movement that expressed opposition to the Townshend duties implemented by Parliament as tax-raising measures on the North American colonies in 1767–8. In 1769, George Mason opposed the slave trade in the fifth resolution of Virginia's non-importation resolutions. This stated that the Old Dominion would not 'import any slaves, or purchase any (hereafter) imported until the said Acts of Parliament are repealed'.[178] This had little impact in practice because Parliament repealed all of the Townshend duties except for that on tea in 1770. A second non-importation association established in Virginia's House of Burgesses on 22 June 1770 also included a similar statement expressing the intention to ban all slave imports, but it was relatively ineffective and ignored by a number of American merchants.[179]

By the late 1760s, newspaper articles and sermons began to attack the slave trade on moral and humanitarian grounds. Thus, a sermon by an anonymous member of the established church appeared in the 30 March 1767 issue of the *Pennsylvania Chronicle* with emotive language to castigate the trafficking of Africans, noting that 'already have the unhappy sons of *Guinea* half darken'd the islands and continent of this new-peopled world: another century or two, if the infernal traffic continues, there is the highest probability that it will totally eclipse the glory of *America*'. In the article, the author also referred to 'the horrid iniquity

---

[176] Du Bois, *The Suppression of the African Slave-Trade*, 8.
[177] Darold D. Wax, '"New Negroes Are Always in Demand": The Slave Trade in Eighteenth-Century Georgia', *Georgia Historical Quarterly*, 68/2 (1984), 204.
[178] Draft of Non-Importation Association, 23 Apr. 1769, and Virginia Nonimportation Resolutions, 18 May 1769, in Rutland, ed., *The Papers of George Mason*, I, 110.
[179] Virginia Nonimportation Association, 22 June 1770, ibid., I, 122; Christian M. McBurney, 'The First Efforts to Limit the African Slave Trade Arise in the American Revolution: Part 3 of 3, Congress Bans the African Slave Trade', *Journal of the American Revolution*, 15 September 2020, n.p., https://allthingsliberty.com.

of the slave trade' and denounced 'so flagitious a commerce'.[180] Another article, emanating from Roxbury, Massachusetts, used an essay by the Puritan divine Cotton Mather to describe 'the slave trade as a spectacle that shocks humanity'; it was an affront to Christian principles, militated against notions of liberty, and compromised New England's position as 'a LAND of LIGHT'.[181] In a 1772 'A Dialogue between two Neighbours, the one *Conscience*, the other *Self-Interest*' the slave trade was singled out as a great stain to the Christian conscience.[182] The Baptist minister Elhanan Winchester's sermon *The Reigning Abominations, Especially the Slave Trade* (1774) was intended to influence both British and American abolitionists. Colonial Virginians were susceptible to numerous vices, according to Winchester, because their participation in the slave trade, referred to as 'a most infamous commerce', blunted the heart against benevolence and promoted avarice and a lack of humanity.[183]

In newspaper articles on the iniquities of the slave trade, emphasis was often placed on the plight of the captives, their anguish in being forced aboard ship, and their 'afflictd condition' in being separated from their families 'and all the Comforts arising from Friendship and Acquaintance, carried amongst a People of Strange Language, to be parted from their fellow Captives, and assign'd to perpetual Slavery and Servitude'.[184] In 1774, an extended 'ADDRESS to Americans upon Slave-Keeping', emphasised the cooperation between African rulers and slave traders in gathering slaves in Africa, referring to this common practice as '*man-stealing* among their subjects' in 'this wicked and barbarous trade'.[185] An earlier article, appearing in the *Virginia Gazette* in mid-1770, was similarly critical of the slave trade, referring to it as depriving 'Mankind, free by nature, of that valuable blessing Liberty' and encouraging 'man-stealing & frequently murder with many other concomitant evils such as the separation forever

---

[180] This was reprinted in the *Newport Mercury*, 20 Apr. 1767.
[181] *Boston Evening-Post*, 15 Apr. 1768. This article was reprinted in *The New-London Gazette*, 13 May 1768, and *The Providence Gazette; and Country Journal*, 14 May 1768, where it was introduced as 'a subject of the most serious nature'.
[182] *The New-London Gazette*, 18 Sept. 1772. For a plea to abolish the slave trade and 'let the *oppressed* Africans go free', see *The Connecticut Gazette; and the Universal Intelligencer*, 15 July 1774. Further moral arguments against the slave trade are reported in *The Essex Journal and Merimack Packet: OR The Massachusetts and New-Hampshire General Advertiser*, 17 Aug. 1774.
[183] Philip Gould, *Barbaric Traffic: Commerce and Antislavery in the Eighteenth-Century Atlantic World* (Cambridge, MA, 2003), 17.
[184] *The New-London Gazette*, 5 Aug. 1768.
[185] *The Connecticut Courant, and Hartford Weekly Intelligencer*, 12 Sept. 1774.

Husbands from Wives and Parents from Children, torn with Violence from their Native Country, Connections, and everything valuable in life in order to supply the demand for that unnatural traffick'.[186]

CONCLUSION

Nine of the thirteen British North American colonies legislated in favour of slave import duties at one time or another. The many attempts by some colonies to restrict slave imports were successful in some instances. Individual colonial assemblies could pass and repeal laws dealing with duties on slave imports for a variety of reasons. Thus, colonies passed such legislation to restrict slave imports when saltwater Africans were not required economically, when there were fears of slave revolts, in order to boost white immigration, manufacturing and trade, and when military costs had to be met. Various colonies used the revenue raised by slave import duties for various purposes, including improving infrastructure and, in one case from Virginia, to rebuild a state house that had burned down. South Carolina made particular use of high slave import duties to stop Africans being imported in the wake of the Stono rebellion of 1739, thereby supporting public safety against protesting slaves. But instances occurred in some colonies, such as Massachusetts, where governors were opposed to laws increasing slave import duties and, in such cases, the legislation was vetoed.

Procedurally, any colonial laws passed in regard to slave import duties needed the assent of the monarch and the imperial parliament. This meant, in effect, that the colonies had to persuade the Board of Trade and the Privy Council in London to accept such legislation. In numerous cases, colonial statutes dealing with this subject were rejected. The British parliament reserved the overall political and constitutional right to decide on the merits of each case and its decisions were binding. As Britain maintained its transatlantic slave trade throughout the eighteenth century, it had no intention of stopping it in the American revolutionary era. The colonies did not combine to form an anti-slave trade stance before the meetings of the First Continental Congress in 1774, and even then the Guinea traffic formed just one element in the North American boycott of British goods in the tense couple of years leading up to the War of American Independence.

---

[186] Excerpt from the *Virginia Gazette*, no exact date specified but mid-1770, as quoted in Haverford College Library, Quaker Collection, Robert Pleasants letterbook (1754–97), fol. 121.

Moral concerns about the slave trade were fairly muted in the North American colonies. The Quakers were at the forefront of anti-slave trade commentary, in pamphlets, correspondence and public statements, but even they took decades to persuade their own membership to relinquish slave importation and slaveholding. New England clergymen joined by the 1770s in their condemnation of the slave trade. But there was no consensus in the North American colonies, not even north of Philadelphia where slave imports had long dried up, that consistent pressure should be exerted to proscribe the transatlantic slave trade. The trade was banned by most colonies in the non-importation protests of 1776–8, 1769–70 and 1774–6, but there were no detailed discussions about the subject at the two Continental Congresses after the Coercive Acts had been implemented in 1774. Abolitionist sentiment lay behind many condemnations of the slave trade by patriots in the American colonies in the mid-1770s but it had not grown into purposeful action.[187]

Robert Pleasants, who thought the slave trade discouraged industry and the settling of white people in Virginia, explained in 1774 that:

our legislature have, both by duties & by petition to the King, endeavour'd to stop the further importations; but while the Guinea merchants receive so much gain, and a corrupt ministry retain their influence, there is little reason to expect relief, by an assent to the one or a compliance to the other. At present there seems to be no other remedy than not to purchase, which indeed some are principled against, as well from a sense of the injustice to that unhappy people, as the good of posterity, and sound policy respecting the security of the state; yet so long as men are actuated more from considerations of present ease, & imaginary interest, than such laudable motives, there will not be virtue enough found to keep them out by those means, and therefore it may be feared the consequences one day or other must be dreadful.[188]

Things may not have turned out in such a future catastrophic scenario as Pleasants predicted, but his assessment of the tensions between economic interest and humanitarian concern were yet to be resolved in respect of the slave trade in the late colonial era, for though efforts were being made by the northern colonies to end the slave trade, African importations were still arriving in a number of southern colonies.[189]

---

[187] Alpaugh, *Friends of Freedom*, 176.
[188] Haverford College Library, Quaker Collection, Robert Pleasants to Charles Pleasants, 12 July 1774, Robert Pleasants letterbook (1754–97), fol. 32. The same letter appears in Library of Congress, Robert Pleasants letterbook (1771–81).
[189] Haverford College Library, Quaker Collection, Anthony Benezet to Robert Pleasants, 7 May 1774, Anthony Benezet correspondence.

2

The Slave Trade and Revolutionary North America, 1774–1787

The continuing deterioration of Anglo–American relations in the 1770s ushered in a new phase of deliberations over whether to continue slave importation in North America, especially after independence was declared in July 1776 and the United States of America was created. Thereafter, the new states had the sovereign right, should they choose to exercise it, over political matters that fell under their jurisdiction. Individual states had important immediate matters of governance to address and establish as newly minted entities, but they all, in the period 1774–87, turned at some point to consider whether they wished to continue with slave importation. There were different mechanisms for dealing with this matter. Legislation was one option, stern resolutions against the slave trade another. Combining opposition to the slave trade with a moral repugnance for slavery and embedding decisions on these issues in a state's constitution was a further option. These ways of tackling continuing slave importation were implemented during the years between the convening of the First Continental Congress (1774) and the Constitutional Convention (1787). Individual states pursued policies often with no particular reference to what other states were doing. This was an early sign of the commitment to states' rights, an integral component of the political history of the United States. As no national government existed before the late 1780s, there was no political mechanism available for a coordinated attempt to proscribe the slave trade across all states of the union. Progress was made on limiting slave importations into some states, but the restrictions introduced were not always permanent.

Criticism of the slave traffic in the American revolutionary era was to be expected at a time when the concepts of liberty and slavery were subject to ever-increasing scrutiny by political commentators.[1] As W. E. B. Du Bois succinctly put it, 'the new philosophy of "freedom" and the "rights of man", which formed the cornerstone of the Revolution, made even the dullest realize that, at the very least, the slave-trade and a struggle for "liberty" were not consistent'.[2] Criticisms of the slave trade emerged in different contexts in the United States in the American revolutionary era. There were private protests, such as that by Benjamin Rush, who stated: 'Let not our united republics be stained with the importation of a single African slave into America.'[3] Opposition to the slave trade began to emerge at town meetings and in print in Massachusetts when moral objections to the traffic were still gaining traction.[4] In 1779, North Carolina Quakers went to court to abolish slave imports, but the state legislature rejected their case.[5] This is a reminder that perceived infringements of states' rights affected the approval or disapproval of committee decisions.

This chapter discusses the main developments in the pursuit of an anti-slave trade posture in the North American colonies and states from the bringing together of the first political combination of those entities in 1774, through to the eve of the Constitutional Convention. Some context for developments covered in the chapter is provided by an initial assessment of the degree to which the slave trade was condemned in North America. This involves returning to a theme examined in Chapter 1, namely the role of the Quakers, in particular Anthony Benezet. The chapter then analyses various strands that led to progress in anti-slave trade activity between 1774 and 1787, including decisions made by the two Continental Congresses; the role of Thomas Jefferson and the Declaration of Independence in condemning the Guinea traffic; the various means through which the slave trade was curtailed in states such as Virginia, Massachusetts and Pennsylvania; the attention paid to the slave trade in the Confederation Congress between 1783 and 1787; and the

---

[1] Bernard Bailyn, *The Ideological Origins of the American Revolution* (Cambridge, MA, 1967; enlarged ed., 1992), 55–93, 232–45.
[2] W. E. B. Du Bois, *The Suppression of the African Slave-Trade to the United States of America, 1638–1870* (Cambridge, MA, 1896), 41.
[3] Benjamin Rush to Nathanael Greene, 16 Sept. 1782, in L. H. Butterfield, ed., *Letters of Benjamin Rush*, 2 vols. (Princeton, NJ, 1951), I, 286.
[4] Christian M. McBurney, 'The First Efforts to Limit the African Slave Trade Arise in the American Revolution: Part 1 of 3, the New England Colonies', n.p., *Journal of the American Revolution*, 14 Sept. 2020, https://allthingsliberty.com.
[5] Maurice Jackson, *Let This Voice Be Heard: Anthony Benezet, Father of Atlantic Abolitionism* (Philadelphia, 2009), 249.

political decisions of the state most opposed to slave trade abolition, namely South Carolina. These disparate developments show that the anti-slave trade cause made numerous gains between 1774 and 1787 – far more than had previously occurred – but that further issues needed to be resolved before there could be national action on the slave trade.

NORTH AMERICAN CONDEMNATION OF THE SLAVE TRADE AND ANTISLAVERY ACTIVITY IN THE AMERICAN REVOLUTIONARY ERA

Just before and during the American revolutionary war, the condemnation of slavery and the slave trade gained wider traction among educated Americans. Quakers were at the forefront of this critical stance among Christian denominations.[6] Regular correspondence between Quakers and their meetings in Philadelphia and London denounced the slave trade among the Society of Friends on moral and humanitarian grounds, with both the British participation in the slave trade and the American reception of imported Africans receiving censure. In July 1774, the Meeting for Sufferings in Philadelphia sent a sympathetic message to its counterpart in London and asked for cooperation in order to suppress 'the iniquity of this inhuman traffic', adding that 'we have grounds to believe that the Testimony against it is increasing'.[7]

The most prominent figure was the Quaker Anthony Benezet, who led an indefatigable assault on the immorality of slavery and the slave trade through his writings, letters, political lobbying, work with Quaker meetings and committees, and exchange of books and pamphlets with sympathetic supporters throughout North America and Europe. These included leading lights of the British abolitionist movement such as Granville Sharp and Thomas Clarkson and, in North America, the anti-slave trade Rhode Island Quaker, Moses Brown, as well as Benjamin Rush and Benjamin Franklin.[8] Benezet's opposition to the slave trade was clearly articulated in publications such as *Observations on the Inslaving, Importing and*

---

[6] Samuel Hopkins to Moses Brown, 29 Apr. 1784, in Edwards Amasa Park, *Memoir of the Life and Character of Samuel Hopkins, D. D.* (Boston, 1854), 120.
[7] Library of the Religious Society of Friends, London, The Meeting for Sufferings in Philadelphia to the Meeting for Sufferings in London, 21 July 1774, Letters passed between the Meetings for Suffering in London and the Meetings for Sufferings in Philadelphia, vol. 1 (1757–1815).
[8] Haverford College Library, Quaker Collection, Anthony Benezet to Moses Brown, Nov. 1773, Anthony Benezet Correspondence; Maurice Jackson, 'Anthony Benezet:

Purchasing of Negroes . . . (1759) and *A Caution and Warning to Great Britain and her Colonies, in a Short Representation of the Calamitous State of the Enslaved Negroes in the British Dominions . . .* (1766).[9]

Benezet believed that Africans lived peacefully and freely before the emergence of the transatlantic slave trade and that the buying and selling of slaves into that traffic was a moral corrosion on Africans and Europeans.[10] He wrote extensively about the capture of slaves in Africa, the privations to which they were subjected and the violence involved in loading them on board ship for the Atlantic crossing for sale in the Americas. Benezet corresponded with English sympathisers to emphasise his 'deep concern' about 'the Negro trade'. He circulated publications drawing attention to 'the great wickedness with which this trade is carried on'.[11] His writings influenced both American and British abolitionism.[12]

Benezet was a leading antagonist of the slave trade, and he called for its abolition.[13] Writing from Philadelphia, in 1774, he expressed dismay that the moral case against the slave trade 'does not abate the zeal of some of our trading men against the traffic'. He observed that 'the inhumanity of the trade and the pernicious tendency of it becomes more and more the

---

Working the Antislavery Cause Inside and Outside of "The Society"' in Brycchan Carey and Geoffrey Plank, eds., *Quakers and Abolition* (Champaign-Urbana, IL, 2012), 112; Anthony Benezet, 'Negroes in Africa, 1762', Benezet to Granville Sharp, 14 May 1772, 29 Mar. 1773; and Benezet to Moses Brown, 9 May 1774, in Roger A. Bruns, ed., *Am I Not a Man and a Brother? The Antislavery Crusade of Revolutionary America, 1688–1788* (New York, 1977), 79, 193, 263, 308–11. The cooperation between Sharp and Benezet is discussed in Peter Stamatov, *The Origins of Global Humanitarianism: Religion, Empires, and Advocacy* (New York, 2013), 129–33.

[9] These publications are reprinted in J. William Frost, ed., *The Quaker Origins of Antislavery* (Norwood, PA, 1980), 193–237.

[10] Maurice Jackson, 'Anthony Benezet and the Dream of Freedom: Then and Now' in Marie-Jeanne Rossignol and Bertram Van Ruymbeke, eds., *The Atlantic World of Anthony Benezet (1713–1784): From French Reformation to North American Antislavery Activism* (Leiden, 2016), xi.

[11] Anthony Benezet to Joseph Phipps, 28 May 1763, in Frost, ed., *The Quaker Origins of Antislavery*, 187.

[12] This is apparent in many of his publications gathered together in David L. Crosby, ed., *The Complete Antislavery Writings of Anthony Benezet, 1754–1783: An Annotated Critical Edition* (Baton Rouge, LA, 2014). For an appraisal of one of his main publications, see Trevor Burnard, 'Anthony Benezet: *A Short History of Guinea* and Its Impact on Early British Abolitionism' in Joy Damousi, Trevor Burnard and Alan Lester, eds., *Humanitarianism, Empire and Transnationalism, 1760–1995: Selective Humanity in the Anglophone World* (Manchester, 2022), 37–59.

[13] Christopher L. Brown, *Moral Capital: Foundations of British Abolitionism* (Chapel Hill, NC, 2006), 397.

subject of conversation amongst all ranks of people here'.[14] Benezet summarised his own publications criticising the slave trade in letters to his associates and concluded by 1783 that his findings needed to be laid before active men in government.[15] Benezet's circulation of his writings to prominent individuals helped them to consider 'the outrages and corruptions attendant on the slave trade and slavery'.[16] Benezet wrote to the Abbé Raynal in France to 'represent to our compatriots the abominable iniquity of the Guinea trade'.[17] He also wrote to Queen Charlotte of Britain to explain the cruelty of slavery and his opposition to the slave trade.[18] In his *Observations on the Inslaving, Importing, and Purchasing of Negroes* (1760), he added an air of authenticity by including accounts from traders who had been to West Africa and had witnessed the cruelties of slave trading there.[19]

However, condemnation of the slave trade extended beyond the numerically limited realm of Quakers.[20] Clergymen took the lead in excoriating the traffic. John Allen, a Baptist minister in Boston, published a sermon entitled *An Oration on the Beauties of Liberty* (1772) containing emotive criticisms of the horrors of the slave trade, which he characterised as the theft of people from Africa. This was later printed as a popular pamphlet.[21] In 1774, the Reverend Levi Hart delivered a sermon in Connecticut that branded the slave trade a crime and rhetorically asked what Africans had done to Americans to justify their being seized and

---

[14] Anthony Benezet to Moses Brown, 5 Sept. 1774, in Frost, ed., *The Quaker Origins of Antislavery*, 190.
[15] HSP, Anthony Benezet to John Pemberton, 10 Aug. 1783, Pemberton Papers, box 39, folder 109.
[16] Roberts Vaux, *Memoirs of the Life of Anthony Benezet* (Philadelphia, 1817), 34.
[17] Haverford College Library, Quaker Collection, Benezet to the Abbé Raynal, n.d., in *The Pennsylvania Evening Post, and Public Advertiser*, 17 June 1782, Allinson Papers, box 4, folder 5.
[18] Haverford College Library, Quaker Collection, Anthony Benezet to Charlotte, Queen of Britain, 25 Aug. 1783, Anthony Benezet correspondence. Benezet's letter to Queen Charlotte was printed in many newspapers over a period of years. For one example, see the *Federal Spy* (Springfield, Massachusetts), 15 Mar. 1803.
[19] Jonathan D. Sassi, 'With a Little Help from the Friends: The Quaker and Tactical Contexts of Anthony Benezet's Abolitionist Publishing,' *PMHB*, 135/1 (2011), 43.
[20] Joane Pope Melish, *Disowning Slavery: Gradual Emancipation and "Race" in New England, 1780–1860* (Ithaca, NY, 1998), 50.
[21] Stewart M. Robinson, *Political Thought of the Colonial Clergy. Words of the Declaration of Independence Foreseen in the Writings of Clergymen prior to July 1776* (n.p., 1956), 36.

taken as enforced transatlantic migrants.[22] Hart pursued links between the abolition of the slave trade, gradual slave emancipation and Christian salvation.[23] In 1775, Deacon Benjamin Colman of Newbury, Massachusetts argued in a newspaper article that the slave trade was tantamount to participation in a serious crime.[24] The Reverend Samuel Hopkins of Newport, Rhode Island, wrote a pamphlet in 1776, that referred to the slave trade as an immoral form of commerce that inflicted 'inhumanity, oppression, and cruelty, exceeding everything of the kind that has ever been perpetrated by the sons of men'.[25] Hopkins regarded the slave trade as an affront to disinterested Christian benevolence.[26] He cited examples of cruelty against Africans on the west African coast and during the Middle Passage in his condemnation of the slave trade.[27]

Despite these criticisms of the slave trade to North America, no political movement to end the traffic in imported Africans occurred during the revolutionary era. Benezet wrote nothing more about the slave trade for almost a decade after 1774.[28] English Quakers, in particular, were lukewarm in their support for their American abolitionist counterparts. The American Revolution interrupted American abolitionism in North America and Benezet's wide-ranging correspondence.[29] In 1788, the French traveller Brissot de Warville claimed that by the mid-1770s 'a

---

[22] Joseph Conforti, *Samuel Hopkins and the New Divinity Movement* (Grand Rapids, MI, 1981), 127.
[23] Molly Oshatz, *Slavery and Sin: The Fight against Slavery and the Rise of Liberal Protestantism* (New York, 2011), 33.
[24] Joshua Coffin, *A Sketch of the History of Newbury, Newburyport, and West Newbury* (Boston, 1845), 339–40.
[25] Samuel Hopkins, *A Dialogue Concerning the Slavery of the Africans: Shewing It to Be the Duty and Interest of the American States to Emancipate All Their African Slaves; With an Address to the Owners of Such Slaves: Dedicated to the Honourable the Continental Congress: To Which Is Prefixed the Constitution of the Society, in New-York, for Promoting the Manumission of Slaves, and Protecting Such of Them as Have Been, or May Be, Liberated* (Norwich, CT, 1776), 6, 17.
[26] Oshatz, *Slavery and Sin*, 35.
[27] McBurney, 'The First Efforts to Limit the African Slave Trade Arise in the American Revolution: Part 1 of 3', n.p.
[28] Robert G. Parkinson, *Thirteen Clocks: How Race United the Colonies and Made the Declaration of Independence* (Chapel Hill, NC, 2021), 57.
[29] Brown, *Moral Capital*, 405, 412; Seymour Drescher, 'Divergent Paths: The Anglo-American Abolitions of the Atlantic Slave Trade' in Wim Klooster, ed., *Migration, Trade, and Slavery in an Expanding World: Essays in Honour of Pieter Emmer* (Leiden, 2009), 264.

general cry' arose against the slave trade in North America.[30] However, this was an exaggeration. By 1774, antislavery activity in the North American colonies, based on the spread of the discourse of natural rights, was beginning to experience decline. Only one significant pamphlet dealing with the abolition of the slave trade appeared in the early years of the revolutionary war, namely Samuel Hopkins's *A Dialogue Concerning the Slavery of Africans* (1776), which attributed early American successes in the War of Independence to God's approval of the decision of the Continental Congress to forbid slave imports.[31] The fragility of the wartime situation chipped away at unity among many Americans on this topic. 'Although sentiment against slave imports continued through the 1770s', Robert G. Parkinson has argued, 'it did not translate into a consensus for abolition'.[32]

THE CONTINENTAL CONGRESSES AND THE SLAVE TRADE

By the mid-1770s, the first attempt to ban the slave trade by the North American colonies as a whole came with a pledge from the First Continental Congress, a meeting of delegates between 5 September and 26 October 1774 from twelve of the thirteen North American colonies at Carpenters' Hall, Philadelphia. Mainly concerned with discussions about boycotting goods imported from Britain in the Anglo–American political crisis rather than moral concerns about the slave trade, the delegates resolved not to import or purchase another slave from 1 December 1774, 'after which time, we will wholly discontinue the slave trade, and will neither be concerned in it ourselves, nor will we hire our vessels, nor sell our commodities or manufactures to those who are concerned in it'.[33]

---

[30] J. P. Brissot de Warville, *New Travels in the United States of America. Performed in 1788* (London, 1788), 269.
[31] Bruns, ed., *Am I Not a Man and a Brother?*, 397.
[32] Robert G. Parkinson, '"Manifest Signs of Passion": The First Federal Congress, Antislavery, and Legacies of the Revolutionary War' in John Craig Hammond and Matthew Mason, eds., *Contesting Slavery: The Politics of Bondage and Freedom in the New American Nation* (Charlottesville, VA, 2011), 54.
[33] Worthington C. Ford et al., eds., *Journals of the Continental Congress, 1774–1789*, 34 vols. (Washington, DC, 1904–37), I, 177. However, some colonies, notably Rhode Island, were averse to this resolution, believing it harmed their slave trading activities: see Duncan J. MacLeod, *Slavery, Race and the American Revolution* (Cambridge, 1974), 32. The pledge from the Continental Congress was anticipated by one month in North Carolina by a general meeting of Deputies at Newbern on 25 Aug. 1774, which resolved that they would neither import nor purchase slaves after 1 November 1774: see *The North Carolina Gazette*, 2 Sept. 1774.

This was one of the first measures issued by the Continental Congress as part of their broader non-importation ban on British goods.[34] It seems that Benezet influenced this determination through his meetings with delegates at the Congress.[35] The decision was greeted warmly by anti-slave trade supporters. The Reverend Samuel Hopkins, for instance, informed a member of the Continental Congress that its members had exercised 'much wisdom and benevolence' in making this decision and had 'rejoiced the hearts of many benevolent, pious persons, who have been long convinced of the unrighteousness and cruelty of that trade, by which so many Hundreds of thousands are enslaved'.[36]

This was the first time the British North American colonies – with one exception, Georgia – had come together to issue such a statement.[37] This was followed by a ban on imported slaves suggested by the Second Continental Congress, held in Independence Hall, Philadelphia from 10 May 1775. This body included delegates from twelve of the thirteen colonies. It is not known who was responsible for drafting the relevant clause relating to the slave trade in the Continental Association agreement, but it was most likely to have been Richard Henry Lee of Virginia who, though he was a slaveowner, had previously spoken about the immorality of the traffic.[38] The decision to include the slave trade in the non-importation agreements did not necessarily mean that all colonies were opposed to slave imports. Indeed, it could be argued that this was more related to colonies expressing their political right to self-determination. South Carolina agreed to the policy to reduce its debts, but it did not want to see the ban on the slave trade become permanent.[39]

The first ban on the slave trade was incorporated into the second of the Articles of Association of the First Continental Congress on 20 October 1774. The second ban was implemented by its successor in

---

[34] Micah Alpaugh, *Friends of Freedom: The Rise of Social Movements in the Age of Atlantic Revolutions* (Cambridge, 2021), 185.
[35] Anthony Benezet to Samuel Allinson, 23 Oct. 1774, in George S. Brookes, *Friend Anthony Benezet* (Philadelphia, 1937), 98.
[36] Samuel Hopkins to Thomas Cushing, 29 Dec. 1775, in Robert J. Taylor, ed., *The Adams Papers. Papers of John Adams. Volume 3. May 1775–January 1776* (Cambridge, MA, 1979), 388–90.
[37] Christian M. McBurney, 'The First Efforts to Limit the African Slave Trade Arise in the American Revolution: Part 3 of 3, Congress Bans the African Slave Trade', *Journal of the American Revolution*, 15 September 2020, n.p., https://allthingsliberty.com.
[38] Ibid.
[39] David Brion Davis, *The Problem of Slavery in the Age of Revolution, 1770–1823* (Ithaca, NY, 1975), 119–20.

April 1776.⁴⁰ Benjamin Rush welcomed the first decision on moral grounds, noting that 'this resolution does our Congress the more honor as it was proposed and defended entirely on *moral* and not political principles'.⁴¹ The English abolitionist lawyer Granville Sharp concurred, referring to the Congress acting 'nobly in forbidding the iniquitous importation of more slaves'.⁴² A contrary view was expressed by Benezet, who thought it would have little effect as it ignored the supply of slaves by Britain to the West Indies and overlooked the possible entry of Africans into North America via the Mississippi River.⁴³ The documentary record is silent over the views and discussions on the slave trade at both Continental Congresses, but it may be that the subject was too controversial to be debated and recorded.⁴⁴

The decision of the First Continental Congress on slave importations had a positive effect on the only colony absent from its meetings. On 6 July 1775 Georgia, which did not send delegates to the Continental Congresses, resolved to neither import nor purchase slaves from Africa or elsewhere 'after this day'.⁴⁵ In April 1776, the Second Continental Congress modified the proscription of British imported goods, however, and stated that a permanent abolition of the slave trade was not intended.⁴⁶ At the time, it was reasonable to assume that prohibition of slave importation would become a permanent policy.⁴⁷

Condemnation of the slave trade by both Continental Congresses was given impetus by political divisions between Britain and her North American colonies rather than representing action based mainly on

---

[40] John P. Kaminski, Gaspare J. Saladino and Richard Leffler, eds., *Commentaries on the Constitution, Public and Private. Volume 2: 8 November to 17 December 1787* (Madison, WI, 1983), 503, 509; John P. Kaminski, Gaspare J. Saladino and Richard Leffler, eds., *Commentaries on the Constitution, Public and Private. Volume 3: 18 December 1787 to 31 January 1788* (Madison, WI, 1984), 437.

[41] Rush to Granville Sharp, 1 Nov. 1774, in John A. Woods, ed., 'The Correspondence of Benjamin Rush and Granville Sharp 1773–1809', *Journal of American Studies*, 1/1 (1967), 13. See also Donald J. D'Elia, 'Dr Benjamin Rush and the Negro', *Journal of the History of Ideas*, 30/3 (1969), 417.

[42] LCP, Granville Sharp to Rush, 18 July 1775, Benjamin Rush correspondence, vol. 28.

[43] Benezet to Granville Sharp, 18 Nov. 1774, as quoted in Bruns, ed., *Am I Not a Man and a Brother?*, 351.

[44] Joseph J. Ellis, *The Cause: The American Revolution and Its Discontents, 1773–1783* (New York, 2021), 34.

[45] Ruth Scarborough, *The Opposition to Slavery in Georgia prior to 1860* (Nashville, TN, 1933), 97.

[46] Mack Thompson, *Moses Brown, Reluctant Reformer* (Chapel Hill, NC, 1962), 106.

[47] Betty Fladeland, *Men and Brothers: Anglo-American Antislavery Cooperation* (Champaign-Urbana, IL, 1972), 29.

humanitarian or economic motives. As Christopher L. Brown has argued, the non-importation agreements highlighted the distinction between British and American identities: 'Bans on the slave trade took shape as a way to displace moral responsibility for colonial slavery onto Britain, and to cast colonial patriots as innocent victims of a mercantile system that not only enslaved them but led them to enslave others. Prohibiting the importation of slaves allowed Americans to declare their innocence and demonstrate their virtue without much changing their economic system.'[48] Thus the decisions made by the Continental Congresses in respect of the slave trade served as part of a wider political economy of resistance to British sovereignty.

The continental Congresses were supported by local patriot committees in individual colonies that reinforced their resolves. These groups respected the decisions made by the two Continental Congresses on the slave trade. Thus in March 1775, when a merchant from Norfolk, Virginia ignored the Continental Association's stipulation to ban slave imports, the local Committee of Correspondence stated that the matter should be publicised, that the Rhode Island merchant, John Brown, a participant in the slave trade, should be singled out as an enemy of American liberty 'and that every person may henceforth break off all dealings with him'.[49] Rhode Island's two delegates in the Continental Congress, the colony's former governor Samuel Ward and Stephen Hopkins, both indicated their support for the ban on importing slaves to North America.[50] Rhode Island, the leading colony in North America involved in the slave trade in the American revolutionary era, was largely successful in fulfilling the Continental Congress's objectives, for only three slavers left Rhode Island for Africa between 1 December 1774 and the end of the War for Independence in 1783.[51]

---

[48] Christopher Leslie Brown, 'The Problems of Slavery' in Edward G. Gray and Jane Kamensky, eds., *The Oxford Handbook of the American Revolution* (New York, 2012), 438.

[49] Proceedings of the Committee of Correspondence, 6 March 1775, in Peter Force, ed., *American Archives, Fourth Series: Containing a Documentary History of the English Colonies in North America, from the King's Message to Parliament, of March 7, 1774, to the Declaration of Independence by the United States*, 6 vols. (Washington, DC, 1837–56), II, 33–4.

[50] McBurney, 'The First Efforts to Limit the African Slave Trade: Part 3 of 3', n.p.; John Russell Bartlett, ed., *Records of the Colony of Rhode Island and Providence Plantations in New England. Volume VII. 1770 to 1776* (Providence, 1862), 264–5.

[51] www.slavevoyages.org. This is a corrective to Jay A. Coughtry, *The Notorious Triangle: Rhode Island and the African Slave Trade, 1700–1807* (Philadelphia, 1981), 31, which states that no Rhode Island slaving vessels sailed in this period.

Both congresses included a delegation from South Carolina, which of all the colonies and states, had the longest history of intransigence on banning the slave trade. The resolutions showed that delegates from various colonies could speak with a united voice. That the South Carolina delegates acceded to this proposed ban on slave imports is explained by the fact that both Continental Congresses acted within the broader context of nonimportation of British goods at this stage of the Anglo–American crisis. In both cases the decisions were influenced by widespread dislike of the traffic in enslaved Africans by many people in the northern colonies and the Upper South. In both cases, too, economic considerations – as outlined above in considering taxes on slave imports into Virginia and South Carolina – were much more important than moral scruples about the slave trade.[52] These resolutions were well observed initially in North America.[53] Yet they had no binding effect because neither the First nor the Second Continental Congress had the political authority to enforce its views: individual colonies were not required to bring their laws into line with the decisions of Congress, which could only signal its intentions.

THOMAS JEFFERSON, THE SLAVE TRADE AND THE DECLARATION OF INDEPENDENCE

In 1776, after the War for Independence started, Thomas Jefferson, a Virginia delegate to the Continental Congress, was the only leading American politician to stick his head above the parapet to denounce the continuance of the transatlantic slave trade. Already in 1774, in *A Summary View of the Rights of British America*, Jefferson had expressed his condemnation of the slave trade: 'The abolition of domestic slavery is the great object of desire in these colonies where it was unhappily introduced in its infant state. But previous to the enfranchisement of the slaves we had, it is necessary to exclude all further importations from Africa. Yet our repeated request to effect this by prohibitions and by imposing duties which might amount to a prohibition have been hitherto defeated by His Majesty's negative.'[54] In the first part of this quotation,

---

[52] Davis, *The Problem of Slavery in the Age of Revolution*, 24.
[53] Du Bois, *The Suppression of the African Slave-Trade*, 47.
[54] Thomas Jefferson, 'A Summary View of the Rights of British America, 1774' in Gordon S. Wood, ed., *The American Revolution: Writings from the Pamphlet Debate, 1764–1776*, 2 vols. (New York, 2015), II, 101–2.

Jefferson was expressing the view that making the slave trade illegal would weaken slavery in North America.[55] In the second part, Jefferson used the issue of the slave trade to attack British sovereignty over the North American colonies and to register his dismay that the British state considered the consent of colonists unimportant. Whether he sincerely believed that the slave trade should be abolished is problematic, however, given that he remained a lifelong slaveowner, as did several other Founding Fathers, including George Washington and James Madison.[56]

Tasked in June 1776 as part of a committee of five with other members of the Continental Congress to draft a declaration of independence, Jefferson was mainly responsible for the draft statement. He bolstered the arguments he had set down in *A Summary View of the Rights of British America* by boldly inserting a slave trade clause into the draft of the Declaration of Independence that introduced additional reasons for the necessity of ending the slave trade to North America. His words were aimed at King George III to justify the revolt against Britain by the American colonists. Jefferson argued that the king had 'waged cruel war against liberty itself, violating its most sacred rights of life and liberty in the persons of a distant population [Africans] who never offended him, capturing and carrying them into slavery in another hemisphere, or to incur miserable death in the transportation thither'. He added that the monarch had 'determined to keep open a market where Men should be bought & sold, he has prostituted his negative for suppressing every legislative attempt to prohibit or restrain this execrable commerce'.[57]

This statement suited Jefferson's political ends in supporting rebellion, but it was straining the argument to blame the monarch for a trade in which Virginia and other American colonies had freely participated.[58] Jefferson's words are phrased in an egregious way. No other delegate to the Continental Congress is on record as supporting this statement. In addition, as already noted, Jefferson was a slaveowner who retained

---

[55] Christa Dierksheide, 'Slavery in Jefferson's Worlds' in Dustin Gish and Andrew Bibby, eds., *Rival Visions: How Jefferson and His Contemporaries Defined the Early American Republic* (Charlottesville, VA, 2020), 191.

[56] Brown, 'The Problems of Slavery', 437.

[57] Quoted in Allan Nevins, *The American States during and after the Revolution 1775–1789* (New York, 1924), 445–6.

[58] Pauline Maier, *American Scripture: Making the Declaration of Independence* (New York, 1997), 146.

his slaves throughout the revolutionary war and beyond.[59] His words on the slave trade in his draft of the Declaration drew no attention to this fact. Nor was there condemnation of the domestic slavery found in the United States. It might be added that, when Jefferson penned his words, Virginia had already, to all extents and purposes, stopped importing Africans and experienced no shortage of black labourers either just before or during the revolutionary war.[60]

Jefferson's draft of the Declaration of Independence was submitted to the Continental Congress on 28 June 1776. It was discussed by that body for two days. Various changes were made which were not to Jefferson's liking. The Continental Congress deleted the draft clause on the slave trade from the final document partly because delegates from the southern states considered it an indirect attack on slavery itself. Another paragraph dealing with slavery was also deleted.[61] Jefferson observed in notes he kept of Congress's proceedings that the deletion was done 'in complaisance to South Carolina & Georgia, who had never attempted to restrain the importation of slaves, and who on the contrary still wished to continue it ... Our Northern brethren also I believe felt a little tender under those censures; for tho' their people have very few slaves themselves yet they had been pretty considerable carriers of them to others'.[62]

Jefferson regretted the deletion of his words on the slave trade in the draft version of the Declaration of Independence, implying that Congress could have taken a bolder step in moving towards abolition in the future.[63] Insufficient evidence is available to assess whether Jefferson had support for his deleted clause, but one correspondent informed John Adams, in what seems an implied reference to Jefferson's draft, that he could wish 'that some great Strokes I saw in a Manuscript Draught had

---

[59] David Armitage, *The Declaration of Independence: A Global History* (Cambridge, MA, 2007), 57–8.
[60] Philip D. Morgan, *Slave Counterpoint: Black Culture in the Eighteenth-Century and Lowcountry* (Chapel Hill, NC, 1998), 62.
[61] Ellis, *The Cause*, 87.
[62] Thomas Jefferson's Notes of Proceedings in Congress, 1–4 July 1776, in Paul H. Smith, ed., *Letters of Delegates to Congress, 1774–1789. Volume 4. 16 May–15 August 1776* (Washington, DC, 1979), 359. Jefferson preserved the deleted passage: see Thomas Jefferson, 'Autobiography' in Merrill D. Peterson, ed., *Thomas Jefferson: Writings* (New York, 1984), 21–2.
[63] Peter S. Onuf, 'Washington and Jefferson: American Nationhood and the Problem of Slavery' in Gish and Bibby, eds., *Rival Visions*, 215.

not been omitted'.[64] Jefferson himself complained about the mutilations to his draft of the Declaration of Independence. He wrote out his full draft in his own hand and circulated it to a number of his Virginia friends. But the deletions were not reinstated and so the Declaration effectively became Congress's document rather than just Jefferson's.[65] The pruning of Jefferson's draft of the Declaration meant that the views he expressed therein on the slave trade were not well known to his contemporaries.[66]

FURTHER NORTH AMERICAN OPPOSITION TO THE SLAVE TRADE IN THE REVOLUTIONARY ERA

The Continental Congress had already agreed to prohibit further importation of slaves in British ships on the basis that such captives were an item of trade, but the deletion of Jefferson's comments from the Declaration of Independence anticipated the way in which slave imports largely remained the prerogative of individual states for the next generation.[67] Nevertheless, the fact that Americans were now 'an independent people' gave hope to those who wished to abolish 'that impious trade' and awakened expectations that 'it will have but a very short duration'.[68] But matters turned out to be more complex than these expectations. After 1776, North Americans were involved not just in the extensive war effort but in drafting and debating constitutions for the new states that made up the United States of America. In these circumstances, it was difficult for them to focus on an effective ban to the slave trade. Disruptions to the transatlantic slave trade in the revolutionary war meant that slave imports into North America were effectively curtailed in any case from 1776 to 1783. Possibly that meant that the slave trade did not appear to be an immediate priority for political action.

The Articles of Confederation, the first formal charter for national government, were drawn up by the Continental Congress in 1776 but

---

[64] Samuel Cooper to John Adams, 14 Aug. 1776, in Robert J. Taylor, ed., *The Adams Papers. Papers of John Adams. Volume 4. February–August 1776* (Cambridge, MA, 1979), 457–8.
[65] Richard R. Beeman, *Our Lives, Our Fortunes and Our Sacred Honor: The Forging of American Independence, 1774–1776* (New York, 2013), 413.
[66] Francis D. Cogliano, *Thomas Jefferson: Reputation and Legacy* (Charlottesville, VA, 2006), 201.
[67] Seymour Drescher, *Abolition: A History of Slavery and Antislavery* (New York, 2009), 125.
[68] *The Boston-Gazette, and Country Journal*, 13 Oct. 1777.

were not published for a further five years owing to serious disagreements over the relative powers of Congress and the states and the ownership of public lands. No clause in the Articles of Confederation and Perpetual Union, the governing constitution of the alliance of US independent states, dealt with the slave trade; under those articles, ratified in 1781, the confederation government did not have the right to regulate commerce. This meant that by 1781 there was no collective agreement among the newly fledged states in relation to slave importation and thereby no means of states acting together on this issue. In any case, to suggest that the states could have combined their efforts on a slave trade clause or on any other significant political issue of the time is to misread history: at the same, individual states jealously guarded their own rights and were in the business of making arrangements that would be put into effect in their own jurisdictions.[69]

The Society of Friends in North America actively censured the slave trade when the revolutionary war ended. By 1780, the Philadelphia Meeting for Sufferings decided that public antislavery lobbying should be revived. It made efforts to persuade English Friends to promote abolitionism.[70] Prominent Pennsylvania Quakers attacked the slave trade. For example, James Pemberton referred in a letter to his brother that the African slave trade was 'a practice detestable to human nature, and sorrowfully disgraceful to any Government under the Christian profession'.[71] In 1783, the Yearly Meeting of Quakers in Delaware, New Jersey, Pennsylvania, western Maryland and western Virginia condemned the slave trade to the Confederation Congress, referring to 'avaricious motives ... contrary to every humane and righteous consideration, and in opposition to the solemn declarations often repeated in favour of universal liberty'. The meeting also criticised in emotive language 'the licentious wickedness of the African trade for slaves, and the inhuman Tyranny and Blood guiltiness inseparable from it'. A petition, signed by 536 Quakers from five states, requested Congress to intervene 'to discourage and prevent so obvious an evil'.[72] Benezet was probably the author of

---

[69] Jack N. Rakove, 'The Articles of Confederation, 1775–1783' in Jack P. Greene and J. R. Pole, eds., *A Companion to the American Revolution* (Oxford, 2000), 281–6.
[70] Brown, *Moral Capital*, 413–14.
[71] HSP, James Pemberton to John Pemberton, 20 Aug. 1783, Parrish and Pemberton Families Papers, Series 1: Pemberton Family Papers, box 1, folder 9.
[72] First and third quotations from Kaminski et al., eds., *Commentaries on the Constitution ...Volume 2*, 503; second quotation from Haverford College, Quaker Collection, Address of the Annual Assembly of the Yearly Meeting in Pennsylvania,

this address, which was delivered to Congress, then decamped to Princeton, New Jersey. Four members of the Quaker committee travelled there to be present at its reading.[73] The President of the Congress, Elias Boudinot, informed them that it was not common practice to allow petitioners an audience. However, he made an exception in this case and James Pemberton, representing the Philadelphia Yearly Meeting, was allowed to read out the Quaker petition before Congress.[74] Benezet also urged Benjamin Franklin to demonstrate leadership in Congress in relation to slavery and the slave trade.[75]

The Continental Congress encouraged states to enact laws against the slave trade compatible with the Articles of Association of 1774–5. In November 1783, the Quaker petition was taken to Annapolis, Maryland, where the Congress was then meeting, and presented to a committee comprising Jefferson, the lawyer David Howell of Rhode Island, and the Maryland lawyer Jeremiah T. Chase. The committee recommended that any action against the slave trade should be taken by individual states in accordance with the non-importation agreement of the First Continental Congress.[76] On 8 January 1784 Congress 'lightly dismissed' the committee report.[77] Dissatisfied with the silence of Congress on the slave trade, the Philadelphia Yearly Meeting revived the matter by sending a letter on the subject to Richard Henry Lee, the president of Congress, on 26 January 1785. His response to this request is unknown, but Congress did not take any action. The Philadelphia Yearly Meeting had reason to believe they had support in Congress in relation to the slave trade, but they had not received any account of public measures disapproving of the traffic.[78]

New Jersey, Delaware and the western parts of Maryland and Virginia, Oct. 1783, Philadelphia Yearly Meeting Minutes.

[73] Fladeland, *Men and Brothers*, 33; Friends Historical Library, London, 'To the United States in Congress Assembled. The Address of the People called Quakers' and 'To the Meeting for Sufferings in Philadelphia', n.d., Miscellaneous MSS.

[74] Gary B. Nash, *Warner Mifflin: Unflinching Abolitionist* (Philadelphia, 2017), 126, 128; HSP, William Dillwyn to John Pemberton, 6 Dec. 1783, Pemberton Papers, vol. 40.

[75] Benezet to Franklin, 5 Mar. 1783, in Brookes, *Friend Anthony Benezet*, 384–7.

[76] Nash, *Warner Mifflin*, 128.

[77] Michael J. Klarman, *The Framers' Coup: The Making of the United States Constitution* (New York, 2016), 278.

[78] Kaminski et al., eds., *Commentaries on the Constitution...Volume 2*, 503; Library of the Religious Society of Friends, London, the Meeting for Sufferings in Philadelphia to the Meeting for Sufferings in London, 16 June 1785, Letters passed between the Meeting for Sufferings in London and the Meeting for Sufferings in Philadelphia, vol. 1 (1757–1815).

STATE ACTION ON THE SLAVE TRADE IN THE REVOLUTIONARY ERA

Between the Declaration of Independence in 1776 and the Constitutional Convention of 1787, many states took action against the slave trade, in a variety of ways and for diverse reasons. The only two states that did not act to restrict or prohibit the slave trade in this period were Georgia and New Hampshire.[79] In Georgia, for example, the state constitution of 1777 had no provision relative to the slave trade.[80] But even though it was often impractical to abolish existing laws, passed while the thirteen colonies were under British sovereignty, some state legislatures authorised new laws on slavery and the slave trade, and sometimes principles on these matters became part of the new state constitutions. Numerous resolutions condemning the slave trade appeared in North American newspapers in the American revolutionary era. Sometimes a humanitarian note was struck in pointing out the inhumanity of the trade to enslaved Africans; but more frequently the slave trade was attacked because it was an affront to virtue, a hindrance to white immigration, and an impediment to the growth of manufacturing.[81]

Individual states had the sovereignty to decide what laws or regulations they would pass after American independence had been declared in 1776. The state legislatures effectively provided governance with little attention paid to the Continental Congress.[82] Delaware was the first state to take action. Though Governor John Penn had vetoed an attempt by the General Assembly of Delaware to prohibit the import and export of slaves in 1775, the state's constitution of 1776 reversed this decision and forbade the importation of slaves for sale or labour. Thus, clause 26 stated that 'no Negro, Indian or mulatto Slave,'[83] ought to be brought into this

---

[79] John P. Kaminski, Gaspare J. Saladino, Richard Leffler, Charles H. Schoenleber and Margaret A. Hogan, eds., *Ratification of the Constitution by the States. Volume 3* (Madison, WI, 2000), 1355.
[80] Ralph Betts Flanders, *Plantation Slavery in Georgia* (Chapel Hill, NC, 1933), 38.
[81] MacLeod, *Slavery, Race and the American Revolution*, 32.
[82] Mark D. Kaplanoff, 'Confederation: Movement for a Stronger Union' in Greene and Pole, eds., *A Companion to the American Revolution*, 465.
[83] 'Mulatto' was racial classification referring to people of mixed African and European ancestry.

state for sale from any part of the World'.[84] However, there was no enforcement mechanism to back up this decision.[85]

Virginia was the next state to follow in a similar line. In October 1778, Virginia introduced a bill to end the slave trade which passed without opposition.[86] This measure was a statute rather than a clause in the state constitution. The law stipulated that any slaves imported after the statute came into effect would be legally free. A penalty of £1,000 per slave illegally entering Virginia was specified for the importer and £500 for the purchaser.[87]

Virginia was one of the first governments in the modern world to end the slave trade. Why the statute was enacted is not absolutely clear. But it may have been connected with an influx of new representatives into the assembly, combining with eastern members to stop slave imports to increase the profits on selling slaves they already owned. Possibly the presence of rebellious slaves during the revolutionary war also persuaded Virginia planters to end the slave trade.[88] An exception to the Virginia law to end the slave trade was made in 1780 when refugees from South Carolina and Georgia were allowed to bring their slaves to Virginia until a year after the end of the revolutionary war.[89]

Jefferson supported the interdiction of the slave trade to Virginia. It is unclear whether he drafted or introduced the act, though some historians suggest he was involved in its composition.[90] There was no indication that such an abolition was connected to a wider antislavery stance.[91] Some Virginia planters thought that continuing the slave trade would

[84] Entry for 20 Sept. 1776 in Claudia L. Bushman, Harold B. Hancock, and Elizabeth Moyne Hamsey, eds., *Proceedings of the Assembly of the Lower Counties on Delaware 1770-1776, of the Constitutional Convention of 1776, and of the House of Assembly of the Delaware State 1776-1781* (Newark, DE, 1986), 223.
[85] James G. Basker, ed., *Early American Abolitionists: A Collection of Anti-slavery Writings* (New York, 2005), 77.
[86] Nevins, *The American States*, 446.
[87] William Waller Hening, ed., *The Statutes at Large: Being a Collection of all the Laws of Virginia, from the First Session of the Legislature in 1619*, 13 vols. (Richmond, VA, 1821), IX, 471-2; Robert McColley, *Slavery and Jeffersonian Virginia*, 2nd ed. (Urbana, IL, 1974), 165.
[88] 'A Bill to Prevent Importation of Slaves', in Hening, ed., *The Statutes at Large*, IX, 22-4; Michael A. McDonnell, *The Politics of War: Race, Class, and Conflict in Revolutionary Virginia* (Chapel Hill, NC, 2007), 331-2.
[89] McColley, *Slavery and Jeffersonian Virginia*, 165.
[90] John E. Selby and Don Higginbotham, *The Revolution in Virginia, 1775-1783* (Charlottesville, VA, 2007), 158.
[91] Eva Sheppard Wolf, *Race and Liberty in the New Nation: Emancipation in Virginia from the Revolution to Nat Turner's Rebellion* (Baton Rouge, LA, 2006), 14, 21.

suffocate slavery by introducing too many Africans for the state's economic needs.[92] Others opposed the slave trade because they wanted to slow down the growth of slavery in the Old Dominion so that agriculture could be promoted without reliance on slave labour. This, it was held, would serve as a superior path towards economic growth in Virginia.[93] In addition, tidewater planters were profiting from the natural increase of their black population which produced surplus labour, hence reducing the need for African imports.[94] The Virginia Act of 1778 was clear in banning the slave trade to the state, but there were loopholes: it excluded slaves brought into Virginia by their owners, slaves entering Virginia with owners who were passing through the state, and slaves owned by people planning to settle in Virginia.[95]

Anti-slave trade resolutions were passed in other states during the revolutionary era. These were the first binding proscriptions on slave trading in United States history.[96] Vermont's Constitution of 1777 banned slavery forever.[97] In Massachusetts, the slave trade was ended by constitutional means rather than through a separate act. John Adams took the lead in drafting the Bill of Rights of the Massachusetts Constitution of 1780, which effectively ended slave imports by declaring all men free and equal. This was specified in Article 1; there was no specific reference to slavery or the slave trade. The state's Supreme Court upheld this principle in dealing with cases brought before it involving black people. Thus, between 1780 and 1783 in three related judicial actions known as the 'Quock Walker cases', the Supreme Judicial High Court used the principle of judicial review to abolish slavery.[98]

When colonial laws came to an end in 1776, Pennsylvania's assembly made no provision for the continuation of prior laws. One law no longer enforced was the Negro duty act of 1773. However, on

---

[92] MacLeod, *Slavery, Race and the American Revolution*, 196, n. 79.
[93] Sheppard, *Race and Liberty in the New Nation*, 22.
[94] David Brion Davis, 'American Slavery and the American Revolution' in Ira Berlin and Ronald Hoffman, eds., *Slavery and Freedom in the Age of the American Revolution* (Urbana, IL, 1983), 266.
[95] McDonnell, *The Politics of War*, 331.
[96] Sean M. Kelley, *American Slavers: Merchants, Mariners, and the Transatlantic Commerce in Captives, 1644–1865* (New Haven, CT, 2023), 156.
[97] HSP, Samuel Hopkins to Anthony Benezet, 8 Dec. 1783, box 11, folder 59, Cox-Parrish-Wharton Papers.
[98] Nevins, *The American States*, 448; Emily Blanck, 'Seventeen Eighty-Three: The Turning Point in the Law of Slavery and Freedom in Massachusetts', *New England Quarterly*, 75/1 (2002), 24–51.

7 September 1778, the assembly passed a law to appoint a collector to gather the duty on slaves entering Pennsylvania after 4 July 1776. This was largely a symbolic gesture, reaffirming the state's right to regulate the slave trade; in practice, the numbers of slaves entering Philadelphia at that time were minuscule.[99] In 1776, Pennsylvania's new Constitution included statements about the right to life and liberty for its citizens but avoided reference to slavery. However, one drafter of that document, George Bryan, urged in May 1778 that the state legislature should support an abolition bill. Bryan's gradual abolition bill was referred to the Executive Council but in 1779, the Assembly produced their own abolition bill. Amongst other matters, this bill prohibited slave importations.[100]

More important decisions regarding slavery and the slave trade in Pennsylvania followed. Pennsylvania's gradual abolition law of 1780 repealed former slave importation duty acts.[101] It is recorded that Benezet interviewed every member of the state's legislature to help secure this statute, which provided for a gradual abolition of slavery.[102] The voting in the assembly amounted to a 34–21 vote in favour of the law.[103] There was no separate legislation specifically ending slave importations to Pennsylvania. After the passing of Pennsylvania's gradual abolition law, abolitionist societies in the state continued to promote slave emancipation and in 1787, reorganised themselves into the Pennsylvania Abolition Society. This body circulated abolitionist literature and remonstrated with the Constitutional Convention in Philadelphia in 1787 to outlaw the slave trade.[104]

Several other states took varied action against the slave trade in 1783–4. New Hampshire had no prohibitory law against the slave trade.[105] However, its state Constitution of 1783, which became effective in the following year, banned slave imports. In the same year, the

---

[99] Darold D. Wax, 'Reform and Revolution: The Movement against Slavery and the Slave Trade in Revolutionary Pennsylvania,' *Western Pennsylvania Historical Magazine*, LVII (1974), 418–19; Du Bois, *The Suppression of the African Slave-Trade*, 224.

[100] Gary B. Nash and Jean R. Soderlund, *Freedom by Degrees: Emancipation in Pennsylvania and Its Aftermath* (New York, 1991), 100–2.

[101] Du Bois, *The Suppression of the African Slave-Trade*, 225.

[102] Vaux, *Memoirs of the Life of Anthony Benezet*, 103.

[103] Wax, 'Reform and Revolution', 420.

[104] Nevins, *The American States*, 446, 448; Paul Finkelman, 'Human Liberty, Property in Human Beings, and the Pennsylvania Supreme Court', *Duquesne Law Review*, 53 (2015), 467; Nash and Soderlund, *Freedom by Degrees*, 125.

[105] Jeremy Belknap to Ebenezer Hazard, 25 Jan. 1788, in *Collections of the Massachusetts Historical Society: The Belknap Papers*, fifth series, vol. 3 (Boston, 1877), 11.

Maryland state legislature enacted a law that ended the slave trade.[106] In 1784, Connecticut passed a gradual abolition law.[107] An act for encouraging and promoting the commerce of Connecticut, set down by the state's General Court in 1784, explicitly discountenanced the trade in slaves from Africa to Connecticut.[108]

In 1784, the Rhode Island Assembly passed a statute that prohibited future importation of slaves into the state but failed to specify any fines for violation. The General Assembly of Rhode Island and Providence Plantations agreed, at its December session in 1783, to follow the resolve of the Continental Congress of 1774 and to require all masters of vessels cleared out for the coast of Africa to give bond to the general treasurer of the state for £1,000 that he would not take on board Africans, transport them and sell and dispose of them as slaves.[109] The Rhode Island merchant Moses Brown was a prominent figure in the condemnation of the slave trade on grounds of conscience. In 1783, he informed a correspondent in a private letter that 'the evils of the slave trade, have been gradually opening more and more for some Years, and that Trade is now generally acknowledged to be unwarrantable upon any just Principle'.[110]

In June 1787, the Rhode Island legislature received a Quaker petition, sponsored by Moses Brown, to prevent the 'cruel and unjust trade' in slaves. The substance of the petition was incorporated into a bill prohibiting citizens or residents of the state from participating in the slave trade. The bill passed the lower house of the Assembly by the wide margin of 44–4 votes and was then sent to the upper house, quickly approved, and passed into law on 31 October 1787.[111] This was the first law to prohibit US citizens from participation in the traffic.[112] Conviction was intended

---

[106] Du Bois, *The Suppression of the African Slave-Trade*, 226.
[107] Bernard C. Steiner, *History of Slavery in Connecticut* (Baltimore, 1893), 30; David Menschel, 'Abolition without Deliverance: The Law of Connecticut Slavery 1784–1848', *The Yale Law Journal*, 111/1 (2001), 183–222.
[108] *The Connecticut Journal*, 9 June 1784.
[109] *The United States Chronicle: Political, Commercial and Historical*, 15 Jan. 1784.
[110] Moses Brown to ?, 26 Aug. 1783, in Frost, ed., *The Quaker Origins of Antislavery*, 258.
[111] Mack Thompson, *Moses Brown: Reluctant Reformer* (Chapel Hill, NC, 1962), 190–2; *United States Chronicle*, 2 Aug. 1787; RIHS, Moses Brown to Samuel Emlen, 6 Nov. 1787, Moses Brown Papers, vol. 6; Moses Brown to ?, 13 Nov. 1787, in Frost, ed., *The Quaker Origins of Antislavery*, 259. For further condemnation of the slave trade by Brown, see Moses Brown to Jeremy Belknap, 28 Jan. 1786, in *Life of Jeremy Belknap, D.D., the Historian of New Hampshire with Selections from His Correspondence and Other Writings* (New York, 1847), 166.
[112] J. Stanley Lemons, 'Rhode Island and the Slave Trade', *Rhode Island History*, 60/4 (2002), 96.

to be easy under this law because the evidence of one seaman belonging to a vessel infringing the act was sufficient to obtain a condemnation.[113] The state law passed in Rhode Island was a progressive measure. Moses Brown congratulated supportive members of the assembly as 'friends to Liberty, Humanity, and the rights of mankind'.[114] It was claimed at the time, however, that Rhode Island's action would not succeed unless Massachusetts and Connecticut adopted similar acts.[115]

The New York legislature banned slave imports in 1785 and authorised substantial fines for those who did not comply. This was one of several measures in the immediate aftermath of the revolutionary war in New York in which legislators sought to move towards the gradual abolition of slavery.[116] On 13 March 1786, Alexander Hamilton and other memorialists signed a petition to the New York legislature requesting an end to slave importation, described as 'a commerce so repugnant to humanity, and so inconsistent with the liberality and justice which should distinguish a free and enlightened people'.[117] This memorial, however, was not followed up.

During the peace negotiations at the end of the American Revolution, the abolitionist Secretary of Foreign Affairs John Jay insisted that British ships should have no right to bring slaves into any US state from any part of the world, 'it being the intention of the United States entirely to prohibit their importation'.[118] No evidence has been found to demonstrate the grounds on which Jay could justify this statement.[119] Moreover,

---

[113] LCP, Jeremy Belknap to Benjamin Rush, 12 Feb. 1788, Benjamin Rush correspondence, vol. 30.

[114] RIHS, Moses Brown to the Committee of the Massachusetts Assembly, 1 Nov. 1787, Moses Brown correspondence.

[115] Edwards Amasa Park, ed., *The Works of Samuel Hopkins, D.D., First Pastor of the Church in Great Barrington, Mass., afterwards Pastor of the First Congregational Church in Newport, R. I., with a Memoir of His Life and Character*, 3 vols. (Boston, 1852), I, 122–3.

[116] Davis, *Problem of Slavery*, 24; Thompson, *Moses Brown*, 182; David N. Gellman, *Emancipating New York: The Politics of Slavery and Freedom 1777–1827* (Baton Rouge, LA, 2006), 52–3; Arthur Zilversmit, *The First Emancipation: The Abolition of Slavery in the North* (Chicago, 1967), 152–3.

[117] Memorial to abolish the slave trade, 13 Mar. 1786, in Harold C. Syrett, ed., *The Papers of Alexander Hamilton. Volume 3. 1782–1786* (New York, 1962), 654–5.

[118] John Jay: Proposals for Inclusion in a Trade Agreement [c. 1 June 1783] in Elizabeth M. Nuxoll, ed., *The Selected Papers of John Jay. Volume 3. 1782–1784* (Charlottesville, VA, 2013), 386–8.

[119] Ibid., 386–8, n. 2.

he exaggerated the extent to which the United States was unanimous in seeking the abolition of the slave trade to America at that time. Nearly a quarter century of further campaigning and changes to legislation were needed before that goal was achieved.

In 1786, Governor William Livingston of New Jersey, who regarded slavery as incompatible with humanity, Christianity and the inalienable rights of mankind, was influenced by the petitions of the Quaker David Cooper and other Friends to oversee an act that banned slave imports and liberalised slave manumissions. A New Jersey act of 1786 was passed that referred to 'the principles of justice and humanity' and prohibited slave importation.[120] However, the slave trade clause of this act was limited because it imposed low fines on violators and did not authorise the freedom of slaves illegally brought into the state. The fines amounted to £50 for each slave brought into New Jersey after 1776 and £20 for each African brought to the state before that year.[121] Livingston and his supporters also tried to follow a plan that had the combined goal of gradual abolition of slavery in New Jersey and the abolition of slave imports to the state. Livingston came to realise, however, that these twin goals were over-ambitious and in seeking both he might lose both, and so he abandoned the plan. The ban on slave imports in 1786 did nothing to prevent the continuance of slavery in New Jersey.[122]

Anti-slave trade sentiments were not welcomed by delegates collectively acting on behalf of the American people. On 27 September 1783, the Philadelphia Yearly Meeting, in its first peacetime meeting for over a decade, agreed to present a memorial to the Confederation Congress to prevent the resumption of the slave trade after the end of the War of Independence. More than a thousand Friends attended the meeting. The petition (dated 4 October 1783) had no stated authorship but was probably the work of Benezet. It argued that some merchants were 'prompted from avaricious motives to renew the iniquitous trade for slaves to the African Coasts' and therefore solicited 'your Christian interposition to

---

[120] Du Bois, *The Suppression of the African Slave-Trade*, 227.
[121] Graham Russell Hodges, *Root and Branch: African Americans in New York and East Jersey, 1613–1863* (Chapel Hill, NC, 1999), 169; Carl E. Prince, Mary Lou Lustig, and David William Voorhees, eds., *The Papers of William Livingston*, 5 vols. (Trenton and New Brunswick, 1979–88), V, 255; Nevins, *The American States*, 447.
[122] James J. Gigantino, II, *The Ragged Road to Abolition: Slavery and Freedom in New Jersey, 1775–1865* (Philadelphia, 2014), 72–3.

discourage & prevent so obvious an evil, in such manner as under the Influence of Divine Wisdom you shall Meet'.[123]

Around the time the petition was presented, the Yearly Meeting passed over management of antislavery activities to the Meeting for Sufferings, which appointed a committee to deal with the issues of slavery and the slave trade.[124] It did not have much initial impact. A three-person congressional committee, led by Jefferson, recommended that each state should deal with the slave trade in its own way in accordance with the antislavery clause of the Non-Importation Association of 1774. This was, in effect, urging all states that had not yet banned the slave trade to do so.[125] Under the Articles of Confederation, however, this recommendation would not have been binding. Southern congressmen voted against this judgment, and the full Congress voted down the committee report.[126]

Discussions concerning slavery were rare in the deliberations of the Confederation Congress, but the matter was raised from time to time. Thus, in January 1784, Congress rejected a report recommending that a Quaker statement about abolishing the slave trade should be circulated to individual states.[127] Clearly, it was not difficult for Congress to ignore Quaker demands partly because their pacifism or professed loyalism in the revolutionary war had lost them political credibility in the United States.[128]

---

[123] 'To the United States in Congress Assembled, The Address of the People Called Quakers,' 4 Oct. 1783, in Gary B. Nash and Michael R. McDowell, eds., *Writings of Warner Mifflin: Forgotten Quaker Abolitionist of the Revolutionary Era* (Newark, DE, 2021), 135–6.

[124] Richard Bauman, *For the Reputation of Truth: Politics, Religion, and Conflict among the Pennsylvania Quakers 1750–1800* (Baltimore, 1971), 198.

[125] Bruns, ed., *Am I Not a Man and a Brother?*, 494–501; Matthew Mason, *Slavery and Politics in the Early American Republic* (Chapel Hill, NC, 2006), 28; A. Glenn Crothers, *Quakers in the Lion's Mouth: The Society of Friends in Northern Virginia, 1730–1865* (Gainesville, FL, 2012), 109; Kenneth R. Bowling, William Charles diGiacomantonio and Charlene Bangs Bickford, eds., *Documentary History of the First Federal Congress of the United States of America. Volume 8. Petition Histories and Nonlegislative Official Documents* (Baltimore, 1988), 314–15.

[126] Nicholas P. Wood, 'Abolitionists, Congress, and the Atlantic Slave Trade: Before and after Ratification' in Douglas Bradburn and Christopher R. Pearl, eds., *From Independence to the U.S. Constitution: Reconsidering the Critical Period of American History* (Charlottesville, VA, 2022), 98.

[127] Paul H. Smith, ed., *Letters to Delegates of Congress, 1774–1789. Volume 21. October 1, 1783-October 31, 1784* (Washington, DC, 1994), 266.

[128] Thomas P. Slaughter, *The Beautiful Soul of John Woolman, Apostle of Abolition* (New York, 2008), 387.

In May 1783, Benezet wrote to Franklin to espouse the anti-slave trade cause against 'a traffick so infamous & cruel in all its parts', arguing that the United States could set a moral and political example to European nations by abolishing slave importation.[129] In January 1785, abolitionists again raised concerns about slavery and the slave trade in Congress. A Quaker address was read to Congress but there is no official record of it.[130] Two months later, petitioners called on the conscience of the delegates to the Continental Congress 'to exert their Influence and Endeavours to discourage and prohibit' the slave trade. To persuade delegates of the necessity for taking this action, they enclosed a copy of Benezet's pamphlet *The Case of Our Fellow Creatures, the Oppressed Africans* (1784).[131] Benezet had long been a critic of the 'avowed abomination' of the slave trade. An address by the Quakers dated Philadelphia 26 January 1785 was also enclosed. How influential these views were in changing the minds of politicians to act on this topic is a debatable matter.[132] Both the Continental Congress and the Confederation Congress played down issues related to slavery and antislavery in order to preserve national unity in the years when the United States was preoccupied with establishing a strong union.[133]

Quakers were active in drafting and presenting further petitions to Congress on the slave trade. In 1786, John Parrish and James Pemberton delivered such a petition on behalf of the Meeting for Sufferings of the Philadelphia Yearly Meeting. The petition referred to 'universal liberty & the common rights of man' but expressed the hope that Congress would encourage action against this 'national iniquity'.[134] No action was taken, but the Quaker antislavery activists persisted with

---

[129] Benezet to Franklin, 5 May 1783, in Ellen R. Cohn, ed., *The Papers of Benjamin Franklin. Volume 39. January 21 through May 15, 1783* (New Haven, CT, 2008), 560.

[130] Wood, 'Abolitionists, Congress, and the Atlantic Slave Trade,' 98.

[131] Whether Benezet was the author of this pamphlet is carefully questioned in Patrick C. Lipscomb, III and Edward H. Milligan, 'A Note on the Authorship of *The Case of Our Fellow-Creatures* (1784)', *Quaker History*, 55/1 (1966), 47–51.

[132] Paul H. Smith, ed., *Letters to Delegates of Congress, 1774–1789. Volume 22. November 1, 1784–November 6, 1785* (Washington, DC, 1995), 284, n. 2; Benezet to Franklin, 8 May 1783 (quotation) in Cohn, ed., *The Papers of Benjamin Franklin. Volume 39*, 575.

[133] Seymour Drescher, 'Divergent Paths: The Anglo-American Abolitions of the Atlantic Slave Trade' in Wim Klooster, ed., *Migration, Trade, and Slavery in an Expanding World: Essays in Honor of Pieter Emmer* (Leiden, 2009), 266.

[134] The quotations are taken from minutes of the Pennsylvania Yearly Meeting as cited in Nicholas P. Wood, 'Considerations of Humanity and Expediency: The Slave Trades and

their attack on the slave trade. In 1787 and 1788, Parrish, Pemberton and Richard Waln, acting on behalf of the Meeting for Sufferings in conjunction with Maryland Quakers, petitioned for an ending to slave imports and exports at state level. In 1787, furthermore, the Pennsylvania Abolition Society requested that the Constitutional Convention in Philadelphia should ensure it discussed the slave trade to the United States. That plea was to be heard in the deliberations and decisions of the convention.[135]

SOUTH CAROLINA AND SLAVE IMPORTS IN THE 1780S

Though many states took decisive action against the slave trade in the decade after the declaration of American independence, some refused to follow suit. South Carolina was the main state continuing with slave imports in the Confederation period. At the end of the War of Independence in 1783, South Carolina's slave trade resumed. Initially, British subjects were prominent in this resumption of the slave trade to Charleston but the purchasers were South Carolinian planters. One Charlestonian critic of the revived traffic concluded that the importing merchants and the planters were to be jointly blamed for this situation – 'the receiver is as bad as the thief'.[136] The physician and historian David Ramsay regretted this occurrence and noted that no debate had taken place on the subject, nor a law passed. Instead, 'this infamous traffic will be resumed without anything being said on the subject'. He feared that 'the mad notions entertained of the separate States sovereignty will forever prevent the interference of the Continental sovereignty on this subject'.[137] However, a prominent Charleston merchant, Henry Laurens, who had imported Africans and was involved in rice plantations based on slave labour, had now emerged as an important spokesman against the Guinea traffic. In 1783, he 'candidly' informed a friend of his wish that 'the further importation of Negroes may be prohibited' on grounds of

---

African Colonization in the Early National Antislavery Movement' (University of Virginia PhD dissertation, 2013), 75.

[135] Ibid., 75–6; Wood, 'Abolitionists, Congress, and the Atlantic Slave Trade', 100–1.
[136] HSP, John Kirk to James Pemberton, 6 Apr. 1784. Pemberton Papers, box 41, folder 42.
[137] David Ramsay to Benjamin Rush, 22 Aug. 1783 and 9 Sept. 1783, in Robert L. Brunhouse, ed., 'David Ramsay, 1749–1815', *Transactions of the American Philosophical Society*, new series, LV, part 4 (1965), 76.

conscience.[138] Leaving aside the morality of the trade, Laurens informed another correspondent that South Carolinians would be ruined by the continuance of the slave trade because 'this Country already overwhelmed with debt will sink deeper & deeper by excessive importations until the evil shall purge itself off'.[139]

Edward Rutledge, a prominent South Carolina politician, joined Laurens in attacking the slave trade. In 1785, he led an unsuccessful bid to ban importations of slaves into the state for three years.[140] Rush thought the commitment of many South Carolinians to slavery and the slave trade was fanatical, referring to it as a prevailing negromania. But he claimed to know several leading men in South Carolina who were secret enemies to the slave trade – possibly including Laurens, as mentioned above – and he had no doubt 'they will seize the first favourable opportunity that offers of abolishing at least that part of their laws that permits them to import the poor creatures from Africa'.[141]

The situation with regard to slave importation in the Palmetto state proved less optimistic than Rush supposed for South Carolina continued 'to *import slaves* contrary to the just resolution of Congress in 1774'.[142] Both in South Carolina and Georgia, many interested parties argued that a supply of young Africans was needed to revitalise the economy of the Lower South.[143] Most Carolinians, faced with meeting pre- and post-war financial obligations, expected the state legislature to aid them.[144] In 1783 South Carolina, having not imported slaves during the revolutionary war, witnessed a renewed demand for African captives from lowcountry rice planters and from backcountry settlers who had recently taken over lands from the Cherokees. These saltwater Africans were needed to replace the approximately 25,000 slaves lost to South Carolina during the American revolutionary war either destroyed by disorders introduced by British

---

[138] Laurens to John Owen, 9 Aug. 1783, in David R. Chesnutt and C. James Taylor, eds., *The Papers of Henry Laurens. Volume 16. September 1, 1782–December 17, 1792* (Columbia, SC, 2003), 259 (quotation). For a similar sentiment, see Laurens to Alexander Hamilton, 19 Apr. 1785, ibid., 553–4.
[139] Laurens to James Bourdieu, 9 June 1785, ibid., XVI, 568–9.
[140] Nevins, *The American States*, 447.
[141] Rush to Sharp, 28 Nov. 1783, in Woods, ed., 'The Correspondence of Benjamin Rush and Granville Sharp', 20.
[142] Sharp to Rush, 10 Oct. 1785, ibid., 28.
[143] Douglas R. Egerton, *Death or Liberty: African Americans and Revolutionary America* (New York, 2009), 154.
[144] Richard Brent Clow, 'Edward Rutledge of South Carolina, 1749–1800: Unproclaimed Statesman' (University of Georgia PhD dissertation, 1976), 203.

troops or carried off by those forces at the end of the conflict. The losses amounted to a quarter of South Carolina's slave population.[145]

Over the next four years, between 1783 and 1787, around 10,000 Africans were imported at Charleston. But while this took place a contentious debate over the slave trade occurred in South Carolina. A group of legislators wanted to ban the slave trade from February 1783 on the grounds that slave purchases were expensive and led to planters increasing their debts and facing credit restrictions. Certainly, indebtedness was leading to many protests by South Carolinian planters during the 1780s. Not all South Carolinians agreed, however, that the slave trade was harmful for the economy in their state. Advocates of keeping the slave trade open made the case for African imports being essential for South Carolina's plantation labour requirements. Slaves, these proponents argued, were essential for maintaining the state's export levels whereas indebtedness was a temporary phenomenon.[146]

By 1785 declining tax collections, a shortage of currency and widespread indebtedness were placing serious strains on South Carolina's economy. The loss of imperial bounties for the export of indigo and naval stores had had a negative impact on the state's economy. A series of poor rice harvests in 1783, 1784 and 1785 made it difficult for planters to repay their pre-war debts and loans for newly imported slaves. One potential solution was to curtail slave imports until the economic crisis passed.[147] Edward Rutledge, as noted above, thought restricting slave imports would restore a favourable balance of trade to the state.[148]

Struggles ensued as the state legislature discussed what to do with the slave trade.[149] On 4 March 1785 a bill was brought before South Carolina's House of Representatives to prevent slave importations for three years, but after a long debate it was rejected by 65–58 votes.[150]

---

[145] John Drayton, *A View of South-Carolina, as Respects Her Natural and Civil Concerns* (Charleston, 1802), 165; James A. McMillin, *The Final Victims: Foreign Slave Trade to North America, 1783–1810* (Columbia, SC, 2005), 8.

[146] Edward B. Rugemer, *Slave Law and the Politics of Resistance in the Early Atlantic World* (Cambridge, MA, 2018), 222-3; Rachel N. Klein, *Unification of a Slave State: The Rise of the Planter Class in the South Carolina Backcountry 1760–1808* (Chapel Hill, NC, 1990), 126-7.

[147] James Haw, *John and Edward Rutledge of South Carolina* (Athens, GA, 1997), 192; Gordon C. Bjork, 'The Weaning of the American Economy: Independence, Market Changes, and Economic Development', *JEcH*, 24/4 (1964), 556; McMillin, *The Final Victims*, 8.

[148] Clow, 'Edward Rutledge', 205.   [149] Drayton, *A View of South-Carolina*, 146.

[150] 'Debate on the Importation of Negroes, 1785' in Donnan, ed., *Documents*, IV, 480.

Lowcountry representatives such as John Rutledge and Charles Cotesworth Pinckney wanted to keep the slave trade open: wealth, they argued, was based on plantation production and planters needed fresh supplies of Africans to produce more crops for the export trade.[151]

The debate over slave importations continued. On 27 September 1785, a committee appointed by the South Carolina legislature under the leadership of Governor William Moultrie debated the issue of the slave trade as part of a wider consideration of the state of commerce and credit in the state. Proscribing the arrival of Africans at Charleston was regarded as one measure that might alleviate the economic problems along with the possibility of state emission of paper money and legal interventions between debtors and creditors.[152] It was clear to South Carolina's politicians that the political independence of the United States had not made the state financially self-sufficient.[153]

Varying views were aired on either side of the debate. David Ramsay argued that slave importations should be stopped 'or else the balance of trade will be ever against us'.[154] On 27 September 1785, Ralph Izard introduced a motion in the South Carolina Assembly to prohibit the slave trade for three years and said a few words in its favour. This was opposed by John Rutledge, who argued that closing Charleston from importing slaves was the wrong policy when additional supplies of Africans were needed. Rutledge had always advocated the deployment of slave labour as an essential part of South Carolina's plantation output. He regarded slaves as productive assets required to increase the state's wealth.[155] He did not want fellow South Carolinians to offer any reproach or reproof for white people importing and buying Africans to help the state's economy recover from war, debts and inflation.[156] Rutledge forcefully provided evidence to demonstrate that the cost of slaves imported to the state since 1783 was far overshadowed by the 'immense quantities of dry goods'.[157]

The suspension of slave imports was twice defeated in September 1785 sessions of South Carolina's legislature but on 28 September, the day after

---

[151] Clow, 'Edward Rutledge', 205. [152] Haw, *John and Edward Rutledge*, 192.
[153] Ulrich B. Phillips, 'The South Carolina Federalists, 1', *The American Historical Review*, 14/3 (1909), 541.
[154] David Ramsay to Benjamin Rush, 31 Jan. 1785, in Brunhouse, ed., 'David Ramsay', 86-7.
[155] 'Debate on the Importation of Negroes, 1785' in Donnan, ed., *Documents*, IV, 481; Haw, *John and Edward Rutledge*, 192; *Charleston Evening Gazette*, 28 Sept. 1785.
[156] Egerton, *Death or Liberty*, 155.
[157] 'Debate on the Importation of Negroes, 1785' in Donnan, ed., *Documents*, IV, 481.

Izard and John Rutledge contributed to the debate, Henry Pendleton, a state judge, reported to the legislature that the committee on the state of the republic recommended the cessation of slave importations for three years.[158] No member of the South Carolina assembly spoke out to condemn the cruelties of the slave trade.[159] The debate continued in the Committee of the Whole, once again led by Izard. Thomas Bee, a former delegate to the Second Continental Congress and lieutenant governor of the state, expressed worries that the current surge in importing slaves could not be sustained owing to the depreciated state of South Carolina's economy. 'The sight of a negroe yard', he stated, 'was too great a temptation for a planter to withstand, he could not leave it without purchasing; in short, there seemed to be a rage for negroes, without any consideration how they were to be paid for'.[160]

The revolutionary war veteran Charles Cotesworth Pinckney argued that 'this country was not capable of being cultivated by white men ... was it not well understood that no planter could cultivate his land without slaves?'[161] Slaves were essential for South Carolina's economy: white men had always been found wanting in cultivating lands. Pinckney cited the example of Georgia under James Oglethorpe to back up this claim.[162] 'Negroes were to this country', Pinckney proclaimed, 'what raw materials were to another country': they increased staple production and brought in about £3 per head in import duties. Pinckney added that banning slave importation from South Carolina would divert ships to North Carolina and Georgia to the benefit of planters wanting to purchase slaves in those states.[163]

South Carolina's planters were wedded to the notion that economic growth needed Atlantic commerce and that plantation staple crops required more slaves.[164] Modern research has shown, in support of Pinckney's position, that additional slave imports were needed in South Carolina after the end of the revolutionary war; the growth of the state's

---

[158] *Charleston Evening Gazette*, 28, 30 Sept. 1785; Haw, *John and Edward Rutledge*, 192.
[159] Egerton, *Death or Liberty*, 157.
[160] 'Debate on the Importation of Negroes, 1785' in Donnan, ed., *Documents*, IV, 482.
[161] *Charleston Evening Gazette*, 1 Oct. 1785.
[162] Oglethorpe and the other Georgia trustees had banned slavery from the new colony of Georgia in 1735 but, faced with labour shortages and poor agricultural profits, reversed this policy in 1751.
[163] 'Debate on the Importation of Negroes, 1785' in Donnan, ed., *Documents*, IV, 483.
[164] Brian Schoen, 'Positive Goods and Necessary Evils: Commerce, Security, and Slavery in the Lower South, 1787–1837' in John Craig Hammond and Matthew Mason, eds., *Contesting Slavery: The Politics of Bondage and Freedom in the new American Nation* (Charlottesville, VA, 2011), 164.

slave population stalled considerably in the 1780s compared with the previous decade; and in 1780s the ratio of slave imports to total black population increase was at its highest point in South Carolina since the 1740s.[165]

On 5 October 1785, the debate was resumed in the Committee of the Whole with a new resolution introduced to suspend slave imports for three years.[166] Edward Rutledge argued against this 'destructive importation' on the grounds that South Carolina's economy was seriously in debt and that allowing more Africans to enter the state would inflame the planters' poor credit situation. He cited the previous decision by South Carolina's legislature to suspend the slave trade in the early 1740s when the colony was experiencing similar problems connected with debt. Rutledge discounted the idea that Georgia could profit from South Carolina's economic woes by continuing to import slaves because Georgia itself was mired in debts that could take three years to collect.[167] Pendleton, however, cautioned that keeping Charleston open as a slave importing centre was unwise at a time when credit was insecure in South Carolina and many planters were already in debt. The House of Representatives voted on Edward Rutledge's proposal against slave importation, which was defeated by 63 votes to 48. Izard's bill to prohibit the slave trade was passed to the lower house of South Carolina's assembly, but it was fairly narrowly defeated by 51 votes to 47.[168]

Georgia, like South Carolina, was fully committed to slave trading in the American revolutionary era. Thus, in a letter of 1784, the Savannah merchant Joseph Clay informed a merchant in London that 'the negro business is a great object with us, both with a View to our Interest individually, and the general prosperity of this State and its commerce, it is to the trade of this country as Soul to the body.'[169] Georgia, like South Carolina, had experienced a heavy loss of slaves during the American revolutionary war, amounting to 10,000 people or two-thirds of the state's pre-war slave population.[170] Therefore, it is unsurprising to

---

[165] Peter C. Mancall, Joshua L. Rosenbloom, and Thomas Weiss, 'Slave Prices and the South Carolina Economy, 1722–1809', *JEcH*, 61/3 (2002), 625.
[166] *Charleston Evening Gazette*, 18 Oct. 1785.
[167] 'Debate on the Importation of Negroes, 1785' in Donnan, ed., *Documents*, IV, 485–6.
[168] Ibid., 489; Ulrich B. Phillips, *American Negro Slavery: A Study of the Supply, Employment and Control of Negro Labor as Determined by the Plantation Regime* (New York, 1918), 134; Arthur H. Schaffer, *To be an American: David Ramsay and the Making of the American Consciousness* (Columbia, SC, 1991), 170–1.
[169] Joseph Clay to James Jackson, 16 Feb. 1784, in 'Letters of Joseph Clay, Merchant of Savannah, 1776–1793', *Collections of the Georgia Historical Society*, 8 (1913), 194–5.
[170] McMillin, *The Final Victims*, 8.

find that, in 1784, Georgia's legislature stated that the Confederation's power over foreign trade did not extend to banning slave importation.[171] In 1786, South Carolina and Georgia refused to give the Continental Congress the authority to regulate the slave trade.[172] By early 1787, only three states – Georgia, South Carolina and North Carolina – still allowed slave imports, though North Carolina had introduced a prohibitive duty on slave imports in 1786.[173] The restrictions in North Carolina consisted of a duty of £5 on each slave imported from Africa and £10 on each from elsewhere.[174]

On 22 March 1787, a lively debate took place in South Carolina's House of Representatives after a slave trade clause was added to a bill for the recovery of debts. A number of comments made in the debate focused on the proposed timing of the measure, for the Senate had inserted the words 'three months' before the prohibition of imports was to occur. Consideration should be made, according to some contributors, to the fact that Charleston merchants had already sent out vessels to purchase Africans. A suggestion was put forward that the time before the bill was enacted should be extended to five months to allow those Charlestonians currently purchasing slaves to have time to dispose of their cargoes. Against this view, it was noted that a great many slaves could be imported and sold within five months and that this would only add to South Carolina's debts.[175] The House of Representatives voted by 83–23 to send the bill to the Senate. A third reading of the bill on 22 March 1787 to recover debts and to proscribe slave imports was approved in South Carolina's House of Representatives by 70–57 and a motion made and seconded that the clause on slave importations be struck out of the bill was defeated by 73–56.[176]

---

[171] Don E. Fehrenbacher with Ward M. McAfee, *The Slaveholding Republic: An Account of the United States Government's Relations to Slavery* (New York, 2001), 25.

[172] John P. Kaminski, Gaspare J. Saladino and Richard Leffler, eds., *Commentaries on the Constitution, public and private. Volume 2: 8 November to 17 December 1787* (Madison, WI, 1983), 504.

[173] Du Bois, *The Suppression of the African Slave-Trade*, 229. This was repealed in 1790 but reinstated in 1794: see Mary Stoughton Locke, *Anti-slavery Activity in America: From the Introduction of African Slaves to the Prohibition of the Slave Trade (1619–1808)* (Boston, 1901), 135.

[174] Adrienne Koch, ed., *Notes of Debates in the Federal Convention of 1787 Reported by James Madison* (Athens, OH, 1966), 506.

[175] 'Debate on the Importation of Negroes, 1787' in Donnan, ed., *Documents*, IV, 492–3.

[176] SCDAH, entry for 22 Mar. 1787 in the South Carolina House of Representatives Journal (1787).

The number of states importing enslaved Africans dropped from three to two when, on 28 March 1787, a couple of months before the Constitutional Convention, South Carolina's legislature passed an act prohibiting slave imports for three years, following Edward Rutledge's proposal of 1785. The vote in the state's House of Representatives was 74–56. The reference to 'three months' in the slave trade clause (referred to above) was struck out.[177] This act was implemented for economic reasons, in order to curtail credit extensions then prevalent in the state, rather than on humanitarian grounds.[178] James Pemberton noted that 'the pernicious effects' of South Carolina's 'vast importation of slaves since 1783 has prohibited the trade for three years'.[179]

The proscription of slave imports was part of the act passed in South Carolina for the recovery and payment of private debts in three annual instalments.[180] This measure was the culmination of contentious debates that began in late September 1785, with some legislators in the state's House of Representatives arguing that slaves had increased South Carolina's wealth and others countering this view by emphasising the insufficiency of the state's current poor export values to pay for imports, including slaves. Eventually, in late March 1787, South Carolina's Assembly voted to close the slave trade. Lowcountry representatives, who were dominant in the assembly, voted 61–17 to close the trade while backcountry representatives, supporting the interior of the state's need for Africans, voted by 29–18 to continue the slave trade. Large slaveholders owning more than twenty slaves voted by 33–16 to close the trade, indicating their preference for maintaining their own investments.[181] The ban lasted for seventeen years.[182] Henry Laurens applauded the state's cessation of slave imports as an important contribution to debtor

---

[177] 'Debate on the Importation of Negroes, 1787' in Donnan, ed., *Documents*, IV, 494. The text of the act is printed in the *Charleston Morning Post*, 29 Mar. 1787.

[178] Jerome J. Nadelhaft, *The Disorders of War: The Revolution in South Carolina* (Orono, ME, 1981), 171; 'Debate on the Importation of Negroes, 1787' in Donnan, ed., *Documents*, IV, 494. For the problems caused for a ship captain entering Charleston who had his slaves seized without knowledge of this change, see James Dennison to His Excellency the Governor and Council of the State of South Carolina, 15 June 1787, in Adele Stanton Edwards, ed., *Journals of the Privy Council 1783–1789* (Columbia, SC, 1971), 195–6.

[179] NYPL, James Pemberton to Granville Sharp, 8 May 1788, Digital Collections.

[180] Clow, 'Edward Rutledge', 208.

[181] Lacy K. Ford, *Deliver Us from Evil: The Slavery Question in the Old South* (New York, 2009), 83.

[182] Rugemer, *Slave Law and the Politics of Resistance*, 223–4.

relief.[183] The historian Winthrop D. Jordan characterised South Carolina's ban on slave imports in 1787 as 'a matter of men denying themselves what they wanted but could not afford'.[184]

The prohibition act of 1787 continued the acrimonious debate among South Carolinians about whether to ban slave imports. This legislation was supported by influential lowcountry planters concerned about poor economic conditions in the state. Federalists assured backcountry planters wanting to purchase slaves that South Carolina's closure of the slave trade was a temporary measure.[185] Despite division among South Carolinians over the continuance of the slave trade, they wanted to maintain their states' rights on this matter. One contributor to the debates on the slave trade argued that legislative interference was not required; instead, there should be a clause in the state's constitution concerning a ban on slave imports; but no other legislator supported this suggestion. In fact, no politicians in South Carolina desired a permanent ban on slave disembarkations; they expected to choose when, and for what reasons, they could restrict or open the trade.[186]

Jefferson congratulated South Carolina's legislature for 'suspending the importation of slaves, and for the glory you have justly acquired by endeavouring to prevent it forever'. Echoing his long-held view that the slave trade must be ended, he added that 'there is a superior bench reserved in heaven for those who hasten it'.[187] South Carolina's prohibition act of 1787 was swiftly followed by an ordinance passed later on the same day that introduced fines as well as forfeitures to those found guilty of illegal slave importation.[188] Early in 1788, the Charleston merchant Alexander Gillon attempted to overturn the prohibition, but he encountered fierce opposition and his motion was defeated by 93 votes to 40.[189]

---

[183] Gregory D. Massey, 'The Limits of Antislavery Thought in the Revolutionary Lower South: John Laurens and Henry Laurens', *JSH*, 63/3 (1997), 527–8.

[184] Winthrop D. Jordan, *White over Black: American Attitudes towards the Negro, 1550–1812* (Chapel Hill, NC, 1968), 318.

[185] Ford, *Deliver Us from Evil*, 83.

[186] Donald L. Robinson, *Slavery in the Structure of American Politics, 1765–1820* (New York, 1971), 298–9; 'Debate on the Importation of Negroes, 1785' and 'Debate on the Importation of Negroes, 1787' in Donnan, ed., *Documents*, IV, 480–9, 492–4; Klein, *Unification of a Slave State*, 131–2; Jerome J. Nadelhaft, 'South Carolina and the Slave Trade, 1783–1787' (University of Wisconsin MA thesis, 1961).

[187] Jefferson to Edward Rutledge, 14 July 1787, in Julian P. Boyd, ed., *The Papers of Thomas Jefferson. Volume 11. 1 January to 6 August 1787* (Princeton, NJ, 1955), 231.

[188] Phillips, *American Negro Slavery*, 135.   [189] Ibid.

In 1788, South Carolina passed a further act that brought in a temporary ban on slave imports until 1 January 1793.[190] This measure was occasioned by the debts contracted by planters; by the necessity for the legislature to secure its payment by postponing instalments; and to prevent opening up a new source of debt before the old one was paid.[191]

DEVELOPMENTS IN OTHER STATES

Those in favour of proscribing the slave trade realised that there was still much work to do before they could achieve their goal. Defenders of slave importation were keen to state their position. Thus, in Rhode Island, which dispatched many vessels in the Guinea traffic, a division arose between the merchant John Brown, a participant in the trade as noted above, and his brother Moses Brown, a sincere anti-slave trade promoter. Moses Brown, who had converted to Quakerism, had once been a slave trader but his participation in the Guinea traffic weighed heavily on his conscience and he had determined to do everything in his power to put it to an end. He was zealous and determined to achieve this goal.[192] In 1786, John acknowledged his brother's opposition to the slave trade but argued that slaves brought to transatlantic markets from the west African coast were positively better off than those left behind. He regarded the slave trade 'as just & right as any trade'.[193] Though many Rhode Island merchants had been largely concerned in the slave trade for the sake of gain, the state passed an act abolishing the traffic in October 1787.[194] However, although it was reported that 'the general

---

[190] Nevins, *The American States*, 447; Du Bois, *The Suppression of the African Slave-Trade*, 233.

[191] Duke de la Rochefoucault Liancourt, *Travels through the United States of North America, the Country of the Iroquois, and Upper Canada, in the Years 1795, 1796, and 1797. With an Authentic Account of Lower Canada*, 2 vols. (London, 1799), I, 574–5.

[192] HSP, Samuel Hopkins to Levi Hart, 27 Nov. 1787, American Colonial Clergy, Case 8, box 23, Simon Gratz Autograph Collection.

[193] RIHS, John Brown to Moses Brown, 27 Nov. 1786, Moses Brown correspondence. For an argument against prohibition of the African slave trade, see RIHS, statement of c. 1784, ibid.

[194] HSP, John Collins to Benjamin Franklin, 12 May 1788, Pennsylvania Abolition Society Papers, series 2.2; Haverford College Quaker Collection, Moses Brown to ?, 13 Nov. 1787, Richard T. Cadbury Collection, MC 954. A copy of the text of the act is published in the *Newport Herald*, 8 Nov. 1787.

sense of the People seems to abhor the slave trade', the Rhode Island government was too weak to prosecute those involved in the trade.[195]

Too many people still had a vested financial interest in the slave trade in the 1780s for it to wither other than by a law or decree. At that point, proscription of the slave trade could only proceed on a state-by-state basis. It was pointed out in 1786 that plenty of people had argued for action to be taken against slave importations 'but unhappily are the minds of some biased by Gain & prejudiced by long habit as to pursue a Conduct so repugnant to every Principle of Justice & Humanity setting aside it being so incompatible with the Christian religion, which injoins "the doing unto others as we would have them do to us"'.[196] Samuel Hopkins lamented that too few of his fellow clergymen, and too few non-Quakers, had spoken out against the continuance of slave imports into the United States by the late 1780s.[197] However, there were some positive shoots of progress. Some states legislated against the slave trade either a short time before or after the Constitutional Convention of 1787. In late 1786, for example, Virginia's Assembly passed a law to prohibit slave importation under a penalty of £1,000 on the transgressor and of £500 on the purchaser, with a declaration that any such slave would be immediately restored to freedom.[198] In October 1788, Connecticut passed a bill banning any of the state's inhabitants from receiving slaves, with a penalty of $1,667 for the use of a ship and of $167 for each slave carried.[199]

In October 1786, Philadelphia Quakers considered delivering another address to Congress condemning the slave trade. They acknowledged that no law could follow from such an initiative as that lay beyond the powers of Congress, but they thought a declaration from them would stimulate state assemblies to act on the issue.[200] Considering the continuing rise of slave imports to some southern states, the Philadelphia Meeting for Sufferings decided action was necessary.[201] James Pemberton, who had

---

[195] HSP, Extract of a letter from Providence, Rhode Island, 23 Aug. 1788, Pennsylvania Abolition Society Papers, series 2.2.
[196] RIHS, John Murray to Moses Brown, 6 Mar. 1786, Moses Brown correspondence.
[197] HSP, Samuel Hopkins to Levi Hart, 27 Nov. 1787, American Colonial Clergy, case 8, box 23, Simon Gratz Autograph Collection.
[198] HSP, James Pemberton to John Pemberton, 29 Oct. 1786, Pemberton Papers, box 47, folder 46.
[199] Bernard C. Steiner, *History of Slavery in Connecticut* (Baltimore, 1893), 31.
[200] HSP, [James Pemberton] to William Dillwyn, 26 Oct. 1786, Pemberton Papers, box 47, folder 14.
[201] HSP, James Pemberton to John Pemberton, 28 Oct. 1786, ibid., box 47, folder 15.

extensive abolitionist connections on both sides of the Atlantic, had reported to them that opposition from the southern states and lack of congressional jurisdiction were holding up the anti-slave trade cause.[202]

In November 1786, a committee of the Quaker Meeting for Sufferings in Philadelphia attended Congress in New York to revive their consideration of action against the slave trade that the Philadelphia Yearly Meeting had presented at Princeton in October 1783. The members of the committee were Isaac Zane, James Thornton, David Cooper, Thomas Lightfoot, Jacob Lindley, John Parrish, William Savery, Jr, John Drinker and James Pemberton. This proved to be a difficult time to receive consideration of their memorial because the delegates selected by the states had not yet gathered for congressional meetings. The committee proceeded cautiously 'by a careful enquiry who of the Delegates from the different Governments were now in this City & likely to continue here; what might be discovered of their several sentiments, and dispositions, and what might be the probable effect of visiting, and conferring with them, and some others, whose weight & influence might be useful to our design'.[203]

Pemberton and his colleagues had fruitful discussions with delegates to Congress about 'the evil of the impious traffic'. They hoped the delegates would make every effort to suppress it.[204] On 15 November 1786, they visited several people amenable to their cause, including James Duane, mayor of New York, Nathaniel Gorham, former President of Congress, Melancton Smith, a delegate from New York, and the foreign affairs minister John Jay, each of whom identified delegates who might be sympathetic to the Quaker memorial. Duane manifested 'a friendly openness and hearty concurrence with us'. Jay afforded the delegation 'such aid & countenance as might be within his power'. Gorham 'evidenced an acceptable disposition much to our satisfaction'. Smith was 'cheerfully disposed to promote our business & views'.[205]

---

[202] Joseph S. Foster, 'James Pemberton' in Craig W. Horle, Joseph S. Foster, Laurie M. Wolfe, Jeffrey L. Scheib, Robert E. Wright, David Haugaard, Dianna DiIllio, Jennifer A. Janofsky and Leigh A. McCuen, eds., *Lawmaking and Legislators in Pennsylvania: A Biographical Dictionary. Volume Three: 1757–1775* (Harrisburg, PA, 2005), 1034. Pemberton's networking among British and American abolitionists is discussed in J. R. Oldfield, *Transatlantic Abolitionism in the Age of Revolution: An International History of Anti-slavery, c.1787–1820* (Cambridge, 2013), 32.

[203] HSP, James Pemberton to John Pemberton, 17 Nov. 1786, Pemberton Papers, box 47, folder 32.

[204] RIHS, James Pemberton to Moses Brown, 12 Jan. 1787, Moses Brown correspondence.

[205] HSP, James Pemberton to John Pemberton, 17 Nov. 1786, Pemberton Papers, box 47, folder 32.

The Quaker committee made further visits on the following day, 16 November, to five delegates from South Carolina, one from North Carolina, one from Georgia, two from Maryland and one from Massachusetts. This led to encouraging discussions, despite some objections from the Southern delegates, who acknowledged nevertheless 'that on a computation it was allowed that twelve thousand slaves had been imported to So[uth] Carolina and Georgia since the commencement of the Peace, & upbraided the People of Rhode Island with carrying on the iniquitous traffic notwithstanding the Prohibitory laws made there and in Massachusetts ag[ains]t the importation among themselves'.[206]

After their friendly reception from delegates, Pemberton and his associates decided it would be prudent to leave their address under the special care of the New York Meeting for Sufferings to present to Congress if an occasion arose. Nothing concrete occurred after these efforts, but the meetings held with the delegates were very useful for gauging the political temperature with regard to the slave trade in different states.[207] James Pemberton believed there were grounds to hope that 'the prohibition of the importation as a political evil will take place when Congress are invested with the powers of regulating commerce'.[208] In the meantime, other anti-slave trade activity continued. Pemberton himself, for instance, agreed to support the distribution of 1,000 new copies of Thomas Clarksonn's *Essay on the Commerce and Slavery of the Human Species* to legislators of US states, especially those in the south, 'the impious traffic of late' having 'greatly increased in South Carolina and Georgia'.[209]

In 1787, the Pennsylvania Abolition Society reorganised itself to coincide with the beginnings of the British Society for Establishing the Abolition of the Slave Trade. The expectation was that competition would ensue between the United States and Britain to determine which nation would be the first to abolish the slave trade. The English abolitionist James Phillips hoped that progress towards ending the slave trade to the United States would occur if Congress achieved powers to regulate commerce and if the influential Benjamin Franklin exercised pressure on the issue.[210] The Pennsylvania Society drew up an address on 2 June 1787 expressing a desire that the Constitutional Convention would make 'the Suppression of the African trade in the United States, a party of their

---

[206] Ibid.   [207] Ibid.
[208] HSP, James Pemberton to John Pemberton, 25 November 1786, ibid., box 47, folder 40.
[209] HSP, [James Pemberton] to William Dillwyn, 26 Oct. 1786, ibid., box 47, folder 14.
[210] HSP, James Phillips to James Pemberton, 17 Feb. 1787, ibid., box 47, folder 139.

important deliberations'. The address referred to the offence caused 'by this inhuman traffic', and argued emotively that the pretensions to a love of liberty and an honourable national character by the American states would not be achieved 'while they share in the profits of a Commerce that can only be conducted upon Rivers of human tears and Blood'. The document was submitted to the Society's president, Franklin, for presentation to the Convention. Franklin, however, decided not to present the address because he thought it advisable to keep quiet on the matter while the Convention was in the middle of its deliberations.[211]

CONCLUSION

Between 1774 and 1787, greater condemnation of the slave trade occurred from mainly Christian individuals and groups, notably Quakers, than was the case before the beginning of the imperial crisis between Britain and her North American colonies. The humanitarian arguments made were replicated in newspaper coverage in the northern colonies and states. But the moral case made against continuation of the slave trade, with evidence presented on the cruelties of slave trafficking in Africa, did not translate into coordinated campaigning against continuance of the slave trade. As Christopher Leslie Brown has observed, 'there was an abolitionist consensus without a national abolitionist movement'.[212] Institutions set up to bring together the various colonies and states in North America were limited in their anti-slave trade stance. Both Continental Congresses banned slave importations as part of a wider package of non-importation measures on British goods, but neither had any authority to impose enforcement measures. Jefferson's attempt to insert a clause into the Declaration of Independence to prohibit slave importations backfired as he penned words stretching far beyond the required remit of such a clause and was forced to withdraw his statement. The Confederation Congress under the Articles of Confederation lacked the political authority to deal with slave imports and was in any case far more concerned with measures to preserve union among the states in the American revolutionary war and its aftermath.

[211] Julie L. Holcomb, *Moral Commerce: Quakers and the Transatlantic Boycott of the Slave Labor Economy* (Ithaca, NY, 2016), 68–9; Pennsylvania Society for the Abolition of Slavery: Address, 2 June 1787, in James H. Hutson, ed., *Supplement to Max Farrand's The Records of the Federal Convention of 1787* (New Haven, CT, 1987), 44–5.

[212] Christopher Leslie Brown, 'Abolition of the Atlantic Slave Trade' in Gad Heuman and Trevor Burnard, eds., *The Routledge History of Slavery* (Abingdon, 2011), 286.

None of this means that progress was absent in proscribing the slave trade during the period from the Coercive Acts to the convening of the Constitutional Convention. In fact, a fair amount of positive activity occurred at state level on this subject. Delaware and Vermont acted to ban the slave trade in their state constitutions of 1776 and 1777 respectively. The Bill of Rights included in the Massachusetts constitution of 1780 proscribed slave imports. The New Hampshire state constitution of 1783 also banned slave imports. Other jurisdictions proscribed the slave trade by law. In 1778, Virginia passed a statute to end slave importations to the state. The Pennsylvania gradual abolition of slavery law in 1780 incorporated a bill in the same state from the previous year that banned slave imports. Many of these measures, especially in the northern states, were influenced by humanitarian considerations, but in some cases, such as Virginia, economic issues relating to the needs of the state were also important. In none of the instances cited was there a protracted set of discussions lying behind the decisions made.

Abolitionist progress in Pennsylvania owed much to the efforts of Benezet in stigmatising the slave trade. Two years after his death in May 1784, Jeremy Belknap acknowledged this in a private letter in which he exclaimed, 'Blessed be the name of Anthony Benezet, for what he has written and done toward abolishing the trade in "Slaves and souls of men"'.[213] After Benezet's death, the torch calling for the ending of the transatlantic slave trade passed to others associated with Philadelphia, such as Rush, Franklin and several prominent Quakers including James Pemberton and Warner Mifflin connected with the Pennsylvania Abolition Society, and to New England abolitionists such as Moses Brown.[214] In early 1786, the latter, based in Providence, Rhode Island, criticised 'the iniquitous trade to Africa for slaves which remains to be carried on in several of the United States to the dishonour of the whole'.[215]

South Carolina was the state where the most acrimonious arguments occurred over the slave trade. The state legislature reopened Charleston to slave importations in 1783 and over the next four years thousands of Africans were brought to the Palmetto state. This was a contentious issue. Supporters of the reopening of South Carolina's slave trade argued that the new arrivals were necessary to meet the state's economic demands in

---

[213] Belknap to Brown, 15 July 1786, in *Life of Jeremy Belknap*, 167.
[214] Their abolitionist efforts are discussed in Chapter 3 below.
[215] Massachusetts HS, Brown to Belknap, 28 Jan. 1786, Belknap Papers.

its staple crop plantation sector, which dominated South Carolina's economy, in the wake of the heavy loss of slaves during the American revolutionary war. More cautious commentators were worried that importing fresh supplies of slaves would lead to credit difficulties, mounting debts and balance of trade problems in a state recovering from the economic difficulties of war and its aftermath. South Carolina's divisions over the slave trade underscored the reality that proscribing the entire slave trade to the United States could only happen under the aegis of national political authority and that was absent in 1787. The achievements of individual states in banning the slave trade were notable between 1774 and 1787 but the prohibition of slave importations to the United States as a whole was unfinished business.

3

The US Constitution, the Debates over Ratification and the Slave Trade, 1787–1788

When the fifty-five delegates to the Constitutional Convention met in Philadelphia on 25 May 1787, slavery and the slave trade were not high on their agenda.[1] Discussions focused on the most important issues facing the American states – the forms of governance, the distinction between legislative, judicial and executive powers, the nature of the franchise, and the role of the new presidency. Regulation of foreign commerce had been weak under the Articles of Confederation, and it was widely expected that such trade, including the importation of slaves, would be discussed.[2] This was a crucial, formative forum in establishing a federal republic and it was approached in an orderly, rational and thorough way as befitted its political and constitutional significance. At the end of the proposed Constitutional Convention, it was expected that delegates would produce a carefully worded draft text that would then be debated in state ratifying conventions.

Twelve of the thirteen states participated in the Convention: Rhode Island did not take part. Forty-two delegates had served in the Continental Congress or in Congress under the Articles of Confederation, so they were well versed in the major political issues that needed to be resolved in creating a federal nation. Twenty-five delegates were slave owners; slaves were critical to the wealth of another sixteen. Thomas Jefferson, who had spoken out publicly against the slave trade in 1776, was not among them as he was then engaged

---

[1] This chapter is derived, in part, from an article published in *Slavery & Abolition* 22/3 (2001), *available online* on 8 September 2010: http://wwww.tandfonline.com/10.1080/714005207.

[2] Douglas R. Egerton, *Death or Liberty: African Americans and Revolutionary America* (New York, 2009), 241.

in a diplomatic role as American minister to France. The elderly Benjamin Franklin was present at the Constitutional Convention, but he chose largely to remain silent in order to ensure that the union was preserved. George Washington was unanimously elected as president of the Convention, in which role he was expected to remain impartial in political debates, something he assiduously maintained.[3] At the time the Convention was assembled, no nation had prohibited the African slave trade.[4]

During the early part of the convention, slavery and the slave trade caused little friction whenever they were discussed. Over the course of the summer, however, these subjects became an important issue of debate. James Madison announced to the assembled delegates that the real division among the states was 'not by their difference of size ... but principally from the effects of their having or not having slaves'.[5] Around 40 per cent of the wealth of the five southernmost states was bound up in slavery at the time of the Constitutional Convention. Northern delegates were mainly predisposed against slavery but a number of them were slaveholders and they were disinclined to push for an antislavery constitution because of their fear of a mass of free black people in the United States. Equally, many delegates were chary of allowing a proslavery constitution to emerge because this was considered a taint on the honour and revolutionary ideals of the new American nation.[6] The key issues in relation to slavery and the slave trade were the form of taxation and representation to be followed in the new House of Representatives and provisions to be made over the foreign slave trade. Meetings about these issues at the convention were held in a secluded room at Independence Hall, Philadelphia, with no spectators allowed and no information about the deliberations conveyed to outsiders. The 4,500 draft of the federal constitution was completed on 17 September.[7]

Over the course of the summer of 1787, the delegates to the Convention debated all articles and clauses of the proposed

---

[3] Mark D. Kaplanoff, 'The Federal Convention and the Constitution' in Jack P. Greene and J. R. Pole, eds., *A Companion to the American Revolution* (Oxford, 2000), 470; Michael J. Klarman, *The Framers' Coup: The Making of the United States Constitution* (New York 2016), 263.

[4] George Ticknor Curtis, *History of the Origin, Formation, and Adoption of the Constitution, of the United States; with Notices of Its Principal Framers*, 2 vols. (New York, 1861), I, 456.

[5] James Madison, *Notes of Debates in the Federal Convention of 1787* (New York, 1966), 224.

[6] Klarman, *The Framers' Coup*, 264.

[7] Linda Colley, 'What Happens when a Written Constitution Is Printed? A History across Boundaries,' *Transactions of the Royal Historical Society*, 6th series, XXXI (2021), 75–6.

Constitution, and this included thorny moral and political issues associated with slavery and the slave trade. Debates on the slave trade took place between 21 and 28 August. Eventually, compromises were reached in order to compile a document that stood a good chance of being endorsed by nine of the thirteen states in state ratifying conventions, which was the bar set for successful adoption of the written rules for the federal government. It took many months for different state conventions to debate the Constitution in their ratifying conventions, and the result was not a foregone conclusion. Eventually, in September 1788, the final ratification was achieved.[8] In recent decades, historians have favoured a proslavery view of the Constitution, focusing on how it preserved slavery and therefore protected the southern states.[9] However, antislavery impulses were evident during the Constitutional Convention and ratification process, notably the fact that the Constitution did not guarantee, in relation to slavery, that there could be property in man.[10]

Among the varied positions put forward by delegates at the Convention, political compromises were made over slavery, the slave trade and the nature, functions and operation of the US government. These compromises have attracted extensive historical commentary.[11] This chapter, in line with the focus of the book, examines the constitutional clause dealing with the slave trade and the debates it engendered at the Convention and during the ratification process. Complex arguments and alignments were made. Individual views are regularly reported

---

[8] Ibid., 77.

[9] Arguments for and against this proposition can be found in many publications, including William M. Wiecek, 'The Witch at the Christening: Slavery and the Constitution's Origins' in Leonard W. Levy and Dennis J. Mahoney, eds., *The Framing and Ratification of the Constitution* (New York, 1987), 167–84; Don E. Fehrenbacher, completed and edited by Ward M. MacAfee, *The Slaveholding Republic: An Account of the United States Government's Relations to Slavery* (New York, 2002); and David Waldstreicher, *Slavery's Constitution: From Revolution to Ratification* (New York, 2009).

[10] Sean Wilentz, *No Property in Man: Slavery and Antislavery at the Nation's Founding* (Cambridge, MA, 2018), 268.

[11] E.g. Staughton Lynd, 'The Compromise of 1787', *Political Science Quarterly*, 81/2 (1966), 225–50; Staughton Lynd, *Class Conflict, Slavery, and the United States Constitution* (Indianapolis, IN, 1967); Paul Finkelman, 'Slavery and the Constitutional Convention: Making a Covenant with Death' in Richard R. Beeman, Edward C. Carter II and Stephen Botein, eds., *Beyond Confederation: Origins of the Constitution and American National Identity* (Chapel Hill, NC, 1987), 195–217; Wiecek, 'The Witch at the Christening', 167–84; Fehrenbacher, *The Slaveholding Republic*, 28–47; Richard R. Beeman, *Plain, Honest Men: The Making of the American Constitution* (New York, 2009).

throughout the chapter to illustrate the intricacies of the positions taken. Two months before the Constitutional Convention met, only two states – North Carolina and Georgia – still allowed slave imports. South Carolina, as Chapter 2 has shown, had closed its slave trade for three years a few months before the Convention met.[12] It might be supposed, therefore, that a Constitution could include an outright ban on the importation of enslaved Africans into the United States; but that proved not to be the case. Instead, the delegates at the Constitutional Convention envisaged a shift from state to federal control in this policy area but slave trade abolition could only be implemented, as we will see, in 1808.[13]

THE CONSTITUTIONAL CONVENTION AND THE SLAVE TRADE

The text of the Constitution was very scrupulously worded and subject to numerous emendations before the final version was confirmed. The process was careful and deliberate for the delegates were fully aware of the historic importance of their role in laying the foundation stones for US government that would be of enduring utility. Article 1, Section 9 of the US Constitution, dealing with the foreign slave trade, stated: 'The Migration or Importation of such Persons as any of the States now existing shall think proper to admit, shall not be prohibited by the Congress prior to the Year one thousand eight hundred and eight but a Tax or duty may be imposed on such Importation, not exceeding ten dollars for each Person.' Article 5 added that no amendment could be made to this clause before 1808.

Though these articles contain brief and simple words, they were controversial for two main reasons. First, the wording contained in Article 1, Section 9 was an ambiguous statement of the Constitution's position on the slave trade: 'Such persons' could be interpreted to mean exclusively enslaved Africans or to include both slaves and white immigrants, while 'migration' could refer either to immigration or to movement between

---

[12] Kenneth Morgan, 'Slavery and the Debate over Ratification of the United States Constitution', *Slavery & Abolition*, 22/3 (2001), 42.
[13] See two studies by David F. Ericson: 'Slave Smugglers, Slave Catchers, and Slave Rebels: Slavery and American State Development, 1787–1842' in John Craig Hammond and Matthew Mason, *Contesting Slavery: The Politics of Bondage and Freedom in the New American Nation* (Charlottesville, VA, 2011), 185; and *Slavery in the American Republic: Developing the Federal Government, 1791–1861* (Lawrence, KS, 2011), 31.

states.[14] The wording resulted from the fact that reference to slaves or the slave trade was a circumspect matter at the Constitutional Convention. In the words of Benjamin Rush, 'no mention was made of *negroes* or *slaves* in the constitution, only because it was thought the very words would contaminate the glorious fabric of American liberty and government'.[15] It was later explained that, if the Constitution had referred to 'the importation of slaves' rather than 'the importation of such persons' then 'many good people would have been alarmed, whose apprehension from the delicate mode of expression there adopted, were never once disturbed from their slumbers'.[16] Second, heightened public awareness of abolitionist attacks on the slave trade in Britain, resulting from the Anglo-American Quaker moral crusade and Thomas Clarkson's nationwide tours throughout Britain gathering evidence about the conduct of the slave trade, spread rapidly to the United States, adding to the urgency of American debates on the interplay between slavery and freedom in their own nation.[17]

The Constitutional Convention offered an opportunity to ban the slave trade to the United States. In June 1787, the Pennsylvania Society for Promoting the Abolition of Slavery prepared a petition to end the slave trade but Tench Coxe, secretary of the society, strongly advised its president, Franklin, not to raise it at the convention, and this was complied with.[18] Between 23 July and 10 September 1787 the Constitutional Convention debated provisions for the slave trade at various points before they were accepted. It proved to be the subject of 'a great diversity of sentiment'.[19] Major issues of government – the composition of Congress

---

[14] William M. Wiecek, *The Sources of Antislavery Constitutionalism in America, 1760–1848* (Ithaca, NY, 1977), 75. It was recognised during the ratification process that 'it is not to be disguised that by "such persons," slaves are principally, if not wholly intended': see Republicus, *Kentucky Gazette*, 1 March 1788, in John P. Kaminski, Gaspare J. Saladino, Richard Leffler, Charles H. Schoenleber and Marybeth Carlson, eds., *Ratification of the Constitution by the States: Virginia. Volume 1* (Madison, WI, 1988), 450.

[15] Benjamin Rush to John Coakley Lettsom, 28 Sept. 1787, in L. H. Butterfield, ed., *Letters of Benjamin Rush*, 2 vols. (Princeton, NJ, 1951), I, 442. See also Klarman, *The Framers' Coup*, 265.

[16] *New-York Commercial Advertiser*, 13 Dec. 1806.

[17] Roger Anstey, *The Atlantic Slave Trade and British Abolition, 1760–1810* (London, 1975).

[18] *Pennsylvania Gazette*, 5 Mar. 1788; John P. Kaminski, Gaspare J. Saladino and Richard Leffler, eds., *Commentaries on the Constitution, Public and Private. Volume 2: 8 November to 17 December 1787* (Madison, WI, 1983), 504.

[19] Luther Martin, 'Genuine Information VII', Baltimore *Maryland Gazette*, 18 Jan. 1788, in John P. Kaminski, ed., *A Necessary Evil? Slavery and the Debate over the Constitution*, Constitutional Heritage 2 (Madison, WI, 1995), 173. Among the newspapers which

and the Senate, voting qualifications, the separation of powers and so forth – dominated the first month of the deliberations at the Convention: arrangements about the constitutional position of the slave trade were only discussed later in the debates. Roger Sherman, an elderly lawyer representing Connecticut, who had been involved in drafting the Declaration of Independence and the Articles of Confederation, made the first statement about the slave trade on 22 August 1787. Though he disapproved of the traffic, he wanted to retain the status quo on this matter. He argued that 'the States were now possessed of the right to import slaves, as the public good did not require it to be taken from them'. In addition, he expected that 'the good sense of the several states' would soon provide impetus to abolish slavery in the United States.[20] Other delegates then offered different views, and it became clear that the question about what to do about the slave trade was highly contentious and not easily resolvable.

THE LOWER SOUTH AND THE SLAVE TRADE AT THE CONSTITUTIONAL CONVENTION

South Carolina's delegation supported a distinctive pro-slave trade and proslavery position. All four of its delegates were wealthy slaveowners who insisted there should be no plans to prohibit or tax the slave trade.[21] Many slaves had deserted to British lines during the revolutionary war, and it was considered important for the survival of South Carolina's plantation economy that numbers of slaves should be maintained. That would require fresh importations. Delegates from the Lower South insisted that the Constitution should protect slavery and that the new national government should not attack a state's right to uphold its decisions on this crucial matter.[22] Ironically, however, three South Carolinian delegates – Charles Pinckney, John Rutledge and Pierce Butler – had voted

---

reprinted this article were the *Pennsylvania Packet*, 25 Jan. 1788; *Pennsylvania Herald*, 26 Jan. 1788; *New York Journal*, 27 Feb., 1, 7 Mar. 1788; and the *State Gazette of South Carolina*, 8, 15 May 1788.

[20] Max Farrand, ed., *The Records of the Federal Convention of 1787*, 4 vols. (New Haven, CT, 1937), II, 369–70.

[21] John P. Kaminski, Charles H. Schoenleber, Jonathan M. Reid, David P. Fields, Michael E. Stevens, Gaspare J. Saladino, Margaret R. Flamingo and Timothy D. Moore, eds., *Ratification of the Constitution by the States: South Carolina* (Madison, WI, 2016), xlv; Klarman, *The Framers' Coup*, 263.

[22] Wilentz, *No Property in Man*, 79.

earlier in the year in their state legislature for a three-year prohibition on slave imports.[23]

Charles Cotesworth Pinckney of South Carolina, second cousin of Charles Pinckney, noted that his state's legislature had argued that an amendment to the Articles of Confederation regulating trade should exclude the matter of slave importations.[24] He drew attention to the differences between the position of South Carolina and Georgia, on the one hand, and Virginia, on the other, in respect of the slave trade. He thought that if regulations over the slave trade were left as they were, South Carolina and Georgia would, of their own accord, eventually stop importation. But he also argued that if South Carolina's delegates were to assent to a Constitution that restricted slave imports, they would not have the support of their constituents because 'S. Carolina & Georgia cannot do without slaves'. Moreover, as Virginia already had all the slaves she wanted, 'it would be unequal to require S.C. & Georgia to confederate on such unequal terms'.[25]

Pinckney and other South Carolinian delegates considered that attitudes and actions towards the slave trade were personal judgements and that the Constitutional Convention had not convened to determine whether a moral case against the Guinea traffic was just.[26] Furthermore, Pinckney was convinced that his constituents would not surrender their right to choose whether to open or close the slave trade. It was for them, apart from anything else, a matter of state pride. The three most southerly states 'acted upon the belief that their constituents would not surrender the right to continue the importation of slaves, although they might, if left to themselves, discontinue the practice at some future time'.[27]

Pinckney's views on the slave trade were unequivocal: 'South Carolina can never receive the plan if it prohibits the slave trade. In every proposed extension of the powers of Congress, that state has expressly & watchfully excepted that of meddling with the importation of negroes. If the States all be left at liberty on this subject, S. Carolina may perhaps by degrees do of herself what is wished, as Virginia & Maryland have

---

[23] Leonardo Marques, *The United States and the Transatlantic Slave Trade to the Americas, 1776–1867* (New Haven, CT, 2016), 45–6.
[24] Kaminski et al., eds., *Ratification of the Constitution by the States: South Carolina*, xlv.
[25] Farrand, ed., *Records of the Federal Convention*, II, 371.
[26] Shirley Sidney Ulmer, 'The South Carolina Delegates to the Constitutional Convention of 1787: An Analytical Study' (Duke University PhD dissertation, 1956), 162.
[27] Curtis, *History of the Origin, Formation, and Adoption of the Constitution*, I, 456, II, 288 (quotation), 308.

already done.'²⁸ Allowing the continuance of the slave trade would be beneficial to the whole American Union, so Pinckney thought, because this would raise the output of produce, the level of consumption and increased revenue for the Treasury.²⁹ He added that he did not think South Carolina would stop slave imports 'in any short time, but only stop them occasionally as she now does'.³⁰

John Rutledge, who had been governor of South Carolina throughout the revolutionary war, attacked the proposal to abolish the slave trade because it was a vital way of ensuring that the slave population of his state was maintained and therefore it needed to be preserved for economic reasons. He added that the northern states would benefit from increasing the size of the American slave population through additional African imports because northern ships carried the commodities produced by plantation slave labour.³¹ Rutledge argued that North Carolina, South Carolina and Georgia would never agree to restrictions on slave importation.³² He was adamant that the plan to abolish the slave trade would never be accepted by the Lower South: 'If the Convention thinks that N.C., S.C. & Georgia will ever agree to the plan, unless their right to import slaves be untouched, the expectation is vain. The people of those States will never be such fools as to give up so important an interest.'³³ For Rutledge, morality and religion were irrelevant in this instance; what mattered was whether the southern states wanted to be a part of the union.³⁴

A less forthright view, but one essentially making the same point, was expressed by Dr James McHenry, a Maryland delegate, who stated that South Carolina and Georgia could not do without slaves and could not confederate on any conditions that restricted them from access to new supplies of Africans. 'They had enjoyed the rights of importing slaves when colonies' that 'they enjoyed as States under the confederation – And if they could not enjoy it under the proposed government, they could not associate or make a part of it.'³⁵ Most Virginians had a different view;

---

28 Adrienne Koch, ed., *Notes of Debates in the Federal Convention of 1787 Reported by James Madison* (Athens, OH, 1966), 503.
29 Farrand, ed., *Records of the Federal Convention*, II, 371.
30 Koch, ed., *Notes of Debates in the Federal Convention*, 507.
31 Wilentz, *No Property in Man*, 80.
32 Kaminski et al., *Ratification of the Constitution by the States: South Carolina*, xlv.
33 Farrand, ed., *The Records of the Federal Convention*, II, 373.
34 Kaminski et al., eds., *Ratification of the Constitution by the States: South Carolina*, xlv.
35 Farrand, ed., *The Records of the Federal Convention*, II, 378.

they supported abolition of the slave trade at national level because their state had already had enough slaves to support its economy and it was considered that ending slave imports would stabilise slavery in the Old Dominion.[36] Oliver Ellsworth, a Connecticut Senator, contrasted the different positions of Virginia and Maryland, on the one hand, and South Carolina and Georgia, on the other, in regard to slavery and the slave trade. As slaves multiplied so fast in the Chesapeake, he noted, 'it is cheaper to raise than import them, whilst in the sickly rice swamps foreign supplies are necessary' and so it would be unjust to meddle with the slave supply of those states in the Lower South. Hugh Williamson of North Carolina considered it was wrong to include any measure in the Constitution that any state found objectionable.[37]

Whether or not South Carolina would have failed to ratify the Constitution if slave importations had been subject to congressional interference might have been a correct prediction, in which case Charles Cotesworth Pinckney and John Rutledge's statements were bluffs; but we cannot tell whether South Carolina was ready to go it alone. Gary B. Nash thinks the delegates should have called the bluff of South Carolina and Georgia at the Constitutional Convention, arguing that severe economic problems meant that both states would have to agree to join the federal union out of necessity. The problem with this interpretation, however, is there is no evidence that the South Carolinians were, in fact, bluffing.[38] Paul Finkelman argued that South Carolina would soon have realised that it needed to ratify the Constitution and, in that case, the First or Second Federal Congress might have banned the trade.[39] That, of course, is pure speculation. The nineteenth-century lawyer and historian George Ticknor Curtis had a shrewd grasp of the issue at stake and his succinct analysis is worth quoting: the southern states 'were unwilling to deprive themselves of the supply of this species of labor for their new and yet unoccupied lands. Those states would not consent to a power of immediate prohibition, and they were extremely reluctant to yield even a power that might be used at a future period. They preferred to keep the whole subject in their own hands, and to determine for themselves when

---

[36] Wilentz, *No Property in Man*, 73.
[37] Koch, ed., *Notes of Debates in the Federal Convention*, 504, 506.
[38] See two studies by Gary B. Nash: *Race and Revolution* (Madison, WI, 1990), 29–30, and *The Forgotten Fifth: African Americans in the Age of Revolution* (Cambridge, MA, 2006), 80–3.
[39] Paul Finkelman, 'The Founders and Slavery: Little Ventured, Little Gained', *Yale Journal of Law and the Humanities*, 13/2 (2001), 436–7.

the importation should cease.' In fact, the Lower South's position on the slave trade at the Constitutional Convention was a concession to what would in two decades' time be a federal power to proscribe slave importations to the United States.[40]

PERSPECTIVES ON THE SLAVE TRADE AT THE CONSTITUTIONAL CONVENTION

It was not just some delegates from the Lower South who attacked the slave trade during the meetings of the Constitutional Convention. Delegates from other states also entered a highly charged debate on the issue. James Wilson, a future Supreme Court Justice, and Gouverneur Morris of Pennsylvania, who had served in the Continental Congress and who wrote the preamble to the US Constitution, both expressed their distaste for the slave trade but adopted different positions in the debate. Morris's position was not entirely clear, for he appears to have inclined towards combining the matter of the slave trade with a navigation act and export taxes. Wilson found reasons to suggest that South Carolina and Georgia would abolish their slave trades and he was therefore prepared to accept the trade if necessary in order to get the Lower South states to support the Constitution.[41] The Maryland trial attorney opened the debate by explaining that the slave trade was 'inconsistent with the principles of the revolution and dishonorable to the American character'.[42] Virginia delegates wanted the slave trade to be curtailed, but it was pointed out by Charles Cotesworth Pinckney that this stance was not motivated by humanitarian concerns but represented self-interest on the part of the Old Dominion: it was likely, in the event of slave trade abolition, that the value of Virginia's slaves would rise.[43]

George Mason, an influential Virginia planter, argued that the slave trade originated from the avarice of British merchants but that it now needed to be dealt with as a matter concerning not just the importing states but the whole American Union. Virginia and Maryland's decisions to end the slave trade would be all in vain, he argued, if South Carolina and Georgia were still permitted to import Africans. Those states could

---

[40] Curtis, *History of the Origin, Formation, and Adoption of the Constitution*, II, 457 (quotation), 460.
[41] Paul Finkelman, 'The Pennsylvania Delegation and the Peculiar Institution: The Two Faces of the Keystone State', *PMHB*, 112/1 (1988), 65–7.
[42] Quoted in Wilentz, *No Property in Man*, 80.   [43] Ibid., 84.

then act as entrepôts for the transfer of Africans taken to western lands in frontier areas.[44] Mason supported white immigration to the United States, which he believed would be harmed by continued slave importation. He also regarded slavery as a moral evil. His conclusion was that a new national government should exercise the right 'to prevent the increase of slavery'.[45]

Mason considered that continued importation of Africans, which he had long viewed as 'a nefarious trade', would 'render the United States weaker, more vulnerable, and less capable of defence'.[46] He castigated the slave trade as 'diabolical in itself, and disgraceful to mankind', and was reluctant to see the southern states admitted to the American Union while the trade continued. He also criticised the continuance of the slave trade for at least two more decades when there was no constitutional arrangement to safeguard slave property already in the United States.[47] Mason informed Jefferson, then American minister to France, that the northern states and the Lower South had made a compromise over the slave trade, which permitted 'the latter to continue the Importation of Slaves for twenty odd Years; a more favourite Object with them than the Liberty and Happiness of the People'.[48]

Other distinctive individual points of view were expressed in the debate over the slave trade at the Constitutional Convention. The solicitor and politician John Dickinson of Delaware argued that the national government should have the final say on the slave trade as the traffic affected most states in one way or another; the decision should not be influenced by 'the States particularly interested'.[49] John Langdon, the president (governor) of New Hampshire, considered it unconscionable to leave such a decision to individual states: it was a matter for the general government. If individual states were allowed to proceed as they saw fit, then Langdon argued that the Lower South would continue importing

---

[44] Robert McColley, *Slavery and Jeffersonian Virginia*, 2nd ed. (Champaign-Urbana, IL, 1974), 167.
[45] Farrand, ed., *The Records of the Federal Convention*, II, 370 (quotation); Jeff Broadwater, *George Mason: Forgotten Founder* (Chapel Hill, NC, 2006), 191.
[46] 'Objections to this Constitution of Government' in Robert A. Rutland, ed., *The Papers of George Mason 1725–1792: Volume III. 1787–1792* (Chapel Hill, NC, 1970), 993, 1,066.
[47] Mason to the Chairman of the Constitutional Convention, 17 June 1788, ibid., III, 1,086; Egerton, *Death or Liberty*, 241–2.
[48] Mason to Jefferson, 26 May 1788, in Julian P. Boyd, ed., *The Papers of Thomas Jefferson. Volume 13. March–7 October 1788* (Princeton, NJ, 1956), 204–7.
[49] Farrand, ed., *The Records of the Federal Convention*, II, 372.

Africans.[50] To leave the conduct of the slave trade beyond congressional interdiction would be to allow the states freedom to do as they pleased.[51]

Luther Martin, the antifederalist attorney general of Maryland, thought it disgraceful that the Constitution did not prohibit slave imports, referring to it as *'the only branch* of commerce, which is *unjustifiable in its nature,* and *contrary* to the *rights* of *mankind'*.[52] The abolitionist Moses Brown of Rhode Island expressed concern that continuation of the slave trade for twenty-one years would undo the efforts made by individual states to end the slave traffic.[53] The slaveowner James Iredell of North Carolina regarded the slave trade as deplorable and inhumane.[54] He argued that it had 'already continued too long for the honor and humanity of those concerned in it'.[55] He added, however, that 'our situation makes it necessary to bear the evil as it is. It will be left to the future legislatures to allow such importations or not'; but 'the interests of humanity will ... have gained something by the prohibition of this inhuman trade, though at the distance of twenty odd years.' Iredell would have liked to see the slave trade terminated in 1788 but realised this was not practical at the time owing to the attitudes of the Lower South delegates.[56]

Discussions on these matters continued for several days, with arguments supporting both the pro-slave trade and anti-slave trade stance.[57] Northerners and some delegates from the Upper South hoped Congress would decide to abolish the African slave trade to the United States.[58] During the debates, however, it became clear that the Lower South states cared more about maintaining their right to keep their options open with regard to the slave trade – in essence, maintaining the position established under the Confederation Congress – than the northern and middle states insisted upon ending the slave trade. Moreover, the experienced delegates from South Carolina approached the matter with confidence and total conviction that their view was the correct way forward for their state on

---

[50] Koch, ed., *Notes of Debates in the Federal Convention*, 507.
[51] *New York Daily Advertiser*, 18 Jan. 1788. [52] *Maryland Gazette*, 22 Jan. 1788.
[53] Mack Thompson, *Moses Brown: Reluctant Reformer* (Chapel Hill, NC, 1962), 193–4.
[54] Willis P. Whichard, *Justice James Iredell* (Durham, NC, 2000), 51.
[55] 'Answers to Mr Mason's Objections to the New Constitution recommended by the late convention at Philadelphia' in Griffith J. McRee, ed., *Life and Correspondence of James Iredell, One of the Associate Justices of the Supreme Court of the United States*, 2 vols. (New York, 1858), I, 213.
[56] Ibid.; Whichard, *Justice James Iredell*, 62. [57] Wilentz, *No Property in Man*, 99–100.
[58] Woody Holton, *Liberty Is Sweet: The Hidden History of the American Revolution* (New York, 2021), 531.

this subject.[59] The Constitutional Convention appointed a Committee of Eleven, later referred to as the Committee of Slave Trade. This comprised one delegate from each state attending the Convention. Though the committee's deliberations were kept confidential, most of its members were opponents of the slave trade.[60] As the prominent Philadelphia Quaker James Pemberton succinctly summarised the situation at the time, 'there was a desire prevailed in the Convention to subvert the enormous traffic, which the representatives from So[uth] Carolina, & the adjacent states being aware of, vigorously opposed'.[61]

The French traveller J. P. Brissot de Warville, who visited the United States in 1788, was scathing about the position of the Lower South on the slave trade at the Constitutional Convention:

> A numerous party still argue the impossibility of augmenting their number without recruiting them in Africa. It is to the influence of this party, in the late general convention, that is to be attributed the only article which tarnishes that glorious monument of human reason, the new federal system of the United States. It was this party that proposed to bind the hands of the new Congress, and to put it out of their power for twenty years to prohibit the importation of slaves ... To avoid the evils, which without meliorating the fate of the Blacks, would attend a political schism, the convention was forced to wander from the grand principle of universal liberty, and the preceding declaration of Congress. They thought it their duty to imitate Solon, to make, not the best law possible, but the best that circumstances would bear.[62]

Madison was keenly aware of this division between the states over the slave trade when he informed Jefferson that South Carolina and Georgia 'were inflexible on the point of the slaves'.[63] If the slave trade to those colonies were banned, South Carolinian and Georgian planters would be obliged to purchase slaves from Virginia at inflated prices.[64] In Madison's view, and others shared in this prediction, there was strong reason to believe that barring the slave trade in 1787–8 would have prevented South Carolina and Georgia from joining the confederation

---

[59] Klarman, *The Framers' Coup*, 286.   [60] Wilentz, *No Property in Man*, 87–8.
[61] RIHS, James Pemberton to Moses Brown, 16 Nov. 1787, Moses Brown correspondence.
[62] J. P. Brissot de Warville, *New Travels in the United States of America. Performed in 1788* (London, 1788), 271–2. The reference to Solon is to the difficult balancing act undertaken in the reforms of this Athenian statesman of ancient times.
[63] Madison to Jefferson, 24 Oct. 1787, in Robert A. Rutland, Charles F. Hobson, William M. E. Rachal and Jeanne K. Sisson, eds., *The Papers of James Madison. Volume 10. 27 May 1787–3 March 1788* (Charlottesville, VA, 1977), 214.
[64] Mary Sarah Bilder, *Madison's Hand: Revising the Constitutional Convention* (Cambridge, MA, 2015), 169.

of states.⁶⁵ As he carefully put it, 'I should conceive this clause to be impolitic, if it were one of those things which could be excluded without encountering greater evils', adding that 'great as the evil is, a dismemberment of the union would be worse'.⁶⁶ Without the compromises reached over slavery and the slave trade at the Constitutional Convention, either no Constitution would have been adopted or a union of some kind would have been agreed from which at least three southern states would have been excluded.⁶⁷ Madison had some sympathy for planters in South Carolina and Georgia, acknowledging that their agricultural economies were not as mature as was the case in Virginia and that the Lower South contained many citizens who had purchased land in the expectation that it would be improved by imported Africans.⁶⁸

Madison was aggrieved at seeing the slave trade continued at a federal level, but even with the compromise over the slave trade clause in the text of the Constitution, he had cause for optimism for the future. Acknowledging that the southern states would not have entered the union without keeping the slave trade open and without allowing slavery to maintain its position in the United States, he argued that the 'temporary permission' accorded to slave imports under the Constitution included a clause through which 'an end may be put to it after twenty years. There is therefore an amelioration of our circumstances. A tax may be laid in the mean time; but it is limited, otherwise congress might lay such a tax as would amount to a prohibition'.⁶⁹ The lawyer John Adams, who had drafted the Massachusetts Constitution, and Judge Francis Dana of Massachusetts similarly agreed that the compromise over the slave trade at the Constitutional Convention had opened the door eventually for proscription of the traffic.⁷⁰ Brissot de Warville explained the situation as follows: 'the Congress will be authorised in twenty years to pronounce definitively on this article. By that time, the sentiments of humanity, and

---

⁶⁵ David C. Hendrickson, *Peace Pact: The Lost World of the American Founding* (Lawrence, KS, 2003), 238.
⁶⁶ Madison to the Chairman of the Constitutional Convention, [17 June 1788] in Robert A. Rutland, Charles F. Hobson, William M. E. Rachal and Jeanne K. Sisson, eds., *The Papers of James Madison. Volume 11. 7 March 1788–1 March 1789* (Charlottesville, VA, 1977), 150.
⁶⁷ Curtis, *History of the Origin, Formation, and Adoption of the Constitution*, II, 315.
⁶⁸ McColley, *Slavery and Jeffersonian Virginia*, 170.
⁶⁹ Madison to the Chairman of the Constitutional Convention [17 June 1788] in Rutland et al., eds., *The Papers of James Madison. Volume 11*, 150.
⁷⁰ Betty Fladeland, *Men and Brothers: Anglo-American Antislavery Cooperation* (Champaign-Urbana, IL, 1980), 47.

the calculations of reason, will prevail; they will no longer be forced to sacrifice equity to convenience, or have anything to fear from opposition or schism'.[71]

Despite these optimistic views, however, in 1787 at Philadelphia it was recognised that the abolition of the slave trade 'could not be secured within any time or any means capable of being foreseen or even conjectured'.[72] Moses Brown lamented, after the Convention had ended, that there was no hope for immediate action from Congress, for 'the door of hope' had been barred for twenty-one years and, he feared, for much longer.[73] The English abolitionist Granville Sharp expressed his concern to Benjamin Franklin about the inability of Congress to intervene on the slave trade at a federal level for twenty years.[74] This was a blow to the high hopes with which abolitionists had approached the Convention as the forum to act decisively and immediately in relation to slavery and the slave trade. However, the Constitutional Convention had for the first time raised the subject of the slave trade as a matter of federal concern.

COMPROMISE OVER THE SLAVE TRADE AT THE CONSTITUTIONAL CONVENTION

After bitter sectional acrimony a compromise was reached whereby the South Carolina delegation supported the commerce clause of Article 1, Section 9 in return for New England agreeing to help to protect the slave trade. Roger Sherman and John Rutledge were the architects of this agreement.[75] Sherman opposed the slave trade but, in circumstances where compromise was necessary to secure the union, he decided that maintaining it for the time being was a lesser evil.[76] On 25 August, the slave trade committee at the Convention considered the slave trade clause in detail. At a debate on the convention floor, a proposal that 1800 should mark the limit for slave importation was struck out and replaced by 1808.

---

[71] Warville, *New Travels*, 273.
[72] Curtis, *History of the Origin, Formation, and Adoption of the Constitution*, I, 458.
[73] Moses Brown to ?, 13 Nov. 1787, in J. William Frost, ed., *The Quaker Origins of Antislavery* (Norwood, PA, 1980), 259.
[74] Sharp to Franklin, 10 Jan. 1788, in Prince Hoare, ed., *Memoirs of Granville Sharp, Esq. Composed from his own Manuscripts and other Authentic Documents in the Possession of his Family and of the African Institution* (London, 1820), 377–8.
[75] Christopher Collier, *All Politics is Local: Family, Friends, and Provincial Interests in the Creation of the Constitution* (Hanover, NH, 2003), 64.
[76] Egerton, *Death or Liberty*, 244.

Charles Cotesworth Pinckney was responsible for this change of date, reflecting South Carolina's commitment to maintaining states' rights over the regulation of slave imports.[77] Massachusetts and Connecticut joined the Lower South in achieving a majority vote for this measure, with Virginia, Pennsylvania, Delaware and New Jersey voting against the proposal.[78] But this was an unwise move according to Madison. He opposed the change of year and argued that 'twenty years will produce all the mischief that can be apprehended from the liberty to import slaves. So long a term will be more dishonourable to the National character than to say nothing about it in the Constitution'.[79] However, the extension to 1808 passed despite Madison's misgivings.[80]

The financier Robert Morris, a representative of Pennsylvania, also disagreed with the suggested change of year for the limit on slave imports. He proposed that only North Carolina, South Carolina and Georgia should have the right to import slaves in order to demonstrate that the compromise reached was owing to the pressures placed on the Convention by those states. Following some debate on this matter, however, Morris withdrew his suggestion after Mason suggested that it might offend persons in those states.[81] Article 1, Section 9 was allowed to stand as it was drafted by a vote of 7–4, with the new date of 1808 incorporated before the slave trade could be dealt with on a national basis. The clause meant exactly what its words said: all applications to Congress for a prohibition before 1808 would be refused.[82]

After considerable debate the delegates to the Convention proposed that Congress should have no power to interfere with the foreign slave trade for twenty-one years but that taxes could be levied on imported Africans. This was achieved despite protestations from the Virginia delegation about protecting the slave trade. Maryland, Georgia, South Carolina and the New England states forged an alliance to secure this

---

[77] Wilentz, *No Property in Man*, 94.
[78] Hendrickson, *Peace Pact*, 237; Edward B. Rugemer, *Slave Law and the Politics of Resistance in the Early Atlantic World* (Cambridge, MA, 2018), 231.
[79] Farrand, ed., *The Records of the Federal Convention*, II, 415.
[80] Jeff Broadwater, *Jefferson, Madison, and the Making of the Constitution* (Chapel Hill, NC, 2019), 151.
[81] Klarman, *The Framers' Coup*, 289.
[82] Jeremy Belknap to Ebenezer Hazard, 7 May 1790, in John P. Kaminski, Charles H. Schoenleber, Gaspare J. Saladino, Richard Leffler, Jonathan M. Reid, Margaret R. Flamingo, Johanna E. Lannér-Crusin, David P. Fields, Patrick T. Conley and Timothy D. Moore, eds., *Ratification of the Constitution by the States: Rhode Island: Volume 3* (Madison, WI, 2013), 857.

arrangement. The cross-sectional agreement was made possible by a compromise made by the South Carolina and New England delegations not to allow Congress to stop slave imports to the United States before 1808 in return for allowing it to pass navigation acts by majorities rather than by a two-thirds vote.[83] Article 1, Section 9 of the Constitution encapsulated this compromise. It was exempted from the power of amendment.[84]

In sticking firm to their commitments to slavery and the slave trade, South Carolina and Georgia had set down a marker that the importation of Africans and the preservation of slavery were fixed and permanent features of their states.[85] Most free residents of South Carolina supported the slave trade clause in the Constitution.[86] David Brion Davis considered that by this juncture 'Americans overwhelmingly opposed the continuation of the African slave trade'.[87] He did not indicate how one could measure that sentiment. More important, though, was the fact that the political means to enforce the issue were not yet available in the nascent federal nation. As Seymour Drescher has explained, 'antislavery sentiment was too diffuse and the priority of the union too strong to engender a sustained majority for immediate federal power over the foreign slave trade'.[88]

James Iredell later pointed out that Congress had no authority to restrain the states from importing slaves before 1808.[89] He argued that 'the interests of humanity' had 'gained something by the prohibition of this inhuman trade, though at the distance of twenty odd years'.[90] Other interested commentators reacted to the slave trade clause in the

---

[83] Erickson, *Slavery in the American Republic*, 31; Don E. Fehrenbacher, 'Slavery, the Framers, and the Living Constitution' in Robert A. Goldwin and Art Kaufman, eds., *Slavery and its Consequences: The Constitution, Equality, and Race* (Washington, DC, 1988), 10.

[84] David Brion Davis, 'American Slavery and the American Revolution' in Ira Berlin and Ronald Hoffman, eds., *Slavery and Freedom in the Age of the American Revolution* (Urbana, IL, 1983), 266.

[85] Finkelman, 'Slavery and the Constitutional Convention', 213–18.

[86] James A. McMillin, *The Final Victims: Foreign Slave Trade to North America, 1783–1810* (Columbia, SC, 2005), 7.

[87] Davis, 'American Slavery and the American Revolution', 267.

[88] Seymour Drescher, 'Divergent Paths: The Anglo-American Abolitions of the Atlantic Slave Trade' in Wim Klooster, ed., *Migration, Trade, and Slavery in an Expanding World: Essays in Honor of Pieter Emmer* (Leiden, 2009), 267.

[89] Jonathan Elliot, ed., *The Debates in the Several State Conventions, on the Adoption of the Federal Constitution, as Recommended by the General Convention at Philadelphia in 1787*, 4 vols. (Washington, DC, 1836), IV, 119.

[90] [James Iredell], 'Answer to Mr Mason's Objections to the New Constitution recommended by the late Convention at Philadelphia, by MARCUS' in McCree, *Life and Correspondence of James Iredell*, II, 213.

Constitution in opposing ways. Benjamin Rush confidently predicted to an English correspondent that there would in 1808 be 'an end of the African trade in America'.[91] The constitutional clause, of course, did not directly state that that would occur then, though it conceded that the national government could, at that juncture, act against slave importations.[92] James Pemberton apologised for the fact that the Constitution had delayed interference with the slave trade for two decades. The Lower South states were responsible for this compromise. But he noted that this was not intended to restrain the legislatures of the states from enacting laws they considered expedient for eliminating slave importations to their own jurisdictions.[93]

Under the provisions of Article 1, Section 9 every state had the right to alter its position on slave importation for twenty-one years because the private laws of each state would submit to the superior jurisdiction of Congress if the Constitution were to be ratified.[94] However, Article 1, Section 9 included no provision that the slave trade would be prohibited after 1788 and no security that this would ever be achieved; instead, it allowed for the possibility of abolition.[95] While the clause restraining Congress from acting on the slave trade remained in operation, legislative acts in individual states could be repealed and 'the odium attending it will be greatly effaced by the sanction which is given to it in the general government'.[96] Moses Brown worried that Article 1, Section 9 would discourage individual states from taking further action on the slave trade, and that they might therefore 'fall back from their present light into great darkness on this subject'.[97]

It is worth adding that many delegates to the Constitutional Convention thought the South was growing faster than the North in economic and demographic terms, and that it could well be that in 1808 Southerners might control the House of Representatives and prevent the passage of a law banning slave importation. Thus, Paul

[91] Rush to John Coakley Lettsom, 28 Sept. 1787, in Kaminski et al., eds., *Commentaries on the Constitution, public and private*, I, 262–3.
[92] Wilentz, *No Property in Man*, 113, 125.
[93] RIHS, James Pemberton to Moses Brown, 16 Nov. 1787, Moses Brown correspondence.
[94] Philadelphia *Freeman's Journal*, 21 Nov. 1787.
[95] In the Pennsylvania ratifying convention, 1 Dec. 1787, William Findley noted that the Constitution included no statement about the power to prevent slave imports: see HSP, James Wilson's notes, Wilson MSS.
[96] *Maryland Gazette*, 22 Jan. 1788.
[97] HSP, Moses Brown to James Pemberton, 17 Oct. 1787, Pemberton Papers, box 48, folder 172.

Finkelman has argued that 'the delegates in Philadelphia were not deferring a vote on the African slave trade in order to kill it later, but were in fact deferring any consideration until a time when everyone assumed the supporters of the trade would have the political strength to prevent a ban on it'.[98] This assumption proved to be incorrect, for the supporters of the slave trade did not have the political support to act in this way in 1807/8.

Reflecting decades later on Article 1, Section 9, John Jay explained, carefully and precisely, that he understood:

the sense and meaning of this clause to be that the power of Congress, although competent to prohibit such migration and importation, was not to be exercised with respect to the *then existing states* (and them only) until the year 1808; but that the Congress were at liberty to make such prohibition as to any one State, which might in the *mean* time be established, and further that from and after *that period*, they were authorized to make such prohibition, as to all the States, whether new or old.[99]

REACTIONS TO THE SLAVE TRADE COMPROMISE AT THE CONSTITUTIONAL CONVENTION

The compromise over the slave trade at the Constitutional Convention enabled South Carolinians who wanted the trade to stay open to return to their states and argue that they had successfully prevented any tampering by the national government in their slave property and that slavery had therefore been preserved in the United States. That was an achievement they were pleased to secure to prevent any interference with their ability to open and close their slave trade according to prevailing economic conditions. But, although that seemed a victory for the Lower South in 1788, the wording of Article 1, Section 9 implied that eventually – to be precise in twenty years' time – the national government would have the right to legislate on the slave trade.[100] In South Carolina, it was reported that 'the planters observe with anguish that in twenty years the new government will prohibit the importation of negroes'.[101] In fact, in that state the main objection to the Constitution was that it invested the

---

[98] Finkelman, 'The Founders and Slavery,' 431 (quotation).
[99] John Jay to Elias Boudinot, 17 Nov. 1819, in Philip B. Kurland and Ralph Lerner, eds., *The Founders' Constitution. Volume Three: Article 1, Section 8, Clause 5 through Article 2, Section 1* (Chicago, 1987), 297–8.
[100] Wilentz, *No Property in Man*, 100.
[101] Jean-Baptiste Petry to le Maréchal de Castries, 16 Nov. 1787, in Kaminski et al., eds., *Ratification of the Constitution by the States: South Carolina*, 41.

federal legislature with the power to regulate or prevent slave importations.[102] Not all South Carolinians were dejected about Article 1, Section 9, however. Some, such as William Loughton Smith, later pointed out that while the Constitution remained unaltered, enemies of South Carolina's position on this matter, including those in Virginia and North Carolina, 'can't touch our negroes for 20 years & perhaps not constitutionally after that time'.[103]

In *The Federalist*, no. 42, Madison provided a carefully worded, lengthier appraisal of the gains made by the insertion of Article 1, Section 9 in the final version of the US Constitution:

It were doubtless to be wished that the power of prohibiting the importation of slaves, had not been postponed until the year 1808, or rather that it had been suffered to have immediate operation. But it is not difficult to account either for this restriction on the general government, or for the manner in which the whole clause is expressed. It ought to be considered as a great point gained in favour of humanity, that a period of twenty years may terminate for ever within these states, a traffic which has so long and so loudly upbraided the barbarism of modern policy; that within that period it will receive a considerable discouragement from the federal government, and may be totally abolished by a concurrence of the few states which continue the unnatural traffic, in the prohibitory example which has been given by so great a majority of the union.[104]

Rush also welcomed Article 1, Section 9. Arguing that any action dealing with slavery in the United States needed to proceed gradually, he contended that 'the Section of the constitution which will put it in the power of Congress twenty years hence to restrain it [i.e. the slave trade] altogether, was a great point obtained from the Southern States'.[105]

Madison later explained that, at the Constitutional Convention, South Carolina and Georgia were averse to any interference to the slave trade 'and solemnly declared that their constituents would never accede to a Constitution containing such an article ... Out of this conflict grew the middle measure providing that Congress should not interfere until the year 1808; with an implication, that after that date, they might prohibit the importation of slaves into the States then existing, & previous thereto,

---

[102] *Pennsylvania Gazette*, 19 Mar. 1788.
[103] William Loughton Smith to Edward Rutledge, 9 Aug. 1789, in George C. Rogers, Jr, ed., 'The Letters of William Loughton Smith to Edward Rutledge, June 6, 1789 to April 28, 1794,' *SCHM*, 69/1 (1968), 21.
[104] James Madison, 'The Powers Conferred by the Constitution further Considered', no. 42, 22 Jan. 1788, in Jacob E. Cooke, ed., *The Federalist* (Middletown, CT, 1961), 405.
[105] Benjamin Rush to Jeremy Belknap, 28 Feb. 1788, in Kaminski et al., eds., *Commentaries on the Constitution, Public and Private. Volume 2*, 530.

into the States not then existing.' South Carolina and Georgia's earnestness on this subject, Madison further explained, 'was farther manifested by their insisting on the security in the V article, against any amendment to the Constitution affecting the right reserved to them'.[106]

The federalist newspaper, the *Pennsylvania Gazette*, viewed the slave trade clause in the constitution as a cause for celebration. Its provisions would enable the federal government to make 'an effectual check to the African trade, in the course of one and twenty years. How honourable to America – to have been the first Christian power that has borne a testimony against a practice, that is alike disgraceful to religion, and repugnant to the true interests and happiness of Society'.[107] The jurist and legal scholar James Kent later argued that 'the constitution evidently looked forward to the year 1808 as the commencement as an epoch in the history of human improvement'.[108] It was pointed out that Article 1, Section 9 only limited the power of the federal legislature in regard to the slave trade; it did not restrain state legislatures from enacting such laws, or supplementing laws already in place, as they judged expedient to prohibit the slave trade within their own territory.[109] Whether Article 1, Section 9 implied that Congress had authority over the interstate slave trade is debatable, but the evidence on balance suggests that such power was not vested in Congress.[110]

Other commentators were far less sanguine about the decisions about the slave trade at the Constitutional Convention. The Rhode Island congregational theologian Samuel Hopkins admitted in a private letter that he was hurt by the decisions of the Convention on this matter:

They have carefully secured the practice of it [i.e. the slave trade] for 20 years, and prevented any Asylum for slaves during that term, unless every individual State, should suppress this trade. They have taken it out of the hands of Congress. We cannot determine that the major part of the delegates were pleased with this.

---

[106] James Madison to Robert Walsh, 27 Nov. 1819, in Kurland and Lerner, eds., *The Founders' Constitution. Volume Three*, 298.

[107] *Pennsylvania Gazette*, 26 Sept. 1787.

[108] James Kent, Commentaries 1: 179–87 (1826) in Kurland and Lerner, eds., *The Founders' Constitution. Volume Three*, 305.

[109] James Pemberton to Moses Brown, 16 Nov. 1787, and Edmund Prior to Moses Brown, 1 Dec.1787, in Kaminski et al., eds., *Commentaries on the Constitution, Public and Private. Volume 2*, 525–6.

[110] For detailed consideration of this issue, see two studies by David L. Lightner: 'The Founders and the Interstate Slave Trade,' *Journal of the Early Republic*, 22/1 (2002), 25–51, and *Slavery and the Commerce Power: How the Struggle against the Interstate Slave Trade Led to the Civil War* (New Haven, CT, 2006), 16–36.

Some of the southern delegates no doubt, insisted upon it that the introduction of slaves should be secured, and obstinately refused to consent to any constitution, which did not secure it. The others therefore consented, rather than have no constitution, or one in which the delegates should not be unanimous.[111]

A Quaker contribution from Philadelphia was more censorious than Hopkins, hoping that some well-disposed people would petition and have the article erased as 'a disgrace to the Annals of America'. This represented an attack on liberty of conscience – a guiding principle of the Society of Friends.[112] An anonymous contribution to the *New York Morning Post* lamented that Congress could not immediately take action against the slave trade, and was 'absolutely precluded from interference with that most flagrant violation of natural justice'.[113]

Numerous condemnations of the slave trade clause on moral grounds were made in the wake of the Constitutional Convention. Three can be cited here. A stinging rebuke to politicians for failing to act over the slave trade came from Jeremy Belknap of Massachusetts. He wrote to Benjamin Rush:

Can you believe that the state of Massachusetts whose first principle is that all men are by nature free & equal still permits her citizens to carry on the terrible traffic in 'Slaves & Souls of men'? When shall we be wise! When shall we be consistent! Why should it not be felony to steal men as much as to steal money & plate? Or why should it not be deemed equally criminal to steal abroad as at home?[114]

A pamphlet by Tench Coxe offered a more measured approach to the subject but made essentially the same point: 'the importation of slaves from any foreign country is, by a clear implication, held up to the world as equally inconsistent with the dispositions and the duties of the people of America'.[115] 'A Countryman' stated that 'all good Christians must agree, that this trade is an abomination to the Lord, and must, if continued, bring down a heavy judgment upon our land. It does not seem to be justice, that one man should take another from his own country, and

---

[111] Samuel Hopkins to Moses Brown, 22 Oct. 1787, in Kaminski et al., eds., *Commentaries on the Constitution, Public and Private: Volume 2*, 510. Hopkins commented further on the slave trade at the Constitutional Convention in the *Providence Gazette*, 13 Oct. 1787.

[112] Timothy Meanwell in Philadelphia *Independent Gazetteer*, 29 Oct. 1787.

[113] *New York Morning Post*, 11 Apr. 1788.

[114] LCP, Jeremy Belknap to Benjamin Rush, 29 Sept. 1787, Benjamin Rush correspondence, vol. 30, box 1.

[115] Tench Coxe, 'An Examination of the Constitution' (1787) in Kurland and Lerner, eds., *The Founders' Constitution. Volume 3*, 282.

make a slave of him; and yet we are told by this new constitution, that one of its great ends, is to establish justice'.[116]

The Rhode Island antislavery advocate Moses Brown feared that Article 1, Section 9 of the Constitution obstructed further consideration of the slave trade at federal level for twenty-one years and that consequently 'the states may fall back from their present Light into great Darkness on this subject, and the Recovery from the Gross Evil, for which this land mourns'.[117] Others echoed his disappointment. Thus, James Pemberton and his associates had hoped that the establishment of a federal government would 'have been more conspicuous on the principles of Equity & Moral Justice by a Provision against the iniquitous slave trade, but the influence of the southern governments has diverted them from that very important object'.[118] The Convention delegates, in Pemberton's view, had not fulfilled their moral duty.[119] Nevertheless, restrictions on acting against the slave trade only operated at a federal level after 1787 and state legislatures could still enact measures to prohibit the slave trade to their jurisdictions.[120]

THE SLAVE TRADE IN THE RATIFICATION DEBATES OVER THE CONSTITUTION: GENERAL ISSUES

After the Constitutional Convention ended, its decisions still needed to be confirmed in state ratifying conventions proposed under Article 5 of the US Constitution, with delegates elected by voters. A relatively new departure for the United States, this was an essential part of the public scrutiny and debate needed to convey legitimacy on the Constitution. The only previous use of ratifying conventions had occurred during the confirmation process of the Massachusetts Constitution (1780) when town meetings approved the text of the foundations of state government after it had

---

[116] 'A Countryman,' 13 Dec. 1787, ibid., III, 285.
[117] HSP, Moses Brown to James Pemberton, 17 Oct. 1787, Pemberton Papers, box 48, folder 172.
[118] HSP, James Pemberton to John Pemberton, 20 Sept. 1787, ibid., box 48, folder 152.
[119] Joseph S. Foster, 'James Pemberton' in Craig W. Horle, Joseph S. Foster, Laurie M. Wolfe, Jeffrey L. Scheib, Robert E. Wright, David Haugaard, Dianna DiIllio, Jennifer A. Janofsky and Leigh A. McCuen, eds., *Lawmaking and Legislators in Pennsylvania: A Biographical Dictionary. Volume Three: 1757–1775* (Harrisburg, PA, 2005), 1035.
[120] HSP, James Pemberton to Moses Brown, 16 Nov. 1787, Pemberton Papers, box 49, folder 6, and HSP, James Pemberton to John Pemberton, 3 May 1788, ibid., box 50, folder 26.

been considered by a state constitutional convention. John Adams was the main advocate of this public approval mechanism.[121] The ratification process of the US Constitution in 1787–8 largely followed the procedures adopted in Massachusetts.

During the constitutional proceedings of the summer of 1787, only delegates had knowledge of the nature of the issues, debates and resolutions: the proceedings of the Convention were kept secret and restricted from public view throughout all of the debates.[122] It was now important for the educated public to debate and consider the proposals. Delegates to the ratification conventions and other Americans had easy access to the printed Constitution and the articles and clauses of that document were subject to wide-ranging appraisals. During this process, slavery and the slave trade generated greater public attention and commentary than ever before. On 26 September 1787, Congress sent out a call for the ratifying conventions to be convened. They took place between late 1787 and May 1790. Though the Constitution became the official framework of federal government on 21 June 1788, only nine states out of thirteen had by then completed the ratification process, but under Article 7 that was the stage when the Constitution became binding. The ratification process was lengthy and by no means a foregone conclusion because antifederalists were active in opposing the proposed strengthening of the federal government that lay at the heart of the discussions.[123] Many substantive governmental issues in the ratifying conventions were debates based on petitions to the state assemblies.[124]

The ratifying conventions in Delaware, New Jersey, Connecticut and Maryland made no mention of the slave trade. There was also very little debate over Article 1, Section 9 in New York. But the clause was discussed in Rhode Island, New Hampshire, North Carolina, Massachusetts, Pennsylvania, Virginia and South Carolina.[125] In the latter state,

---

[121] C. Bradley Thompson, *John Adams and the Spirit of Liberty* (Lawrence, KS, 1998), 40–1.
[122] This is well articulated in HSP, James Pemberton to John Pemberton, 20 Apr. 1788, Pemberton Papers, box 50, folder 3.
[123] These matters are explained fully in Pauline Maier, *Ratification: The People debate the Constitution, 1787–1788* (New York, 2010).
[124] Stephen A. Higginson, 'A Short History of the Right to Petition Government for the Redress of Grievances', *The Yale Law Journal*, 96/1 (1986), 155.
[125] As the material discussed below shows, Jed Handelsman Shugerman is incorrect in stating that South Carolina was the only state whose ratifying convention concentrated on the slave trade clause: see his article 'The Louisiana Purchase and South Carolina's Reopening of the Slave Trade in 1803', *Journal of the Early Republic*, 22/2 (2002), 268.

according to the French consul at Charleston, repeal of the constitutional clause dealing with the slave trade was one of the major issues which would likely be brought forth and discussed in the South Carolina legislature.[126] The Massachusetts ratifying convention, in particular, gave detailed consideration to the proposed rule over the slave trade. Comparisons with the Articles of Confederation (1781), which omitted clauses on slavery and the slave trade, did not feature in the arguments; instead commentators focused on the slave trade in relation to Christian morality, republican notions of liberty and the extent of congressional power over the traffic.[127] In the Rhode Island House of Deputies in late 1787, a bill proposed by the Quakers to prohibit the slave trade passed by a very large majority.[128] The Rhode Island state ratifying convention debated the issue of the slave trade in detail and concluded that, even though it was nugatory to propose an amendment to Article 1, Section 9, it was nevertheless morally right for this state body to recommend it to indicate the strength of feeling against a clause that was 'so inconsistent with the Spirit of a free Government'.[129]

THE SLAVE TRADE IN THE RATIFICATION DEBATES OVER THE CONSTITUTION: OPPONENTS

Opponents of the constitutional clause on the foreign slave trade highlighted various deficiencies in the agreed statement. All sections of the nation included critics who opposed it on moral grounds. The antifederalist Quaker preacher James Neal, in the Massachusetts ratification convention debates, objected to the notion that the slave trade could flourish for another twenty years because it favoured 'the making merchandise of the bodies of men; and unless his objection was removed, he would not put his hand to the constitution'.[130] A leading New England lawyer

---

[126] Jean-Baptiste Petry to Comte de Montmorin, 26 Dec. 1787, in Kaminski et al., eds., *Ratification of the Constitution by the States: South Carolina*, 59.
[127] W. E. B. Du Bois, *The Suppression of the African Slave-Trade*, 68, n. 3; Samuel Bannister Harding, *The Contest over the Ratification of the Federal Constitution in the State of Massachusetts* (New York, 1896), 71.
[128] Proceedings of government, 32 Oct.–3 Nov. 1787, in John P. Kaminski, Charles H. Schoenleber, Gaspare J. Saladino, Richard Leffler, Jonathan M. Reid, Margaret R. Flamingo, Patrick D. Conley and Timothy D. Moore, eds., *Ratification of the Constitution by the States: Rhode Island: Volume 1* (Madison, WI, 2011), 43.
[129] *Providence Gazette*, 13 Mar. 1790.
[130] Massachusetts Ratification Convention Debates, 25 Jan. 1788 (quotation) in Kaminski, ed., *A Necessary Evil?*, 88.

Theophilus Parsons, however, responded to this opinion by construing that Article 1, Section 9 offered 'a dawn of hope for the final abolition of the horrid Traffick'.[131] An article in the *Massachusetts Centinel* argued that if Massachusetts were to agree to the slave trade clause, it would be repudiating its own state constitution, which begins with the words 'All men are born free and equal'. To adopt the Federal Constitution as it then stood would be to 'rase [i.e. raze] our own to the very foundation'. Voting for Congress to be expressly restricted from making any provision against the slave trade for twenty-one years meant repudiating 'freedom and equity' as 'the natural rights of every man born into the world'. The author of the article was shocked that Congress would not currently be allowed to prevent slave imports to the United States.[132]

In New Hampshire, the lawyer Joshua Atherton, a delegate from Amherst, who led the antifederalist forces in the state ratifying convention, echoed this sentiment by arguing in a speech to the convention that the continuation of the slave trade made Americans *'consenters to and partakers in the* sin and guilt of this abominable traffic, at least for a certain period, without any positive stipulation that it shall even then be brought to an end'. By 1808, he added, 'Congress may be as much or more puzzled to put a stop to it then as we are now. The clause has not secured its abolition'. For Atherton, there should be a move 'to abolish the detestable custom of enslaving the Africans' rather than 'our becoming guarantees for its exercise for a term of years'.[133] Similar arguments were made in the *Exeter Freemen's Oracle* on 8 February 1788:

this cruel and barbaric practice is not to be prohibited by Congress for twenty years to come, and even then, it is not said, it shall cease – Here is a permission granted, for the enslaving and making miserable our fellow men, totally contrary to all the principles of reason, justice, benevolence and humanity, and all the kind and compassionate dictates of the Christian religion. Can we then hold up our

---

[131] Jeremy Belknap to Benjamin Rush, 12 Feb. 1788, in John P. Kaminski, Gaspare J. Saladino, Richard Leffler, Charles H. Schoenleber and Mary A. Hogan, eds., *Ratification of the Constitution by the States: Massachusetts. Volume 4* (Madison, WI, 2001), 1588.

[132] *Massachusetts Centinel*, 21 Nov. 1787, in John P. Kaminski, Gaspare J. Saladino, Richard Leffler and Charles H. Schoenleber, eds., *Ratification of the Constitution by the States: Massachusetts. Volume 2* (Madison, WI, 1998), 872.

[133] Joseph B. Walker, *A History of the New Hampshire Convention for the Investigation, Discussion, and Decision of the Federal Constitution: And of the Old North Meeting House of Concord, in Which It Was Ratified by the Ninth State, and thus Rendered Operative, at One O'clock p.m., on Saturday, the 21st Day of June 1788* (Boston, 1788), 113.

hands for a Constitution that licences this bloody practice? Can we who have fought so hard for Liberty give our consent to have it taken away from others? May the powers above forbid.[134]

These were arguments advanced with no local economic or social interest, for slavery had naturally whittled itself down to a numerically small institution in New Hampshire. Rather, it reflected the way in which some New Hampshire politicians spoke about slavery to define their own notions of the larger questions of freedom and tyranny. Federalists in that state compromised on the issue of slavery because they concluded that the Constitution did not condone slavery in principle. New Hampshire's antifederalists, by contrast, found a compromise between slavery and the Constitution difficult to accept because they believed that republican government should be based on a common moral and religious foundation.[135]

Other New England commentators decried the brutality of the slave trade and argued that the Constitution preserved a miserable trafficking of black Africans that ran counter to the compassionate creeds of Christianity.[136] Three antifederalists writing in Northampton's *Hampshire Gazette* thought it monstrous that Christians should support the slave trade. They eloquently evoked the pain of the Guinea traffic by asking what feelings their readers would have if their own children were carried off into slavery: 'Where is the man who can lay his hand upon his heart and say, I am willing my sons and my daughters should be torn from me and doomed to perpetual slavery? We presume that man is not to be found amongst us: And yet we think the consequence is fairly drawn, that this is what every man ought to be able to say, who voted for this Constitution'.[137] Possibly the moral and religious

---

[134] 'A Friend to the Rights of the People: Antifederalist 1', *Exeter Freemen's Oracle*, 8 Feb. 1788, in John P. Kaminski, Charles H. Schoenleber, Jonathan M. Reid, Gaspare J. Saladino, Margaret R. Flamingo, Timothy D. Moore and David P. Fields, eds., *Ratification of the Constitution by the States: New Hampshire* (Madison, WI, 2017), 116.

[135] Jean Yarbrough, 'New Hampshire: Puritanism and the Moral Foundations of America' in Michael Allen Gillespie and Michael Lienesch, eds., *Ratifying the Constitution* (Lawrence, KS, 1989), 245–9.

[136] 'Adelos', Northampton *Hampshire Gazette*, 6 Feb. 1788; 'A Friend to the Rights of the People: Antifederalist 1', Exeter *Freeman's Oracle*, 8 Feb. 1788, in Kaminski, ed., *A Necessary Evil?*, 96, 98.

[137] Consider Arms, Malachi Maynard and Samuel Field, Dissent to the Massachusetts Convention, *Hampshire Gazette*, 9 Apr. 1788, in Kaminski et al., eds., *Ratification of the Constitution by the States: Massachusetts. Volume 4*, 1737.

legacy of puritanism in New England influenced the stance taken against the slave trade by many in that region.[138]

After Massachusetts ratified the Constitution on 6 February 1788 by the relatively slim margin of 187–168 votes, three opponents of the decision from Hampshire County, Massachusetts singled out the slave trade clause as one of the reasons for their opposition. Referring to the *'nefarious trade'* of enslaving the Africans and singling out the epithet *nefarious* as indicative of 'something peculiarly wicked and abominable', these delegates wondered how a constitution could be created with retention of the slave trade, which ran counter to their principles and ideas of government. Advocates of ratification explained to them that congressional interdiction with the slave trade was only a matter of twenty-one years, stating 'how much more glorious would the acquisition have been, was such abolition to take place the first moment the constitution should be established. If we had said that after the expiration of a certain term the practice should cease, it would have appeared with a better grace; but this is not the case, for even after that, it is wholly optional with the Congress, whether they abolish it or not'.[139]

In the Middle states, the slave trade clause also elicited criticism on grounds of conscience. It was attacked for 'entailing endless Servitude on Millions of the human Race,' and for ensuring that 'poor Africans' were doomed to 'endure a continuance of depredation, rapine, and murder, for 21 years to come.'[140] Another source, from New York, referred to the inhuman traffic in transporting slaves to the United States.[141] Such a deplorable situation occurred, as one newspaper report put it, 'notwithstanding the *patriotic* convention, at which a Washington presided' that had 'declared that this abominable traffic shall be continued for TWENTY years by the people of America!'[142] If future legislatures persisted in maintaining the slave trade after twenty-one years, it was noted that this would be a matter between God and their own consciences and,

---

[138] Yarbrough, 'New Hampshire', 249.
[139] Consider Arms, Malachi Maynard and Samuel Field, Dissent to the Massachusetts Convention, *Hampshire Gazette*, 9, 16 Apr. 1788, in John P. Kaminski, Gaspare J. Saladino, Richard Leffler and Charles H. Schoenleber, eds., *Commentaries on the Constitution, Public and Private. Volume 5: 1 April to 9 May 1788* (Madison, WI, 1995), 42, 47.
[140] *New York Morning Post*, 11 Apr. 1788, in Kaminski, ed., *A Necessary Evil?*, 150.
[141] *New York Journal*, 15 Nov. 1787.
[142] 'A Caution', Philadelphia *Independent Gazetteer*, 6 May 1788, in Kaminski, ed., *A Necessary Evil?*, 153. This was reprinted in the *New York Journal*, 16 May 1788; *Boston Gazette*, 19 May 1788; and Winchester's *Virginia Gazette*, 21 May 1788.

though it was necessary in 1787 to 'bear the evil as it is,' humanity would have gained something if it was ended in 1808.[143]

An alternative view was that the congressional power to deal eventually with the slave trade should be a matter for rejoicing rather 'than to regret that its exercise should be postponed for twenty years.'[144] James Wilson emphasised, in debates in the Pennsylvania Convention, that it was not the intention of Article 1, Section 9 to admit slave importation after 1808. On the contrary, Congress could then act against the slave trade 'notwithstanding the disposition of any state to the contrary.' Wilson hoped that this would lay a foundation for banishing slavery from the United States, following the principle of gradual emancipation followed by Pennsylvania.[145]

The views of Pennsylvania Quakers were naturally of particular importance given their avowed abolitionist stance and political influence. They had hoped the Constitution would eradicate the slave trade in terms of equity and natural justice, and were dismayed that the wording of Article 1, Section 9 forbade congressional interference with it for twenty-one years.[146] Some Quakers found the entire document incompatible with the principles of the Religious Society of Friends.[147] The Pennsylvania Abolition Society petitioned the Constitutional Convention to suppress the slave trade on humanitarian grounds.[148] A good many antifederalists in Pennsylvania tried to exploit Quaker repugnance for slavery and the slave trade in order to win their support. But though Friends objected to the Constitution's clauses on slavery, they mainly supported ratification because as a religious society they were not concerned with setting up or pulling down governments.[149]

---

[143] *Norfolk and Portsmouth Journal*, 19 Mar. 1788.
[144] Thomas McKean in Debates of the Pennsylvania Convention, 28 Nov. 1787, in Merrill Jensen, John P. Kaminski and Gaspare J. Saladino, eds., *Ratification of the Constitution by the States: Pennsylvania* (Madison, WI, 1976), 417.
[145] James Wilson in the Pennsylvania Convention debates, 3 Dec. 1787, ibid.
[146] James Pemberton to John Pemberton, 20 Sept. 1787, in Jensen et al., eds., *Ratification of the Constitution by the States: Pennsylvania*, 133.
[147] Timothy Meanwell in the Philadelphia *Independent Gazetteer*, 29 Oct. 1787, in Kaminski, ed., *A Necessary Evil?*, 120.
[148] The Pennsylvania Abolition Society Petition to the Constitutional Convention, *Pennsylvania Gazette*, 5 Mar. 1788, reprinted in the Philadelphia *Independent Gazetteer*, 7 Mar. 1788, ibid., 148.
[149] Owen S. Ireland, *Religion, Ethnicity and Politics: Ratifying the Constitution in Pennsylvania* (University Park, PA, 1995), 81; James Thornton, Sr to Moses Brown, 17 Dec. 1787, in Kaminski, ed., *A Necessary Evil?*, 140.

In addition to debates over the slave trade during the Pennsylvania ratifying convention, in January 1788 the Pennsylvania Society for Promoting the Abolition of Slavery approached the state legislature 'in favour of a law to prohibit the fitting out, owning, or insuring vessels in Pennsylvania that are to be employed directly or indirectly in the African slave trade. It is expected this law will meet with no opposition.'[150] The Society drafted a petition to be presented to the state legislature to pass an act that extended the 1780 gradual emancipation law in Pennsylvania. The petition was signed by 2,000 people and submitted to the legislature, which passed the law in line with the specifications outlined above. Benjamin Rush, who was closely involved with the petition, hailed the success of this move to end the slave trade in relation to Pennsylvania.[151]

In the South, there was not so much of an appeal to conscience in relation to the slave trade clause in the Constitution. Of course, any such attitudes in South Carolina and Georgia were unlikely to produce printed justifications; but in the Upper South there were occasional attacks on the immorality of the slave trade using volatile language and appeals to the conscience of those involved. 'Republicus' in the *Kentucke Gazette* pointed to the innocence of Africans and the guilt of those who purchased slaves.[152] James Iredell thought, however, that the evil of the slave trade had to be endured for the time being because not all states were willing to prohibit the importation of African captives. He added that 'if any, in violation of their clear conviction of the injustice of this trade, persist in pursuing it, this is a matter between God and their own consciences.'[153] Iredell also made the point that Article 1, Section 9 did not restrain individual states from doing what they pleased in respect of the slave trade over the next twenty years.[154]

In New England and the Middle states, but infrequently in the South, people complained that the South was authorised to continue slave trading for another twenty-one years without an opportunity to amend Article 1, Section 9.[155] Some perceived an uneasy contrast between

---

[150] Benjamin Rush to Jeremy Belknap, 8 Jan. 1788, in Butterfield, ed., *Letters of Benjamin Rush*, I, 448.
[151] Rush to Belknap, 6 May 1788, ibid., I, 460.
[152] 'Republicus' in the *Kentucke Gazette*, 1 Mar. 1788, in Kaminski, ed., *A Necessary Evil?*, 179–80.
[153] Marcus V (James Iredell) in *Norfolk and Portsmouth Journal*, 19 Mar. 1788, ibid., 182.
[154] Elliot, ed., *The Debates in the Several State Conventions*, IV, 119.
[155] Massachusetts Ratification Convention Debates, 25 and 26 Jan. 1788; 'A Friend to the Rights of the People', Antifederalist 1, Exeter *Freeman's Oracle*, 8 Feb. 1788, in Kaminski, ed., *A Necessary Evil?*, 88–9, 98.

northern states refusing to engage in the slave trade but acquiescing in the Constitution's statement that the traffic should not experience interference until 1808. Thus, in the New Hampshire ratifying convention, it was stated that 'there is a great distinction in not taking part in the most barbarous violation of the sacred laws of God and humanity, and our becoming guarantees for its exercise for a term of years'.[156] A writer in Philadelphia's *Independent Gazetteer* was worried that the slave trade ('a disgrace to the annals of America') could not be amended under the Constitution for twenty-one years and there was no guarantee that it would not be dealt with thereafter. This point was also made by Luther Martin of Maryland, delegate of that state at the Constitutional Convention, later a founding member of the Maryland Society for the Abolition of Slavery, and frequent lambaster of the Constitution and a strong national government.[157]

Another report in Philadelphia's *Independent Gazetteer* interpreted the slave trade clause as giving southern states the right to import enslaved Africans for another twenty-one years 'against the declared sense of the other states to put an end to an odious traffic in the human species'.[158] An antifederalist comment in the *New York Journal* went further by suggesting that Article 1, Section 9 of the Constitution was 'purposely so contrived for reviving that wicked and inhuman trade to Africa', adding that this would permanently secure the slave trade.[159] Antifederalists in Pennsylvania argued that the northern states had no right to interfere with slave importations to the southern states, claiming that it was 'a matter of domestic notice & that they should be allowed to import them forever'.[160]

---

[156] Joshua Atherton's speech in the New Hampshire Ratifying Convention, c.13 Feb. 1788, ibid., 99–100.

[157] Timothy Meanwell in the Philadelphia *Independent Gazetteer*, Oct. 1787, ibid., 120; 'Genuine Information VIII,' Luther Martin, in the Baltimore *Maryland Gazette*, 22 Jan. 1788, ibid., 175; Paul S. Clarkson and R. Samuel Jett, *Luther Martin of Maryland* (Baltimore, 1970), 139; Jack N. Rakove, *Original Meanings: Politics and Ideas in the Making of the Constitution* (New York, 1996), 137. For the further argument that Article 1, Section 9 allowed the states to do as they pleased over the slave trade, see the *New York Daily Advertiser*, 18 Jan. 1787.

[158] Centinel III (Samuel Bryan) in Philadelphia *Independent Gazetteer*, 8 Nov. 1787, in Kaminski, ed., *A Necessary Evil?*, 126.

[159] 'A Countryman from Dutchess County I (Hugh Hughes)' and 'A Countryman from Dutchess County II (Hugh Hughes),' *New York Journal*, 21 and 23 Nov. 1787, ibid., 131–2.

[160] David Ramsay to Benjamin Rush, 21 Apr. 1788, in Kaminski et al., eds., *Ratification of the Constitution by the States: South Carolina*, 261.

Another line of attack laid emphasis on Congress's impotence to deal with the slave trade on a national basis over the next generation. Thus, Samuel Hopkins, pastor of the First Congregational Church in Newport, Rhode Island, was upset because the issue of the slave trade appeared to be taken away from the hands of Congress: any asylum for slaves was prevented until 1808 'unless every individual state should suppress this trade'. Hopkins ended up reluctantly endorsing the Constitution even though he thought the revolutionaries had lost sight of their moral concerns over slavery.[161] An added suspicion, in some quarters, was that if the Constitution was adopted, the southern states' right to import slaves might prevail forever and could be entered into by all states in the Union.[162]

Other critiques of the slave trade clause insisted that it was immoral, inconsistent with the actions of the Continental Congress, and at odds with cherished republican principles of liberty and justice. Three antifederalists writing together noted that the First Continental Congress had voted on 5 September 1774, to stop the buying of slaves after 1 December 1774. They compared this decision taken before American independence with that of the slave trade clause in the Constitution and asked: 'Can we suppose that what was morally evil in the year 1774, has become in the year 1788, morally good? Or shall we change evil into good and good into evil, as often we find it will serve a turn?'[163] To these writers, the constitutional handling of these issues was a retrograde step and one that demonstrated moral confusion. A more commonly cited argument was the general inconsistency of authorizing continuation of the slave trade while espousing republican ideas and

---

[161] Samuel Hopkins to Moses Brown, 22 Oct. 1787, in Kaminski, ed., *A Necessary Evil?*, 73. Hopkins's abolitionist career has been analysed in several studies: Elizabeth Donnan, 'Agitation against the Slave Trade in Rhode Island, 1784–1790' in *Persecution and Liberty: Essays in Honor of George Lincoln Burr* (New York, 1931), 473–82; David S. Lovejoy, 'Samuel Hopkins: Religion, Slavery and Revolution', *New England Quarterly*, 40/2 (1967), 227–43; Stanley K. Schultz, 'The Making of a Reformer: The Reverend Samuel Hopkins as an Eighteenth-Century Abolitionist', *Proceedings of the American Philosophical Society*, 115/5 (1971), 350–65; Joseph A. Conforti, *Samuel Hopkins and the New Divinity Movement: Calvinism, the Congregational Ministry, and Reform in New England between the Great Awakenings* (Grand Rapids, MI, 1981), 125–41; and James D. Essig, *The Bonds of Wickedness: American Evangelicals against Slavery, 1770–1808* (Philadelphia, 1982), 88-94.

[162] Algernon Sidney in Philadelphia *Independent Gazetteer*, 21 Nov. 1787, in Kaminski, ed., *A Necessary Evil?*, 131.

[163] Consider Arms, Malachi Maynard and Samuel Field in Northampton *Hampshire Gazette*, 9 and 16 Apr. 1788, ibid., 107.

notions of liberty: one commentator wondered how such a practice could be reconciled with the gracious sentiments expressed in John Dickinson's *Letters from a Farmer in Pennsylvania* (1767).[164] As an antifederalist put it succinctly in February 1788, 'Can we who have fought so hard for Liberty give our consent to have it taken away from others?'[165] (A Southern reply to this sentiment, of course, would have emphasized that the South also fought for its liberty during the War of Independence and that its interests, including slaves as property, should be upheld.) Some New Englanders feared that the keystone of the Massachusetts Constitution of 1780 – that all men are born free and equal – might prove unworkable now that the federal Constitution did not explicitly attack the slave trade.[166]

In the South, two further arguments against the slave trade were put forward by George Mason, a Virginia delegate to the Constitutional Convention, and the elderly Charlestonian lawyer Rawlins Lowndes, the chief antifederalist opponent to ratification in South Carolina. In the Virginia ratifying convention debates, Mason, who had refused to sign the Constitution, stated that the trade was 'nefarious' and 'disgraceful'; at the same time he supported slavery in the Old Dominion and wished that the Constitution had done something to protect that institution. Mason's denunciation of slave importations, despite its strong adjectives, was not really based on moral outrage but on a wily attempt to protect the peculiar position of Virginia, with a surplus of slaves and a rapidly growing black population. Thus, Mason argued that curtailment of the slave trade would be an important step towards strengthening the institution of slavery. There was deep-seated hostility to the slave trade in Virginia at this time. John Tyler and other members of the state's convention attacked the wickedness of the traffic. But Mason's views – condemning the slave trade but condoning slavery – were criticised as inconsistent even by fellow Virginians.[167]

---

[164] For example, Samuel Hopkins to Levi Hart, 29 Jan. 1788; 'A Countryman from Dutchess County, II (Hugh Hughes)', *New York Journal*, 23 Nov. 1787; and Luther Martin, 'Genuine Information, VIII' in the Baltimore *Maryland Gazette*, 18 Jan. 1788, in Kaminski, ed., *A Necessary Evil?*, 95, 102, 132, 174.

[165] 'A Friend to the Rights of the People: Antifederalist 1,' Exeter *Freeman's Oracle*, 8 Feb. 1788, ibid., 98.

[166] 'Adelos' and Consider Arms, Malachi Maynard and Samuel Field in Northampton *Hampshire Gazette*, 6 Feb., 9 and 16 Apr. 1788, ibid., 97, 106.

[167] Virginia Ratifying Convention Debates, 11 and 17 June 1788, ibid., 185–8; Donald L. Robinson, *Slavery in the Structure of American Politics, 1765–1820* (New York, 1971), 295; Duncan J. MacLeod, *Slavery, Race and the American Revolution* (Cambridge, 1974), 38–9.

The slave trade clause played a major part in the ratification process in South Carolina.[168] By the spring of 1788, some South Carolinians, such as Rawlins Lowndes, were arguing that the northern states had no right to interfere with the Palmetto state's importation of Africans, that the matter was one of state decisions and control, and that South Carolina should be allowed to import them forever.[169] Lowndes argued that the northern states were jealous of South Carolina's slave trade, and that Article 1, Section 9 prohibited the slave trade into the United States 'by an ungenerous limitation of twenty years ... under the specious pretext of humanity'.[170] He further criticised the slave trade clause in the Constitution because it was a compromise with the northern states that avoided any stipulation that they should pay duties on their shipping. The South, by contrast, would be heavily taxed and future control of the slave trade had been relinquished.[171] Lowndes approved of South Carolina's state law prohibiting slave imports for three years but found no arguments presented against the view that the state's politicians might change their minds and decide to open Charleston for further importations.[172] However, Lowndes's views proved as idiosyncratic as Mason's: both

---

[168] Howard A. Ohline, 'Politics and Slavery: The Issue of Slavery in National Politics, 1787–1815' (University of Missouri, Columbia, PhD dissertation, 1969), 87.

[169] David Ramsay to Benjamin Rush, 21 Apr. 1788, in Robert L. Brunhouse, ed., 'David Ramsay, 1749–1815: Selections from His Writings', *Transactions of the American Philosophical Society*, new series, 55/4 (Philadelphia, 1965), 120. The impact of slavery on the ratification process in South Carolina is discussed in Robert M. Weir, 'South Carolina: Slavery and the Structure of the Union' in Gillespie and Lienesch, eds., *Ratifying the Constitution*, 20–34.

[170] South Carolina House of Representatives debates, 16 Jan. 1788, in Kaminski et al., eds., *Ratification of the Constitution by the States: South Carolina*, 108.

[171] South Carolina House of Representatives: Debate over the Calling of a State Ratifying Convention, in Kaminski, ed., *A Necessary Evil?*, 167–78; Carl J. Vipperman, *The Rise of Rawlins Lowndes, 1721–1800* (Columbia, SC, 1978), 247. In a speech in the South Carolina House of Representatives on 16 Jan. 1788, Lowndes eccentrically argued that the slave trade was justifiable on the grounds of religion, humanity and justice because it allowed Americans to transfer 'a set of human beings from a bad country to a better': see *Massachusetts Centinel*, 23 Feb. 1788, in John P. Kaminski, Gaspare J. Saladino, Richard Leffler, Charles H. Schoenleber and Margaret A. Hogan, eds., *Ratification of the Constitution by the States: Massachusetts. Volume 3* (Madison, WI, 2000), 1357. Lowndes's speech was reprinted in the *Connecticut Journal*, 12 Mar. 1788; the *Worcester Magazine*, 13 Mar. 1788; the *Pennsylvania Packet*, 17 Mar. 1788; the *Pennsylvania Gazette*, 19 Mar. 1788; and the New Jersey *Brunswick Gazette*, 25 Mar. 1788.

[172] Speeches of Rawlins Lowndes in the South Carolina Legislature, 1788' in Herbert J. Storing, ed., *The Complete Anti-federalist. Volume 5: Maryland and Virginia and the South* (Chicago, 1981), 150.

were overturned in the debates held in their respective states.[173] Lowndes found his position so isolated that he was not asked to be a delegate at the South Carolina ratifying convention in May 1788.[174]

In the debates held in South Carolina's House of Representatives on 17 January 1788, Charles Cotesworth Pinckney spoke at length about the importance of the slave trade to South Carolina. His views are worth quoting at length:

> On this point your delegates had to contend with the religious and political prejudices of the Eastern and middle states, and with the interested and inconsistent opinion of Virginia, who was warmly opposed to our importing more slaves. I am of the same opinion now as I was two years ago ... that while there remained one acre of swamp land uncleared in South Carolina I would raise my voice against restricting the importation of negroes ... the flat swampy situation of our country oblige us to cultivate our lands with negroes, and that without them S. Carolina would soon be a desart waste.[175]

Pinckney continued with an explanation of the objections that had been offered to his point of view: 'It was alledged by some of the members who opposed an unlimited importation, that slaves increased the weakness of any state who admitted them' and 'that they were a dangerous species of property that an invading enemy could easily turn against ourselves & the neighbouring states.' Pinckney then summarised the compromise reached at the Constitutional Convention to take account of the opposing views of South Carolina (insisting on state control of slave importation) and the middle states and Virginia (who were in favour of an immediate and total prohibition). Pinckney concluded that the matter was settled 'after a great deal of difficulty'.[176] Rawlins Lowndes also defended slave importation to South Carolina as a necessity to clear the land and turn forests and swamps into fields for productive use.[177]

---

[173] 'Civis', David Ramsay, in Charleston *Columbian Herald*, 4 Feb. 1788; David Ramsay to Benjamin Lincoln, 29 Jan. 1788; Virginia Ratifying Convention Debates, 11–25 June 1788, in Kaminski, ed., *A Necessary Evil?*, 175, 177, 185–96.

[174] Jerome J. Nadelhaft, 'South Carolina: A Conservative Revolution' in Patrick T. Conley and John P. Kaminski, eds., *The Constitution and the States: The Role of the Original Thirteen in the Framing and Adoption of the Federal Constitution* (Madison, WI, 1988), 173.

[175] Charles Cotesworth Pinckney in the South Carolina House of Representatives debates, 17 Jan. 1788, in Kaminski et al., eds., *Ratification of the Constitution by the States: South Carolina*, 123.

[176] Ibid.

[177] S. Max Edelson, *Plantation Enterprise in Colonial South Carolina* (Cambridge, MA, 2006), 260.

Another South Carolina delegate, John Barnwell, offered a different approach to the constitutional clause on the slave trade. He welcomed Article 1, Section 9 because it had not left the matter open and had effectively closed consideration of it for twenty-one years. He was confident that, when that time had expired, Congress would not interfere with the slave trade because the commercial prosperity of many states would depend on exporting America's products. An attempt to prohibit slave imports would have a deleterious effect upon the production of those commodities. This persuaded Barnwell that politicians would not curtail the slave trade because of its essential support for export products. He believed that the slave trade to South Carolina would continue for ever unless banned by state law.[178] These various approaches to slave importation in South Carolina lend support to the view that this issue was the principal ground of objection to ratifying the Constitution.[179]

THE SLAVE TRADE IN THE RATIFICATION DEBATES OVER THE CONSTITUTION: SUPPORTERS

The existence of negative views about Article 1, Section 9 of the Constitution was counterbalanced by a good many positive views in the ratification process. Some commentators judiciously acknowledged that the southernmost states had determined the agenda on this issue. An encouraging view of the slave trade clause needed to take account of this recalcitrance. Thus, James Pemberton thought the delegates to the Constitutional Convention did the best they could in the circumstances. He looked forward to firm central authority being adopted by securing the Constitution. Furthermore, the slave trade clause was not intended to inhibit individual states from enacting laws pertaining to the traffic.[180] James Iredell, a leading proponent of ratification, challenged strong antifederalist views in North Carolina. He noted that it was impossible to end the slave trade at the Constitutional Convention because of the position taken by South Carolina and Georgia; but he differed from Pemberton in

---

[178] John Barnwell in South Carolina House of Representatives debates, 17 Jan. 1788, in Kaminski et al., eds., *Ratification of the Constitution by the States: South Carolina*, 133.
[179] *Pennsylvania Gazette*, 19 Mar. 1788.
[180] James Pemberton to Moses Brown, 16 Nov. 1787, in Kaminski, ed., *A Necessary Evil?*, 129. Cf. A Native of Virginia, *Observations upon the Proposed Plan of Federal Government*, 2 Apr. 1788, ibid., 183–4; Thomas E. Drake, *Quakers and Slavery in America* (New Haven, CT, 1950), 102.

arguing that, if the Constitution were not adopted, it would be within the power of every state to continue the slave trade forever.[181]

Madison devoted considerable attention to the question of the slave trade. He noted the inflexibility of the southernmost states on this issue but argued in the Virginia ratifying convention debates – partly to counteract Mason's views – that the greater evil of the southern states not entering into the Union would have resulted if 'temporary permission of that trade' had not been permitted. Under the Articles of Confederation, he reminded delegates, the slave trade would have continued forever; but Article 1, Section 9 meant that it could be ended in 1808. 'Is the importation of slaves permitted by the new Constitution for twenty years?' he asked, adding, 'By the old, it is permitted forever'.[182] Madison underscored the point that slave importation was prohibited by Virginia's laws 'and we may continue the prohibition'. If South Carolina and Georgia were excluded from the Union, 'the consequences might be dreadful to them and to us'.[183] In *The Federalist* papers, Madison suggested that the slave trade would be strongly discouraged by government up to 1808 and might even be abolished by some states. Arguing that attempts 'to pervert this clause into an objection against the Constitution' were misplaced, he cited the provisions made over the slave trade as an achievement that might terminate a traffic in human beings for ever from the United States.[184]

A few months earlier, similar points had been made in the Massachusetts ratification convention debates. Some contributors to the debates were optimistic about the ability of Congress after twenty years to 'totally annihilate the slave trade', pointing out that there was no provision under the Confederation for it ever being abolished. Moreover, because 'all the states, except two, have passed laws to this effect, it might

---

[181] North Carolina Ratifying Convention Debates, 26 July 1788, in Kaminski, ed., *A Necessary Evil?*, 199; Louise Ivery Trenholme, *The Ratification of the Federal Constitution in North Carolina* (New York, 1932), 119–22, 163.

[182] James Madison to Thomas Jefferson, 24 Oct. 1787; Virginia Ratifying Convention Debates, 17 June 1788; *The Federalist*, 38, 12 Jan. 1788, in Kaminski, ed., *A Necessary Evil?*, 141, 163, 187. Cf. 'Philanthrop' in Northampton *Hampshire Gazette*, 23 Apr. 1788, ibid., 108.

[183] Madison in the Virginia Convention Debates, 17 June 1788, in John P. Kaminski, Gaspare J. Saladino, Richard Leffler, Charles H. Schoenleber and Marybeth Carlson, eds., *Ratification of the Constitution by the States: Virginia. Volume 3* (Madison, WI, 1993), 1339.

[184] 'Publius (James Madison)' in *The Federalist*, 42, 22 Jan. 1788, in Kaminski, ed., *A Necessary Evil?*, 141–2.

reasonably be expected, that it would then be done – in the interim, all the states were at liberty to prohibit it'.[185] Thomas Daws, an architect, builder and politician, asked what more could the Constitution have done, given that Southerners, like New Englanders, had their prejudices. The merchant and politician Tristram Dalton suggested that the Constitution gave Congress a right in time to abolish the slave trade. The reverend Isaac Backus, a New England Baptist leader, thought a check to slave trading had been gained that did not exist under the Articles of Confederation, and hoped in time that the trade would stop. Supporters of the slave trade clause 'rejoiced that a door was now to be opened, for the annihilation of this odious, abhorrent practice, in a certain time'. Backus, who favoured ratification, had not spoken out about slavery or the slave trade before 1788; but his speech in the Massachusetts ratifying convention agreed with the view that the Constitution would eventually give the national government the power to end the slave trade.[186] A writer in the strongly federal newspaper the *Massachusetts Centinel* endorsed this view: 'If, for no other consideration than that it opens a door for the abolition of the Slave Trade, in America, in a given number of years – the new proposed Constitution for the United States is incomparably preferable to the old-one, in which no provision is made either for the suppression or circumscription of this wicked trade.'[187]

Though these comments supporting the slave trade clause reflect optimistic hopes, some anti-slave trade advocates in the middle states wrote with more certitude and conviction about what should happen to the slave trade at federal level. Benjamin Rush, a lifelong opponent of slavery but a supporter of ratification, thought the slave trade clause 'was a great point obtained from the Southern States' that gave Congress the right to restrain it altogether in twenty years' time.[188] In the Pennsylvania ratifying convention debates, Anthony Wayne echoed Madison's point that the Articles of Confederation provided no limit on the slave trade. His fellow delegate, James Wilson, another pro-Constitution opponent of

---

[185] Jeremy Belknap, Notes of Convention Debates, 25 Jan. 1788, in Kaminski et al., eds., *Ratification of the Constitution by the States. Volume 3*, 1354.
[186] Massachusetts Ratification Convention Debates, 25 and 26 Jan., 4 Feb. 1788, in Kaminski, ed., *A Necessary Evil?*, 88–9, 91; William G. McLoughlin, *Isaac Backus and the American Pietistic Tradition* (Boston, 1967), 199.
[187] *Massachusetts Centinel*, 14 June 1788, in Kaminski, ed., *A Necessary Evil?*, 112.
[188] Benjamin Rush to John Coakley Lettsom, 28 Sept. 1787; to Elizabeth Ferguson, 25 Dec. 1787; to Jeremy Belknap, 28 Feb. 1788, ibid., 117, 140, 147.

slavery and the slave trade, added that the restraint proposed under the Constitution was twenty-one years with the import duty of $10 for each person acting as a partial prohibition. After 1808, Wilson suggested, Congress 'will have the power to prohibit such importation, notwithstanding the disposition of any state to the contrary'.[189] Robert Waln, a wealthy Philadelphia merchant, was also convinced that Congress would have the power at the end of twenty-one years to stop 'that iniquitous traffic.'[190] A similar view was expressed in the *Pennsylvania Gazette* on 26 September 1787. Here, it was noted, the Constitution 'provides an effectual check to the African trade, in the course of one and twenty years. How honourable to America – to have been the first Christian power that has borne a testimony against a practice, that is alike disgraceful to religion, as repugnant to the true interests and happiness of Society'.[191]

The wording of the slave trade clause in the Constitution reassured some interested parties, such as those cited above, that 1808 would mark the end of the slave trade to the United States. However, the words used were open to the opposite interpretation because they only allowed for Congress not to interfere legislatively with the slave trade for twenty-one years; they did not state that, at that juncture, slave imports to the United States would definitely be curtailed once and for all. Some commentators thus argued that the Constitution supported the continuation of the slave trade, and that there was no firm commitment to abolish it in 1808.[192]

Virginia had ended slave imports in 1778, but commentators from the Old Dominion were keen to seek a compromise with the Lower South over slave importations while reiterating Virginia's stance on the slave trade. Because South Carolina and Georgia were inflexible in their opposition to tampering with the slave trade, an anonymous Quaker from Virginia thought that Article 1, Section 9 of the Constitution was 'the

---

[189] Pennsylvania Ratifying Convention Debates, 3 Dec. 1787, ibid., 136; Geoffrey Seed, *James Wilson* (Millwood, NY, 1978), 83–4. Cf. Plain Truth to Timothy Meanwell, Philadelphia *Independent Gazetteer*, 30 Oct. 1787, in Kaminski, ed., *A Necessary Evil?*, 121.

[190] Robert Waln to Richard Waln, 3 Oct. 1787, in Kaminski, ed., *A Necessary Evil?*, 118. For an argument that Article 1, Section 9 'expressly confirmed' Congress' power to prohibit the slave trade eventually, see Fehrenbacher, *The Slaveholding Republic*, 42–3.

[191] *Pennsylvania Gazette*, 26 Sept. 1787, in Kaminski, ed., *A Necessary Evil?*, 117.

[192] See Granville Sharp to John Jay, 1 May 1788, in Henry P. Johnson, ed., *The Correspondence and Public Papers of John Jay*, 4 vols. (New York, 1891), III, 330; Samuel Hopkins, *A Discourse upon the Slave Trade and the Slavery of the Africans* (Providence, RI, 1793); Elliot, ed., *Debates*, II, 107, 120, 203–4; Farrand, ed., *Records*, II, 355–76, 415.

best compromise that could be made'.[193] And, of course, the clause did not affect the law of Virginia, which prohibited slave importation.[194] It was pointed out in this regard that the power of the legislature of each state, even after the adoption of the Constitution, was sufficient to maintain prohibition if it already existed and that 'the exercise of this power of the state governments can *in no wise* be controuled or restrained by the federal legislature'.[195]

During the months when Americans debated the constitutional status of slavery and the slave trade, individual states passed laws to solidify their commitment to slave trade abolition. It seems clear that the extensive attacks on the slave trade during the Constitutional Convention and during the course of the ratification debates emboldened legislators in making these decisions. For two years, from the summer of 1787, Quaker Yearly Meetings campaigned for state laws to forbid the fitting out of vessels for the slave trade. Thus, the New England Yearly Meeting sent memorials to Massachusetts and Rhode Island to this effect.[196] On 22 February 1788, New York passed a law which made it an offence to sell any slave imported into the state since 1 June 1785 on pain of a $100 fine. Just over a month later, on 25 March, Massachusetts passed an act to prevent the 'iniquitous and inhuman practice' of the slave trade and thereby to protect the lives of 'many innocent persons' sacrificed 'to the lust of gain'. The law introduced fines of £50 for every person taken on board ship as a slave and £200 for every vessel fitted out for the trade. In such circumstances any insurance on a ship and its cargo would become null and void. This measure aroused angry feelings in Massachusetts among those who feared it would influence South Carolina not to ratify the Constitution; but that proved not to be the case. On 29 March, Pennsylvania enacted a law prohibiting its citizens from involvement in the slave trade. Any shipowner found guilty of failing to meet this requirement would have to forfeit the vessel and all

---

[193] *Virginia Independent Chronicle*, 12 Mar. 1788, in Kaminski et al., eds., *Ratification of the Constitution by the States: Virginia. Volume 1*, 482.
[194] 'A Native of Virginia. Observations upon the Proposed Plan of Federal Government', 2 Apr. 1788, in John P. Kaminski, Gaspare J. Saladino, Richard Leffler, Charles H. Schoenleber and Marybeth Carlson, eds., *Ratification of the Constitution by the States: Virginia. Volume 2* (Madison, WI, 1990), 675.
[195] 'An American', *Pennsylvania Gazette*, 21 May 1788, ibid., 836.
[196] Sydney V. James, *A People among Peoples: Quaker Benevolence in Eighteenth-Century America* (Cambridge, MA, 1963), 297.

its appurtenances and pay a fine of £1,000.[197] Tench Coxe, Secretary of the Pennsylvania Society for the Abolition of Slavery, greeted this measure by noting that 'the commerce in African slaves has breathed its last in Pennsylvania'.[198] Coxe, on behalf of the society, corresponded with abolitionists and foreign sympathisers to spread the anti-slave trade message.[199]

Further measures concerning the slave trade were soon raised at state level. By early 1788, Rhode Island had banned by law the buying and selling of slaves in foreign ports and, to render conviction easy, only the testimony of a seaman on a vessel was necessary to secure the conviction.[200] James Pemberton noted that this redounded to the credit of the Rhode Island government, but he was doubtful whether the law was 'sufficiently explicit to prevent evasion'.[201] His correspondent, Moses Brown, though believing that most Americans abhorred the slave trade, nevertheless feared that those who had a love of gain would still participate in the slave trade without fear of prosecution.[202] Pemberton himself managed to get a Massachusetts law dealing with the slave trade republished in a newspaper with the widest circulation in Massachusetts as well as presenting anti-slave trade petitions to various state governments.[203] But he realised that further action was required because 'the stain of dutiful reproach ... has long lain on the Christian name by the detestable traffic in human flesh and the horrors attending it'. He believed that 'thro the Divine Blessing deliverance will be obtained for the afflicted Africans'.[204]

---

[197] Du Bois, *The Suppression of the African Slave-Trade*, 230–4; *Dunlap and Claypoole's American Daily Advertiser* (Philadelphia), 27 Mar. 1788; Charlene Bangs Bickford, Kenneth R. Bowling, William Charles diGiacomantonio and Helen E. Veit, eds., *Documentary History of the First Federal Congress of the United States of America. Volume 16. Correspondence, First Session, June–August 1789* (Baltimore, MD, 2004), 739.

[198] Tench Coxe to Henry Bromfield, 6 May 1788, in Kaminski et al., eds., *Commentaries on the Constitution, Public and Private. Volume 5*, 390–1.

[199] Jacob E. Cooke, *Tench Coxe and the Early American Republic* (Chapel Hill, NC, 1978), 93.

[200] LCP, Jeremy Belknap to Anthony Benezet, 12 Feb. 1788, Benezet correspondence.

[201] HSP, James Pemberton to Moses Brown, 16 Nov. 1787, Pemberton Papers, box 49, folder 6.

[202] HSP, Moses Brown to James Pemberton, 23 Aug. 1788, ibid., box 50, folder 156.

[203] New York HS, Gilder Lehrman Collection, GLC#04980, James Pemberton to Moses Brown, 17 May 1788.

[204] NYPL, James Pemberton to Granville Sharp, 8 May 1788, Digital Collections.

On 9 September 1788, New England Quakers, meeting in Providence, Rhode Island, approved a petition to the Connecticut legislature calling for an end to the slave trade. Franklin wrote to the governor of Connecticut to explain the slave trading voyages 'were repugnant to the political principles & forms of government lately adopted by the Citizens of the United States'. In October 1788, the General Court of Connecticut brought in fines of £50 for each slave boarded on one of its vessels and £500 for each vessel used in the transportation of slaves. On 3 February 1789, a supplementary act for Delaware stipulated that anyone found to be involved in a vessel carrying slaves would be subject to a fine of £500.[205] These developments support James Pemberton's view that the Constitution did 'not restrain the Assemblys of the Separate States from passing any prohibitory laws which they may judge expedient to abolish that infamous traffic'.[206] This of course was the situation that obtained before the Constitutional Convention and the ratification process. But though Article 1, Section 9 had forbidden any constitutional decision on slave imports to the United States for twenty-one years, politicians in the Lower South were still on their guard over this matter: as William Loughton Smith of South Carolina put it, 'those who were better acquainted with human nature' realised 'that some indirect attempt to interpose would be made' within that time period.[207]

CONCLUSION

The Constitutional Convention held in Philadelphia over the summer of 1787 was an essential forum for political debates over the formation of a stronger union and federal government for the United States and, as part of its remit, slavery and the slave trade were debated in detail. The subject of the slave trade was acrimonious and divisive. It had never before been discussed at such length by virtually all of the states and many divergent views were expressed about the wording of a constitutional clause

---

[205] Du Bois, *The Suppression of the African Slave-Trade*, 230–4; Jeremy Belknap to Ebenezer Hazard, 18 Apr. 1788, in Kaminski et al., eds., *Ratification of the Constitution by the States: South Carolina*, 531; *New Haven Gazette*, 23 Oct. 1788; New York HS, Gilder Lehrman Collection, GLC#07485.01, Franklin to Samuel Huntington, 12 Jan 1788.
[206] HSP, James Pemberton to John Pemberton, 3 May 1788, Pemberton Papers, box 50, folder 26.
[207] William Loughton Smith to Edward Rutledge, 28 Feb. 1790, in Rogers, Jr, ed., 'The Letters of William Loughton Smith to Edward Rutledge', 107.

pertaining to the subject. Article 1, Section 9 of the Constitution was the agreed outcome devised by the delegates. It carefully avoided the use of the words 'slave' or 'slave trade', preferring the more anodyne 'migration' and 'such persons' to avoid undue controversy. It signalled that the federal government through Congress would have the right to interpose in regulating the slave trade for the whole of the United States in the future but this could not occur for twenty-one years until 1808. This was guaranteed by Article 5. A compromise had been hammered out between the northern and southern states, with a bargain made that there would be no federal inference in the right of an individual state to open or close its slave trade before 1808 while a Navigation Act would protect the commerce of the northern states.

James Madison, who had played a pivotal role in drafting the Constitution, was dismayed at this outcome for he would have preferred that constitutional means could have been found to end slave importations to the United States once and for all in 1788. But he realised that compromise was necessary. Unlike some historians who regard the slave trade clause in the Constitution as a lost opportunity to act against the Guinea traffic immediately, Madison realised that South Carolina and Georgia delegates would never agree to this on behalf of their constituents, that they expected and intended to deal with the slave trade as a matter of personal judgement and according to the political wishes of individual states, that they were not bluffing when they said they would not agree to the constitution if their wishes were not granted, and that the need to forge a federal union among the states was a higher imperative than moves against the slave trade at this moment in time.

Constitutional arrangements over the slave trade left plenty of areas of debate on the subject during the ratification conventions of 1787–8. Some commentators were disappointed at the compromise struck there and the effective tying of hands of the federal government on this issue for twenty-one years. Among them were people who feared that the federal government had failed to grasp the nettle on this subject, that delays would be harmful to the anti-slave trade clause, and that there was no guarantee that there would be action against the slave trade at the earliest opportunity, in 1808, or afterwards. Others exercised their patience and were willing to wait until 1808, comforting themselves that action would then be taken promptly. Many northern states expressed their opposition to the slave trade on moral grounds in their ratifying conventions while South Carolina and Georgia avoided public debate about the humanitarian desire to get rid of slave importations. In 1788, before the

Constitutional Convention met, South Carolina at state level banned slave importation for five years but reopened the domestic slave trade, thereby reversing a ban imposed in the previous year.[208] The sheer amount of commentary on the subject in speeches, newspapers and debates indicated that prohibition of the slave trade was a lively topic of political debate that would continue for some years to come.

---

[208] Lacy K. Ford, *Deliver Us from Evil: The Slavery Question in the Old South* (New York, 2009), 83–4.

4

Opposition to the Slave Trade in the Early National Period, 1789–1802

The debates over the slave trade clause in the US Constitution and in the ratification debates in individual states had indicated that conflicting positions were held about opposition to the transatlantic slave trade, but a temporary halt to the possibility of further action on this matter resulted from congressional restraints against slave trade abolition for twenty-one years. However, the slave trade continued to be a divisive issue in American public life. At the time of the ratification debates, the Quakers were increasing their opposition to the Guinea traffic through debates and petitions associated with their major bodies such as the Pennsylvania Abolition Society and a greater transatlantic cooperation among the Society of Friends was emerging on the matter. Activists in the fight against the slave trade increased the sophistication and interaction of their transatlantic networks. Organised antislavery societies proliferated in the late 1780s in the United States in cities such as Baltimore, Maryland; Richmond, Virginia; Providence, Rhode Island; and New Haven, Connecticut.[1] In April 1790, the Philadelphia Quaker abolitionist James Pemberton argued that 'the principles of Justice and Sound Policy' were gaining ground in relation to slavery, and that the states of Delaware, New Jersey, Connecticut and Rhode Island had lately taken action to prohibit the African slave trade.[2]

---

[1] J. R. Oldfield, *Transatlantic Abolitionism in the Age of Revolution: An International History of Anti-slavery, c.1787–1820* (Cambridge, 2013), 21–2.

[2] HSP, James Pemberton to the Society for the Relief of Free Negroes & Others Unlawfully Held in Bondage Lately Established in Washington County in This State, 20 Apr. 1789, Pennsylvania Abolition Society letterbook (1789–94), Pennsylvania Abolition Society Papers.

In addition, the British parliament, for the first time, began to consider extensive testimony submitted on the British slave trade in 1788, which added to the international scrutiny of shipping enslaved Africans across the Atlantic.[3] Slaveholders within the United States were aware of the growing international scrutiny bestowed upon slavery and the slave trade, and they made efforts in some states to absorb parts of the abolitionist cause. In 1789, the Maryland Society for the Abolition of Slavery argued, for example, that action against slaveholding was now a timely direction to follow, while both the Virginia and Maryland legislatures narrowly failed to support moves to abolish slavery.[4]

However, abolitionist moves against slavery took many years to come to fruition even where states enacted gradual emancipation laws, and the matter of the foreign slave trade remained controversial and incapable of resolution on a national scale before 1808. The slave trade was widely considered to be a matter for individual states to decide what action they wished to take. South Carolina and Georgia, which had extensive plantations, remained adamantly opposed to interference with their rights to conduct their own slave trade because they wanted to determine, as part of their states' rights, whether they needed to increase or stem the flow of enslaved Africans into their jurisdictions. In addition, American merchants were increasing their commitment to slave trading in the new nation and they, too, wanted to pursue their commercial interests in the trade without federal interference.[5]

This chapter analyses anti-slave trade activity in the United States during the period from the convening of the First Federal Congress in 1789, up to the point when South Carolina was about to reopen its slave trade in 1803, after a hiatus of sixteen years. This was a time when consideration of the slave trade continued at state level, notably in places where an outright ban on slave importations had yet to be determined, but for the first time, discussions of transatlantic slaving relating to the United States were debated in a national legislative forum, the federal Congress, and recorded verbatim in the pages of the *Annals of Congress*. After a preliminary discussion of anti-slave trade views expressed in the United States between 1788 and 1792, the chapter focuses on the divisive and contentious debates on the slave trade in the first Federal Congress of

---

[3] Roger Anstey, *The Atlantic Slave Trade and British Abolition, 1760–1810* (London, 1975), 266.
[4] Elija H. Gould, *Among the Powers of the Earth: The American Revolution and the Making of a New World Empire* (Cambridge, MA, 2012), 159–60.
[5] David Eltis, 'The U.S. Transatlantic Slave Trade, 1644–1867: An Assessment', *Civil War History*, 54/4 (2008), 347–78.

1790, when Quaker petitions on the subject were presented to the House of Representatives, and on subsequent attempts by Congress to implement laws against the participation of US citizens in the foreign slave trade. There is also consideration of the abolition societies formed in the United States to combat slave trading and of the political divisions in South Carolina, always the state with potentially the largest interest in slave imports, at a time when the slave trade to that state remained closed. Overshadowing all of these developments was the restriction on Congress acting against the slave trade because of Article 1, Section 9 of the Constitution.

ANTI-SLAVE TRADE VIEWS IN THE UNITED STATES, 1788–1792

American anti-slave trade activists increased their lobbying activities between 1788 and 1792 to continue their attacks on restricting slave imports to the United States. They brought pressure on state legislatures, distributed books and pamphlets, many of them British, and helped to generate extensive press coverage for their campaign.[6] The Pennsylvania Abolition Society played a leading role in this lobbying activity. In 1789, it suggested that the Constitution was a 'testimonial' against the slave trade and that individual states should be expeditious in abolishing it.[7] Most meetings of the Pennsylvania Abolition Society received and considered epistles, letters, petitions and essays on antislavery. These were circulated to members and other abolitionist sympathisers.[8]

Quaker antislavery committees focused their efforts on attempts to persuade states to single out the iniquity of the slave trade. Thus, in 1788–9, the Pennsylvania Abolition Society and the Philadelphia Yearly Meeting presented petitions to the state legislatures of Pennsylvania and Delaware on this topic. Some gains were made. In Pennsylvania, a law passed to bolster the terms of the 1780 gradual abolition act and the proscription on slave imports was extended to any forms of the slave trade, foreign or domestic. In Delaware, the state legislature banned participation in the carrying trade in slaves.[9] However, with the new

---

[6] Oldfield, *Transatlantic Abolitionism*, 73–4.
[7] David Brion Davis, *The Problem of Slavery in the Age of Revolution, 1770–1823* (Ithaca, NY, 1975), 326.
[8] James Alexander Dun, 'Philadelphia not Philanthropolis: The Limits of Pennsylvanian Antislavery in the Era of the Haitian Revolution', *PMHB*, 135/1 (2011), 80.
[9] Nicholas P. Wood, 'Considerations of Humanity and Expediency: The Slave Trades and African Colonization in the Early National Antislavery Movement' (University of Virginia PhD dissertation, 2013), 76–7.

federal government just getting under way in 1789, the Pennsylvania Abolition Society thought it should allow it some months to settle down rather than introducing slavery and the slave trade as a matter for public debate and discussion. 'Our Continental Government is now beginning operations', James Pemberton wrote in mid-1789, 'but the necessary arrangement of public affairs has so much engaged their time that we have not yet thought it expedient to lay the subject of slavery before them'.[10]

This view did not prevent the circulation of anti-slave trade views. Newspapers in New England and the Middle Atlantic states particularly advocated slave trade abolition. The print of the Liverpool slave ship *Brooks*, showing Africans packed next to one another on the lower deck of a slaving vessel, was then being widely circulated in Britain as part of an abolitionist assault against the British slave trade. It was reproduced as a broadside in the United States and distributed to antislavery supporters. Matthew Carey also included the print in his magazine, *American Museum*, a widely read publication. Such initiatives were important in keeping alive the matter of slave trade abolition in the United States.[11] In the 1790s, occasional sermons were also given in the northern states against the slave trade.[12]

In private correspondence, those sympathetic to slave trade abolition also voiced their views. The Massachusetts merchant and politician Tristram Dalton, one of the first US senators, referred in correspondence to 'the cursed African trade'.[13] The Virginia Quaker Robert Pleasants, who favoured gradual emancipation of slavery in Virginia, attacked the

---

[10] HSP, James Pemberton to the Committee of the Society Instituted at London for Effecting the Abolition of the Slave Trade, 24 June 1789, Pennsylvania Abolition Society Papers, series 2.1, loose correspondence outgoing (1783–1914).

[11] Oldfield, *Transatlantic Abolitionism*, 73–4; Gary B. Nash, *Warner Mifflin: Unflinching Abolitionist* (Philadelphia, 2017), 162–3.

[12] For example, James Dana, *The African Slave Trade. A Discourse Delivered in the City of New-Haven, September 9, 1790, before the Connecticut Society for the Promotion of Freedom* (New Haven, 1790); Jonathan Edwards, *The Injustice and Impolicy of the Slave Trade, and of the Slavery of the Africans: Illustrated in a Sermon Preached before the Connecticut Society for the Promotion of Freedom, and for the Relief of Persons Unlawfully Holden in Bondage, at Their Annual Meeting in New-Haven, September 15, 1791* (New Haven, 1791); William Patten, *On the Inhumanity of the Slave-Trade, and the Importance of Correcting It. A Sermon Delivered in the Second Congregational Church, Newport, Rhode Island, September 15, 1792* (Providence, RI, 1793); and Samuel Hopkins, *A Discourse upon the Slave-Trade, and the Slavery of the Africans. Delivered in the Baptist Meeting-House before the Providence Society for Abolishing the Slave-Trade &c. At Their Annual Meeting on May 17, 1793* (Providence, RI, 1793).

[13] Tristram Dalton to Caleb Strong, 23 Aug. 1789, in Charlene Bangs Bickford, Kenneth R. Bowling, William Charles diGiacomantonio and Helen E. Veit, eds., *Documentary*

slave trade in a private letter of 1791 in which he hoped that nations would 'abolish that most abominable traffic in human flesh'. He had no doubt that nations would prohibit such a trade, 'which to the disgrace of humanity, as well as Christianity, hath been prosecuted for many years, at the expence, no doubt, of the lives of millions of the unhappy Africans'.[14] There were, however, two main stumbling blocks to achieving this goal. One was the fact that the US still had a strong commitment to the slave trade in the early years of the new nation. Owing to state-level proscriptions, between 1791 and 1800 the relatively small number of 13,085 Africans arrived in the Carolinas and Georgia and 262 reached the northern states.[15] However, US vessels were very active in supplying ships to take thousands of slaves to foreign territories in the 1790s, such as Rio de la Plata, the Danish West Indies, the Dutch Americas, Cuba and the Mascarene Islands in the Indian Ocean. The Transatlantic Slave Trade Database indicates that the number of slave embarkations on US-flagged vessels amounted to 16,000 in the 1780s, 50,344 in the 1790s, and 55,000 for the period from 1800 to 1807.[16] The second problem for anti-slave trade supporters between 1789 and 1802 was the division among US politicians over what could be done to end the slave trade, as the discussion below will show.

SLAVE TRADE DEBATES IN THE FIRST FEDERAL CONGRESS, FEBRUARY 1790

The First Federal Congress, meeting in New York, was the most obvious place that offered the opportunity for further public debates on the slave trade. It met less than two years after the Constitutional Convention and before all thirteen states had undertaken ratification. It was charged with putting into practice all the decisions about federal and state government included in the Constitution.[17] This was an administration dominated by slaveholders. President George Washington, Secretary of State Thomas

History of the First Federal Congress of the United States of America. Volume 16. Correspondence. June–August 1789 (Baltimore, MD, 2004), 1,378.

[14] Haverford College Library, Quaker Collection, letter of 15 Sept. 1791, Robert Pleasants letterbook (1754–97), fol. 196.

[15] David Eltis and David Richardson, 'A New Assessment of the Transatlantic Slave Trade' in David Eltis and David Richardson, eds., *Extending the Frontiers: Essays on the New Transatlantic Slave Trade Database* (New Haven, CT, 2008), 48.

[16] www.slavevoyages.org.

[17] Fergus M. Bordewich, *The First Congress: How James Madison, George Washington, and a Group of Extraordinary Men Invented the Government* (New York, 2016), 1.

Jefferson and Attorney General Edmund Randolph were large slave-owning Virginia planters. Twenty-nine of sixty-five representatives of the lower house (45 per cent) and ten of twenty-six senators (38 per cent) were from the southern states. They included fourteen representatives and eight senators who were planters. These congressmen could therefore bring personal knowledge of slaveholding to bear on issues raised about slavery and the slave trade.[18]

Despite the prevalence of slaveowners in Congress, however, it seems that many representatives were already convinced of the iniquity of the slave trade and looked forward to its prohibition. One would like firmer evidence on this point from the documentary record, but it was claimed by Owen Biddle of Philadelphia in 1790 that there was 'so large a majority in the house favorable' to the abolition of the slave trade.[19] A correspondent of Moses Brown found that 'all orders of men' were averse to the slave trade and seemed pleased with efforts to suppress it, though the correspondent disliked the abolitionist efforts of the Quakers and their allies.[20]

The issue of the slave trade was raised in the First Federal Congress after the ratification debates on 13 May 1789, almost two weeks after Washington became the first president of the United States. Josiah Parker, a planter from Virginia, proposed that a duty of $10 per imported slave be added to a tariff bill.[21] This met with a strong rebuttal from the Georgia planter and politician James Jackson, who insisted that the tax would discriminate against his state and should therefore be opposed. Madison, now a Virginia congressman, defended Parker's proposal on the grounds that it would support a national disapproval of the slave trade.[22] Nevertheless, he asked Parker to withdraw his proposed amendment, which he did after complaints were made that it was improper to insert human beings in a bill to collect duties on goods and merchandise. Representatives from South Carolina and Georgia were opposed to the bill.[23]

---

[18] Adam Rothman, *Slave Country: American Expansion and the Origins of the Deep South* (Cambridge, MA, 2005), 5.
[19] HSP, Owen Biddle to John Parrish, 23 Mar. 1790, box 1, folder 15, Cox-Parrish-Wharton Papers.
[20] RIHS, William Rotch, Jr to Moses Brown, 16 May 1789, Moses Brown correspondence.
[21] Donald L. Robinson, *Slavery in the Structure of American Politics, 1765–1820* (New York, 1971), 299–302.
[22] Sean Wilentz, *No Property in Man: Slavery and Antislavery at the Nation's Founding* (Cambridge, MA, 2018), 154.
[23] [Philadelphia] *Independent Gazetteer*, 9 Nov. 1789; William Smith to Edward Rutledge, 6 June 1789, in Bickford et al., eds., *Documentary History of the First Federal Congress. Volume 16*, 711.

Parker revised his proposal four months later as an independent bill. The House of Representatives postponed consideration of it, no doubt recognising it could inflame opposing interests in Congress. The bill was not taken up again. Duty-free slave imports were therefore maintained for individual states.[24] The hesitations over Parker's bill provided an early foretaste of the difficulties that would be encountered in discussing the slave trade at congressional level. On 19 September 1789, Congress received a bill concerning slave importations prior to 1808, but after a first reading further consideration of the bill was postponed until the next session of Congress.[25] While these matters relating to the slave trade were in progress, several New York assemblymen argued that foreign commerce was exclusively controlled by the federal government but that recently passed state laws prohibiting the slave trade might become void.[26]

The issue of the slave trade was soon raised in petitions. The right to petition local assemblies had been firmly established in colonial America. A petition clause in the First Amendment to the Constitution – in the Bill of Rights, proposed on 25 September 1789 – included the duty of government to consider petitioners' grievances. The early federal Congresses aimed to comment favourably or unfavourably on every petition.[27] Lower South representatives usually opposed abolitionist petitions, expressing underlying worries that such memorials would influence wider government intervention against southern slavery.[28]

Two such petitions on the slave trade reached the second session of the First Congress – convened in New York City – on 11 February 1790. The location for the congressional meetings was Federal Hall on Wall Street.[29] One petition came from the Quaker Yearly Meeting of Pennsylvania, New Jersey, Delaware, western Maryland and Virginia. This had been

---

[24] Don E. Fehrenbacher and Ward M. McAfee, *The Slaveholding Republic: An Account of the United States Government's Relations to Slavery* (New York, 2001), 137–8; Robin L. Einhorn, *American Taxation, American Slavery* (Chicago, 2006), 152–3; Wood, 'Considerations of Humanity and Expediency', 80.

[25] Linda Grant De Pauw, Charlene Bangs Bickford and LaVonne Siegel Hauptman, eds., *Documentary History of the First Federal Congress of the United States of America. Volume 3. House of Representatives Journal* (Baltimore, MD, 1977), 215.

[26] Howard A. Ohline, 'Slavery, Economics, and Congressional Politics, 1790', *JSH*, 46/3 (1980), 339.

[27] Stephen A. Higginson, 'A Short History of the Right to Petition Government for the Redress of Grievances', *The Yale Law Journal*, 96/1 (1986), 142–3.

[28] Richard S. Newman, *The Transformation of American Abolitionism: Fighting Slavery in the Early Republic* (Chapel Hill, NC, 2002), 57.

[29] Gary B. Nash and Michael R. McDowell, eds., *Writings of Warner Mifflin: Forgotten Quaker Abolitionist of the Revolutionary Era* (Newark, DE, 2021), 265.

adopted on 3 October 1789 by the Philadelphia Yearly Meeting of Friends, which had nearly a thousand members. Twenty-three members were charged with presenting the memorial to Congress.[30] A committee including James and John Pemberton, Nicholas Waln, Samuel Emlen and Henry Drinker took the petition to New York.[31] The Quaker abolitionist Warner Mifflin was prominent among the petition's supporters.[32]

The memorial recalled the Quaker petition presented to the Confederation Congress in 1783, which the delegates 'generally acknowledged, yet, not being vested with the powers of legislation, they declined promoting any public remedy against the gross national iniquity of trafficking in the persons of fellow-men'.[33] The petition, signed by nine Quakers, called for 'serious Christian attention' to some of the 'enormities' practised 'under the federal countenance given to this abominable commerce'; it hoped there would be a 'sincere and impartial inquiry' into 'the licentious wickedness of the African trade for slaves'; and that this would be followed by an immediate end to the slave trade from Africa to the United States. The petition also admonished Congress for infringing the principles of the Declaration of Independence.[34] The other petition, submitted by Quakers from New York and western New England, was a short document with the more limited intention of seeking congressional help to maintain a policy of legal containment of slavery in New York.[35]

---

[30] William C. diGiacomantonio, '"For the Gratification of a Volunteering Society": Antislavery and Pressure Group Politics in the First Federal Congress', *Journal of the Early Republic*, 15/2 (1995), 172; Kenneth R. Bowling, William Charles diGiacomantonio and Charlene Bangs Bickford, eds., *Documentary History of the First Federal Congress of the United States of America. Volume 8. Petition Histories and Nonlegislative Official Documents* (Baltimore, MD, 1988), 315; 'Appointment of Committee to Present Petition to Congress', 3 Oct. 1789, in Nash and McDowell, eds., *Writings of Warner Mifflin*, 309.

[31] Richard Bauman, *For the Reputation of Truth: Politics, Society, and Conflict among the Pennsylvania Quakers 1750–1800* (Baltimore, 1971), 199; Henry E. Huntington Library, San Marino, California, James Pemberton to Robert Pleasants, 28 Feb. 1790, Pleasants Family Papers (1745–1898), R. A. Brock Collection, box 12.

[32] Gary B. Nash, 'Warner Mifflin (1745–98): The Remarkable Life of an Unflinching Abolitionist' in Maurice Jackson and Susan Kozel, eds., *Quakers and Their Allies in the Abolitionist Cause, 1754–1808* (London, 2015), 18.

[33] Memorial of the Philadelphia Yearly Meeting, 3 Oct. 1789, 11 Feb. 1790, in Bowling et al., eds., *Documentary History of the First Federal Congress. Volume 8*, 322.

[34] Nash, 'Warner Mifflin', 18; 'Memorial of the Philadelphia Yearly Meeting to Congress', 3 Oct. 1789, in Nash and McDowell, eds., *Writings of Warner Mifflin*, 306–7.

[35] Memorial of the New York Yearly Meeting, 10–11 Feb. 1790, in Bowling et al., eds., *Documentary History of the First Federal Congress. Volume 8*, 323–4; Joseph J. Ellis,

On 12 February 1790, another petition was presented to Congress by the Pennsylvania Abolition Society – endorsed by the elderly and frail Franklin, as president of the society – that urged Congress to disregard its constitutional limitations and to take action against the slave trade. The petition was drafted by leading members of the Pennsylvania Abolition Society such as Tench Coxe, Nicholas Waln and James Pemberton.[36] Franklin forwarded the memorial to John Adams at the request of the Pennsylvania Abolition Society.[37] It was the last public paper he signed before his death.[38] The memorial had been in gestation for some time, but Coxe, an influential conservative member of the society, had confidentially urged that it should be held back because it was 'an overzealous act of honest men'. He referred to the subject being 'much tortured' and to the 'errors of the Quakers in point of decorum'. His conclusion was that 'the address of the friends is impolitic and unhandsome'.[39]

Despite Coxe's reservations, however, the petition, based on moral and humanitarian principles, was forwarded to Congress by a vote of forty-three to eleven in the House of Representatives.[40] Coxe hoped its moderate tone would obviate sectional differences when it was debated.[41] The petitioners urged Congress to ignore the constitutional limitation on tampering with the slave trade – perhaps the cause of Coxe's qualms – and to promote the abolition of slavery in the United States. James Pemberton, chairman of the committee of correspondence of the Pennsylvania Abolition Society, provided the main leadership on the submission. He was confident that the memorial greatly advanced the cause of slave trade abolition.[42] However, the Pennsylvania Abolition

---

Founding Brothers: The Revolutionary Generation (New York, 2001), 81–3; Nash, *Warner Mifflin*, 164.

[36] Newman, *The Transformation of American Abolitionism*, 48.

[37] Franklin to Adams, 9, 15 Feb. 1790, in Bowling et al., eds., *Documentary History of the First Federal Congress. Volume 8*, 324. The Memorial of the Pennsylvania Abolition Society, 3, 15 Feb. 1790, is printed in ibid., 324–6.

[38] Extract of a letter from Providence, Rhode Island, 26 Mar. 1791, *Salem Gazette*, 5 Apr. 1791.

[39] Tench Coxe to James Madison, 31 Mar. 1790, in Charles F. Hobson and Robert A. Rutland, eds., *The Papers of James Madison. Volume 13: 20 January 1790–31 March 1791* (Charlottesville, VA, 1981), 130–3.

[40] Entry for 12 Feb. 1790 in De Pauw et al., eds., *Documentary History of the First Federal Congress. Volume 3*, 295.

[41] Jacob E. Cooke, *Tench Coxe and the Early American Republic* (Chapel Hill, NC, 1978), 149.

[42] HSP, James Pemberton to the Committee of the Society in London for Effecting the Abolition of the Slave Trade, 2 Apr. 1790, Pennsylvania Abolition Society letterbook (1789–94), Pennsylvania Abolition Society Papers.

Society's demands exceeded the remit of the two yearly meeting petitions. Thus, the society's petition went beyond proscribing the slave trade to endorse the need for full slave emancipation.[43] This, of course, was political dynamite as far as many Southern representatives were concerned and, unsurprisingly, led to a heated congressional debate.[44]

Petitions had long been a vehicle for allowing popular participation in the legislative process, with abundant examples that could be cited from the colonial period. These petitions against the slave trade provided the most passionate and rhetorical commentary in the first Federal Congress.[45] No other petitions presented to the first Congress were debated so fervently, nor did any other petitions absorb so much of Congress's time.[46] As John C. Meleney has argued, they 'were the product of a calculated and well-organized campaign; and nothing else could have served so well to arouse the outraged indignation of the representatives of the states of the deep South'.[47] Gary B. Nash, with slight exaggeration, noted that 'the Quaker petitions set Congress aflame as if a lightning bolt had struck Federal Hall'.[48]

The Senate voted to lay the first two petitions on the table but refused to take further action: This was a tactic used to prevent debate. But the petitions were not entirely dismissed because the House set up a select committee to scrutinise them.[49] It was intended that the committee should include representatives from all the states, but every southern state except for Virginia refused to participate.[50] The petitions were then debated in a

---

[43] Oldfield, *Transatlantic Abolitionism*, 75; Ohline, 'Slavery, Economics, and Congressional Politics, 1790', 340; David Waldstreicher, *Runaway America: Benjamin Franklin, Slavery, and the American Revolution* (New York, 2004), 236; Robert G. Parkinson, *The Common Cause: Creating Race and Nation in the American Revolution* (Chapel Hill, NC, 2019), 633.
[44] Bordewich, *The First Federal Congress*, 203.
[45] Bowling et al., eds., *Documentary History of the First Federal Congress. Volume 8*, 314.
[46] William C. diGiacomantonio, 'Petitioners and their Grievances: A View from the First Federal Congress' in Kenneth R. Bowling and Donald R. Kennon, eds., *The House and the Senate in the 1790s: Petitioning, Lobbying, and Institutional Development* (Athens, OH, 2002), 36.
[47] John C. Meleney, *The Public Life of Aedanus Burke: Revolutionary Republican in Post-Revolutionary South Carolina* (Columbia, SC, 1989), 187.
[48] Nash, 'Warner Mifflin', 19.
[49] David F. Ericson, *Slavery in the American Republic: Developing the Federal Government, 1791–1861* (Lawrence, KS, 2011), 32; Nicholas P. Wood, 'Abolitionists, Congress, and the Atlantic Slave Trade: Before and After Ratification' in Douglas Bradburn and Christopher R. Pearl, eds., *From Independence to the U.S. Constitution: Reconsidering the Critical Period of American History* (Charlottesville, VA, 2022), 105–6.
[50] Bordewich, *The First Federal Congress*, 203.

public session based on the committee's report.⁵¹ Quakers were determined that the petitions should be debated but they received plenty of opposition from the Lower South representatives. John Pemberton reported to his brother James that 'the southern members seem very averse to a prohibition of the wicked traffic'.⁵² One prominent Quaker, John Parrish, referred to the lobbying as 'a kind of warfare'.⁵³

The petitions were controversial and inflammatory for several reasons. Some politicians thought the Quaker petitions of 1790 were raising too large a question about the future of the United States when it had just become a federal nation and when Congress was only just beginning its activities. Southern congressmen felt pressurised by this lobbying, which they resented because the petitioners were not their constituents. They asked whether the procedures followed were constitutional in the light of Article 1, Section 9 of the Constitution. They were also determined to prevent any further attempts to submit petitions to Congress on the slave trade.⁵⁴

The debate about the petitions opened in Congress on 11 February 1790, when Thomas Fitzsimons of Pennsylvania introduced them on the floor of the House of Representatives. Josiah Parker of Virginia drew immediate attention to the importance of the slave trade, paid tribute to the respectable arguments made by the Quakers and hoped Congress could 'ascertain what can be done to restrain a practice so nefarious'.⁵⁵ Madison sought to calm nerves among congressmen over the slave trade, reminding members that 'the constitution secures to the individual States the right of admitting, if they think proper, the importation of slaves into their own territory ... subject, however, to a tax, if Congress are disposed to impose it, of not more than ten dollars on each person'.⁵⁶ That was a succinct recapitulation of what had been decided at the Federal

---

[51] Bruce A. Ragsdale, *Washington at the Plow: The Founding Farmer and the Question of Slavery* (Cambridge, MA, 2021), 217.

[52] John Pemberton to James Pemberton, 11 Feb. 1790, in Charlotte Bangs Bickford, ed., *Documentary History of the First Federal Congress. Volume 18: October 1789–March 14, 1790: Correspondence: Second Session* (Baltimore, MD, 2011), 496–7.

[53] Haverford College Library, Quaker Collection, John Parrish to Henry Drinker, 25 Feb. 1790, Vaux Family Papers, box 2.

[54] Jeffrey L. Pasley, 'Democracy, Gentility, and Lobbying in the Early U.S. Congress' in Julian E. Zelizer, ed., *The American Congress: The Building of Democracy* (Boston, 2004), 49–50.

[55] *Annals of Congress*, 1st Congress, 2nd session, House of Representatives, 11 Feb. 1790, 1226.

[56] Ibid.

Convention in 1787, and nothing legally had since changed. Madison's views were extended further while the petitions were still being considered by a committee of the whole.[57] In a letter to Benjamin Rush, written just over a month after the Congressional debates on the slave trade in 1790, Madison referred to South Carolina and Georgia as 'intemperate beyond all example and even all decorum' by arguing for 'the lawfulness of the African trade itself'.[58]

Many contributions to the lengthy congressional debate of 11 February 1790 were divided about the position adopted by the Quakers. The contributions raised broad issues about the right of American citizens to refer an important matter of moral concern to the Federal Congress on a matter that had been deemed beyond congressional power to act for two decades. On the one hand, those sympathetic to the anti-slave trade petition pointed out that the substance of their memorial was a subject concerning moral behaviour in relation to the increase of a 'licentious traffic', and that it ought to be heard in Congress because it did not contain anything unconstitutional. Quakers as citizens, it was argued, had a right to give their opinion on public measures and there was no intention that Congress, after considering it, would resort to any unconstitutional act. On the other hand, those opposing consideration of the petitions accused the Quakers of meddling in a business in which they had no direct interest, and one in which they would face no direct consequences. There was also the consideration that any attention paid by Congress to the petition might appear an implicit attack on southern property and an indication of support for slave emancipation. The South Carolina physician and state representative Thomas Tudor Tucker forthrightly condemned the petition because its purpose was to criticise a certain type of commerce on moral grounds and 'to request the interposition of Congress to effect its abrogation', which that body did not have the constitutional authority to do.[59]

---

[57] A committee of the whole was 'a committee that is formed by the House resolving itself into a committee. At this time the speaker leaves the chair and is supplanted by another member as chairman of the committee. Any legislation favorably acted on by the committee of the whole must be reported to the House by the chairman of the committee for further action'. De Pauw et al., eds., *Documentary History of the First Federal Congress. Volume 3*, xxii.

[58] Madison to Rush, 20 Mar. 1790, in Hobson and Rutland, eds., *The Papers of James Madison. Volume 13* (Charlottesville, VA, 1981), 109.

[59] *Annals of Congress*, 1st Congress, 2nd Session, House of Representatives, 11 Feb. 1790, 1,228–9, 1,232 (quotation).

Congressmen attacking the Quaker petitions strenuously attempted to discredit the antislavery role of the Society of Friends. Southern members, according to one influential Quaker, attacked the petition 'with much acrimony, but they were not without able advocates'.[60] It was argued that Quaker pacifism had been tantamount to disloyalty against the American revolutionary cause and had undermined American military security. A Georgian congressman claimed that the Quakers had been enemies to the American revolutionary cause but were now interfering with others' concerns in times of peace.[61] The South Carolinian lawyer William Loughton Smith argued that the Quakers were too few in number to constitute a body that could claim to represent public opinion at large. A defence of the Quaker position appeared in the New York *Daily Advertiser*, but the attacks by Southern congressmen on the Friends highlighted 'the vulnerability of an abolition movement associated too tightly with Quakers'.[62]

The debates on the petitions on the floor of Congress were the fullest public exchange of views on slavery that had yet occurred in the new American Republic. They were reported in detail in two New York newspapers and in one Philadelphia newspaper.[63] The debates took place in the House of Representatives: the Senate refused to consider them.[64] The Quaker petitioners mounted a more sophisticated lobbying campaign than had yet been witnessed in congressional affairs.[65] Their tactical activities were persistent, and they succeeded in capturing national attention.[66]

---

[60] HSP, James Pemberton to the Committee of the Society at London for Effecting the Abolition of the Slave Trade, 28 Feb. 1790, Pennsylvania Abolition Society letterbook (1789–94), Pennsylvania Abolition Society Papers.

[61] Robert G. Parkinson, *Thirteen Clocks: How Race United the Colonies and Made the Declaration of Independence* (Chapel Hill, NC, 2021), 180.

[62] David N. Gellman, *Emancipating New York: The Politics of Slavery and Freedom, 1777–1827* (Baton Rouge, LA, 2006), 96–7.

[63] Ellis, *Founding Brothers*, 88; Gary B. Nash, *Race and Revolution* (Madison, WI, 1990), 38. For congressional debates on the petitions, see *Annals of Congress*, 1st Congress, 2nd Session, House of Representatives, 11 Feb. 1790, 1,224–32, and Helen E. Veit, Charlotte Bangs Bickford, Kenneth R. Bowling and William C. diGiacomantonio, eds., *Documentary History of the First Federal Congress: Debates in the House of Representatives. Volume XII. Second Session: January to March 1790* (Baltimore, MD, 1994), 270–3, 282–92, 295–313.

[64] Rothman, *Slave Country*, 5.

[65] diGiacomantonio, 'For the Gratification of a Volunteering Society', 169.

[66] Nash and McDowell, eds., *Writings of Warner Mifflin*, 266.

On 12 February 1790, the House of Representatives debated whether to commit the petitions on the slave trade. The procedure used here needs to be clarified. 'Committed' meant that the House could discuss the petition further, but not always. Not every item referred to committee received further consideration. However, no petitions were summarily dismissed, and all were acknowledged by legislators and the subject of each petition read aloud in the House. The sheer number of petitions was large: 567 were submitted to the House and sixty-eight to the Senate in the First Federal Congress.[67] Given these considerations, petitioners knew that if their memorials were tabled they would be set aside whereas if they were committed at the very least their contents would be communicated to Congress and they might be further considered by a select committee.

Some Southern representatives opposed to the petitions made criticisms that extended beyond the specific details included in the memorials. Here are some, though not all, of the criticisms made. Tucker thought it regrettable that the House should be considering the memorials because, in his view, they constituted 'so glaring an interference with the Constitution'. He argued that Article 1, Section 9 meant that Congress could do nothing about the matter at this juncture. In his view, the petitions were a direct attack on the rights and property of the southern states.[68] He pointed out, in relation to the Pennsylvania Abolition Society's petition, that Franklin 'ought to have known the Constitution better'.[69] The South Carolina slaveholder and state judge Aedanus Burke supported Tucker's views, arguing that the petitions were subversive of the Constitution; they served to blow 'the trumpet of sedition in the Southern States'.[70] The lawyer and slaveholder James Jackson of Georgia ranged even more broadly in his criticism of the petitions, which he apprehended would lead to 'revolt, insurrection, and devastation' in the southern states. Abraham Baldwin forcibly deprecated the consequences of considering the memorials as Congress could not constitutionally declare and interpose on the subject of the slave trade.[71]

The congressional debate of 12 February 1790, however, was not one-sided. The lawyer and military veteran John Lawrence (sometimes spelled

---

[67] Richard R. John and Christopher J. Young, 'Rites of Passage: Postal Petitioning as a Tool of Governance in the Age of Federalism' in Bowling and Kennon, eds., *The House and Senate in the 1790s*, 107.
[68] *Gazette of the United States*, 17 Feb. 1790 (quotation); Edward B. Rugemer, *Slave Law and the Politics of Resistance in the Early Atlantic World* (Cambridge, MA, 2018), 232.
[69] Veit et al., eds., *Debates in the House of Representatives. Volume 12*, 302.
[70] *Gazette of the United States*, 17 Feb. 1790.   [71] Ibid.

Laurance) of New York thought the subject of the slave trade would undoubtedly come before Congress and that it was a good time to consider the claims of his opponents now that memorials had been submitted for examination. Congress could then decide how far it could constitutionally interfere. 'Surely there is no danger of our exceeding our powers', he stated, for 'we know what they are, and shall undoubtedly keep within their limits in all our deliberations and decisions'. Congressman John Page of Virginia – later a governor of the state – wanted the memorials committed because they were not asking for the total abolition of slavery: they were only requesting Congress to consider them in the light of its constitutional position. The merchant and diplomat Elbridge Gerry of Massachusetts opposed the slave trade and thought the petitions should be considered because Congress, despite its limitations in terms of action at present, had the right to regulate the business.[72]

Eleven Quaker petitioners sat in the gallery as the debates proceeded to remind the legislators that they were waiting upon a response from Congress. They included senior representatives of the Society of Friends in the United States, including John Pemberton, Warner Mifflin, Samuel Emlen, Jr and John Parrish, Jr. Mifflin had been present when the Philadelphia Yearly Meeting's petition on the slave trade had been presented to the Confederation Congress in 1783, and he now took it upon himself to call privately on several members of Congress to present his case. As the Quaker petitioners watched the proceedings on the floor of the House from the gallery, an observer commented that 'the dignity and Honor of the House were greatly lessened by the torrent of abuse' inflicted by Southern members on the Quaker petitioners. Members of the Quaker delegation also wrote private letters to congressmen and sent them Scriptural texts dealing with the iniquity of bondage.[73]

The Quakers found themselves on the receiving end of verbal attacks.[74] 'Never was a subject more warmly debated', wrote Brissot de Warville, a supporter of Warner Mifflin and co-founder of the Société des Amis des Noirs, 'and, what never happened before in America, it gave occasion to the most atrocious invectives from the adversaries of

---

[72] All the information in this paragraph is taken from ibid.
[73] HSP, Elias Boudinot to William Bradford, Jr, 25 Mar. 1790, Wallace Papers; Bowling et al., eds., *Documentary History of the First Federal Congress. Volume 8*, 316–18; diGiacomantonio, 'Petitioners and their Grievances', 37.
[74] Nash, 'Warner Mifflin', 20.

humanity'.[75] James Pemberton wrote that the presentation and reception of the Pennsylvania Abolition Society's memorial to Congress, composed by people of various Christian denominations, was 'violently opposed by a train of invective speeches from the southern delegates disgraceful to themselves and degrading to the dignity of the Representative body'.[76] Thus, several congressmen from the Lower South – William Loughton Smith, Burke and Tucker of South Carolina, and Baldwin and Jackson from Georgia – 'protested in the strongest terms' about committing them because they were requesting something unconstitutional, but their opposition was ineffectual.[77] Tucker argued that the Quaker memorials were an improper interference with the Constitution. He was dismayed that Friends thought Congress 'should intermeddle in the internal regulations of the particular states' over a matter that was 'a direct attack on the rights and property of the Southern States'.[78] Southern members in Congress were clearly rattled by the persistent focus of the Quaker petitions on the anti-slave trade cause.[79]

Loughton Smith, who was known for his proslavery speeches, was entirely opposed to the Quakers.[80] He supported Tucker's critical appraisal of their memorials, which he hoped would not be committed. Burke attacked Quaker loyalism in the War of Independence as a way of branding them as the enemies of America.[81] His reprobation of the Quaker petition argued that it was subversive of the Constitution; he

---

[75] J. P. Brissot de Warville, *New Travels in the United States of America. Performed in 1788* (London, 1788), 299 (quotation); Nash and McDowell, eds., *Writings of Warner Mifflin*, 266.

[76] HSP, James Pemberton to the Committee of the Society in London Instituted for Effecting the Abolition of the Slave Trade, 2 Apr. 1790, Pennsylvania Abolition Society Papers, series 2.1, loose correspondence outgoing (1783–1914).

[77] William Loughton Smith to Edward Rutledge, 13, 28 Feb. 1790, in George C. Rogers, Jr, ed., 'The Letters of William Loughton Smith to Edward Rutledge, June 6, 1789 to April 28, 1794', *SCHM*, 69/2 (1968), 103, 107; Meleney, *The Public Life of Aedanus Burke*, 187. Further discussion of South Carolina's attack on the Quaker petitions is included in Stanley Kenneth Deaton, 'Revolutionary Charleston, 1765–1800' (University of Florida PhD dissertation, 1997), 321–3.

[78] Jonathan Elliot, ed., *The Debates in the Several State Conventions on the Adoption of the Federal Constitution; As Recommended by the General Convention at Philadelphia in 1787*, 5 vols. (Washington, DC, 1836–45), IV, 410.

[79] Jeffrey L. Pasley, 'Private Access and Public Power: Gentility and Lobbying in the Early Congress' in Bowling and Kennon, eds., *The House and the Senate in the 1790s*, 65.

[80] See South Carolina HS, Charleston, William Loughton Smith to 'My Dear Sir', 24 Nov. 1790, Miscellaneous Manuscripts Collection, volume 1.

[81] Robert G. Parkinson, '"Manifest Signs of Passion": The First Federal Congress, Antislavery, and the Legacies of the Revolutionary War' in John Craig Hammond and

would refuse to serve on any committee considering it if it was committed. Baldwin, one of Georgia's two signatories to the Constitution, agreed with these sentiments, emphasising that Congress could not constitutionally interfere in the business; he hoped the house would proceed no further on the subject.[82] In a private letter, South Carolina's Charles Cotesworth Pinckney aired the opinion that the federal government would not intermeddle with slavery and the slave trade because they were a matter of domestic regulation.[83]

On 12 February 1790, Congress considered another petition presented on the slave trade by the Pennsylvania Abolition Society, with Franklin's name appended. It was read after a second reading had been given to the Quaker petition on the slave trade debated on the previous day.[84] Tucker immediately expressed his disapproval of the Pennsylvania Abolition Society's petition, arguing that it was likely to alarm the southern states. He worried about the broader impact on the southern states of any congressional consideration of the slave trade at this juncture. In particular, he was concerned that a detailed consideration of the slave trade would modulate into discussion of slavery itself. And on this point, he offered a prescient rhetorical reflection: 'Do these men expect a general emancipation of slaves by law? This would never be submitted to by the Southern States without a civil war.'[85]

Other speakers in the debate feared that the Pennsylvania Abolition Society's petition sought to promote an unconstitutional move, and that it might 'blow the trumpet of sedition in the Southern States'. But there were also regrets that the Constitution had determined that Congress could not immediately act to interdict the slave trade and to reprobate 'the traffic in human flesh'. Another perspective was to express disappointment that such a delicate matter for some states had ever been brought before Congress. Still another view was that the Quaker petitions should be discounted by Congress because they dealt with an issue that was still only capable of being decided within individual states for individual

---

Matthew Mason, eds., *Contesting Slavery: The Politics of Bondage and Freedom in the New American Nation* (Charlottesville, VA, 2011), 51.

[82] Elliot, ed., *Debates*, IV, 410–11.
[83] SCL, Pinckney to 'Dear General', 31 Mar. 1790, Charles Cotesworth Pinckney Papers.
[84] *Annals of Congress*, 1st Congress, 2nd session, House of Representatives, 12 Feb. 1790, 1,239–40.
[85] Ibid., 1,240 (both quotations).

states.⁸⁶ Loughton Smith argued it was unnecessary to commit a petition to Congress, which could not act upon it, and, as a reminder to his colleagues, that 'in the Southern States, difficulties had arisen on adopting the Constitution, inasmuch as it was apprehended that Congress might take measures under it for abolishing the slave trade'.⁸⁷ These interventions showed that a sharp division of opinion on the slave trade existed in Congress even though in 1790 there was no congressional power available to resolve the situation.⁸⁸

Some congressmen from South Carolina and Georgia attacked Quakers and other Northern emancipationists about the petitions. They focused not just on arguments dealing with Article 1, Section 9, but on the entire abolitionist thrust on slavery. The slave trade was not always condemned separately; it was often attacked as the embodiment of all that was immoral about slavery.⁸⁹ Some critics also impugned the character of Quaker petitioners and charged them with antifederalist motives, notably Franklin's support of the Pennsylvania Abolition Society's petition. Northerners, supported by some members from Maryland and Virginia, asked for a clearer definition of the Constitution's powers to regulate the slave trade.⁹⁰ Critics of the slave trade made the sectional argument that Northerners who wanted to end imports of enslaved Africans to the United States were motivated by the desire to sell off their own surplus slaves to Southern purchasers. Interestingly the anti-slave trade rhetoric deployed by some Virginians in the debates never extended to a definite call for action to prevent slave imports to individual states.⁹¹

Madison, listening carefully to the various points of view, commented on the constitutional niceties of the debate and indicated that any attempt to challenge Article 1, Section 9 would be unacceptable. But he still thought that Congress should consider the Quaker petitions, for there were 'a variety of ways by which it could countenance the abolition, and regulations might be made in relation to the introduction of them into the new States to be formed out of the Western Territory'.⁹² This was a reference to the Northwest Ordinance, passed by Congress on

---

⁸⁶ Ibid., 1,241 (both quotations), 1,242–3.   ⁸⁷ Ibid., 1,243.
⁸⁸ Rugemer, *Slave Law and the Politics of Resistance*, 232.
⁸⁹ Duncan J. MacLeod, *Slavery, Race and the American Revolution* (Cambridge, 1974), 36.
⁹⁰ Edgar S. Maclay, ed., *Journal of William Maclay* (New York, 1890), 196; Thomas E. Drake, *Quakers and Slavery in America* (New Haven, CT, 1950), 102–5.
⁹¹ Einhorn, *American Taxation*, 154.
⁹² *Annals of Congress*, 1st Congress, 2nd session, House of Representatives, 12 Feb. 1790, 1,246.

13 July 1787, which provided for government in territories west of the Appalachian mountains and set down a formal method for states to be carved out of those areas.

Madison argued that the Quaker memorial should be committed but without any debate upon the subject. He recapitulated the overall reasons for the adoption of the Constitution and explained the limitation of the powers of Congress to interfere in the regulation of the commerce in slaves. He defended the right of Congress to interpose in the regulation of the slave trade despite Article 1, Section 9.[93] Madison saw no harm in committing the Quaker memorials, considering that South Carolina's representatives had exaggerated their importance.[94] By tabling two congressional reports on the petitions, Madison hoped the debate over the memorials would be concluded.[95] Thus, Madison facilitated the printing of the reports by the select committee and the Committee of the Whole in the House Journal. These reiterated the point that Congress could not take any action on the foreign slave trade before the date set in the Constitution, but was able to ban US citizens from supplying the enslaved to other nations and to regulate the handling of slaves imported on ships owned by American citizens.[96]

From the perspective of the Lower South, the objections raised by congressmen from those states to the Quaker petitions about the slave trade had a salutary effect. Thus, Loughton Smith explained that:

> our early & violent opposition had this good effect it convinced the house that So. Car. & Georgia look with a jealous eye on any measure in which the negroes are at all concerned – we did not admit that even after 1808 Congress would be authorized to prohibit the importation, but that the clause was inserted for greater Caution & to quiet the minds of our people – we assured them that whenever Congress should directly or indirectly attempt any measure levelled at our particular rights in this respect, they must expect a revolt in those States, which would never submit to it, & that the most violent opposition would be given to every step which might appear to interfere in any manner with our negro property.[97]

Loughton Smith summarised South Carolinians' irritation at the Quaker petitions by noting that Congress had 'had a great deal warm debate two days about these cursed negro Petitions, & I think we so

---

[93] Ibid.
[94] Jeff Broadwater, *James Madison: A Son of Virginia & Founder of the Nation* (Chapel Hill, NC, 2012), 191.
[95] Nash, 'Warner Mifflin', 21.   [96] Ragsdale, *Washington at the Plow*, 218.
[97] Smith to Rutledge, 28 Feb. 1790, in 'The Letters of William Loughton Smith to Edward Rutledge', 108.

effectually tired the members out & embarrassed them that they will not be in a hurry to bring the subject on again'.[98] The debates in Congress were clearly a blow for abolitionists, who struggled to have their views on the slave trade considered. John Oldfield has aptly summarised the abolitionists' negative reception of the Pennsylvania Abolition Society's petition: 'try as they might to put on a brave face, pointing to the action already taken by individual states against the slave trade, the decision came as a grave disappointment to American activists, who had wanted the Federal government to put its mark on abolition, not least as a way of reaffirming its commitment to the revolutionary principles that lay at the heart of the country's struggle with the British'.[99]

In a vote taken at the end of the debate on 12 February, forty-three congressmen voted in favour of the petitions being committed against eleven opposing such action: seven of the opponents were from the Lower South.[100] This was the trigger to appoint a special committee to consider the petitions. Representatives from Maryland and Virginia hoped for full consideration of the memorials.[101] Madison wanted the committee to explore the parameters of Congress' power over slavery and the slave trade.[102] The House special committee comprised six Northerners and a Virginian. Behind the scenes, Quaker abolitionists, including James Pemberton and Warner Mifflin, worked closely with committee members. This ensured that the petitions received a favourable hearing.[103]

The fact that the petitions were referred to a committee rather than tabled was a positive development for the abolitionists.[104] The presence of the Quaker petitioners in the House gallery to listen to the debates on their memorials irritated some congressmen present. Proslavery speakers in the debate attacked the Quakers on various grounds, notably their pacifism in the revolutionary war, vilifying them as non-citizens who should play no part in influencing the laws of a nation that they had not fought to form.[105] On 15 February, Vice President John Adams, after

---

[98] Smith to Rutledge, 13 Feb. 1790, ibid., 104.
[99] Oldfield, *Transatlantic Abolitionism*, 75.
[100] *Annals of Congress*, 1st Congress, 2nd session, House of Representatives, 12 Feb. 1790, 1247; Wilentz, *No Property in Man*, 313 n. 12.
[101] Gary B. Nash, *The Forgotten Fifth: African Americans in the Age of Revolution* (Cambridge, MA, 2006), 88.
[102] Nash and McDowell, eds., *Writings of Warner Mifflin*, 313.
[103] Wilentz, *No Property in Man*, 159, 313 n. 13; Nash, *Warner Mifflin*, 166–72.
[104] Betty Fladeland, *Men and Brothers: Anglo-American Antislavery Cooperation* (Champaign-Urbana, IL, 1980), 57.
[105] diGiacomantonio, 'For the Gratification of a Volunteering Society', 183–5.

delaying, read the petitions to the Senate.[106] Senators from South Carolina and Georgia reportedly attacked the petitions in a fiery manner but there is no detailed record of the debate that occurred in that chamber.[107] Adams himself, it should be noted, did not support what he described later as 'the silly petition of Franklin and his Quakers'.[108]

The select House committee report was presented on 5 March 1790.[109] Though the report expressed sympathy with antislavery goals, Friends were disappointed with its specific conclusions: the committee could not find constitutional grounds for interfering with foreign slave imports before 1808 but hoped that individual states could revise their laws periodically to promote the matters raised in the antislavery memorials.[110] The committee report, echoing the evasive language used to avoid the word *slave* in the Constitution, reiterated the decision 'that the General Government is expressly restrained from prohibiting the importation of such persons as any of the states now existing shall think proper to admit until the year 1808'. It also implied that scruples about continuation of the slave trade would have to be dealt with on a state-by-state basis.[111]

However, the report had some positive outcomes. It included two resolutions to regulate the Atlantic slave trade before 1808 and to ban the foreign slave trade.[112] On the matter of slave importations, however, the congressional committee handling the Quaker memorials had acted in a lukewarm manner and the result was to confirm that the Constitution provided protection against federal intervention against slave imports until 1808.[113] James Pemberton, writing on behalf of the Pennsylvania Abolition

---

[106] Nash and McDowell, eds., *Writings of Warner Mifflin*, 313.
[107] Bordewich, *The First Federal Congress*, 205.
[108] Massachusetts HS, John Adams to Thomas Crafts, 25 May 1790, Papers of John Adams.
[109] The report is printed in Bowling et al., eds., *Documentary History of the First Federal Congress. Volume 8*, 335-7.
[110] Nash and McDowell, eds., *Writings of Warner Mifflin*, 326-7.
[111] *Annals of Congress*, 1st Congress, 3rd session, House of Representatives, 8 Mar. 1790, 1,465; Gellman, *Emancipating New York*, 95-9. For further analysis of the Quaker petitions to Congress in 1790, see Donald L. Robinson, *Slavery in the Structure of American Politics, 1765-1820* (New York, 1971), 302-10; Ohline, 'Slavery, Economics, and Congressional Politics', 355-60; Stuart E. Knee, 'The Quaker Petition of 1790: A Challenge to Democracy in Early America', *Slavery & Abolition*, 6/3 (1985), 151-9; and Richard S. Newman, 'Prelude to the Gag Rule: Southern Reaction to Antislavery Petitions in the First Federal Congress', *Journal of the Early Republic*, 16/4 (1996), 571-99.
[112] Wood, 'Considerations of Humanity and Expediency', 85.
[113] Gellman, *Emancipating New York*, 99.

Society, hoped that the Quaker petitions on the slave trade would be further promoted 'when the general government is more perfectly settled'.[114]

SLAVE TRADE DEBATES IN THE FIRST FEDERAL CONGRESS, MARCH 1790

Quaker petitions on the slave trade were considered by both a special committee and a committee of the whole in Congress between 16 and 23 March 1790. On 15 March, Ralph Izard and Pierce Butler, wealthy planters of South Carolina, gave long speeches in the Senate against the Pennsylvania Abolition Society's petition. They focused on sensitive issues raised by the memorial but veered off into areas that clearly lay beyond the specific intentions of the Quakers. Izard railed against what he termed Quaker fanaticism while Butler accused Franklin of signing the petition in an antifederal attempt to overturn the Constitution.[115] On 16 March, several Southerners made pointed remarks in the House of Representatives about the 'impolicy' of the Quaker petitions and Smith of South Carolina argued that 'an evil Spirit Actuated' Friends in their submission. But John Pemberton reported that Quaker sympathisers in Congress recognised that Southerners were using these tactics to delay consideration of the petitions.[116] Warner Mifflin also addressed Congress on 16 March, raising the question 'whether it is not the duty of every friend to humanity, delegated in congress with the power of legislation, to exert the utmost strength thereof, as speedily and efficaciously as circumstances will admit, to prevent any further progress in the African slave trade'?[117]

On 16 and 17 March, Southern members repeatedly tried to prevent consideration of the petitions, but debates continued for a week. Much

---

[114] HSP, James Pemberton to the Committee of the Society at London for Effecting the Abolition of the Slave Trade, 3 May 1790, Pennsylvania Abolition Society letterbook (1789–94), Pennsylvania Abolition Society Papers.

[115] Entry for 15 Feb. 1790 in Kenneth R. Bowling and Helen E. Veit, eds., *Documentary History of the First Federal Congress of the United States of America. Volume 9. The Diary of William Maclay and Other Notes on Senate Debates* (Baltimore, MD, 1988), 202.

[116] John Pemberton to James Pemberton, 16 Mar. 1790, in Charlotte Bangs Bickford, Kenneth R. Bowling, Helen E. Veit and William Charles diGiacomantonio, eds., *Documentary History of the First Federal Congress. Volume 19. Correspondence: Second Session: 15 March–June 1790* (Baltimore, MD, 2011), 883–4 (quotation on 883).

[117] Warner Mifflin's Address to Members of Congress, 16 Mar. 1790, in Bowling et al., eds., *Documentary History of the First Federal Congress. Volume 8*, 337.

wrangling occurred during the sessions.[118] Tucker was disappointed that the House of Representatives gave the memorial a second reading as he considered it 'a glaring ... interference with the Constitution' that might end with interference into 'the rights and property of the Southern States'. But this view was immediately challenged by the farmer and lawyer Joshua Seney of Maryland who could see no challenge to the Constitution in the memorial.[119] Several other congressmen favoured consideration of the Quaker memorial. Thomas Scott of Pennsylvania and Roger Sherman of Connecticut adopted this position. Elbridge Gerry also favoured committal, suggesting that the memorial did not infringe anything in the Constitution. John Page offered a similar perspective, concluding that South Carolina and Georgia's apprehensions were unfounded because Congress was restrained from interference in relation to slave imports to those states. Elias Boudinot of New Jersey, the former president of the Continental Congress, favoured the committal of the memorial because it only contained 'a request that Congress would interfere their authority in the cause of humanity and mercy', but he re-emphasised the point that Congress was constitutionally forbidden to interfere with the slave trade for another twenty years.[120]

Discussion of the report of the select committee on the memorials of the Quakers concerning the slave trade took place between 17 and 19 March 1790.[121] A long debate took place on the floor of the House on 17 March. Representatives from South Carolina and Georgia took a great interest in the matter and demonstrated their opposition to the measure. They were alarmed because Congress had 'no right to interfere in any Manner' with the slave trade prior to the Year 1808'.[122] Loughton Smith opened proceedings by lamenting that the subject of the slave trade had been brought before the House because he felt it would lead to 'a very unpleasant discussion' and would raise the anxieties of Southern representatives. Smith attacked the Quakers' attempt to meddle in politics with their petitions over

---

[118] The position of members from the Lower South is summarised in Bordewich, *The First Federal Congress*, 214–17.
[119] *Gazette of the United States*, 17 Feb. 1790, in Veit et al., eds., *Documentary History of the First Federal Congress of the United States of America. Volume 12*, 302.
[120] *Annals of Congress*, 1st Congress, 2nd session, House of Representatives, 22 Mar. 1790, 1517–18.
[121] 'From Our Correspondent: Slave Trade', *Massachusetts Centinel* (Boston), 31 Mar. 1790.
[122] Jonathan Trumbull to David Trumbull, 20 Mar. 1790, in Bickford et al., eds., *Documentary History of the First Federal Congress, Volume 19*, 937.

'a business with which they had no concern'. To Smith, Quakers were acting like busy-bodies and attempting to gain a hearing on matters relating to slavery, such as manumission and emancipation, which lay within the political and legal purview of the states, not the national government.[123]

Smith, the sole and lengthy speaker on 17 March, offered an impassioned defence of slavery and the slave trade in the lowcountry: 'Without the rice swamps of Carolina, Charleston would decay, so would the commerce of that city: this would injure the back country. If you injure the Southern States, the injury would reach our Northern and Eastern brethren; for the states are links of one chain: if we break one, the whole must fall to pieces.'[124] Smith argued that the memorials attacked the character of the southern states, commenting on the 'detestation' found in the wording of the petitions against 'the licentious wickedness of the African trade, and the inhuman blood tyranny and blood guiltiness inseparable from it'.[125] Smith's speech was so lengthy and so irksome to some Northern representatives that John Pemberton commented privately that he 'was heard with more patience than he Deserved, for he wearied himself and his hearers ... except his friend Jackson'.[126]

Matters reached a peak of high tension in the congressional debate on 17 March in response to Smith's speech. According to a witness from Pennsylvania, it 'was conducted with an unusual degree of warmth & not without severe Invective against the Quakers, who seating in the gallery, bore the basteing [sic], as they termed it, with all the Composure of true Philosophers'. The 'Boisterous Commotions' died down on the two subsequent days, however, and a special committee of the whole discussed the petitions 'with great Calmness and moderation'. The writer thought that 'the small Degree of Authority in the National Government' precluded any action being taken that would upset the Lower South.[127]

---

[123] *Annals of Congress*, 1st Congress, 2nd session, House of Representatives, 17 Mar. 1790, 1.503–5 (quotations on 1503). See also Rothman, *Slave Country*, 7.

[124] *Annals of Congress*, 1st Congress, 2nd session, House of Representatives, 17 Mar. 1790, 1,510.

[125] Ibid., 1,503.

[126] John Pemberton to James Pemberton, 17 Mar. 1790, in Bickford et al., eds., *Documentary History of the First Federal Congress. Volume 19*, 895. For further commentary on the tactics pursued in the debates by representatives from the Lower South, see Fisher Ames to George Richards Minot, 23 Mar. 1790, in Seth Ames, ed., *Works of Fisher Ames*, 2 vols. (Boston, 1854), 1, 75–6.

[127] Henry Wynkoop to Reading Beatty, 18 Mar. 1790, in Joseph M. Beatty, Jr, ed., 'The Letters of Judge Henry Wynkoop, Representative from Pennsylvania to the First Congress of the United States', *PMHB*, 38/2 (1914), 192. The 'spirit of acrimony'

James Pemberton also referred to the Pennsylvania Abolition Society's memorial being discussed in Congress 'and being violently opposed by a train of invective speeches from the southern delegates'.[128]

Nothing about the debate was mentioned in the *Annals of Congress* on 18 March 1790, when the committee considered each section of the report.[129] No further detailed comments from the floor of the House were reported until 22 March when Boudinot tried to calm any fears in the southern states about what Congress would consider on slavery and the slave trade by asking rhetorically, 'Can there be any foundation for alarm, when Congress expressly declare, that they have no power of interference prior to the year 1808?' Boudinot defended the Quakers against the bilious attacks on their motivations aired in the debate a few days previously. He did not name names but was clearly referring back to the long diatribe of William Loughton Smith on 17 March. He voted against striking out the Quaker memorial as he could not see that it had committed an impropriety.[130]

On 23 March, four members of the House argued that the Quaker memorials should be dropped and allowed, as it were, to go to sleep because of the dissension caused by the congressional debates. But a decision had to be taken on the two reports on the memorials – one made by a House select committee and another put together by a committee of the whole. Both reports were similar. A motion for taking up the report of the House committee on the subject was debated and finally passed in the affirmative by one vote. But a motion to take up the report of the committee of the whole was defeated by a vote of 21–24.[131] The outcome of these votes, by the narrowest of margins, points to the contentious nature of the slave trade. It was resolved, by twenty-nine votes to twenty-five, that both reports could be inserted in the House journal.[132] This

against the Quakers in this debate is also noted in Fisher Ames to [William Eustis], 17 Mar. 1790, in Bickford et al., eds., *Documentary History of the First Federal Congress, Volume 19*, 891. For the striking appearance of some Quakers in the gallery of the House during the debate, see John Pemberton to James Pemberton, 21 Mar. 1790, ibid., 955.

[128] HSP, James Pemberton to the Committee of the Society in London instituted for effecting the abolition of the slave trade, 2 Apr. 1790, Pennsylvania Abolition Society Papers, series 2.1, Committee of Correspondence letterbook, 1789–94.

[129] Howard A. Ohline, 'Politics and Slavery: The Issue of Slavery in National Politics' (University of Missouri, Columbia, PhD dissertation, 1969), 151 n. 42.

[130] *Annals of Congress*, 1st Congress, 2nd session, House of Representatives, 22 Mar. 1790, 1,517 (quotation), 1,520–1.

[131] Nash and McDowell, eds., *Writings of Warner Mifflin*, 327.

[132] *Annals of Congress*, 1st Congress, 2nd session, House of Representatives, 23 Mar. 1790, 1,523.

tabled the petitions but also gave them official recognition.[133] It was not clear, however, whether the reports would be taken up or not.[134]

This ended the five-week acrimonious consideration of the slave trade by Congress. It is a moot point whether this represented 'an important victory for the abolitionists,' as Nicholas P. Wood has argued.[135] In the only recorded vote on the report, the regional breakdown of the votes showed that only the Lower South representatives voted totally against this decision (by 8–0). The report of the special committee informed the memorialists 'that in all cases to which the authority of Congress extends, they will exercise it for the humane objects of the memorialists, so far as they can be promoted on the principles of justice, humanity, and good policy'.[136] The report of the committee of the whole house suggested several amendments to the memorial, indicating that Congress had no right to interfere with slavery or slave emancipation but did have the right 'to restrain the citizens of the United States from carrying on the African trade, for the purpose of supplying foreigners with slaves, and of providing, by proper regulations, for the humane treatment, during their passage, of slaves imported by the said citizens into the States admitting such importation'.[137]

Madison took the view that had the memorial been committed in the federal legislature, no notice would have been taken of it beyond the chamber, but that the many different objections to whether it should be committed could alarm politicians. Congressmen could vote for the commitment of the petition, he noted, without implying that they would support its request. Nobody contemplated that the petition could ever be construed in Congress as indicating 'a decision of the question of respecting the discouragement of the African slave-trade, nor alarm the owners with an apprehension that the General Government were about to abolish slavery in all the States; such things are not contemplated by any gentleman'.[138] Madison's intervention in the debate was decisive in the

---

[133] Ericson, *Slavery in the American Republic*, 33.
[134] John Pemberton to James Pemberton, 23 Mar. 1790, in Bickford et al., eds., *Documentary History of the First Federal Congress. Volume 19*, 970.
[135] Nash and McDowell, eds., *Writings of Warner Mifflin*, 327; Wood, 'Abolitionists, Congress, and the Atlantic Slave Trade' (quotation), 107.
[136] *Annals of Congress*, 1st Congress, 2nd session, House of Representatives, 23 Mar. 1790, 1,524.
[137] Ibid., 1,524–5 (quotation on 1,525).
[138] Ibid., 1st Congress, 2nd session, House of Representatives, 11 Feb. 1790, 1,231.

committal of the memorial.[139] He chaired a committee appointed to oversee the debates, and supported measures banning American citizens from taking slaves to foreign ports.[140]

Madison remained silent for most of the debate, but amended the wording of the fifth resolution so that it read as follows: 'That Congress have authority to restrain the citizens of the United States, who are concerned in the African trade, from supplying foreigners with slaves; and to provide for their humane treatment while on their passage to the United States.' This amendment was adopted. Southerners opposed taking up the petition in Congress. Madison wanted the deliberations over the slave trade memorial to be recorded in the journals of the House for public information to indicate that Congress would utilise its powers under the Constitution in appropriate cases but to re-emphasise that Congress had no power to proscribe the slave trade before 1808.[141] He referred to the variety of ways Congress could countenance the abolition of the slave trade, including setting down new regulations for states to be created in the west; but he did not provide any further particulars.[142]

Consideration of the Quaker memorials was controversial. Madison considered the style of the debates on the Quaker petitions 'shamefully indecent' and the matter 'evidently misjudged'. He thought the Southerners' tactics were to allow the debate on the memorials to continue for as long as possible in order to underscore 'the restraints imposed by the Constitution' on action against the slave trade.[143] Another observer noted that the matter had become one of serious conversation among interested parties but regretted that it had been raised at all in Congress: the debate was fruitless because it 'could not possibly be productive of any kind of effect'.[144] There was the possibility that the Quaker action would backfire and lead to attacks on the Society of Friends. Thus, one of

---

[139] Manisha Sinha, *The Slave's Cause: A History of Abolition* (New Haven, CT, 2016), 105.
[140] Broadwater, *James Madison*, 192.
[141] Slave Trade petitions, [23 Mar.] 1790, in Hobson and Rutland, eds., *The Papers of James Madison*, volume 13, 116–18. Full reports on the debates appeared in the New York *Daily Gazette*, 17–27 Mar. 1790, and the New York *Daily Advertiser*, 18–25 Mar. 1790.
[142] David L. Lightner, *Slavery and the Commerce Power: How the Struggle against the Interstate Slave Trade Led to the Civil War* (New Haven, CT, 2006), 38.
[143] James Madison to Edmund Randolph, 21 Mar. 1790, in Bickford et al., eds., *Documentary History of the First Federal Congress, Volume 19*, 953.
[144] Edward Carrington to Madison, 7 Apr. 1790, in Hobson and Rutland, eds., *The Papers of James Madison*, volume 13, 142.

Washington's correspondents felt 'particular umbrage that the Quakers should be so busy in this business.' He concluded that 'they will raise up a storm against themselves'.[145] Some Southerners attacked the character of Friends as a religious society and accused them of supporting the British with arms and provisions during the War of Independence.[146] Some Northern congressmen thought the presentation of the Quaker petitions was poorly managed and two – Thomas Fitzsimons and George Clymer – absented themselves before the House debated the reports.[147]

On 22 March, the report of the committee of the whole house, comprising six Northerners and a Virginian, suggested some amendments to particular phrases in the Quaker memorials but restated the clause noting that slave importations 'cannot be prohibited by Congress, prior to the year one thousand eight hundred and eight'.[148] Boudinot was relieved when the representatives 'were done with the Negro business, which has been ... carried by the Southern Gent[lemen] to a most unreasonable length'.[149] Another commentator, the representative and judge Henry Wynkoop of Pennsylvania, hoped the attention given to the Quaker memorials would not disgrace the national government and that it would be best to draw a veil over the debates on the slave trade. The whole affair, in Wynkoop's view, was 'a disagreeable business'.[150]

Loughton Smith summed up the South Carolinian view of the Quaker petitions in a letter to a fellow member from his state:

Some memorials from the Quakers and the Penylva. Society for the abolition of Slavery which were presented to our House have thrown us into a flame which is now fortunately extinguished after a considerable loss of time – two unmeaning resolutions have been passed to gratify the memorialists, (Who are much displeased with them by the bye) and we obtained an explicit declaration that Congress have no power to interfere with the emancipation of slaves. The

---

[145] David Stuart to Washington, 15 Mar. 1790, in Dorothy Twohig, Mark A. Mastromarino and Jack D. Warren, eds., *The Papers of George Washington. Presidential Series. Volume 5. 16 January 1790–30 June 1790* (Charlottesville, VA, 1996), 235–8.

[146] John Pemberton to James Pemberton, 21 Mar. 1790, in Bickford et al., eds., *Documentary History of the First Federal Congress. Volume 19*, 955.

[147] John Pemberton to James Pemberton, 18 Mar. 1790, ibid., 909; Ohline, 'Politics and Slavery', 147.

[148] Report of the Committee of the Whole House, 22 Mar. 1790, in Bowling et al., eds., *Documentary History of the First Federal Congress. Volume 8*, 338 (quotation); Rothman, *Slave Country*, 5.

[149] HSP, Boudinot to William Bradford, Jr, 25 Mar. 1790, Wallace Papers.

[150] Henry Wynkoop to Reading Beattie, 18 and 25 Mar. 1790, in Beatty, ed., 'Letters of Judge Wynkoop', 191, 193.

Quakers are gone home much discontented and the House has been censured by the public for taking up the business.[151]

Loughton Smith here expressed his disapproval of the Quaker petitions but made it clear that it was their statements on the future of slavery that were the main contentious issue. A succinct summary of the arguments on both sides of the debate appeared in the *Massachusetts Centinel* on 31 March 1790: 'The southern members view their States as ruined and undone, if any interference takes place. The other members view an interference as an act of benevolence, humanity and national policy.'[152]

REACTION TO THE QUAKER PETITIONS ON THE SLAVE TRADE, 1790

The businessman, publisher and former US postmaster general Ebenezer Hazard was scathing about the Quaker petitions in a private letter to his friend the Massachusetts minister Jeremy Belknap: 'Did you ever see such a piece of work as Congress has made of the Quakers' Petition about slaves? They were thrown into a great ferment by it, and some very indecent expressions fell from some of the members. Many who are anxious for the honor and dignity of the National Government were extremely hurt by such deviations from the rules of propriety'.[153] Belknap's response was highly critical of the Quakers. Owing to Article 1, Section 9 of the Constitution, Belknap considered that:

all applications to Congress for such prohibition are absolutely precluded; and I apprehend that the stirring up a controversy on this subject may endanger the Union. I was not pleased with the petition of the Quakers. I think them very contemptible politicians. They are governed by their feelings, and they do not reason. They think all mankind must submit to what their impulses dictate … I wish the Quakers would lie still and mind their own business, and let Government mind theirs, without any more meddling.[154]

The exchange between the two men on this subject continued. Hazard did not approve of the application made by the Quakers to Congress or of the manner in which it was conducted. He stated that:

---

[151] William Smith to Gabriel Manigault, 26 Mar. 1790, in Ulrich B. Phillips, ed., 'South Carolina Federalist Correspondence, 1789–1797', *The American Historical Review*, 14/4 (1909), 778.
[152] Bickford et al., eds., *Documentary History of the First Federal Congress. Volume 19*, 960.
[153] Ebenezer Hazard to Jeremy Belknap, 27 Mar. 1790, in *Collections of the Massachusetts Historical Society: The Belknap Papers*, fifth series, Volume 3 (Boston, 1877), 219.
[154] Belknap to Hazard, 7 May 1790, ibid., 221.

> If, as I understand the Quakers meant no more than to request Congress to lay the African trade under such restrictions as the Constitution allowed, there certainly was nothing improper in it; and it ought to have been done. I believe this was all that was intended; but one of the petitions mentioned *abolition*, and this alarmed the Southern members, and excited violent opposition, which was accompanied with a degree of illiberality and personal invective that was truly distressing to those who had the honour and dignity of the Union at heart.

He added that 'the application of the Quakers was ill-timed, and discovered more zeal than knowledge. They discovered, in my opinion, a forwardness and obstinacy and stubbornness in the business, which were unbecoming'.[155]

Madison was dismayed at the Southern congressmen for publicising on the floor of the House a potentially divisive issue that would have been more discreetly handled in committee.[156] He wrote privately to Benjamin Rush that the reaction of the representatives from South Carolina and Georgia was 'intemperate beyond all example and decorum' as they pleaded 'for the lawfulness of the African trade itself', lavishing 'the most virulent language on the authors' of the memorials.[157] Madison thought anyone reading the content and tone of the debates would be astonished at improper arguments that charged the House of Representatives 'with a design to usurp the power of prohibiting the importation of slaves'.[158]

John Parrish wrote to Madison as the most likely person to revive the anti-slave trade discussions in the next Congress, but Madison was cautious about raising further an issue that could lead to acrimonious debate.[159] The issue of the slave trade should not be revived, in Madison's opinion, during the present congressional session unless it appeared that any states were fitting out foreign vessels for the African trade or American bottoms to supply foreigners with slaves, in which case Congress would have the authority to intervene without infringing on the Constitution.[160] Madison acknowledged that some vessels from Rhode Island were employed in the African trade (mainly carrying captives to Cuba) but reiterated the point that Congress could only deal with this

---

[155] Hazard to Belknap, 5 June 1790, ibid., 223–4.
[156] Douglas R Egerton, *Death or Liberty: African Americans and Revolutionary America* (New York, 2009), 255.
[157] Madison to Rush, 20 Mar. 1790, in Hobson and Rutland, eds., *The Papers of James Madison*, volume 13, 109.
[158] Madison to Tench Coxe, 28 Mar. 1790, ibid., volume 13, 128–9.
[159] Wood, 'Considerations of Humanity and Expediency', 101–2.
[160] John Parrish to Madison, 28 May 1790, in Hobson and Rutland, eds., *The Papers of James Madison*, Volume 13, 232–3.

matter in a way that respected the Constitution. He thought further consideration of the slave trade by Congress at this juncture would be 'unseasonable & unsuccessful'.[161] One of Madison's Southern correspondents also warned against further discussion of the slave trade in Congress. He thought it 'very improper' to introduce the topic there because 'it interfered with other, perhaps more important business, and that its discussion could not fail to produce great intemperance of debate, which tends to weaken the government'.[162]

James Pemberton wrote to Robert Pleasants to emphasise the significance of this favourable reaction in Congress: 'it is generally acknowledged that the cause of humanity has been advanced by its being agitated in that public body whose powers are too restricted to do what many of the members are disposed to promote'.[163] He argued that abolitionists were nearer to 'the desired issue of suppressing the most abominable traffic that callousness & ambition ever promoted'.[164] This was over-optimistic, however, because Congress had not created new legislation dealing with the slave trade as a result of the consideration of the Quaker petitions. The Pennsylvania Society for Promoting the Abolition of Slavery realised its petition had not met with the success expected but it was satisfied that it 'evidently served to disseminate our principles, by exciting a Commotion on the subject'.[165]

This sense of optimism for the abolitionist cause led to no definite gains or action for the petitioners other than, as Pemberton noted, a sense that many congressmen might well support the condemnation of the slave trade. However, after voting to print both reports, most members of the House of Representatives decided to move on to consideration of matters other than the slave trade.[166] One should not overestimate the gains made by those condemning the slave trade when considering the two reports,

---

[161] Madison to Parrish, 6 June 1790, ibid., volume 13, 240. The supply of slaves by Rhode Island merchants to Cuba is discussed in Sean M. Kelley, *American Slavers: Merchants, Mariners, and the Transatlantic Commerce in Captives, 1644–1865* (New Haven, CT, 2023), 150–5.

[162] Thomas Pleasants, Jr to Madison, 10 July 1790, in Hobson and Rutland, eds., *The Papers of James Madison*, Volume 13, 269–74.

[163] Huntington Library, James Pemberton to Robert Pleasants, 20 Apr. 1790, Robert Pleasants Papers, Brock Collection, box 12.

[164] Huntington Library, James Pemberton to Robert Pleasants, 9 May 1790, ibid.

[165] HSP, Pennsylvania Society for Promoting the Abolition of Slavery to the Society of the Friends of the Blacks at Paris, 30 Aug. 1790, Pennsylvania Abolition Society Papers, series 2.1, loose correspondence, outgoing, 1783–1914.

[166] Wood, 'Considerations of Humanity and Expediency', 100.

but the debates on this issue did show that the Lower South was unable to suppress abolitionist influence in the federal legislature. That was a positive step in moral terms for those who wanted a proscription of the slave trade.[167]

Warner Mifflin had arranged to meet Washington about the Quaker petitions concerning slavery and the slave trade, and when he did so he explained the motivation and purpose of the memorials. Washington noted in his diary, however, that, as this was a matter that might come before him for an official decision, he would not express his sentiments on the question before this happened.[168] Washington also privately wrote that the Quaker petitions were awkward and revived an issue that the Constitution had deferred until 1808. He hoped that 'the Memorial of the Quakers (& a very malapropos one it was)' had been put to sleep. The presentation of the petitions interrupted congressional consideration of Alexander Hamilton's plan for federal funding of state debts.[169] Clearly, Washington believed that immediate discussion of pressing financial difficulties in the United States should take precedence over any raking of the coals about what to do about the slave trade, which Congress had already determined upon until 1808. More broadly, he avoided speaking publicly about slavery because of his awareness of important sectional divisions in Congress on this subject.[170]

Others shared Washington's views. Thus, for instance, Jeremy Belknap cautioned against the tactic of petitioning Congress on the slave trade in 1790. He did not think that organising an elite group of protesters would be effective at that time on the federal level because the Constitution had forbidden any federal action against the slave trade until 1808. He was concerned that the Quaker petitions would produce sectional discord and therefore damage the new American Union. John Adams, vice president and leader of the Senate, agreed with Belknap on this subject and argued

---

[167] Douglas Bradburn, *The Citizenship Revolution: Politics and the Creation of the American Union, 1774–1804* (Charlottesville, VA, 2009), 248–50.
[168] Entry for 16 Mar. 1790 in Donald Jackson and Dorothy Twohig, eds., *The Diaries of George Washington. Volume 6: 1 January 1790–13 December 1799* (Charlottesville, VA, 1979), 47.
[169] George Washington to David Stuart, 28 Mar. 1790, in Dorothy Twohig, ed., *The Papers of George Washington: Presidential Series*, 21 vols. (Charlottesville, VA, 1987–2020), V, 288; Waldstreicher, *Runaway America*, 237.
[170] Paul F. Boller, 'Washington, Quakers, and Slavery', *Journal of Negro Slavery*, XLVI/2 (1961), 87.

that the slave trade should be slowly reduced in order to limit sectional bitterness when national harmony was desired.[171]

The Quakers themselves were influenced by these reservations. Warned by politicians that an attempt to persuade Congress in 1790 to eradicate the slave trade would cause political instability in the new nation, petitioners from the Pennsylvania Abolition Society backtracked, abandoned further petitions in the same vein, and concentrated instead on laws to alleviate conditions in the slave trade.[172] Quakers were discouraged at the outcome of congressional debates on the slave trade memorials because no steps were taken to regulate the slave trade even though the report permitted this to happen.[173] However, by the autumn of 1790, the Pennsylvania Abolition Society wrote in a circular letter to abolition societies in various states to exhort Congress to revive the issue of proscribing the slave trade.[174]

QUAKER PETITIONS AGAINST THE SLAVE TRADE, 1791–1792

The failure of the Quaker submissions to Congress on the slave trade marked a watershed in attempts to influence government policy on this matter. They indicated that until 1808 any attempt to adopt a federal policy on the slave trade could be sabotaged by pro-slave trade congressmen. Thus, in 1790, a suggestion from Rhode Island that there should be a constitutional amendment to the slave trade clause was unsuccessful: this simply was not feasible because of Article 5 of the Constitution. In October, the Pennsylvania Abolition Society tried to coordinate further petitions attacking the slave trade with other abolition societies, but this initiative did not progress very far. A Quaker petition in 1791 that made an 'improper' request for federal intervention in the foreign slave trade was returned after representatives from the Lower South indicated their disapproval.[175] In June 1791, Robert Pleasants urged Madison to present

---

[171] Newman, *The Transformation of American Abolitionism*, 32–3.
[172] The Quaker antislavery advocate Warner Mifflin, however, sent a detailed defence of the Quaker petitions to the House of Representatives in May 1790: see Nash, *Warner Mifflin*, 177.
[173] Ohline, 'Politics and Slavery', 166.
[174] HSP, James Pemberton to the London committee, 25 Oct. 1790, Pennsylvania Abolition Society letterbook (1789–94), Pennsylvania Abolition Society Papers.
[175] Newman, *The Transformation of American Abolitionism*, 48–9, 57; Davis, *The Problem of Slavery in the Age of Revolution*, 326, n. 68; Bowling et al., eds., *Documentary History of the First Federal Congress. Volume 8*, 318.

another memorial attacking the slave trade, but Madison refused to do so out of respect for his public position in the House of Representatives, which was based on support from Virginia's slaveholders.[176]

Nine Quaker petitions on slavery submitted to Congress on 8 December 1791 by antislavery societies in Connecticut, Rhode Island, New York, Pennsylvania, Maryland and Virginia were referred to a committee appointed by the speaker of the House, Nathaniel Macon of North Carolina. The committee comprised men who were indifferent to, or opposed to, the subject at hand and so, unsurprisingly, a report was not issued. No further action on these petitions was taken. A Quaker memorial from the Yearly Meeting at Rhode Island in 1793 called upon Congress 'to exercise the authority vested in them by the Constitution for the suppression of the slave trade'. This was considered in Congress on 20 January 1794. The petition was discounted and ordered to lie on the table, with no further discussion. It was clear that the Quakers were losing influence over Congress on the slave trade.[177]

After the extensive debates concerning the Quaker petitions submitted to Congress in 1790, the federal government accepted that nothing could be done to end the slave trade immediately because of constitutional limitations, but it showed concern to limit importation where possible. Clearly the abolitionist message had made a deep impression on many legislators, and abolitionists continued to attack the cruelties and injustices of the slave trade.[178] In November 1792, a petition on slavery and the slave trade presented to the House of Representatives by Warner Mifflin was denounced by a Southern representative as the work of a fanatic and the memorial withdrawn without debate.[179] The Pennsylvania Society for the Abolition of Slavery decided in 1793 to send

---

[176] Broadwater, *James Madison*, 192; Robert Pleasants to Madison, 6 June, 6 Aug. 1791, and Madison to Pleasants, 30 Oct. 1791, in Robert A. Rutland and Thomas A. Mason, eds., *The Papers of James Madison. Volume 14. 6 April 1791–16 March 1793* (Charlottesville, VA, 1983), 30, 70, 91–2.

[177] *Annals of Congress*, Senate, 3rd Congress, 1st session, 21 Jan. 1794, 36; *Aurora General Advertiser* (Philadelphia), 21 Jan. 1794; Drake, *Quakers and Slavery in America*, 107; Sarah A. Batterson, '"An Ill-Judged Piece of Business": The Failure of Slave Trade Suppression in a Slaveholding Republic' (University of New Hampshire PhD dissertation, 2013), 36–7.

[178] See, for example, an address given before the Connecticut Society for the Promotion of Freedom, dated 15 Sept. 1791, and printed as Jonathan Edwards, *The Injustice and Impolicy of the Slave Trade and of the Slavery of the Africans: Illustrated in a Sermon*, 2nd ed. (Boston, 1822).

[179] Dun, 'Philadelphia not Philanthropolis', 95–6.

no more petitions to Congress until they stood the chance of a better reception.[180] James Pemberton observed in a private letter that Congress continued to ignore the subject of 'the odious Slave Trade'.[181] The Pennsylvania Society for the Abolition of Slavery did not forward treatises against the slave trade to politicians but it did print nine memorials against the slave trade when Congress kept them silently under a committee in 1792.[182]

After the disappointment of 1790, American activists turned to coordinating a nationwide petitioning campaign against the foreign slave trade, involving the carrying of slaves by US citizens, which Congress was permitted to consider and take action against. This entailed dealing with abolition societies in Rhode Island, Connecticut, New York, Pennsylvania, Maryland and Virginia between December 1790 and November 1791. Individual associations, such as the Providence Society for Abolishing the Slave Trade, printed diatribes against the Guinea traffic.[183] The Pennsylvania Abolition Society, imbued with a strong sense of civic virtue, took the lead as the clearinghouse for these abolition societies and also cultivated international connections.[184] At the beginning of 1791 the society was informed that 'a *very very large majority of the citizens of the northern states*' opposed their own citizens supplying foreigners with slaves and wanted to prevent foreigners from fitting out vessels in any US state for Africa. The writer

---

[180] Seymour Drescher, 'Divergent Paths: The Anglo-American Abolitions of the Atlantic Slave Trade' in Wim Klooster, ed., *Migration, Trade and Slavery in an Expanding World: Essays in Honor of Pieter Emmer* (Leiden, 2009), 268.

[181] HSP, Rhode Island Society for the Abolition of Slavery to Alexander Addison, 12 Feb. 1793, Pennsylvania Abolition Society Papers, series 2.1, loose correspondence, outgoing, 1783–1914.

[182] Ohline, 'Politics and Slavery', 236.

[183] For example, William Patten, *On the Inhumanity of the Slave Trade, and the Importance of Correcting It. A Sermon, Delivered in the Second Congregational Church, Newport, Rhode Island, August 12, 1792* (Providence, RI, 1793) and Samuel Hopkins, *A Discourse upon the Slave Trade and the Slavery of the Africans, Delivered before the Providence Society for Abolishing the Slave Trade ... May 17, 1793* (Providence, RI, 1793).

[184] Richard Newman, 'The Pennsylvania Abolition Society and the Campaign for Racial Justice' in Richard Newman and James Mueller, eds., *Antislavery and Abolition in Philadelphia: Emancipation and the Long Struggle for Racial Justice in the City of Brotherly Love* (Baton Rouge, LA, 2011), 124–5. A fair amount of material compiled by these various abolition societies is preserved in HSP, Pennsylvania Abolition Society Papers, series 5.16–5.26, but much of it is very scrappy, including crossed-out minutes and incomplete correspondence drafts.

indicated his disgust for the slave trade by referring to 'those floating ships for the sale of human flesh'.[185]

In October 1791, the Committee of Correspondence laid before the Pennsylvania Abolition Society a memorial on the slave trade, which was read, carefully considered and approved. It resolved that Congress should have authority to restrain US citizens from carrying on the African trade for the purpose of supplying foreigners with slaves. It also decided that Congress should have authority to prohibit foreigners from fitting out vessels from any American port to transport Africans to any foreign port. This memorial, along with similar ones from the abolition societies of Rhode Island, Connecticut, New York, Maryland and Virginia, was presented to Congress and referred to a select committee.[186]

The Philadelphia Yearly Meeting was disappointed that by 1792 their efforts to proscribe the slave trade through congressional channels had failed. 'The oppressed state of the afflicted Blacks continues unredressed', the Philadelphia Meeting for Sufferings informed its counterpart in London, and 'the constitutional powers of Congress being as they alledge inadequate to their just & desirable relief, no way has clearly opened to us for the renewal of our solicitation to that body on the behalf of these distressed people'.[187] In November 1792, Warner Mifflin addressed a memorial to the president and Congress of the United States condemning American acceptance of the slave trade. He argued that slavery and the slave trade conflicted with the claims made in the Declaration of Independence that all men are created equal and entitled to life, liberty and the pursuit of happiness. It remained 'obligatory' for Congress to consider those rights, but Mifflin wrote rhetorically:

How then have those rights become alienated, that Americans should be permitted to continue to ravage the coast of Africa, thereby promoting murder, pillaging, plundering and burning its towns, and enslaving its inhabitants? And in the United States, while some of those very men, who perhaps with their own hands subscribed the aforesaid declaration, remain in the supreme Legislature, that

---

[185] HSP, George Benson to Thomas Harrison, 5 Jan. 1791, Pennsylvania Abolition Society Papers, series 2.2, loose correspondence incoming, 1784–95.
[186] Edward Needles, *A Historical Memoir of the Pennsylvania Society for Promoting the Abolition of Slavery* (Philadelphia, 1848), 39–40.
[187] Library of the Religious Society of Friends, London, The Meeting for Sufferings in Philadelphia to the Meeting for Sufferings in London, 15 Mar. 1792, Letters Passed between the Meeting for Sufferings in London and the Meeting for Sufferings in Philadelphia, Volume 1 (1757–1815).

avaricious men should be permitted to pass through the country, steal, buy, traffic, barter and exchange the blacks, as though they were indeed brute beasts.[188]

Mifflin's powerful diatribe highlighted the greed of the slave trade, but further action was necessary before the stain could be eradicated.

ABOLITION SOCIETIES AND THE SLAVE TRADE

Antislavery discussions were maintained throughout the United States over the next few years through meetings of abolition societies to discuss collective action. By this stage of proceedings, the Pennsylvania Abolition Society had decided it would limit the wording in its petitions to those aspects of the slave trade which Congress could regulate.[189] Memorials on the slave trade from various associations were referred to Congress, soliciting the House of Representatives to exercise their powers on this subject, but though the memorials were read and referred to a committee, nothing was done.[190] Abolitionists presented petitions on the slave trade to Congress in January 1794 and travelled to the capital to lobby in their favour. Similar meetings of delegates from abolition societies were convened in 1795, 1796 and 1797.[191]

Nine societies from six states gathered in Philadelphia at the American Convention of Abolition Societies between 1 and 7 January 1794, after the New York Manumission Society had urged this change of tactic in the abolitionist opposition to the slave trade.[192] They published antislavery pamphlets and sent petitions to state governments and the federal government to oppose the slave trade and slavery and to establish more abolition societies to support the welfare and condition of black

---

[188] *The Memorial of Warner Mifflin to the President, Senate, and House of Representatives of the United States* (Philadelphia, 1792) in Frost, ed., *The Quaker Origins of Antislavery*, 282.

[189] Leonardo Marques, *The United States and the Transatlantic Slave Trade to the Americas, 1776–1867* (New Haven, CT, 2016), 27.

[190] Library of the Religious Society of Friends, London, The Meeting for Sufferings in Philadelphia to the Meeting for Sufferings in London, 15 Mar. 1792, Letters Passed between the Meeting for Sufferings in London and the Meeting for Sufferings in Philadelphia, Volume 1 (1757–1815).

[191] Oldfield, *Transatlantic Abolitionism*, 75–6, 110, 112, 116; Wood, 'Considerations of Humanity and Expediency', 106.

[192] HSP, John Rogers to the Pennsylvania Abolition Society, 4 Mar. 1793, Pennsylvania Abolition Society Papers, series 2.2, loose correspondence, incoming, 1784–95.

Americans.[193] This was an attempt to provide a national group to combat the iniquities of the slave trade. It was, in Ohline's words, 'the first national convention of a pressure group designed to influence the policy of the national government'.[194]

In January 1794, the delegates drew up a petition against the slave trade and submitted it to Congress when they thought it would be considered. The committee, under the leadership of Benjamin Rush, disclaimed any desire to request a general emancipation of slaves already in the United States. Instead, they stated that their only object was to obtain a congressional act prohibiting the trade carried on by US citizens for the purpose of supplying slaves to foreign nations, and to prevent foreigners from fitting out vessels for the slave trade in the ports of the United States.[195] In the same month, New England Quakers submitted to Congress a petition attacking the slave trade.[196]

Taking slaves in American ships to foreign ports was the one branch of transatlantic slaving that Congress could legitimately proscribe constitutionally, and by 1794 it was clear that many American slave traders were supplying Africans to Spanish colonies.[197] The steering committee of the American Convention of Abolition Societies, which had Quaker representatives such as Mifflin, brought pressure to bear on Congress to take action.[198] In January 1793, Mifflin had written a pamphlet addressing the lack of action by Congress on the slave trade, while acknowledging the constitutional limitation on what could currently be achieved: 'Had congress done as much towards removing this national guilt, as by the tenor of their own vote they have power to do, there is no doubt with me, but that it would at least have given a very powerful check, if not a total stop to the odious traffic; notwithstanding the plea of restriction in the constitution of the general government.' He added sharp moral condemnation to these words, informing Congress that it is 'my duty to tell you plainly, that I believe the blood of the slain, and the oppression exercised in Africa, promoted by Americans, and in this country also, will stick to

---

[193] Jennifer Randazzo, 'A Convention of Delegates from the Abolition Societies' in James G. Basker, ed., *Early American Abolitionists: A Collection of Antislavery Writings 1760–1820* (New York, 2005), 218.
[194] Ohline, 'Politics and Slavery', 239–40.
[195] Untitled article, *American Minerva* (New York), 6 Mar. 1794; Fladeland, Men and Brothers, 65.
[196] Ohline, 'Politics and Slavery', 240.
[197] Wood, 'Abolitionists, Congress, and the Atlantic Slave Trade', 112.
[198] Nash and McDowell, eds., *Writings of Warner Mifflin*, 270.

the shirts of every individual of your body, who exercise the powers of Legislation, and do not exert their talents to clear themselves of this abomination'.[199]

Whether or not Congress took account of Mifflin's strictures is unknown, but on 11 February 1794, a congressional committee recommended that a law be introduced against the foreign slave trade. The bill was presented to the House on 28 February. The Senate failed to suppress the bill and it passed without a record vote.[200] The act strengthened federal power over foreign commerce and the slave trade. Such a law would have been unachievable under the Confederation government.[201] Government agents could now take action against US citizens aiding and abetting the slave trade of foreign powers.[202] Samuel Hoare suggested that the next convention should adopt a plan for looking over violations of the foreign slave trade. Committees should be vigilant in seeking out breaches of the law and provide money to enable prosecutions to be carried out.[203]

The convention resumed its work in 1795, putting more effort into coordinating state abolition societies. It sent memorials to South Carolina and Georgia, which had no abolition societies, to end their slave importations and to pass manumission and gradual emancipation laws. In 1794 and 1795, the convention sent addresses to all states that had not banned slave importation.[204] There are no clear signs, however, that the activities of the American Convention of Abolition Societies achieved positive results despite the energy and commitment they displayed for the abolitionist cause. An effort to petition state legislatures to press for a constitutional amendment to end slave imports in the United States before 1808 failed.[205]

---

[199] Warner Mifflin, *A Serious Expostulation with the Members of the House of Representatives of the United States* (Philadelphia, 1794), reprinted in J. William Frost, ed., *The Quaker Origins of Antislavery* (Norwood, PA, 1980), 273.

[200] Ohline, 'Politics and Slavery', 242–3.

[201] Wood, 'Abolitionists, Congress, and the Atlantic Slave Trade', 113.

[202] Andy Cabot, '"Why May Not Our Country Be Enriched by that Lucrative Traffic?" The Slave Trade and the Failed Politics of Federal Proscription in the Early American Republic (1787–1808)', XVII–XVIII. *Revue de la Société d'études anglo-américaines des XVII*e *et XVIII*e *siècles*, issue 77 (2020), paragraph 18, https://journals.openedeition.org/1718/6037.

[203] HSP, Samuel Hoare to the Pennsylvania Society for Promoting the Abolition of Slavery, 10 July 1794, box 14, folder 23, Cox-Parrish-Wharton Papers.

[204] Locke, *Anti-slavery in America*, 105.

[205] Stanley Harrold, *American Abolitionism: Its Direct Political Impact from Colonial Times into Reconstruction* (Charlottesville, VA, 2019), 30.

Though the Convention of Abolition Societies had a national remit, it was slow to take action and, in the words of James Alexander Dun, it 'became mired in efforts to collect information and present petitions towards limited goals'.[206] After 1798 the American Convention meetings became biennial and its activities diminished. New England sent no delegates to the annual convention after 1798; the Maryland and Virginia societies became inactive; and the Convention failed to meet in 1799 and 1802. By 1806, the annual meetings ended and several state abolition societies, in New England and the southern states, fell by the wayside.[207]

CONGRESSIONAL ACTS ON THE SLAVE TRADE, 1794 AND 1800

Congressional acts of 1794 and 1800 forbade US citizens and residents from carrying on the slave trade to foreign countries. The 1794 legislation originated from a petition from several abolitionist societies presented to Congress in January 1794. Howard A. Ohline has argued that this action 'forced Congress to pass a law against the foreign slave trade in 1794'.[208] The memorialists argued that 'this cruel commerce' weakened the United States and warned against allowing foreigners to use American ports to load slave vessels. This was the first slave trade law passed by Congress, where it succeeded after little debate because it specifically disavowed any intention to abolish slave imports to the United States. Brought in to Congress as 'An Act to Prohibit the Carrying On the Slave Trade from the United States to any Foreign Place or Country', it was referred by a committee of the whole to a congressional committee specifically intended to handle the bill.[209] The bill became a regulatory act that encountered little opposition in either house of Congress; it was signed into law by Washington on 22 March 1794.[210] It prohibited American ship captains

---

[206] James Alexander Dun, *Dangerous Neighbours: Making the Haitian Revolution in Early America* (Philadelphia, 2016), 132.
[207] Ibid.; Sinha, *The Slave's Cause*, 110; Winthrop D. Jordan, *White over Black: American Attitudes toward the Negro, 1550–1812* (Chapel Hill, NC, 1968), 344.
[208] Ohline, 'Politics and Slavery', 212–13. This law is discussed in Kelley, *American Slavers*, 161–3.
[209] RIHS, Moses Brown to Almy & Brown, 17 Feb. 1794, Moses Brown correspondence. For the text of the act, see *Gazette of the United States*, 4 Apr. 1794, and Batterson, 'An Ill-Judged Piece of Business', 261.
[210] Wood, 'Considerations of Humanity and Expediency', 111–12; *Gazette of the United States*, V, 49, 7 Feb. 1794; Batterson, 'An Ill-Judged Piece of Business', 19, 41.

from carrying slaves to foreign destinations or dispatching ships in American ports for use by slave traders from other countries.[211]

The act represented the apex of the abolitionists' lobbying and petitioning efforts since 1783. Nicholas P. Wood argues that the 1790 congressional debates on the Quaker petitions dealing with slavery and the slave trade were not a setback for the abolitionists; that they influenced the context in which the Foreign Slave Trade act of 1794 was considered and debated; and that that law was a 'moral victory for the abolitionists'. To support their lobbying, abolitionists reprinted newspaper reports on slave revolts to persuade the American public of the validity of their case.[212] Another stimulus lay in public opposition to the slave trade. Many American newspaper reports in 1794 expressed fear of slave revolts and condemned the slave trade.[213] In addition, northern states were keen to support a law that sought to put an end to violation of state laws and lobbying activity of the abolitionist societies could no longer be discounted. Southern members of Congress accepted the measure because it did not interfere with domestic slavery.[214]

This act laid down a heavy penalty of $2,000 for anyone caught importing slaves, divided equally between the United States and the prosecutor, but had no specific means for policing the traffic. It forbade US citizens or foreigners resident in the United States from fitting out ships to carry slaves to any foreign country. The penalty for not observing this regulation was forfeiture of the vessel. The act also introduced a bonding procedure for all foreign vessels clearing for Africa and an additional $200 fine for each slave carried, to be divided between the United States and the prosecutor. The act included various loopholes, which made evasion relatively easy: These included the lack of a provision to condemn vessels at sea.[215] In fact, merchants found ways of evading the law and sought help from their allies in state courts.[216]

---

[211] Nash, *Warner Mifflin*, 189.
[212] Wood, 'Considerations of Humanity and Expediency', 107-8, 113-15 (quotation on 113).
[213] On fear of slave uprisings, see Du Bois, *The Suppression of the African Slave-Trade*, 80; Drake, *Quakers and Slavery*, 108. On public opposition to the slave trade, see Ohline, 'Politics and Slavery', 243, and Wood, 'Considerations of Humanity and Expediency', 107-8.
[214] Ohline, 'Politics and Slavery', 243-4.
[215] Jay Coughtry, *The Notorious Triangle: Rhode Island and the African Slave Trade, 1700-1807* (Philadelphia, 1981), 213; Marques, *The United States and the Transatlantic Slave Trade*, 27.
[216] Batterson, 'An Ill-Judged Piece of Business', 48-52.

Various abolition societies, dominated by Quakers, made efforts to enforce the 1794 law by bringing action against violators. It was discovered in Pennsylvania that some ships were flying the Danish flag to evade the law and that a few vessels were leaving American ports with legal cargo shipments but also taking a handful of slaves to sell in foreign ports. The Pennsylvania Abolition Society traced more than fifty cases of slave trade violations.[217] Massachusetts citizens were forbidden from participation in the slave trade from 1788 onwards, but in the early 1790s slave ships were still sent out from Salem without facing prosecution under state law.[218] Massachusetts, Connecticut and Rhode Island likewise despatched slaving vessels that evaded capture, as merchants devised various subterfuges to circumvent laws. Merchants from many of the eastern seaboard states were active in supplying slaves to Havana, Cuba in the 1790s.[219]

Enforcement mechanisms were lacking for the 1794 federal law. John Adams's administration of the late 1790s was unwilling to enforce it.[220] In some cases of malfeasance it was not clear what action should be taken. Thus, in 1801, seven years after the law was enacted, governor James Monroe of Virginia was alerted to the fact that thirty Africans had been found aboard a New England vessel off Cuba. Monroe did not know what action could be taken in these circumstances. He received a letter stating that the congressional act was silent on how this situation should be handled.[221]

Unresolved problems over the slave trade continued in the 1790s, notably many unproductive efforts to enforce anti-slave trade laws in New England.[222] A society for abolishing the slave trade was established in Providence, Rhode Island, on 29 January 1789. It had about sixty members initially and had to overcome staunch opposition from slave

---

[217] Marques, *The United States and the Transatlantic Slave Trade*, 27.
[218] An exception occurred in 1792, when action was brought against Joseph Waters, owner of the *Abeona*, and Captain John Sinclair, both of whom were found culpable. See Peabody Essex Institute, Salem, Cleveland v. Waters and Sinclair, Essex Count Court of Common Pleas, volume 14. Sean M. Kelley kindly provided this reference.
[219] George H. Moore, *Notes on the History of Slavery in Massachusetts* (New York, 1866), 225–6; Ohline, 'Politics and Slavery', 214–17, 220–1; Friends' Historical Library, Swarthmore College, James Pemberton to Edmund Prior, 4 Feb. 1790, Wood Manuscripts, RG 5 192.
[220] Ohline, 'Politics and Slavery', 248.
[221] Batterson, 'An Ill-Judged Piece of Business', 48–9; Philip Norborne Nicholas to Governor James Monroe, 11 Feb. 1801, in Donnan, ed., *Documents*, IV, 167.
[222] Mack Thompson, *Moses Brown: Reluctant Reformer* (Chapel Hill, NC, 1962), 200–1.

trade supporters in the state. It held regular meetings and considered received correspondence dealing with the slave trade.[223] Reporting from Rhode Island, a correspondent of the Pennsylvania Abolition Society noted in January 1791 that 'the great body of the people in this state are extremely averse' to the slave trade 'but many Persons in Newport and a number of influential characters in this town [Providence] seem determined to support it till Congress shall interfere & forbid it'.[224]

Some Rhode Island merchants continued their slave trading activities in the belief that prohibitive laws would not be used against them.[225] Thus, in 1795 alone, thirty-two slave ships fitted out at Newport, Rhode Island for Africa.[226] Moses Brown lamented the fact that his merchant brother, John Brown, wanted to send a vessel to Africa with the approval of fellow traders to test the strength of Rhode Island's law against the slave trade. The voyage was intended to deliver Africans to Cuba. It violated the federal law of 1794 banning Americans from taking slaves to ports outside the United States. Moses Brown disapproved of his brother's intentions for the voyage and indicated his disdain for the slave trade, referring to merchants in that trade as 'deadening their humanity' through their 'love of money'. In a lengthy letter to his brother, he stated his belief that it is 'right for every thoughtful citizen to discourage such commerce in every place'.[227] John Brown defended his position by noting that he had only participated in one Guinea voyage in twenty years.[228]

The legislation was not completely ineffectual, however, because a number of prosecutions occurred, notably a federal court trial of John

---

[223] RIHS, Providence Society for Abolishing the Slave Trade Minute book (1789–1827); HSP, Moses Brown to James Pemberton, 8 March 1789, Pemberton papers, box 52, folder 4.

[224] HSP, George Benson to Thomas Harrison, 5 Jan. 1791, Pennsylvania Abolition Society Papers, series 2.2, incoming loose correspondence, 1784–95. For a similar comment, see HSP, Moses Brown to James Pemberton, 2 Sept. 1789, Pemberton Papers, box 52, folder 182.

[225] HSP, Extract of a letter from Rhode Island, 23 Aug. 1788, Pemberton Papers, box 52, folder 182.

[226] James A. McMillin, *The Final Victims: Foreign Slave Trade to North America, 1783–1810* (Columbia, SC, 2005), 43–4.

[227] RIHS, Moses Brown to John Brown, 15 Mar. 1797, Moses Brown correspondence (https://repository.library.brown.edu/studio/item/bdr:303530/). For contextual information on the Brown brothers and the slave trade, see James Francis Reilly, 'Moses Brown and the Rhode Island Anti-slavery Movement' (Brown University MA thesis, 1951).

[228] RIHS, John Brown to Moses Brown, 17 Nov. 1797, Moses Brown correspondence (https://repository.library.brown.edu/studio/item/bdr:303540/). For John Brown's slaving activities, see James B. Hedges, *The Browns of Providence Plantations: Colonial Years* (Cambridge, MA, 1952), 82–4.

Brown concerning his illegal shipment of slaves in an American vessel to Cuba. John Brown, who had been outspoken in his support for the slave trade, was accused of being the main opponent to Rhode Island's law against the slave trade. He accused Moses and his fellow members of the Providence Abolition Society of vindictively singling him out for trial when other Rhode Islanders had a more extensive involvement in the trade.[229] John was put on trial. On 5 August 1797, he was found guilty of infringing the act of 1794 – for which his brother Moses had lobbied – by sending out a vessel intended to carry slaves. His penalty was the forfeiture of the ship, which was sold at public auction. A number of other prosecutions followed but the first of these did not occur until 1799.[230] After being found guilty of ignoring the 1794 act, John Brown assured Moses that he would never, either directly or indirectly, be involved in the trade again; he wanted 'all disputes on the abolition business closed & the hatchet buried'.[231]

It proved difficult to enforce the 1794 act because the United States Treasury Department, which had jurisdiction over the law, failed to send instructions about enforcement to customs officials. A second act of 1800 extended the scope of prohibition, increased the penalties to include imprisonment for a maximum of two years and authorised US naval ships to take slave vessels as prizes. It forbade US citizens from ownership in a slaving vessel, whether American or foreign, and Americans were barred from serving aboard such vessels. A $200 penalty and a two-year gaol sentence could be brought against seamen who flouted this stipulation. Naval commanders were enjoined to detain anyone found on captured slaving vessels and to transport them to US soil for trial. These two acts therefore attempted to suppress American participation in the slave trade without having any authority to prohibit slave imports to US ports.[232] By late 1799, rumours circulated that John Adams's administration intended to support a congressional repeal of the 1794 act, but it was

---

[229] RIHS, John Brown to Moses Brown, 29 July 1797, Moses Brown correspondence (https://repository.library.brown.edu/studio/item/bdr:303537/).
[230] Coughtry, *The Notorious Triangle*, 93, 212–22; Marques, *The United States and the Transatlantic Slave Trade*, 34; Massachusetts HS, Boston, Theodore Foster to Dwight Foster, 6 Mar. 1798, Dwight Foster Papers.
[231] RIHS, John Brown to Moses Brown, 17 Nov. 1797, 28 Aug. 1798 (quotation), Moses Brown correspondence.
[232] Coughtry, *The Notorious Triangle*, 93, 212–22; Fehrenbacher and McAfee, *The Slaveholding Republic*, 140, 382, n. 25.

noted that such action would be 'as indignantly received as a proposal for legalizing piracy, arson or murder'.[233]

On 11 December 1799, two Northern representatives put forward the case for both houses of Congress to alter the 1794 law. Both houses set up committees to consider the subject.[234] In April 1800, the House of Representatives resolved itself into a committee on a bill from the Senate dealing with an act to prohibit carrying on the slave trade to any foreign place or country. In the debate over this bill, it was pointed out that the law did not prevent the exportation of slaves from Africa. James A. Bayard of Delaware argued that it would be dishonourable for Congress to support such a bill that was 'contrary to all those principles held dear in the United States, and which ought to be promoted'.[235] John Rutledge, Jr of South Carolina supported this view, arguing that it was one of the most defective bills that had ever come before Congress. The committee was discharged on 28 April 1800. Six congressmen voted against the bill, including John Brown, but the legislation was enacted.[236]

However, divergence occurred over what should happen next. Bayard hoped the bill would be referred to a select committee but Rutledge opposed this, arguing that the bill was unnecessary because the former act of 1794 had already done everything that was necessary or practicable to be done. A motion for a recommitment 'was carried by a very large majority' in the House of Representatives.[237] On 3 May, after a lively debate, and after several attempts to postpone the measure, the House voted by 67 votes to 5 to pass the bill prohibiting the slave trade to any foreign country. Two of the five dissenting votes came from South Carolina (which had four representatives), and one each came from congressmen for Rhode Island, Maryland and North Carolina. Neither of Georgia's two representatives opposed the bill.[238]

SOUTH CAROLINA AND THE SLAVE TRADE

Proscription on federal intervention over the slave trade until 1808 meant that restriction of slave imports had still to proceed on a state-by-state basis. This remained the only way to tackle the problem in the Federalist

---

[233] Connecticut HS, Hartford, Oliver Wolcott to Davis L. Barnes, 4 Oct. 1799, Oliver Wolcott, Jr Papers.
[234] Ohline, 'Politics and Slavery'. 252.
[235] *Annals of Congress*, 6th Congress, 1st session, House of Representatives, 28 Apr. 1800, 688.
[236] Ibid.   [237] Ibid., 689–90 (quotation on 690).   [238] Ibid., 3 May 1800, 699–700.

era even though influential figures, such as John Adams when vice president, favoured prohibition of the importation of 'new Negroes'.[239] Restrictions on slave imports to individual states came about through as many diverse factors as had been the case in the colonial era, except that now the spectre of slave rebellion was more potent because of resonances occurring from the dramatic disruption to the French Caribbean slave society in Saint-Domingue in the 1790s, resulting from a massive slave revolt there. In Saint-Domingue, over 100,000 slaves rose up and defeated their French overlords in the one large slave victory in a rebellion in the modern world. The cataclysmic events in that French Caribbean territory send shockwaves around the western world.

In South Carolina, the struggle over slave importation had been acrimonious ever since the American Revolution.[240] South Carolina kept its slave trade closed between 1787 and 1803 because it suited the state's leading politicians to do so. Though the slave trade was discussed in legislative sessions, no roll call votes on this subject were conducted between 1793 and 1801.[241] In 1791, the slave trade was discussed in two sessions in the South Carolina legislature – in February and December. Governor Thomas Pinckney wrote that 'great pains were used to effect a total prohibition, but upon the question being taken in the Senate it was lost by so decided a majority that I think we may consider it as certain this state will after March 1793 import as largely as they ever did'.[242]

In 1792 fears over slave insurrection – stimulated by the spread of rebellious ideas, inspired by the emphasis on liberty, equality and fraternity of the French Revolution emanating from the Saint-Domingue slave revolt – induced South Carolina to keep the slave trade closed.[243]

---

[239] John Adams to Jeremy Belknap, 22 Oct. 1795, in Sara Georgini, Sara Martin, R. M. Barlow, Gwen Fries, Amanda M. Norton and Hobson Woodward, eds., *The Adams Papers: Papers of John Adams. Volume 21. March 1791–January 1797* (Cambridge, MA, 2022), 418.

[240] Mark D. Kaplanoff, 'Making the South Solid: Politics and the Structure of Society in South Carolina, 1790–1815' (University of Cambridge PhD dissertation, 1979), 60.

[241] Patrick S. Brady, 'The Slave Trade and Sectionalism in South Carolina, 1787–1808', *JSH*, 38/4 (1972), 608.

[242] Michael E. Stevens and Christine M. Allen, eds., *The State Records of South Carolina: Journals of the House of Representatives 1791* (Columbia, SC, 1986), xvii; Charles Pinckney to George Washington, 8 Jan. 1792, in Mark A. Mastromarino, ed., *The Papers of George Washington. Presidential Series. Volume 9. 23 September 1791–29 February 1792* (Charlottesville, VA, 2000), 404–6.

[243] Brady, 'The Slave Trade and Sectionalism', 609; Lacy K. Ford, *Deliver Us from Evil: The Slavery Question in the Old South* (New York, 2009), 84–5.

Carolinians worried that republican ideas would spread to their state if Frenchmen migrated there and circulated their political views among slaves.[244] Ralph Izard feared French revolutionary ideas would spread and 'cannot fail of producing a convulsion which will be severely felt by the southern states'. In such circumstances, 'the property in Negroes will be rendered of no value'.[245] The closure of South Carolina's slave trade was maintained for the rest of the 1790s. It proved difficult, however, for South Carolina's public officials to implement the prohibition of slave importation according to the legislative acts passed on 21 December 1792 and 20 December 1794.[246]

Support for keeping the slave trade to South Carolina closed in 1792 was expressed in a petition from a citizens' committee in St Luke's parish. This claimed that Virginia had been sending slaves southwards, which was seen as detrimental to peace in the wake of the spread of potential slave uprisings. The petition also expressed disapproval of the formation of abolition societies in other states. Pierce Butler argued that 'if our state legislature do not pass some laws to prevent the importation of Negroes from the West Indies, and if in their power from the northern states, our Property in Carolina is held by a slender tye I would include Virginia Negroes among the proscribed if it can be done for they are strongly tinctured'.[247]

The South Carolinian planter Gabriel Manigault was firmly opposed to slave importation. He thought the state's House of Representatives should continue to agree to stop the traffic but was apprehensive that the Senate would determine otherwise.[248] In the event, Manigault's wishes were granted. James Green Hunt, a representative from Richland District, brought in a bill to ban domestic slave imports forever and imports of Africans for four years. The House of Representatives changed the latter provision to two years. In December 1792, the South Carolina legislature, partly influenced by the successful slave revolt in Saint-Domingue, considered these measures and voted 64–41 to pass an act to ban the

---

[244] SCL, Ralph Izard to Matthias Hutchinson, 20 Nov. 1794, Ralph Izard Papers.
[245] HSP, Ralph Izard to Edward Rutledge, 28 Sept. 1792, Ralph Izard Papers.
[246] SCDAH, A. Vanderhorst to the President and the Senate, 1 Dec. 1795, General Assembly: Governors' Messages.
[247] SCL, Pierce Butler to John Bee Holmes, 5 Nov. 1793, Pierce Butler letterbook (1792–6).
[248] SCL, Gabriel Manigault to Mrs Gabriel Manigault, 7 Dec. 1792, Manigault Family MSS, box 1.

domestic slave trade altogether and to prevent slave importations into the state for two years from 1 January 1793.²⁴⁹

The official record of the debate includes few details but the clerk's notes indicated that eight members of the House spoke in favour of the ban (including Edward Rutledge and Henry Laurens, Jr) and five opposed it (including John Drayton and John Rutledge, Jr, former chief justice of South Carolina).²⁵⁰ The debates were contentious, divisive and long-winded. Many planters strongly opposed prohibition of the slave trade, and this increased in proportion as their estates were cleared of debt.²⁵¹ Gabriel Manigault reported on 7 December that 'we have had today a most tedious debate on the subject of stopping the importation of Negroes for four years, & adjourned without coming to any determination, but shall resume it tomorrow. Two members spoke between them three hours, & you can have no idea how tedious it was'.²⁵² The Senate passed the bill by nineteen votes to fifteen and the House rejected an attempt to overturn it by fifty-seven votes to thirty-eight.²⁵³

In December 1794, the South Carolina legislature extended this act until 1 January 1797.²⁵⁴ At this time slave imports into South Carolina from other states were also banned.²⁵⁵ In December 1796, the same body considered it 'highly impolitic to import Negroes from Africa' and therefore brought in an act to abolish the importation of enslaved Africans into the state until 1 January 1799. In 1797, Duke de la Rochefoucault Liancourt, travelling through South Carolina, thought it likely that those in favour of keeping the slave trade closed would prevail in the state legislature. He supported his view by noting that the demand for South

---

²⁴⁹ *Acts of the General Assembly of the State of South Carolina, from February, 1791, to December, 1794, Both Inclusive. Volume 1* (Columbia, SC, 1808), 215–16; Michael E. Stevens, ed., *The State Records of South Carolina: Journals of the House of Representatives 1792–1794* (Columbia, SC, 1988), xiv–xv; Ford, *Deliver Us from Evil*, 84.
²⁵⁰ Stevens, ed., *The State Records of South Carolina: Journals of the House of Representatives 1792–1794*, xv.
²⁵¹ Duke de la Rochefoucault Liancourt, *Travels through the United States of North America, the Country of the Iroquois, and Upper Canada, in the Years 1795, 1796, and 1797: With an Authentic Account of Lower Canada*, 2 vols. (London, 1799), I, 575.
²⁵² SCL, Gabriel Manigault to Mrs Gabriel Manigault, 7 Dec. 1792, Manigault Family MSS, box 1.
²⁵³ Stevens, ed., *The State Records of South Carolina: Journals of the House of Representatives 1792–1794*, xv.
²⁵⁴ *Acts of the General Assembly of the State of South Carolina, from February 1791, to December, 1794*, 391–3.
²⁵⁵ Ford, *Deliver Us from Evil*, 85.

Carolina indigo had increased and, as a result, less slaves were needed in the backcountry to cultivate it instead of corn, wheat and tobacco.[256]

In 1798, Governor Charles Pinckney warned about any slave or free person of colour being imported into South Carolina from the French West Indies. The South Carolina legislature later passed further acts to extend the prohibition on imported slaves until 1 January 1801 and then to 1 January 1803.[257] Cotton planters in South Carolina's backcountry had pressurised the state legislature to resume slave importations in 1802 but a vote of 86–11 turned down the proposal.[258]

During the 1790s, South Carolina exhibited a clear sectional divide on the slave trade. Inland planters from upcountry areas wanted to maintain the flow of slave imports into the Palmetto state because they needed new labourers for their plantations. Planters in lowcountry areas, however, many of whom had been established for decades before the growth of upcountry agricultural enterprise, wanted to close the slave trade to Charleston because they had surplus slaves and feared the introduction of Africans into communities with a high black majority would cause social instability. However, agriculturalists in South Carolina were less concerned about acculturated slaves arriving in the state from neighbouring states. Thus, in 1803, no lowcountry representative supported a ban on the importation of slaves into South Carolina from other states while more than two-thirds of the upcountry representatives hoped the influx would occur. Two years later, upcountry senators blocked another proposed ban on slave imports.[259]

PROHIBITING THE SLAVE TRADE IN VARIOUS STATES

In 1794, North Carolina finally prohibited the legal trade in slaves after seven years in which it first laid duties on slave imports (in 1787) and then (in 1790) repealed that statute. Tennessee adopted North Carolina's prohibition when it became a state in 1796. In 1798, Congress forbade slave importation from abroad into the Mississippi Territory (later

---

[256] Liancourt, *Travels through the United States of North America*, 578.
[257] *Acts of the General Assembly of the State of South-Carolina, from December, 1795, to December, 1804, Both Inclusive*. Volume II (Columbia, SC, 1808), 90–1, 215–16, 339, 344; Rachel N. Klein, *Unification of a Slave State: The Rise of the Planter Class in the South Carolina Backcountry, 1760–1808* (Chapel Hill, NC, 1990), 234.
[258] Marques, *The United States and the Transatlantic Slave Trade*, 49; Kaplanoff, 'Making the South Solid', 62.
[259] Klein, *Unification of a Slave State*, 254–5.

comprising parts of the states of Alabama and Mississippi). This was extended, in 1804, to a congressional ban on slaves imported to the Orleans Territory and to the rest of the Louisiana Purchase south of the 33rd parallel (incorporated into the American Union in 1812 as the state of Louisiana).[260] These actions imply that Congress wished to act to end the slave trade to the United States, but at this time it could only do so constitutionally for the territories rather than the existing states. In 1793, Georgia passed an act prohibiting slave imports from the West Indies, the Bahamas and Florida, a statute inspired by fears of the spread of slave unrest from Saint-Domingue. But in 1794, Georgia was still importing 'that unhappy race of mankind'.[261] Georgia permanently outlawed the slave trade from Africa in its new state constitution of 1798 and by an act in its legislature in the same year. At the same time the Georgia legislature also banned the interstate slave trade.[262]

After that decision, all US states were, in fact, closed to slave imports. But this did not mean that African arrivals ended at American ports, because there was the option, backed by the Constitution, for states to reopen their harbours to slave imports if they so wished. In other words, proscription by degrees, on a state basis, could never fully end the African slave trade to the United States. Thus, a petition by Philadelphia's black residents in 1800 calling for a ban on slave imports to the United States was doomed to failure. Introduced in Congress by Robert Waln, a wealthy Quaker representative from Pennsylvania, it drew indignation from opponents of slave trade restriction, notably John Rutledge Jr.[263] The growth and spread of slavery into the western federal territories, and the increased productivity of cotton production after the invention in 1793 of the cotton gin, meant that slaves were drawn away from states such as South Carolina where economic circumstances might lead to their replacement by Africans. These imports might comprise illegal shipments

---

[260] W. E. Minchinton, 'The Seaborne Slave Trade of North Carolina', *North Carolina Historical Review*, 71/1 (1994), 17–18; Robinson, *Slavery in the Structure of American Politics*, 297, 299; Fehrenbacher and McAfee, *The Slaveholding Republic*, 136.

[261] Haverford College Library, Quaker Collection, Robert Pleasants to John Eliot, 9 June 1794, Robert Pleasants letterbook (1754–97), fol. 221.

[262] Ruth Scarborough, *The Opposition to Slavery in Georgia prior to 1860* (Nashville, TN, 1933), 108–10; Ford, *Deliver Us from Evil*, 86; William Omer Foster, Sr, *James Jackson: Duelist and Militant Statesman 1757–1806* (Athens, GA, 1960), 89.

[263] Nash, *Race and Revolution*, 79; Jordan, *White over Black*, 328.

of slaves or legitimate disembarkation of Africans in any state that chose to reopen its slave trade.[264]

In 1803, an act of Congress for the first time forbade the importation of 'any negro, mulatto, or other person of colour' to states that banned the foreign slave trade. The wording, perhaps taking its cue from the Constitution, meant, but did not state, slaves. The act authorised government officials to intervene in instances where this occurred. It received firm southern support and was given impetus by fears of an influx of troublesome slaves and free blacks from the French West Indies. The implementation of enforcement immediately by the US collector of customs at Charleston, by seizing a brig recently arrived with enslaved Africans, alarmed planters and played its part in South Carolina's reopening of the slave trade in late 1803, which brought around 40,000 captives through Charleston in four years. These came from West Africa. A ban on importing slaves into South Carolina from the Caribbean was retained because of fears that West Indian slaves might bring with them the spirit of defiance demonstrated in the Saint-Domingue slave revolt.[265]

CONCLUSION

The slave trade was immediately raised as a matter for debate in the First Federal Congress. In February and March 1790, Quaker petitions on the subject were presented to both the House of Representatives and the Senate. Members of the Pennsylvania Abolition Society, a body mainly composed of Quakers, took the lead in presenting these memorials and some of their members, notably James Pemberton and Warner Mifflin, were especially active in providing support through lobbying, correspondence and meetings with prominent political figures who were thought amenable to favourable discussion on the subject. Plenty of contemporary commentary survives on the presentation and reception of the petitions. The South Carolina delegates in Congress tried hard to divert attention away from the moral claims of the memorialists. The issue proved to be too divisive for extensive consideration by Congress at a time when politicians were putting all their efforts into the smooth and sustained

---

[264] Fehrenbacher and McAfee, *The Slaveholding Republic*, 141.
[265] Ibid., 141-2; Adam Rothman, *Slave Country: American Expansion and the Origins of the Deep South* (Cambridge, MA, 2005), 38.

operation of a national government. James Madison realised prolonged attention to the petitions would be too divisive within that context, and he carefully arranged that the petitions should be placed on the table of Congress but not further considered. Madison made the point that Congress was forbidden from interference with the slave trade on a national level until at least 1808, but he encouraged anti-slave trade campaigners to continue their attacks on aspects of the slave trade that fell outside the remit of Article 1, Section 9.

For most of the 1790s, the American Convention of Abolition Societies met annually to coordinate anti-slave trade activity and to pressurise Congress to act in relation to those aspects of the slave trade where it could legitimately intervene. Many petitions, letters and memoranda followed but the American Convention of Abolition Societies never translated their good intentions into a wide-ranging anti-slave trade campaign. It proved difficult, for instance, to sustain networks beyond the main Quaker core of those societies. Eventually, the limitations of the abolition societies were exposed; in 1798, the American Convention of Abolition Societies started to hold meetings biennially; and by 1806, the frequency of meetings had further declined. Despite this diminution of the vigour and impact of the abolition societies, they did pressurise Congress to introduce laws in 1794 and 1800 to restrict the participation of American citizens in the foreign slave trade. The 1794 act was the first law passed by Congress to restrict slave trading at a national level. It forbade Americans from being concerned in ships fitting out for Africa from US ports and succeeded because it made no attempt to tamper with slave importation, thereby avoiding the restrictions imposed by Article 1, Section 9 of the Constitution. The act of 1800 forbade the continuance of the slave trade to any foreign country. Though some prosecutions occurred for those charged with breaking these laws, it proved quite difficult for the legislation to be enforced.

The elephant in the room of slave trade restriction in the 1790s was South Carolina, which kept its ports closed to African importations throughout the decade and up to 1803 after repeated renewals of the 1787 measure taken in that state to close the slave trade. Abolitionist activity had little impact on the closures. Instead, prohibiting slave imports resulted from the South Carolina legislature deciding that the economic demand for slave labour was low during that period. But this was a contentious matter, for a sectional divide had emerged in South Carolina between upland planters who needed to recruit additional

Africans to grow cotton and indigo and tidewater planters who had sufficient black workers cultivating rice. Many smuggled slaves were brought into South Carolina at the turn of the nineteenth century and it only needed (as indeed happened) a change in the state's prospective economic circumstance to put pressure on a change to laws relating to the slave trade.

5

Final Controversies over the US Slave Trade, 1803–1807

The year 1803 was important in the history of the slave trade to the United States because, on 16 December, South Carolina reopened its borders to slave imports with no time restriction.[1] This bold move occurred when all the states in the union had closed their slave trades.[2] The scale of imports amounted to 44,450 Africans brought by US vessels, 19,327 on British vessels and 86 on Danish vessels, presumably US- or British-owned, between 1804 and 1808 – more than twice as many as in any previous five-year period in South Carolina's history.[3] These arrivals augmented the size of the Palmetto state's slave population, which had shown signs of natural increase from the early 1750s, from 97,170 in 1800 to 110,711 in 1810.[4] Substantial slaveholding benefited staple crop production mainly for export markets and enabled South Carolina's planters to achieve financial gains. A contemporary estimated that the richest planters in the state in the first decade of the nineteenth century drew a yearly revenue from their slaves to the amount of $40–50,000

---

[1] *Charleston Courier*, 21 Dec. 1803.
[2] St George Tucker, 'Blackstone's Commentaries 1: App. 290, 1803' in Philip B. Kurland and Ralph Lerner, eds., *The Founders' Constitution. Volume Three. Article 1, Section 8, Clause 5 through Article 2, Section 1* (Chicago, 1987), 297.
[3] Estimates taken from www.slavevoyages.org. See also Leonardo Marques, *The United States and the Transatlantic Slave Trade to the Americas, 1776–1867* (New Haven, CT, 2016), 20; Ira Berlin, *Many Thousands Gone: The First Two Centuries of Slavery in North America* (Cambridge, MA, 1998), 308.
[4] Philip D. Morgan, 'Black Society in the Lowcountry, 1760–1810' in Ira Berlin and Ronald Hoffman, eds., *Slavery and Freedom in the Age of the American Revolution* (Charlottesville, VA, 1983), 85.

while many other planters enjoyed an annual income of $12–20,000 from their slaves.[5]

South Carolina's attachment to the slave trade reflected commercial greed. After it reopened in 1803, it was 'followed with an eagerness which the thirst for gold ever stimulates: no matter through what unworthy means it may be obtained'. A critic of 'the horrid traffic' noted that 'all the other states have prohibited the admission of fresh slaves, while South Carolina alone, regardless of the stigma, continues the importation with double exertion'.[6] But South Carolina also reopened its slave trade for several other reasons: the need to supply the state with new black workers to maximise cotton production; the intention that a legal supply of slaves would eradicate illegal shipments from the Caribbean; the possibility, and perhaps probability, that Congress would prohibit slave importations to the United States in 1808; and the prospects held out by the Louisiana Purchase of 1803, achieved through a treaty of cession, to extend slavery to vast new western territories bought from Spain and France. This important land acquisition, which doubled the territory of the United States, was ratified by the federal government in November 1803, just one month before South Carolina reopened its slave trade.[7] This had implications for debates over the slave trade because Louisiana already had a multiethnic population boosted by slave deliveries by the Spanish and French and close connections with Saint-Domingue. Whether Congress would prohibit the slave trade into Louisiana was then unknown, though the act incorporating the territory into the United States (26 March 1804) declared the trade illegal.[8]

The Louisiana Purchase was partly made possible by the destruction of the French armies in Saint-Domingue, which had led Napoleon to abandon his plan to use North America to provide food supplies to the French

---

[5] Charles William Janson, *The Stranger in America: Containing Observations Made in a Long Residence in that Country, on the Genius, Manners and Customs of the People of the United States; with Biographical Particulars of Public Characters; Hints and Facts relative to the Arts, Sciences, Commerce, Agriculture, Manufactures, Emigration, and the Slave Trade* (London, 1807), 356.
[6] Both quotations are taken from ibid., 359.
[7] Jed Handelsman Shugerman, 'The Louisiana Purchase and South Carolina's Reopening of the Slave Trade in 1803', *Journal of the Early Republic*, 22/2 (2002), 253–90. See also Carl Harrison Brown, 'The Reopening of the Foreign Slave Trade in South Carolina, 1803–1807' (University of South Carolina MA thesis, 1968).
[8] J. R. Oldfield, *Transatlantic Abolitionism in the Age of Revolution: An International History of Anti-slavery, c. 1787–1820* (Cambridge, 2013), 174.

Caribbean.⁹ The cotton boom in Georgia and South Carolina could now extend westwards within US jurisdiction to Louisiana and its important port of New Orleans, which could acquire African slaves from Charleston. Louisiana was divided into a large upper portion designated the 'District of Louisiana' and a smaller southern district named 'the Orleans Territory', which became the state of Louisiana on 30 April 1812. The division between the two parts of Louisiana was drawn at the 33rd parallel.¹⁰

The fact that 3,000 illegally smuggled slaves had arrived in South Carolina between 1800 and 1803 indicated a continuing demand for fresh supplies of African captives and helped arguments in favour of reopening the state's importation of slaves. Indeed, in his annual message of 1803 the planter James B. Richardson, South Carolina's new governor, had given his opinion that the slave trade could not be stopped.¹¹ A coalition of upcountry planters needing workers to meet the cotton boom and lowcountry planters recognising business opportunities was instrumental in persuading South Carolina's legislature to reopen the trade, though some representatives opposed the decision.¹² Those who favoured keeping the slave trade closed argued that freshly imported slaves would devalue the state's existing slave population and add to fears of domestic security.¹³ But these apprehensions were overcome. In a message of 24 November 1803 Richardson argued that smuggling of slaves into South Carolina was rife, despite the prohibition. He was supported in his arguments by a statement made in Congress by the lawyer and planter William Lowndes.¹⁴ He defended the repeal of the

---

⁹ James Alexander (Alec) Dun, 'Atlantic Antislavery, American Ambition: The Problem of Slavery in the United States in an Age of Disruption, 1770–1808' in Andrew Shankman, ed., *The World of the Revolutionary American Republic: Land, Labor, and the Conflict for a Continent* (New York, 2014), 237.

¹⁰ Padraig Riley, *Slavery and the Democratic Conscience: Political Life in Jeffersonian America* (Philadelphia, 2016), 102, 104.

¹¹ John Harold Wolfe, *Jeffersonian Democracy in South Carolina* (Chapel Hill, NC, 1940), 189. Most of Richardson's speech is transcribed and printed in Brown, 'The Reopening of the Foreign Slave Trade', appendix A, 62–3. See also the *Charleston Courier*, 5 Dec. 1803.

¹² Lacy K. Ford, *Deliver Us from Evil: The Slavery Question in the Old South* (New York, 2009), 96–102, 105. For some views of those opposing the decision, see Wolfe, *Jeffersonian Democracy in South Carolina*, 190.

¹³ Marques, *The United States and the Transatlantic Slave Trade to the Americas*, 49.

¹⁴ Ulrich B. Phillips, *American Negro Slavery: A Study of the Supply, Employment, and Control of Negro Labor as Determined by the Plantation Regime* (New York, 1918), 136; *Charleston Courier*, 5 Dec. 1803; Ford, *Deliver Us from Evil*, 96.

South Carolina prohibitory act against the slave trade in 1803 on the grounds that the state had been unable to enforce the law and had received no assistance in this regard from Congress.[15] The governor initially wanted to close the slave trade, arguing that slave imports would increase 'our weakness, not our strength'.[16] But he later urged the South Carolina Assembly to reopen the trade because the ban had an uneven impact on different parts of the state. Enforcement of the ban was difficult because many South Carolinians sympathised with smugglers of illegal slaves.[17] An article in Boston and New York newspapers sympathised with this view, noting that the South Carolina legislature had proved ineffectual in preventing the large-scale smuggling of slaves into the state 'to the injury of those, who conformed to the laws; and to the advantage of those who infringed them'.[18]

This chapter concentrates on the views expressed and actions undertaken in relation to the final years of the slave trade to the United States. South Carolina was the one state on the eastern seaboard that could take substantial numbers of Africans in the first decade of the nineteenth century. Accordingly, it assumes centre stage in this chapter, as developments with regard to slave importations at both state and national level are considered. Fierce arguments still raged between supporters and opponents of the slave trade. Within South Carolina, the debates were contentious and by no means one-sided. Votes were taken regularly in the state legislature about the slave trade. This chapter considers the reasons for the reopening of South Carolina's slave trade in 1803 after sixteen years of closure, and it does so particularly in relation to the acquisition of Louisiana and its potential for absorbing Africans to work on its sugar and cotton plantations. In late 1806, Thomas Jefferson issued a presidential message looking forward optimistically to the date in 1808 when Congress had the power to intervene constitutionally over the slave trade.[19] This brought the slave trade once again to the attention of the

---

[15] Mary Stoughton Locke, *Anti-slavery in America: From the Introduction of African Slaves to the Prohibition of the Slave Trade (1619–1808)* (Boston, 1901), 143, n. 2.
[16] Quoted in Patrick S. Brady, 'The Slave Trade and Sectionalism in South Carolina, 1787-1808', *JSH*, 38/4 (1972), 617.
[17] Ford, *Deliver Us from Evil*, 97; Brown, 'The Reopening of the Foreign Slave Trade', 5.
[18] Anonymous article from the *Boston Gazette* reprinted in the *New-York Commercial Advertiser*, 22 Sept. 1804.
[19] Kenneth Morgan, 'Proscription by Degrees: The Ending of the African Slave Trade to the United States' in David T. Gleeson and Simon Lewis, eds., *Ambiguous Anniversary: The Bicentennial of the International Slave Trade Bans* (Columbia, SC, 2012), 1.

federal legislature. In the ensuing debates in Congress, technical issues were raised over the means by which the slave trade could be proscribed, but there was virtually no debate about the morality of trafficking in Africans. A congressional bill passed in 1807 ended the slave trade to the United States from 1 January 1808.

THE REOPENING OF SOUTH CAROLINA'S SLAVE TRADE

South Carolina's decision to reopen the slave trade demonstrated a rapid shift in the state's political decision-making, but it involved highly complex manoeuvring on a contentious and divisive issue. In 1802, the South Carolina Senate voted to continue the ban on slave imports without a roll call, while the House of Representatives voted 86–11 to keep the trade closed. Only seven backcountry and four lowcountry votes were registered for reopening. However, in late 1803, with virtually the same membership in both houses, the situation was reversed and the House voted 55–46 to reopen. The backcountry voted 30–19 in favour; the lowcountry voted 27–25 against.[20] The Senate and the House of Representatives came to different conclusions about slave importations. The Senate sent to the House a bill for reopening the trade on 6 December 1803. The House was less enthusiastic about reopening and set up a five-person committee, dominated by anti-slave trade representatives, who drafted a bill to prevent slave importation.[21]

The Senate bill to repeal all laws preventing slave imports on 6 December 1803 was challenged by Robert Barnwell, who had served in the revolutionary war, had been a member of the Continental Congress and would later be elected as Speaker of the South Carolina House of Representatives.[22] He argued that it would lead to an oversupply of slaves and a depreciation of commodities based on slave labour that would ruin the state's commerce: 'Our citizens would purchase at all hazards, and

---

[20] Ford, *Deliver Us from Evil*, 98; Shugerman, 'The Louisiana Purchase and South Carolina's Reopening of the Slave Trade', 264, n.2, 271, 279; SCDAH, entry for 18 Dec. 1802 in South Carolina Senate Journal (1802).

[21] Ford, *Deliver Us from Evil*, 98–9; SCDAH, entry for 9 Dec. 1803 in South Carolina House of Representatives Journal (1803). See also Brown, 'The Reopening of the Foreign Slave Trade', 6. It should be noted that neither the House of Representatives Journal nor the Senate Journal summarised discussions and debates. Thus, one can find details of amendments to bills, the roll call votes and the names of representatives voting in the affirmative or negative, but that is all.

[22] Brown, 'The Reopening of the Foreign Slave Trade', 7.

trust to fortunate crops and favorable markets for making their payments; and it would be found that South Carolina would in a few years, if this trade continued open, be in the same situation of debt, and subject to all the misfortunes which the situation had produced, as at the conclusion of the revolutionary war.' Barnwell feared over-speculation in purchasing slaves would occur after the trade was reopened.[23] He proved to be in the minority, however, because most of his fellow legislators wanted the slave trade to reopen to South Carolina.[24] As Carl Harrison Brown has put it, 'the real crux of the problem was that the demand for labor in South Carolina overshadowed the intense fear of a servile revolt' even though the tense and volatile situation in Saint-Domingue had stoked fears of rebellious ideas spreading from the French Caribbean to the Palmetto state.[25]

The shenanigans over whether to reopen the slave trade continued in both houses of South Carolina's legislature. Lacy K. Ford has provided the best analysis of the political decisions. Here are the details. On 14 December 1803, an amendment to open the domestic slave trade but not the foreign slave trade was defeated 66–36. Lowcountry representatives voted unanimously (56–0) against the measure. Then the House of Representatives defeated a bill to continue the prohibition of both the foreign and domestic slave trades by 58–45. More than a third of the lowcountry representatives voted to defeat continued prohibition. Their voting proved crucial in preparing the ground to reopen the slave trade. On 17 December a bill prepared by the Senate was passed by a 55–7 vote in favour of reopening both the foreign and domestic slave trade. Lowcountry representatives from parishes south of Charleston were crucial in securing the passage of the bill. Three factors affected the vote for reopening: Africans could be imported to support cotton cultivation in the Sea Island districts, a chain of over a hundred tidal and barrier islands off the Atlantic coast of South Carolina and Georgia; family, friends and constituents could benefit from a revival of slave importations; and there was an extensive demand for slaves arriving at Charleston and intended for the Louisiana Territory. Thus, within one year, the political sentiment in South Carolina towards reopening the slave trade had altered.[26]

[23] *Charleston Courier*, 26 Dec. 1803 (quotation); Theodore D. Jervey, *The Slave Trade: Slavery and Color* (Columbia, SC, 1925), 24.
[24] 'Debate on the Importation of Negroes, 1803' in Donnan, ed., *Documents*, IV, 502.
[25] Brown, 'The Reopening of the Foreign Slave Trade', 9.
[26] Ford, *Deliver Us from Evil*, 99–102. On the reopening of South Carolina's slave trade in late 1803, see also Moses Young to Charles Pinckney, 9 Jan. 1804, in Constance

Divisions emerged within South Carolina towards reopening the foreign slave trade. Lowcountry legislators (supported by much public opinion) largely opposed reopening the slave traffic, while upcountry representatives favoured a law to this effect. In fact, upcountry legislators had been pressing for a reopening of South Carolina's slave trade for several years.[27] None of South Carolina's eight-member delegation to Congress nor any of the neighbouring states wished to see a resumption of slave imports.[28] A debate ensued over the right of South Carolina to impose a $10 tax on each imported slave but a bill intended to include this measure was delayed until 1806 and never passed into law.[29]

South Carolina's reopening of the slave trade in 1803 'shocked and outraged the rest of the nation'.[30] Among the adverse commentary on South Carolina's decision to reopen the slave trade was an incisive verdict in an extract from a letter reprinted from 1776 in the *National Intelligencer* (Washington, DC) in June 1804. The anonymous writer stated that 'it was not enacted by any law of this nation, nor of any state, that slaves might be imported. Men, *free* in 1776 in *Africa*, could not be transformed on any equitable or legal ground, into slaves in *America* in 1777'. The author argued that, after the Declaration of Independence, 'a slave could not afterwards be imported into these states'.[31] This was clearly not the case, as slave importation was still occurring three decades later. The former slave trader Thomas Branagan wrote a book in which he expressed the hope that American states would 'protest against the deleterious policy of a Sister state in renewing the slave trade' and would

---

B. Schulz, ed., *The Papers of the Revolutionary Era: Pinckney Statesmen: Digital Edition* (2016).

[27] Stephen J. Goldfarb, 'An Inquiry into the Politics of the Prohibition of the International Slave Trade', *Agricultural History*, 68/2 (1994), 29; Howard A. Ohline, 'Politics and Slavery: The Issue of Slavery in National Politics, 1787–1815' (University of Missouri, Columbia, PhD dissertation, 1969), 351.

[28] Elija H. Gould, *Among the Powers of the Earth: The American Revolution and the Making of a New World Empire* (Cambridge, MA, 2012), 161.

[29] Nicholas P. Wood, 'John Randolph of Roanoke and the Politics of Slavery in the Early Republic', *VMHB*, 120/2 (2012), 116.

[30] David Brion Davis, 'American Slavery and the American Revolution' in Ira Berlin and Ronald Hoffman, eds., *Slavery and Freedom in the Age of the American Revolution* (Charlottesville, VA, 1983), 267.

[31] 'Extract of a Letter to a Very Eminent & Venerable Public Character in the Delaware State, upon the Subject of the Revival of the Slave Trade in South-Carolina, Dated in the Spring of the Current Year', *National Intelligencer* (Washington, DC), 18 June 1804.

lobby for an amendment to the Federal Constitution to prohibit the further importation of slaves into the American republic.[32]

Northern newspapers offered scathing critiques on South Carolina's reopening of the slave trade. Here are some examples, all of which were published anonymously. A short article in the *Providence Gazette* in early 1804 condemned this move as a contradiction to American notions of liberty and equality. The writers cold not understand how 'these *good democrats* of South-Carolina, who pretend to be all on fire with love for the *rights* of *man* can deliberately sit down and frame a law by which every principle of justice and natural rights is violated'.[33] Another article, published in a Boston newspaper a few days later, also referring to the reopening of South Carolina's slave trade, stated that 'this abhorred traffic in human flesh calls for the severest reprehension of every government, and every man who countenances or upholds it'.[34] In June 1804, an article in Philadelphia's *Aurora General Advertiser* reminded South Carolina that every other state in the union 'seemed convinced of the injustice and impolicy of dealing in the commerce of the human species, and were doing all in their power to prevent it'. The article also referred to 'the entire abandonment of every noble feeling, by one of our sister states'.[35] A few months later, another article in the *Aurora General Advertiser*, referring to 'the trade in slaves we *deprecate* and *detest*', looked forward towards 'its complete and total abrogation in these states'.[36]

---

[32] Thomas Branagan, *Serious Remonstrances Addressed to the Citizens of the Northern States, and Their Representatives, Being an Appeal to Their Natural Feelings & Common Sense, Consisting of Speculations and Animadversions, the Recent Revival of the Slave Trade, in the American Republic* (Philadelphia, 1805), 27–8.

[33] 'Slave Trade', *Providence Gazette*, 11 Feb. 1804.

[34] 'Slave Trade', *Independent Chronicle*, 20 Feb. 1804.

[35] 'Slave Trade', *Aurora General Advertiser*, 14 June 1804, and 'Slave Trade', *The New Hampshire Gazette*, 3 July 1804. The article was reprinted south of the Mason-Dixon line: see 'Slave Trade', in the *Republican Star or Eastern Shore Advertiser*, 26 June 1804; the *Alexandria Expositor*, 21 June 1804; and the *Maryland Herald and Hager's Town Weekly Advertiser*, 27 June 1804. For further condemnation of South Carolina's reopening of the slave trade in northern newspapers, see 'The Slave Trade', *The Sun* (Pittsfield, Massachusetts), 26 Nov. 1804; 'Slave Trade' in *Spooner's Vermont Journal*, 11 Dec. 1804; and [South Carolina; Legislature] in *The Albany Register*, 4 June 1805. For a plea that Congress should abolish the slave trade to the United States without delay when it was constitutionally permitted to do so, see 'The Slave Trade' in *Republican Farmer* (Danbury, CT), 6 Nov. 1805.

[36] *Aurora General Advertiser*, 31 Dec. 1804.

Outside the state, the reopening of South Carolina's slave trade in 1803 had the broader implication that slave importations to the United States could not be fully proscribed by state laws.[37] The Virginian John Randolph, in a private letter, offering a stirring rebuttal of the traffic: 'I tremble for the dreadful retribution which this horrid thirst for African blood, which the legislators of that state [South Carolina] are base enough to feel yet more base enough to avow, may bring upon us.'[38] Randolph thought the reopening of the slave trade redounded to the 'indelible disgrace' of South Carolina, for 'she has legalized this abomination'.[39] Newspapers pointed out that South Carolina's decision went against the grain of current political opinion on the slave trade. 'Congress have repeatedly expressed their abhorrence of the slave trade', an article in *The Charleston Daily Courier* proclaimed in early 1806, 'by inflicting in all cases where they were allowed to make laws to operate, the most severe penalties on those who were concerned in this inhuman traffic'.[40]

Writing from Philadelphia, Thomas Branagan thought the southern states were upsetting the political balance of the American Union and the rights of non-slaveholding states by allowing more slave importations.[41] Ann Alexander of Philadelphia published a pamphlet imploring South Carolina to end the slave trade, 'which was so repugnant to every principle of humanity and justice',[42] Joseph Stanton of Rhode Island argued that South Carolina's decision to reopen the slave trade shook 'the pillars of public security' and 'tarnished the American character'.[43] Petitions were drawn up in Virginia, North Carolina and Tennessee to disapprove of South Carolina's reopening of the slave traffic.[44] Within South Carolina, at least two members of the state's House of Representatives opposed the slave trade on moral grounds.[45]

An article in the *Aurora General Advertiser* took stock of the situation as 1804 drew to a close:

---

[37] Locke, *Anti-Slavery in America*, 144.
[38] University of North Carolina, Chapel Hill, John Randolph to Littleton Waller Tazewell, 28 Jan. [1804], Randolph correspondence.
[39] Quoted in David Johnson, *John Randolph of Roanoke* (Baton Rouge, LA, 2012), 72.
[40] Letter from Friend Relf, 22 Jan. 1806, in *The Charleston Daily Courier*, 14 Feb. 1806.
[41] James Alexander Dun, *Dangerous Neighbours: Making the Haitian Revolution in Early America* (Philadelphia, 2016), 233.
[42] Ann Alexander, *An Address to the Inhabitants of Charleston, South Carolina* (Philadelphia, 1805), 5. An abbreviated version of her thoughts appeared in *Poulson's American Daily Advertiser* (Philadelphia), 19 June 1805.
[43] Quoted in Ford, *Deliver Us from Evil*, 105.   [44] Ibid.
[45] Brown, 'The Reopening of the Foreign Slave Trade,' 52.

Within the last two years ... a South Carolina legislature sanctioned, by a law, the further introduction of blacks: the public sentiment was decidedly and generally expressed against this measure, and congress undertook to legislate, but what was the result? – on the suggestion of a member that South Carolina herself would repeal the law, congress declined interfering. South Carolina, however, did not repeal the law, and at the commencement of the present session of congress it was hoped, a remedy would no longer be left unemployed.[46]

News of the reopening of South Carolina's slave trade was noticed across the Atlantic, for William Wilberforce, the leading anti-slave trade campaigner in the British parliament, was concerned about reopening the trade. He was pleased to hear, in 1804, from James Monroe, then United States minister to the United Kingdom, that the general sentiment prevailing in America opposed slave importation and that Congress would prohibit the traffic as soon as the law permitted. Wilberforce praised the honour of the United States in trying to put a stop to 'this unjust traffic' without the benefit of the same level of abolitionist campaigning on the issue as had occurred in Britain.[47] Two years later, however, Wilberforce informed Monroe that British abolitionists had been 'a good deal discouraged' by accounts of the extent to which the slave trade was carried on through the port of Charleston.[48]

In the autumn of 1804, an attempt was made in South Carolina's legislature to repeal the bill for reopening the foreign slave trade in the Senate; but on 8 December this was lost by one vote (17–16) with two absentees. It was ordered by the Senate that the yeas and nays be printed.[49] Six lowcountry senators voted with the backcountry to achieve this narrow result intended to keep slave importation open to the state. The House of Representatives, which had been slower to react to the situation, now made its views known. On 14 December 1804, it resolved by a vote of 69–39 that it was 'inexpedient and impolitic' to allow slave importation to the state. The loss of the measure in the Senate, however, meant that no change was made to the law. The conclusion of an anonymous writer in the *Aurora General Advertiser* (Philadelphia) was

---

[46] *Aurora General Advertiser*, 28 Dec. 1804.
[47] Wilberforce to Monroe, 6 and 7 June 1804, in Daniel Preston, ed., *The Papers of James Monroe. Volume 5. Selected Correspondence and Papers January 1803–April 1811* (Santa Barbara, CA, 2014), 228–9.
[48] Wilberforce to Monroe, 21 Aug. 1806, ibid., 515–16.
[49] SCDAH, entry for 8 Dec. 1804 in South Carolina Journals of the Senate (1804). The senators voting for and against South Carolina's slave trade bill in 1804, 1805 and 1806 are listed in Brown, 'The Reopening of the Foreign Slave Trade', appendix D, 71–2.

that 'this foul blot must remain for another year on the character of S. Carolina, for it cannot be said to stain that of the union'.[50] Another article in the same newspaper was afforded satisfaction by knowing that every other southern state was opposed to the introduction of slaves 'and are in favour of a gradual removal of the evil now existing'.[51]

The discrepancy between the majority of the House of Representatives being in favour of keeping South Carolina's slave trade closed and the narrowest of majorities in the Senate for opening it meant that the subject was revisited in the 1805 session. After a detailed debate in the House in December of that year, a bill prohibiting slave importation was subject to two proposed amendments – one dealing with an exception for slaves brought from any neighbouring states with an intention to live in South Carolina, the other stating that those bringing in slaves to South Carolina from sister states should be doing so for their own use and not for speculation. Both were easily defeated (by votes of 74–23 and 66–26, respectively).[52] The bill was then read for a second time in the South Carolina House of Representatives and sent to the Senate with a vote of 56–28.[53] The bill was rejected there by one vote – fifteen ayes versus sixteen nays.[54]

All restrictions on the African slave trade to South Carolina were now removed.[55] An immediate upsurge ensued in vessels bringing slave cargoes to Charleston.[56] The Africans imported were far in excess of the requirements of South Carolina's plantation economy. The surplus slaves were mainly reshipped to New Orleans and Natchez.[57] Slave importations continued 'in full activity' through to late 1805 even though the rest of Charleston's market activities were stagnant. The Africans were

---

[50] 'Slave Trade', *Aurora General Advertiser*, 8 Jan. 1805. [51] Ibid., 28 Dec. 1804.
[52] SCDAH, entry for 3 Dec. 1805 in South Carolina Journal of the House of Representatives (1805).
[53] Shugerman, 'The Louisiana Purchase and South Carolina's Reopening of the Slave Trade', 287; Jervey, *The Slave Trade*, 26–7, 30; *Charleston Courier*, 13 Dec. 1805; SCDAH, entry for 11 Dec. 1805 in South Carolina Journal of the House of Representatives (1805).
[54] SCDAH, entry for 14 Dec. 1805 in South Carolina Journals of the Senate (1805).
[55] Phillips, *American Negro Slavery*, 136–7; *Charleston Courier*, 26 Dec. 1803; *Charleston City Gazette*, 22 Dec. 1803.
[56] Lists of some of the ships bringing Africans to Charleston in 1804–6 are printed in 'Debate on the Importation of Negroes, 1803' in Donnan, ed., *Documents*, IV, 504–6, 508–9, 513–16.
[57] Matthew E. Mason, 'Slavery Overshadowed: Congress debates Prohibiting the Atlantic Slave Trade to the United States, 1806–1807', *Journal of the Early Republic*, 20/1 (2000), 62.

mainly sold to buyers from upcountry areas.[58] Though South Carolina's governor opposed this change, attempts to close the slave trade failed in 1804, 1805 and 1806.[59]

The law which reopened the slave trade to South Carolina in 1803 made a firm distinction between the importation of slaves from Africa and bringing in slaves from the Caribbean. Only the former were legally allowed. Slaves emanating in the West Indies were excluded from importation, with a special limitation placed upon slaves who had been resident in any of the French West Indian islands. Clearly, the spectre of slave resistance and rebelliousness from the Haitian slave revolt still carried a strong resonance.[60]

The revival of the slave trade to South Carolina had further ramifications. Throughout much of the South, the fear of slave revolt was strong at this time. Reopening the slave trade ran the risk of adding to the numbers of slaves likely to rebel.[61] In South Carolina itself, the incorporation of large numbers of Africans into the existing slave labour force between 1804 and 1807 led to some collective acts of resistance.[62] Beyond South Carolina, the reopening of the slave trade was widely deplored. As Winthrop D. Jordan wrote, 'when South Carolina reopened the slave trade the rest of the nation reacted as if orders had been placed for shiploads of rattlesnakes'.[63] The *Washington Expositor*, referring to 39,000 Africans brought to Charleston between 1804 and 1807, asked how anybody 'who prides himself upon the independence of his country' could react with anything other than embarrassment.[64]

Virginians attacked South Carolina for reopening the slave trade in 1803, but a notice in the *Charleston Courier* (22 January 1806) replied that this was a disingenuous argument that neglected to point out that Virginia's interstate domestic slave trade would be harmed by admitting

---

[58] SCL, Henry William De Saussure to Ezekiel Pickens, 10 Sept. 1805, Henry William de Saussure Papers, 1795–1837.
[59] Goldfarb, 'An Inquiry into the Politics', 29–30.
[60] Marques, *The United States and the Transatlantic Slave Trade*, 49.
[61] Adam Rothman, *Slave Country: American Expansion and the Origins of the Deep South* (Cambridge, MA, 2005), 37–8.
[62] Michael P. Johnson, 'Runaway Slaves and the Slave Communities in South Carolina, 1799 to 1830', WMQ, 3rd series, 38/3 (1981), 419.
[63] Winthrop D. Jordan, *White over Black: American Attitudes toward the Negro, 1550–1812* (Chapel Hill, NC, 1968), 400.
[64] Quoted in Gould, *Among the Powers of the Earth*, 161. The slave influx was actually larger than the figure cited here.

more Africans into Charleston.⁶⁵ In December 1804, the North Carolina legislature adopted resolutions to request that their congressmen seek to secure an amendment to the Federal Constitution to prohibit the further importation of slaves from Africa and the West Indies. These requests resulted in no definite action because politicians knew that it was only a matter of two or three years before Congress would have the constitutional right to take action on the slave trade.⁶⁶

Charleston newspapers in 1806, frequently published editorials attacking criticism of the state's slave trade from other states. Brushing aside considerations of morality, emphasis was laid on the importance of slave imports for the economic necessities of South Carolina in providing necessary labourers for land cultivation. One editorial explained that 'the delegates of the people when sitting in solemn general assembly, deemed it essentially necessary for the interest of the state to permit the importation of slaves from Africa, and those merchants who embark in this trade, do no more than carry the intentions and wishes of the government of their country into operation'.⁶⁷

Robin Blackburn has argued that South Carolina's reopening of the slave trade in 1803 'created a climate in which Congress was eager to prevent further imports as soon as possible'.⁶⁸ Thus, South Carolina's decision to reopen the slave trade in 1803 was largely criticised by Northern legislators. They realised slavery would grow in the Louisiana Territory now it was part of the United States, but they wanted to curtail the expansion by controlling slave importation. Against this position, though, South Carolina federalists fiercely countered the northern Jeffersonian attempt to tax African slave imports at a rate of $10 per imported slave.⁶⁹

This proposal stemmed from January 1804 when the Presbyterian legislator David Bard of Pennsylvania, who opposed slavery on religious grounds, introduced a resolution into Congress to impose such a tax on every slave imported into any part of the United States. This revived a proposal made by the Virginian Josiah Parker fifteen years earlier. At the

---

⁶⁵ Steven M. Deyle, *Carry Me Back: The Domestic Slave Trade in American Life* (New York, 2006), 24.
⁶⁶ Phillips, *American Negro Slavery*, 138–9.
⁶⁷ For example. *Charleston Courier*, 22 Jan., 10, 12 July 1806. The quotation is from 'Reply to Criticism of Slave Trade, 1806' in Donnan, ed., *Documents*, IV, 518.
⁶⁸ Robin Blackburn, *The Overthrow of Colonial Slavery, 1776–1848* (London, 1988), 286.
⁶⁹ Marques, *The United States and the Transatlantic Slave Trade*, 49; Riley, *Slavery and the Democratic Conscience*, 103, 108.

time Congress did not have the power to prohibit the slave trade altogether, but it did enjoy the power of taxation and that was what was proposed in order to restrict slave importation.[70]

Bard argued that slavery presented a national moral problem to the United States, and that Congress therefore needed to respond firmly to South Carolina's actions. Some Virginians supported the moral arguments made against South Carolina's continued participation in the slave trade.[71] Bard favoured preventing the increase of slaves coming into the United States, and he supported the gradual abolition of slavery. He considered his proposal justifiable on moral grounds, but did not think his resolution could be carried into law. At the time there was some prospect that South Carolina would close her harbours against slave importation at the next meeting of the state's legislature in May 1804. As a result, Bard thought it better to let the matter rest rather than such a bill be defeated.[72]

The proposal for a $10 tax on slaves was constitutionally legitimate for it was 'a proper subject of taxation'.[73] However, that was not the view of the lawyer and planter Thomas Lowndes of South Carolina when Bard's resolution as debated in the national House of Representatives on 14 March 1804. Lowndes opposed what he referred to as a complicated tax. South Carolina, he argued, would be unable to enforce such an impost because it would be impossible to patrol the many navigable rivers that penetrated its coastline. He thought a $10 tax would not prevent the introduction of a single slave into South Carolina, and that already large numbers of Africans were illegally brought into the province. Moreover, with the immense accession of the Louisiana Territory many people in the southern states would strengthen their interest in the slave trade and would not be discouraged from trafficking in saltwater slaves by a tax on imports.[74]

An anonymous writer in the *Philadelphia Gazette* for 22 January 1806 argued that 'if South Carolina be the only one that imports, the only one that is, or supposes herself to be enriched by this traffic she of course

---

[70] *Annals of Congress*, 8th Congress, 1st session, House of Representatives, 14 Feb. 1804, 994, 999–1,000.
[71] Riley, *Slavery and the Democratic Conscience*, 108–9.
[72] Friends' Historical Library, Swarthmore College, David Bard to ?, 26 Mar. 1804, box 2, Parrish Family Papers, 1780–1866 (Record Group 5 229).
[73] Untitled article from the *Philadelphia Gazette*, 22 Jan. 1806, reprinted in the *Charleston Courier*, 14 Feb. 1806.
[74] *Charleston Courier*, 15 Mar. 1804.

ought to be taxed'.⁷⁵ In practice, however, this never occurred. On neither occasion when the $10 tax was suggested did Congress levy it. Slaves continued to enter the United States duty-free.⁷⁶ It was claimed that the failure to introduce the $10 tax arose from some of South Carolina's congressional representatives stating they would use their endeavours to procure the reintroduction of the prohibition if the measure was relinquished.⁷⁷ Many contributions to the congressional debate ranged far beyond the specific issue of whether there should be an import tax on Africans brought to the United States to broader issues relating to the morality or immorality of slavery.⁷⁸

On 16 February 1804, Bard's resolution was brought in as a bill and referred to a committee of the whole house. Its passage was postponed until March (by a vote of 56–50) to allow South Carolina sufficient time to repeal her recent act. On 8 February 1805, the subject was revived by Henry Southard of New Jersey, and again on 10 December 1805, by James Sloan of the same state. By that time, South Carolina still had not repealed her act. On 27 January 1806, Sloan's proposal reached the stage where a bill was proposed. Southard's proposal did not get as far as that stage.⁷⁹

A vigorous debate on the floor of the House of Representatives occurred in February 1804. Ostensibly, it concerned the right of Congress to raise such an import tax, which was permitted by the Constitution, but contributions to the debate also reiterated the constitutional proscription on banning the slave trade to the United States before 1808. Thomas Lowndes claimed that 'the period has passed when the interests of the country required and her policy dictated that an end should be put to it'.⁸⁰ But because that could not happen until at least 1808, he argued that the proposed tax would fall almost entirely on South Carolina even though the resolution for the debate did not single out that

---

⁷⁵ Untitled article from the *Philadelphia Gazette*, 22 Jan. 1806, reprinted in the *Charleston Courier*, 14 Feb. 1806.
⁷⁶ Robin L. Einhorn, *American Taxation, American Slavery* (Chicago, 2006), 154.
⁷⁷ 'State of the American Slave Trade', *Pittsfield Sun*, 4 Nov. 1805; 'Slave Trade', *Kline's Carlisle Weekly Gazette* (Pennsylvania), 27 June 1804.
⁷⁸ *Annals of Congress*, 8th Congress, 1st session, House of Representatives, 14 Feb. 1804, 994–1,000.
⁷⁹ Locke, *Anti-Slavery in America*, 145.
⁸⁰ 'Speech of Mr. Lowndes in the National House of Representatives, the 14th ult. When the Resolution of Mr Bard, for Imposing a Tax of Ten Dollars on Every Slave Imported into the United States, Was under Consideration', *The Charleston Daily Courier*, 15 Mar. 1804.

state. Though he hoped Congress would legislate conclusively on the slave trade in 1808, which he supported, a tax on imported slaves would make it more difficult later for Congress to effect a full ban. Congressman Andrew Gregg of Pennsylvania agreed: 'Sanction the trade by imposing the tax,' he stated, 'and soon the traders will demand your protection'. Northerners in the debate pointed out that a large number of people at the Constitutional Convention of 1787 opposed the slave trade. Joseph Stanton Jr. of Rhode Island went further by characterising the slave trade compromise as 'one of the most humiliating concessions made by that venerable Convention which framed the Constitution'.[81]

After the debate, Congress postponed a decision on the proposed tax on imported slaves to the second Monday in March 1804. Most of those who voted for the postponement thought it would give South Carolina's legislature an opportunity to revoke the act that had reopened the slave trade to their state.[82] The last roll call vote supported the bill by rejecting a motion for indefinite postponement by 69–42. Nothing then happened to the measure because Congress devoted most of its time to consideration of British proposals to restrict in wartime the goods that the United States could send to British Caribbean colonies and within two years the US implemented its own procedures for ending slave importation. Though Congress failed to impose the tax, congressional discussions on the proposed tax on imported slaves continued from time to time in 1805 and 1806. During this period, all eight South Carolina delegates, along with half the other Southerners and many Northerners, opposed both the $10 tax and the reopening of the slave trade by South Carolina.[83]

The legislatures of North Carolina, Tennessee, Maryland, Massachusetts, New Hampshire and Vermont tried unsuccessfully to persuade their federal congressmen to request a constitutional amendment that would close slave imports on a federal level at once.[84] These requests were all stymied for various reasons. Thus, the Massachusetts request was tabled in the House of Representatives while the New

---

[81] *Annals of Congress*, 8th Congress, 1st session, House of Representatives, 14, 17 Feb. 1804, 991–2, 999, 1,003–4, 1,014 (quotation), 1,017 (quotation), 1,027, 1,034.
[82] Ibid., 1,036.
[83] Ohline, 'Politics and Slavery', 403, 406–8; Don E. Fehrenbacher with Ward M. McAfee, *The Slaveholding Republic: An Account of the United States Government's Relations to Slavery* (New York, 2001), 143.
[84] Phillips, *American Negro Slavery*, 138–9; Herman V. Ames, *The Proposed Amendments to the Constitution of the United States during the First Century of Its History*, 2 vols. (Washington, DC, 1897), II, 208–9, 326–8.

Hampshire request led to the Federalist William Plumer reminding Governor John Langdon of New Hampshire that Article 1, Section 9 of the Constitution forbade any tampering with the slave trade and that, even if it were possible, it would be an unwise course of action to follow.[85]

Other Northern representatives, including Bard and Stanton, took the opportunity to criticise the slave trade on humanitarian grounds and to argue that its reopening was unwise for security reasons and served as a stain on the American character. South Carolina's delegation offered varied perspectives on their state's reopening of the slave trade. Thomas Lowndes explained that South Carolina had partly taken this decision because it had lacked federal assistance in enforcing prohibition of the trade. The rice planter Benjamin Huger, who opposed the trade, warned that federal intervention would meet with resistance in South Carolina. The planter and former soldier Thomas Moore, who also disliked the trade, warned Congress that South Carolinians were adamantly in favour of keeping the trade open and buying slaves.[86]

LOUISIANA AND THE SLAVE TRADE

The purchase of the Louisiana Territory was greeted favourably by many politicians in South Carolina, whether Republican or Federalist, and the state legislature applauded the acquisition.[87] Beyond South Carolina, however, this territorial purchase received differing assessments. By 1804, existing states exercised responsibility over whether slave imports to their jurisdictions were allowed or not, but the slave trade was a federal responsibility in the territories.[88] On 23 January 1804, the antislavery convention of delegates, meeting in Philadelphia, submitted a petition to the Senate requesting that Congress should prevent slave importation into Louisiana. Little attention was given to the memorial. It was merely read in the Senate. In the House it was referred to the committee dealing with the government for Louisiana.[89] The Quakers

---

[85] Ohline, 'Politics and Slavery', 409; Plumer to Langdon, 3 Feb. 1806, in Lynn W. Turner, *William Plumer of New Hampshire 1759–1850* (Chapel Hill, NC, 1962), 161.
[86] Ford, *Deliver Us from Evil*, 105.   [87] Ibid., 97.
[88] David F. Ericson, *Slavery in the American Republic: Developing the Federal Government, 1791–1861* (Lawrence, KS, 2011), 33.
[89] Locke, *Anti-slavery Activity*, 147.

submitted a memorial requesting an end to slave importation to the United States.[90]

On 24 January, the Senate debated a plan drawn up by Jefferson and Senator John Breckenridge of Kentucky, head of the committee to organise the Louisiana Territory. The plan included a proposal to ban both the foreign and domestic slave trades to Louisiana. The second part of the plan was effectively an attack on South Carolina's reopening of the slave trade in 1803.[91] Jefferson tried to intervene in these arrangements by secretly writing to Breckinridge to request that the bill drawn up should include a clause permitting the domestic slave trade (as Virginians had surplus slaves to dispose of) but banning foreign slave imports into Louisiana. But this had no effect as the Louisiana Ordinance bill of 1804 prohibited the domestic and international slave trades to the territory.[92]

In 1804, discussions took place in the Senate about opening Louisiana to the slave trade and permitting unrestricted slave importations there. Those in favour of this position argued that only an influx of slaves could cultivate and improve the land and its resources in the Louisiana Territory.[93] One commentator indicated the controversial nature of whether to allow slave imports into the Louisiana Territory by stating in a private letter that 'if a stop is put to the importation of slaves there must be an army to enforce the law, such is the want of hands to cultivate the soil and the deep rooted prejudice of the inhabitants to all innovation in this particular'.[94]

Part of the intention of the Breckenridge-Jefferson plan was to prevent a rebellion on the scale of the Haitian revolt occurring in the United States. Several senators opposed the plan to stop slave importation into Louisiana. James Jackson of Georgia disagreed with the plan because he

---

[90] Library of the Religious Society of Friends, London, 'To the Senate and House of Representatives of the United States in Congress Assembled. The Memorial of the People Called Quakers', n.d., in Letters to and from Philadelphia, volume 1.

[91] John Craig Hammond, '"They Are Very Much Interested in Obtaining an Unlimited Slavery": Rethinking the Expansion of Slavery in the Louisiana Purchase Territories', *Journal of the Early Republic*, 23/3 (2003), 360; Sean Wilentz, *No Property in Man: Slavery and Antislavery at the Nation's Founding* (Cambridge, MA, 2018), 174–5.

[92] Steven Deyle, 'An "Abominable" New Trade: The Closing of the African Slave Trade and the Changing Patterns of U.S. Political Power', *WMQ*, 3rd series, 66/4 (2009), 838.

[93] Connecticut HS, James Hilhouse to Jonathan Trumbull, Jr, 3 Feb. 1804, Jonathan Trumbull, Jr Papers: Correspondence with Congressmen, volume 2 (1801–18).

[94] New Jersey HS, Daniel Clark to Jonathan Dayton, 24 Jan. 1804, Jonathan Dayton Papers.

thought Louisiana needed additional slaves to develop the territory. Jonathan Dayton of New Jersey was concerned that Southerners would send poor quality slaves into Louisiana and therefore he joined Jackson in opposing the plan. Stephen R. Bradley of Vermont objected to federal regulation of the slave trade. John Quincy Adams did not think banning slave importation would prevent the increase of slavery in Louisiana. Samuel Smith of Maryland noted that Louisianans had requested extra slaves and that they should be allowed to import them.[95]

James Hilhouse of Connecticut, who considered slavery an evil, agreed with the Jefferson-Breckenridge plan but, on encountering opposition in the Senate, proposed an amendment that limited the administration's proposals by suggesting a ban on the introduction of slaves from foreign ports.[96] A ban on slave imports would seriously affect sugar plantation owners in the Louisiana Territory who needed a continuing influx of African labour.[97] The Senate voted 21–6 to support this amendment. Bradley and Jackson were among those voting against the measure while Smith and Dayton did not vote because they did not want to be recorded as supporting the slave trade. The voting result was sympathetically received in some northern newspapers.[98]

Hilhouse proposed a further amendment that it should be illegal to bring any slave into Louisiana after the reopening of South Carolina's slave trade, and that only settlers from southern states could take slaves into Louisiana. The Senate approved this amendment by a vote of 21–7. Hilhouse put forward another amendment which recommended that only US citizens be allowed to take slaves into the Louisiana Territory. This was agreed by a vote of 18–11. In February 1804, the Senate passed the Louisiana government bill, which proscribed the importation of foreign slaves and the domestic slave trade in the Louisiana Territory.[99]

Slave imports to Louisiana had occurred erratically, with long periods of closure, since 1719, when the first African slaving vessel reached

---

[95] Ohline, 'Politics and Slavery', 362, 364–5. [96] Ford, *Deliver Us from Evil*, 107.
[97] Wilentz, *No Property in Man*, 173.
[98] For example, *Aurora General Advertiser*, 31 Jan. 1804.
[99] Ohline, 'Politics and Slavery', 365–7, 370, 376; Hammond, 'They Are Very Much Interested in Obtaining an Unlimited Slavery', 355; Sean M. Kelley, *American Slavers: Merchants, Mariners, and the Transatlantic Commerce in Captives, 1644–1865* (New Haven, CT, 2023), 191. Helpful context about these developments is provided in Jennifer M. Spear, 'Liberty, Slavery, and the Louisiana Purchase of 1803: The Incorporation of the Territory of Orleans' (2018) in *Oxford Research Encyclopedia of American History*. https://oxfordre.com/americanhistory/

French New Orleans.[100] In the two decades before the Louisiana Purchase, Louisiana had experienced complexities over the importation of slaves, with groups of influential individuals either opposing or supporting the inflow.[101] In 1796, Spanish Louisiana had closed a thriving slave traffic owing to fears of the slave rebellion in Saint-Domingue spreading to mainland America, but in 1800 the Spanish authorities reopened the trade.[102] The Louisiana territorial constitution (1804) banned slaves from being brought into the territory except for legitimate settlers bringing them for their own personal use.[103] In March 1804, public meetings were convened in New Orleans with the intention of petitioning Congress to allow slave importation into Louisiana.[104] Influential planters from New Orleans complained that prohibition of the slave trade rendered their plantations of little value.[105] The general sentiment in New Orleans appeared to be in favour of the slave trade.[106]

A resident of New Orleans, Lewis Kerr, explained the complexities of current considerations over the slave trade to the Louisiana Territory. Kerr, an opponent of the slave trade, explained the apprehension in New Orleans that the slave trade would be abolished: 'This has excited considerable alarm among the numerous traders in that valuable article. And as those gentlemen are among the richest and most influential characters in this city the subject makes not a little noise. And that noise, as usual, is arrogantly termed "the voice of the people."' Kerr's view, however, was that only a relatively minor part of New Orleans's population thought the slave trade was popular 'because they have their own views in wishing it to be so'. Kerr thought it would be 'extremely difficult on grounds of policy to justify a continuation of that cruel and wicked traffic'. If slaves were to be admitted to the territory, the fear existed that many would come from the French islands and therefore pose a threat to public safety. On the other hand, if foreign slaves were excluded, Louisianans would draw off slaves from the western states, especially Kentucky and

---

[100] Jean-Pierre le Glaunec, 'Blackness without Ethnicity: Some Hypotheses on the End of the African Slave Trade in 1808, Race, and the Search for Slave Identity in Early American Louisiana' in Gleeson and Lewis, eds., *Ambiguous Anniversary*, 161.
[101] Paul F. Lachance, 'The Politics of Fear: French Louisianans and the Slave Trade, 1786–1809', *Plantation Society in the Americas*, 1/2 (1979), 162–97.
[102] Ford, *Deliver Us from Evil*, 104.   [103] Ericson, *Slavery in the American Republic*, 33.
[104] Ohline, 'Politics and Slavery', 380.
[105] Hatch Dent to James H. McCulloch, 14 July 1804, in Clarence Edwin Carter, ed., *The Territorial Papers of the United States. Volume 9. The Territory of Orleans 1803–1812* (Washington, DC, 1940), 265.
[106] Governor Claiborne to the President, 30 Aug. 1804, ibid., 285.

Tennessee 'and thereby at least extenuate the general evil'. Kerr concluded his letter by condemning those 'who wish to speculate in human flesh at the expense of our national character and our feelings'.[107]

When Louisiana became a US territory in 1803, it already participated in the foreign slave trade. But, as Kerr's letter indicated, this was an issue of controversial debate in the territory, and also at national level, by March 1804. As it happened, just a couple of days after Kerr wrote his letter, Congress outlawed the international and domestic slave trades to Louisiana. This proscription was partly prompted by fears once again of a slave revolt. Some support for the ban in the Senate arose from the self-interest of Virginia representatives who calculated that cutting off new African arrivals would raise the price of existing slaves in Virginia and enable the surplus to be sold profitably to Louisiana.[108] The ban appeared in section 10 of an act dated 26 March 1804, which became effective on 1 October.[109] After the act was passed, the only slaves legally allowed to be taken to Louisiana were those already in the United States before 1798, who were going with their masters.[110] In effect, therefore, Congress still permitted Georgia and South Carolina to import foreign slaves but those states could not sell or transfer those Africans to Louisiana. However, Congress allowed the Charleston loophole to expire in 1805. Thereafter, Charleston became the chief supplier of Africans to Louisiana.[111]

Governor William C. C. Claiborne of the Louisiana Territory was critical of the 'barbarous' nature of the slave trade.[112] Nevertheless, he informed Secretary of State James Madison that Louisianans regarded the slave trade as a lucrative business and that they objected to the fact that South Carolinians could import slaves but they could not. French Louisianans could only be content with their new political connection with the US government if their economic welfare was accounted for, and that included slave importation.[113] During the course of 1804, white

---

[107] Maryland Center for History and Culture, Lewis Kerr to Isaac Briggs, 24 Mar. 1804, Family Correspondence, Briggs-Stabler Papers.
[108] Riley, *Slavery and the Democratic Conscience*, 109.
[109] Richard Peters, ed., *The Public Statutes at Large of the United States of America, Volume 2 (1700–1813)* (Boston, 1845), 283, 286, 289.
[110] Marques, *The United States and the Transatlantic Slave Trade*, 50.
[111] Hammond, 'They Are Very Much Interested in Obtaining an Unlimited Slavery', 362.
[112] Ford, *Deliver Us from Evil*, 104.
[113] Ibid., 113; William C. C. Claiborne to Madison, 10 Mar. 1804, in Dunbar Rowland, ed., *Official Letterbooks of W. C. C. Claiborne, 1801–1816*, 6 vols. (Jackson, MS, 1917), II, 25–6.

Louisianians protested against possible congressional measures to curtail the slave trade, complaining that their agricultural products could not survive successfully without access to new supplies of Africans.[114] Daniel Clark, the first senator from the Orleans Territory to the US House of Representatives, also hoped the prohibition on slave importation to Louisiana could be repealed because a high demand existed for slaves in the new territory.[115]

By the end of 1804, Louisianans were still keen for slaves to be imported even though fears were frequently raised about the possibility of slave insurrections.[116] A Quaker petition drawn up in association with the Pennsylvania Abolition Society was presented to Congress on 21 January 1805 to counter pressure from Louisiana to allow citizens there to import slaves but the senators, after three hours of discussion, refused to submit it to their committee on Louisiana. The Louisiana Ordinance Bill of 1805 lifted the ban on the domestic slave trade but forbade the introduction of foreign slaves into territory, something that proved difficult to prevent.[117]

White Louisianans vigorously debated the pros and cons of the decision. During 1804, Governor Claiborne's reports to Washington, DC always emphasised Louisianan complaints about the law of 1804.[118] Claiborne advised Madison that 'the continuation of the Slave trade for a few years is viewed by the inhabitants as essential to the welfare of this province and no act of Congress would excite more discontent, than an immediate prohibition'.[119] One source privately claimed that Claiborne

---

[114] Ford, *Deliver Us from Evil*, 115.
[115] New Jersey HS, Daniel Clark to Jonathan Dayton, 26 Aug. 1804, Jonathan Dayton Papers.
[116] William C. C. Claiborne to ?, 31 Dec.1804, in Rowland, ed., *Official Letterbooks of W. C. C. Claiborne*, II, 35; Claiborne to the Secretary of State, 3 Oct. 1804, in Carter, ed., *The Territorial Papers of the United States. Volume 9*, 305; Lachance, 'The Politics of Fear', 182.
[117] Ohline, 'Politics and Slavery', 385–6, 393; Deyle, 'An "Abominable" New Trade', 838, n. 8.
[118] Marques, *The United States and the Transatlantic Slave Trade*, 50.
[119] William C. C. Claiborne to James Madison, 16 Mar. 1804, in Mary A. Hackett, J.C.A. Stagg, Ellen J. Barber, Anne Mandeville Colony and Angela Krieder, eds., *The Papers of James Madison, Secretary of State Series. Volume 6. 1 November 1803–31 March 1804* (Charlottesville, VA, 2002), 593. A similar sentiment is expressed in Claiborne to Madison, 12 and 13 July 1804, in David B. Mattern, J. C. A. Stagg, Ellen J. Barber, Anne Mandeville Colony, Angela Krieder and Jeanne Kerr Cross, eds., *The Papers of James Madison, Secretary of States Series. Volume 7. 2 April–31 August 1804* (Charlottesville, VA, 2005), 445, 449.

had been deceived to some degree by the outcry raised over continuance of the slave trade – an interesting suggestion but one that is unproven.[120] Another source stated, though this was exaggerated, that Louisianans had almost 'an universal sentiment in favour of this inhuman traffic, and the prohibition thereof is the great source of discontent'. Francophone planters particularly wanted to keep the territory's slave trade open. But this was a one-sided, partisan view. Louisiana planters divided over whether banning slave imports would stymie any attempt at slave rebellion or whether it would curtail a supply of new slaves to Louisiana when plantation society there was growing. There was a particular fear of slaves being admitted from the West Indies 'that have been concerned in the insurrections of St. Domingo'.[121] Throughout 1804, Louisiana's citizens continued to express discontent over problems associated with the slave trade and the province.[122]

The ban was ineffective, however, because in October 1805 the domestic slave trade to Louisiana was opened after Congress relented owing to the pressure placed on it by Louisianan planters.[123] This was shortly after Louisiana had received an upgrade in its territorial government.[124] So strong were the feelings on the slave trade demonstrated in the legislature in the debates over whether to allow Louisiana to import Africans 'that no doubt can be entertained of a final period being put to the American Slave Trade, whenever the time shall arise when Congress is constitutionally authorized to abolish it'.[125]

---

[120] Maryland Center for History and Culture, Baltimore, Lewis Kerr to Isaac Briggs, 24 Mar. 1804, Family Correspondence, Briggs-Stabler Papers.

[121] Claiborne to Madison, 5 and 12 July 1804, in Mattern et al., eds., *The Papers of James Madison, Secretary of State Series*. Volume 7, 422, 445 (quotations); John Craig Hammond, *Slavery, Freedom, and Expansion in the Early American West* (Charlottesville, VA, 2007), 30, 37–8, 46–7, 187; Everett S. Brown, ed., 'The Senate Debate on the Breckinridge Bill for the Government of Louisiana, 1804', *American Historical Review*, 22/2 (1917), 345–50; Ford, *Deliver Us from Evil*, 112–14; James A. Scanlan, 'A Sudden Conceit: Jefferson and the Louisiana Bill of 1804', *Louisiana History*, 9/2 (1968), 152–5.

[122] William C. C. Claiborne to Thomas Jefferson, with Jefferson's Note, 29 May 1804, in James P. McClure, ed., *The Papers of Thomas Jefferson. Volume 43. 11 March–30 June 1804* (Princeton, NJ, 2017), 504–6, and Claiborne to Jefferson, 1 July 1804, in James P. McClure, ed., *The Papers of Thomas Jefferson. Volume 44. 1 July–10 November 1804* (Princeton, NJ, 2019), 7–9; John Quincy Adams to Abigail Smith Adams, 19 Dec. 1804, Founders Online. https://founders.archives.gov

[123] Marques, *The United States and the Transatlantic Slave Trade*, 50.

[124] James A. McMillin, *Final Victims: Foreign Slave Trade to North America, 1783–1810* (Columbia, SC, 2005), 98.

[125] 'State of the American Slave Trade', *Pittsfield Sun*, 4 Nov. 1805.

The opening of the domestic slave trade to Louisiana from October 1805 led to a rapid surge in slave imports. Between 1805 and 1808, Louisiana took slaves from ships that had touched at Charleston – some from Africa, others from Cuba – as well as smuggled slaves from Texas and Spanish West Florida. Between 7,000 and 8,000 slaves arrived in Louisiana through New Orleans, from overland and overseas, in those four years. The 1805 Territorial Acts, dealing with the Louisiana and Orleans territories, failed to close the South Carolina loophole. This allowed Louisiana continued access to African slave imports until 1808.[126]

SOUTH CAROLINA DEBATES THE SLAVE TRADE, 1806–1807

On 2 December 1806, a Committee of the Whole from South Carolina's House of Representatives met at the State House, in Columbia, to debate the slave trade. Speaker Joseph Alston and Keating Lewis Simons, a Charleston lawyer, were in favour of shutting the ports whereas Major James Miles, Major John Taylor of Columbia and John Izard Wright were against it. Simons spoke for twenty minutes on the subject, emphasising the inhumanity of the traffic and the potential security issues associated with having a very large number of blacks in South Carolina. Alston offered some similar arguments about the injustice of the slave trade but added that 'the increase of slaves tends to destroy that equality that is the basis of our republican institutions, and insisted that it is not only unjust to bring them in, but demonstrably injurious to the real interests of the state'. Varied arguments were presented by those who wanted to open Charleston to the slave trade. Miles conceded that religion, justice and humanity could all be brought to bear against the slave trade but argued that the debate should focus on economic matters. He was worried that keeping ports closed to slave imports would increase smuggling of illegal entries that would prejudice planters in the upcountry who needed to purchase Africans as opposed to lowcountry planters who were already supplied with sufficient slaves. Taylor had once advocated closing the ports, but he now wanted to keep them open, for two reasons: one was to prevent smuggling which would otherwise be impracticable

---

[126] Hammond, *Slavery, Freedom, and Expansion*, 50, 188; Jean-Pierre Le Glaunec, 'Slave Migrations and Slave Control in Spanish and Early American New Orleans' in Peter J. Kastor and François Weil, eds., *Empires of the Imagination: Transatlantic Histories of the Louisiana Purchase* (Charlottesville, VA, 2009), 214, 216.

unless South Carolina were to acquire some revenue vessels; the other was to give upcountry planters an opportunity to purchase more Africans in order to place them on a similar footing to their lowcountry brethren. Taylor thought the federal Congress would doubtless deal with the slave trade in two years' time, when the constitutional restriction on its action ended, and that it would therefore be wise to wait for it to act on the matter. At the conclusion of the debate, the majority of the House passed the resolution. A further short debate on the slave trade took place in the Senate on 9 December 1806.[127]

On 11 December 1806, the bill for the abolition of the slave trade received a second reading and was considered clause by clause. Despite some exceptions, most lowcountry members favoured the prohibition while those from the upcountry opposed it. Edward Hooker, an observer of the debate, noted in his diary that 'the minority appear chagrined that the bill meets with such encouragement, and they are constantly trying some side blow to defeat its object'.[128] The bill passed the lower house and its second reading in the Senate on 13 December. Discussion there offered different views on the enslavement of Africans. One view was that it was an act of humanity to bring in Africans to South Carolina because, it was claimed, they were often prisoners of war in Africa who would otherwise be tortured or killed. But Ralph Izard contradicted this argument by denying that wars were started by white people in Africa in order to acquire slaves. Hooker was not convinced that this was the end of the matter: 'there is still room, however, at the final question, for the opposers of the bill who are a strong party, to make further resistance and perhaps overthrow it'.[129]

South Carolina experienced much controversial debate as a result of the closing of the foreign slave trade to Louisiana while its domestic slave trade was allowed. In 1805 and 1806, planters and legislators fiercely contested whether South Carolina should keep its reopened slave trade. Opponents argued that the state's economy was in debt, that it was being drained of specie, and that the slave trade threatened public safety. Those who supported the status quo reiterated the prospects for business gain through providing additional African captives to meet the southwestern cotton boom. Among the arguments set out, the question of whether the

---

[127] J. Franklin Jameson, ed., 'Diary of Edward Hooker, 1805–1808', *Report of the Historical Manuscripts Commission for the American Historical Association for 1896*, 867, 868 (quotation), 869–70, 873–4.
[128] Ibid., 878.   [129] Ibid., 879.

slave trade to South Carolina should be banned on moral or humanitarian grounds was not a major issue.[130]

In 1806, the mechanics of the voting were dead even in the upper house, where a resolution that the Senate should proceed to a second reading of the bill to prevent slaves from being imported at Charleston resulted in a 16–16 tied vote. This outcome determined against the motion. Therefore the bill was not read a second time.[131] Newspapers referred to the Senate's rejection of the House's bill to end slave imports as a 'deep wound on the national character'.[132] The outgoing governor of the state, the Democratic-Republican Charles Pinckney, also disagreed with the Senate's decision. In the *Charleston Courier* (17 December 1806), he argued that South Carolina 'should cease to practice what every other state in the union discountenances'.

South Carolina's reopening of the slave trade had resonances beyond the state's borders. In February 1805, the Massachusetts legislature instructed their senators and representatives in Congress to prepare for a constitutional amendment to prohibit slave importation from Africa and the West Indies.[133] On 3 March, a motion was made and seconded in the federal House of Representatives that both houses of Congress resolved to propose to state legislatures a constitutional amendment should be made to enable the United States to proscribe slave importation provided that three-quarters of the state legislatures ratified the amendment.[134] In 1806–7, the legislatures of Vermont, New Hampshire, Maryland and Ohio made similar requests.[135]

CONGRESS PROSCRIBES THE SLAVE TRADE, 1806–1807

Newspaper commentary anticipated the date when the US slave trade could be legitimately proscribed at federal level. 'Thanks to the framers of the federal Constitution', one writer observed in late 1805, 'the day is fast approaching when the foul blot which the Slave-Trade fixes on the American character can be wiped out by the veto of the National

---

[130] Ford, *Deliver Us from Evil*, 121–3.
[131] SCDAH, entry for 17 Dec. 1806 in South Carolina Journals of the Senate (1806).
[132] Quoted in the *Richmond Enquirer*, 3 Feb. 1807, and the *National Intelligencer and Washington (DC) Advertiser*, 7 Jan. 1807.
[133] Locke, *Anti-Slavery in America*, 149.
[134] *Annals of Congress*, 8th Congress, 2nd session, House of Representatives, 3 Mar. 1805, 1222.
[135] Locke, *Anti-slavery in America*, 149.

Legislature – and every friend of Humanity will hope that a moment's delay will not take place when the period arrives at which Congress have a Constitutional right to prohibit the infamous traffic'.[136] In January 1806, the American Convention for Promoting the Abolition of Slavery urged state societies to draw up and dispatch memorials to Congress urging it to pass a law prohibiting slave importation to the United States at the earliest opportunity.[137]

Even in South Carolina, there was recognition that attitudes had moved against the slave trade. Thus, on 14 February 1806, the *Charleston Courier* noted that 'Congress have repeatedly expressed their abhorrence of the slave trade, by inflicting, in all cases where they were allowed to make laws to operate, the most severe penalties on those who were concerned in this inhuman traffic. Since the adoption of the Constitution, no state has allowed the importation of slaves, till a year since, the state of South Carolina'.[138] A comment such as this, expressing condemnation of the slave trade, would not have appeared in a South Carolina newspaper a decade beforehand.

The legal proscription of the foreign slave trade to the United States as a whole was a 'quiet abolition'.[139] There were no public announcements about it. Nor was it the result of a vigorous abolition campaign. Nevertheless, it ended in a distinctive way. In December 1805, Senator Stephen Bradley called for a law to be passed prohibiting slave imports into the United States from 1 January 1808, in line with the expiration of Article 1, Section 9, of the Constitution. In the course of a discussion in the Senate, 'it was allowed on all hands, that as soon as the time arrived when Congress shall possess the constitutional power of prohibiting the importation of slaves it would be proper for them to exercise it'.[140] The House set up a committee to consider the matter. The Senate's vote on the matter led to a 14–14 tie and Vice President George Clinton decided the question in favour of postponement. However, the Senate proceeded to

---

[136] 'Slave Trade!', *Independent Chronicle* (Boston), 21 Oct. 1805. In Aug. 1806 Wilberforce, writing from England, also hoped there would be no delay in the United States abolishing its slave trade as soon as Congress had the power to do so: see Oldfield, *Transatlantic Abolitionism*, 183.

[137] Oldfield, *Transatlantic Abolitionism*, 183–4. [138] *Charleston Courier, 14 Feb. 1806.*

[139] Robin Blackburn, *The Overthrow of Colonial Slavery, 1776–1846* (London, 1988), 286.

[140] Ninth Congress – First Session, Senate of the United States, 14–17 Dec. 1805, in the *Columbian Centinel* (Boston), 1 Jan. 1806.

pass Bradley's bill on 27 January 1806.[141] Two months later, a Massachusetts senator reinforced this call. But opponents considered it too soon for such a proposal to be drafted. The matter was particularly controversial, of course, for South Carolina. An editorial in the 10 July 1806 edition of the *Charleston Courier* revealed the resentment felt by pro-slave trade supporters in the state against outside criticism of the slave traffic by northern states or even by those in the Upper South.[142]

At federal level, Jefferson, after remaining quiet on the subject in public for nearly two decades, decided to act swiftly to prevent public agitation by anti-slave trade groups. His influence was crucial in securing the consideration and passing of a bill dealing with slave importation.[143] Jefferson had bided his time on slave trade abolition since the Constitutional Convention of 1787, and he had not forgotten that action on this issue would soon be possible. He took the lead on this subject in late 1806 by invoking natural rights.[144] On 2 December 1806, his sixth presidential address proudly referred directly to the impending end of the constitutional restriction on restraining slave imports:

> I congratulate you on the approach of the period at which you may interpose your authority, constitutionally, to withdraw the citizens of the United States from all further participation in those violations of human rights, which have been so long continued on the unoffending inhabitants of Africa, and which the morality, the reputation, and the best interests of our country, have long been eager to proscribe. Although no law you may pass can take prohibitory effect till the first day of the year one thousand eight hundred and eight, yet the intervening period is not too long to prevent, by timely notice, expeditions which cannot be completed before that day.[145]

Jefferson knew, when he issued this statement, that such a prohibition to the trade would not disturb the institution of slavery in the United States.[146]

Jefferson may have kept fairly quiet on the matter of the slave trade since the Constitution was drafted and ratified, but occasionally he

---

[141] Ibid.; Phillips, *American Negro Slavery*, 140; Wilentz, *No Property in Man*, 182.
[142] 'Reply to Criticism of Slave Trade, 1806' in Donnan, ed., *Documents*, IV, 517–19.
[143] Ohline, 'Politics and Slavery', 412.
[144] James Sidbury, 'Thomas Jefferson in Gabriel's Virginia' in James Horn, Jan Ellen Lewis and Peter S. Onuf, eds., *The Revolution of 1800: Democracy, Race, and the New Republic* (Charlottesville, VA, 2002), 205–6.
[145] Thomas Jefferson, 6th annual presidential message, *Annals of Congress*, 9th Congress, 2nd session, Senate, 2 Dec. 1806, 14.
[146] Oldfield, *Transatlantic Abolitionism*, 185.

revealed his thoughts on the subject, as in 1803 when he referred in a letter to 'the unhappy human beings ... forcibly brought away from their native country'.[147] Article 1, Section 9 of the Constitution did not state that the slave trade would automatically end in 1808: it was necessary for Congress to pass a law for that to happen.[148] Jefferson's presidential address quoted above ensured that the matter was acted upon swiftly. His remarks on the slave trade were referred to a House select committee, which drafted a bill.[149] At the time, various commentators pointed out that Britain was simultaneously at an advanced stage in parliamentary attempts to abolish its own slave trade. There was a certain amount of competitive pride in determining whether the United States or the United Kingdom would be the first significant slave trading power to end participation in the Guinea traffic.[150]

Jefferson's proposal that Congress should immediately exercise its right to abolish the slave trade from the last day of 1807 was endorsed in the *The Democratic Press*. An article in that newspaper stated that 'the sense of this country has been deliberately expressed by a large majority of the states, and, indeed, by all but one, for several years. The finishing hand is now put to the business, through the wise, humane and worthy forecast of the President'. According to the same article, Congress had been thinking about a bill to abolish slave importations at the next December session, but the President had pre-empted this by agreeably surprising the public on this matter.[151]

Congress acted swiftly to abolish the international slave trade to the United States as soon as the Constitution permitted. Little discussion about the source of its authority occurred. No one spoke out in principle about the subject, but there were detailed, and occasionally arcane, discussions and disagreements about how it should be done.[152] However, Congress at this stage of proceedings was, in John Oldfield's

---

[147] Thomas Jefferson to Christopher Ellery, 9 May 1803, in Barbara B. Oberg, ed., *The Papers of Thomas Jefferson. Volume 40. 4 March–1 July 1803* (Princeton, NJ, 2013), 338.
[148] Sidbury, 'Thomas Jefferson in Gabriel's Virginia', 205.
[149] Locke, *Anti-Slavery Activity*, 149.
[150] Matthew Mason, 'Necessary but not Sufficient: Revolutionary Ideology and Antislavery Action in the Early Republic' in John Craig Hammond and Matthew Mason, eds., *Contesting Slavery: The Politics of Bondage and Freedom in the New American Nation* (Charlottesville, VA, 2011), 18.
[151] *The Democratic Press* (Philadelphia), 8 Apr. 1807.
[152] David P. Corrie, *The Constitution in Congress: The Jeffersonians 1801–1829* (Chicago, 2001), 7.

words, 'relatively at one on the issue' because South Carolina's near southern neighbours had criticised the flow of slaves into the Palmetto state while Northerners regarded slave trade abolition as a means to slow down black population growth in southern states and hence their political influence in federal government.[153] On 3 December 1806 in Congress, just one day after South Carolina's legislature began to debate slave importations, and the day after Jefferson made his presidential announcement on the subject, Senator Bradley gave notice that Congress intended to bring forward legislation on slave importations. A committee of seven charged with oversight of the bill discussed proscribing the slave trade to the United States. They agreed on the main points quickly and reported on 15 December 1806 the chief details encapsulated in the act of 1807.[154]

No Southerner in Congress was willing to defend the international slave trade at this juncture.[155] In this final phase of African slave imports to the United States, there was broad agreement among both Northerners and Southerners that the slave trade was inhumane but less agreement about how to prevent it.[156] However, there were considerable differences of opinion about the details of three aspects of slave importation: the penalty for bringing blacks illegally to the United States, whether the federal government could regulate the domestic seaborne slave trade, and what penalties should be put in place for those violating the law.[157]

On 16 December 1806, Congress moved to bring in a bill to prohibit the importation of slaves into the United States after 31 December 1807. Jefferson avoided the argumentative congressional sessions on this subject.[158] The bill penalised anyone found guilty of breaching it with a forfeit of $10,000 as well as surrendering the ship and all its furnishings carrying slaves to American ports. This was to apply to those preparing ships for voyages to Africa and those located in US jurisdictional territories that flouted the law. The president of the United States was authorised to employ whatever number of armed vessels he deemed necessary in order to bring this law into effect. Any newly imported slave found within the United States after 31 December 1807 was to be forfeited. All

---

[153] Oldfield, *Transatlantic Abolitionism*, 185.
[154] Ruth Scarborough, *The Opposition to Slavery in Georgia prior to 1860* (Nashville, TN, 1933), 112.
[155] Ford, *Deliver Us from Evil*, 125.
[156] Dun, 'Atlantic Antislavery, American Ambition', 237.
[157] Mason, 'Slavery Overshadowed', 64; Kelley, *American Slavers*, 204.
[158] Sidbury, 'Thomas Jefferson in Gabriel's Virginia', 206.

penalties and forfeitures made under the law could be sued for and recovered through the courts.[159]

Much debate ensued on section 4 of the proposed bill in which it was stated that any 'negro, mulatto or person of colour' found in the United States. after 31 December 1807 would be forfeited. Discussion centred on whether 'forfeited' meant free or slave. It was pointed out, for example, that the most likely result of importing Africans who were then forfeited would be that they were sold into slavery. Thus, Willis Alston, Jr of North Carolina considered that forfeiture would not work, for once Africans had been imported there was no way to prevent them from becoming slaves; the only way to stop that happening, in his opinion, was to block the importation in the first place.[160] Barnabas Bidwell of Massachusetts argued that forfeiture was a misapplied concept because it implied that human beings could be construed as property.[161]

Congress agreed on the object of the bill – the prevention of slave imports into the United States – but found it more difficult to concur on the means to achieve this end. Differences of opinion were aired on the penalties for importing Africans in the future, focusing on whether they should be in the form of fines, imprisonment or treated as a capital offence. It was finally decided to strike out a clause stipulating the punishment of death on owners and masters of vessels employed in the slave trade, and to include a clause prescribing imprisonment for not more than ten, nor less than five, years.[162]

In late December 1806, a committee of the whole had an extensive debate on whether the slave trade bill should include provisions for the forfeiture of slaves. Sensitivities arose over whether, as the bill stated, the federal government should have the exclusive right to sell slaves illegally imported into the United States. There was also disquiet expressed about whether every state would adopt the new regulations. But the two main objections to the bill were, first, that forfeiture appeared necessary to deprive importers of every motive to introduce slaves into the United States and thereby make the proscription effective, and second, that if the slaves were emancipated and turned loose in the southern states, they would be a destructive nuisance to the people of those states. In addition,

---

[159] *Annals of Congress*, House of Representatives, 9th Congress, 2nd session, 17 Dec. 1806, 167.
[160] Ibid., 169. For further debate on the clause dealing with forfeiture, see ibid., 221–2.
[161] Mason, 'Slavery Overshadowed', 66.
[162] *Annals of Congress*, House of Representatives, 9th Congress, 2nd session, 17, 23 and 31 Dec. 1806, 167, 170–2, 221–2, 240, 243–4.

the notion of forfeiture implied that the importer had a right to the slaves. If it were retained in the bill, it would be a recognition that property could exist in human beings, which the Constitution had never claimed, and 'the term forfeiture implied that the importer had a right till divested by statute'.[163] The debate returned to Article 1, Section 9 of the Constitution: this section 'which forbids us to prohibit the importation of slaves till 1808, clearly implies, that were it not for the restraining clause, we should now have the right of preventing any aliens coming to this country. Otherwise, why this restraint inserted in the Constitution?'[164]

Debates continued over the appropriate and proportionate punishments to be included in the bill for those found guilty of importing slaves in the future. Theodore Dwight of Connecticut explained that his congressional colleagues were agreed that slave importation to the United States should cease but they were in disagreement about the means to effect this object.[165] He reminded fellow congressmen that those of their number who came from the northern and eastern states where slavery had withered would have different attitudes on the subject to representatives from the southern states where slavery had always existed and still did so. Division now centred on whether slave importation should be a capital offence or subject instead to fine and imprisonment. A vote was eventually taken on this matter and, by 63–53 votes, it was decided to take out from the first section of the bill a statement to the effect that death should be the punishment inflicted on the masters and owners of vessels found to be employed in the slave trade.[166]

Controversy in the congressional debates of 1807 concentrated less on preventing the slave trade, but on what to do with illegally imported slaves after 1808, how to punish smugglers and how to regulate the domestic slave trade.[167] Southerners wanted a provision that traders would forfeit smuggled slaves to the federal government, which would then sell them at auction.[168] A joint committee met to discuss the limits on the domestic slave trade, and decided that the coastal trade in slaves should be limited to vessels of forty tons.[169]

---

[163] Ibid., 201–3, 220–1, 224 (quotation).   [164] Ibid., 226.
[165] For further debates on 11 Feb. 1807, over the wording of various sections of the bill, see ibid., 483–4.
[166] Ibid., 240, 243.   [167] Wood, 'John Randolph of Roanoke', 117.
[168] Robin Einhorn, 'The Early Impact of Slavery' in Julian E. Zelizer, ed., *The American Congress: The Building of Democracy* (Boston, 2004), 88–9.
[169] Wood, 'John Randolph of Roanoke', 117.

The legislative history of the measure proscribing the slave trade to the United States was complex, because two bills on this issue were proposed – the Senate bill already mentioned and a different bill from the House of Representatives.[170] By the end of January 1807, both houses of Congress had printed seven different proposals, which indicates the variety of possible ways in which the subject could be treated.[171] Between 17 December 1806 and 8 January 1807, the House of Representatives debated their own bill to end slave importation, prepared by a committee of four Northerners and three Southerners under the chairmanship of Peter Early of Georgia.[172]

Congressional debates did not focus on proscription, for several reasons: all states except South Carolina had closed slave importations to their jurisdictions; the moral arguments over the slave trade had long been accepted even by many South Carolinians; and it was expected that the constitutional clause restraining Congress from acting over the slave traffic would expire in 1808 and be overturned. In addition, stopping slave imports would benefit many Americans: Northerners would increase their political power by slowing down population growth in the South; Chesapeake planters could request higher prices for the surplus slaves they wanted to sell to the Southwest; slaveholders in the Lower South would lessen the risk of slave revolt by reducing the influx of slaves from the Caribbean imbued with a rebellious spirit.[173] Besides these points the Lower South, contrary to some expectations held in 1788, was too weak to prevent an abolition of slave imports: the North had grown faster than the South within twenty years, the new western territories did not support African slave imports, and the New England economy was linked to a further influx of slaves.[174]

Congressmen fiercely debated section 4 of the proposed legislation. Some were opposed to the forfeiture of imported slaves by the federal government, preferring that this should be left to individual states; but a

---

[170] Du Bois, *The Suppression of the African Slave-Trade*, 105–6.
[171] John Quincy Adams to John Adams, 27 Jan. 1807, in Worthington C. Ford, ed., *Writings of John Quincy Adams*, 7 vols. (New York, 1913–17), III, 158; Ohline, 'Politics and Slavey,,' 413.
[172] Ohline, 'Politics and Slavery', 413–14.
[173] Duncan J. Macleod, *Slavery, Race and the American Revolution* (Cambridge, 1974), 156–7; Anthony A. Iaccarino, 'Virginia and the National Contest over Slavery in the Early Republic, 1780–1833' (University of California, Los Angeles, PhD dissertation, 1999), 126.
[174] Paul Finkelman, 'The Founders and Slavery: Little Ventured, Little Gained', *Yale Journal of Law and the Humanities*, 13/2 (2001), 432–3.

majority of representatives disagreed with their views and did not want the matter to be subject to state laws.[175] Discussion concentrated on whether *forfeited* meant that such persons would be free or slaves, whether penalties for those caught importing slaves in the future should be a fine or imprisonment, and whether the crime constituted a capital offence.[176] The debate on the death penalty was bitterly divisive, but in the end Northerners prevailed in ensuring this did not pass in the House of Representatives. Their main objection lay in classifying the slave trade as a felony.[177]

Neither forfeiture nor the death penalty were sectional issues but a sectional division emerged over the question of what to do with captured Africans after they were forfeited, with Southerners opposed to the federal government having control over this process. A motion to delete 'forfeiture' from the proposed legislation was defeated in the House by 77–39 votes on 7 January 1807. The conflict over enforcement mechanisms appeared to be heading for stalemate.[178] Benjamin Tallmadge of Connecticut feared, as the debates over slave trade restriction dragged 'heavily along', that 'we shall get no Bill at all, or one so ineffectual in its provisions as to be good for nothing'.[179] By mid-January, Timothy Pitkin of Connecticut concluded despondently that 'the ideas of the Southern and Northern members, are so different on this subject that it seems next to impossible for us to agree in the details of a Bill. The gentlemen from the southern states are determined that in case any Negros are imported after 1808 that they shall be sold as slaves by the United States. To this the northern gentlemen object, as in fact establishing slavery by law'.[180] Nevertheless, somewhat tortuous arguments on slave importation continued in Congress and agreement was finally reached. Eventually it was decided to strike out a clause that stipulated death as the punishment for owners and masters of vessels employed in the slave trade and to include a clause prescribing imprisonment for not less than five and not more than ten years for those who defied the law. The Senate bill eventually became

---

[175] Ohline, 'Politics and Slavery', 415–17.
[176] *Annals of Congress*, 9th Congress, 2nd session, House of Representatives, 17, 23 and 31 Dec. 1806, 167, 170–2, 221–2, 240–4.
[177] Ohline,' Politics and Slavery', 420–3.   [178] Ibid., 415, 418–19.
[179] Connecticut HS, Hartford, Benjamin Tallmadge to Jonathan Trumbull, 13 Jan. 1807, Jonathan Trumbull, Jr Papers.
[180] Connecticut HS, Timothy Pitkin to John Treadwell, 12 Jan. 1807, John Treadwell Papers.

law rather than the House of Representatives' bill.[181] As Lacy Ford put it, 'South Carolina yielded quietly to federal action'.[182]

Details of the bill were amended several times as the measure was debated in Congress. The final version made slave importations a misdemeanour punishable with imprisonment. It required masters of larger vessels taking slaves on coastwise voyages to declare that the slaves had not been imported after the beginning of 1808. And it stipulated that all smuggled slaves seized under the act should be disposed of according to the laws of the state or territory where the seizure took place. These conclusions were confirmed after divisions between northern and southern states had emerged in Congress on the matter of the slave trade. The South had been careful to ensure the bill was not seen to infringe states' rights or implicitly attack slaveholders while the North was divided between opposition to slavery and a desire to see an effective act passed to stop slave importations. Most Northerners took an antislavery posture towards ending the slave trade in 1808, while many Southerners stood firm to ensure domestic slavery within the United States was protected. After the House of Representatives voted in favour of a federal ban on slave imports by 63 votes to 49, Jefferson signed the bill into law on 2 March 1807.[183] This now meant that the federal government, for the first time, had the authority to make laws against the slave trade.[184] However, as Padraig Riley has argued, there was no 'consensual antislavery intent in the legislation'.[185] None of the four leading newspapers in the United States offered any commentary on the passage of the bill.[186]

The congressional debate on the slave trade in 1806 revealed the sectional divisions between the North and the South over slavery. It foreshadowed the greater sectional tension over slavery that sparked strong controversy in the United States from the era of the Missouri Compromise (1819–21) through the Civil War.[187] The debates over the slave trade in Congress in 1807 avoided humanitarian rhetoric, indicating

---

[181] For a summary of the debates, see Du Bois, *The Suppression of the African Slave-Trade*, 96–108, and Donald L. Robinson, *Slavery in the Structure of American Politics, 1765–1820* (New York, 1971), 324–37.
[182] Lacy Ford, 'Reconfiguring the Old South: "Solving" the Problem of Slavery', *Journal of American History*, 95/1 (2008), 104.
[183] Phillips, *American Negro Slavery*, 145–7; Wood, 'John Randolph of Roanoke', 117.
[184] Ericson, *Slavery in the American Republic*, 34.
[185] Padraig Riley, 'Slavery and the Problem of Democracy in Jeffersonian America' in Hammond and Mason, eds., *Contesting Slavery*, 235.
[186] Blackburn, *The Overthrow of Colonial Slavery*, 286.
[187] Mason, 'Slavery Overshadowed', 59–81.

that the ending of the African slave trade to the United States was not the result of a moral crusade. It was not surprising that an ethical tone was absent from the debates because during the previous generation, stretching back to the first Federal Congress in 1789–90, there had been no general debate in the legislature or elsewhere in the public sphere pertaining to the morality of the slave trade.[188] However, most Congressmen were now agreed that slave importation to the United States should end. As Sean Wilentz has argued, 'the slave trade battle revealed ... that northern antislavery sentiment was sizable, articulate, and far from passive'.[189]

The slave trade act passed by Congress in 1807 had ten sections. Among the most important issues established were the following: slave importation to the United States would become illegal after 1 January 1808; it would be illegal for a citizen to build or bring a slaving vessel to the United States; any such vessel could be apprehended and forfeited to the United States, with a forfeiture fine of $20,000; it would be illegal for a citizen to take on board ship any person to be sold as a slave in the United States, with a fine of $5,000 for anyone caught doing this in addition to the forfeiture of the ship; slaves on such ships were subject to state laws; people shipping slaves could be found guilty of 'high misdemeanour', imprisoned for between five and ten years and fined between $1,000 and $10,000; it would be illegal to import slaves from adjoining foreign territory; and the president had the authority to deploy the Navy to enforce the act.[190]

CONCLUSION

By the end of 1803, it appeared that the controversies over the transatlantic slave trade had been largely overcome in the United States. All states by then had stopped slave importations, including South Carolina, the most recalcitrant state dealing with this issue, where slave arrivals had been prevented by successive state laws passed since 1787. The expectation in late 1803 must therefore have been a quiet period before Congress would have the authority to intervene in the matter in 1808, if it chose to do so and that was by no means a certainty. However, the issue of the slave trade came to the fore dramatically as a political issue with the

---

[188] Seymour Drescher, *Abolition: A History of Slavery and Antislavery* (Cambridge, 2009), 135–6.
[189] Wilentz, *No Property in Man*, 185.   [190] Ohline, 'Politics and Slavery', 427–8.

acquisition of the Louisiana Territory by the United States in 1803, and the subsequent reopening of South Carolina's slave trade for the first time since the debates over the ratification of the Constitution.

The massive increase in US-owned territory through the Louisiana Purchase held out the possibility of further demand for slave labour, with Charleston acting as an entrepôt for furnishing new African imports across the southwest United States to New Orleans and Natchez. But there was no consensus among politicians either at federal or state level that this was a desirable outcome. The years between 1803 and 1806 were therefore marked by bitter controversies about whether to reopen the slave trade to South Carolina and then, after that had taken place, whether the trade should remain open. Divisions emerged in South Carolina between various sections of the state and between different planters. Regular debates on the status of the slave trade within the South Carolina legislature led to bills introduced in the state assembly and a series of votes that demonstrated divisions between the House of Representatives and the Senate and upcountry and lowcountry legislators. The subject also attracted detailed discussions in both houses of the federal Congress, with different political positions taken on the subject.

Jefferson's presidential message of December 1806, looking forward to the time when Congress could intervene constitutionally to prohibit the slave trade, gave notice that the issue would be subject to detailed scrutiny in the national legislature at the first available opportunity. Debates on the slave trade accordingly were regularly held in Congress and in South Carolina's state legislature in late 1806 and 1807 and the final result was for Congress to prohibit the slave trade to the United States from 1 January 1808. This was achieved, unlike in the contemporaneous British abolition of the slave trade, without significant abolitionist pressure or campaigning. In Congress, few representatives dwelt upon the morality and cruelty of the slave trade. Those aspects of the Guinea traffic had been extensively explored in previous years, and it seems to have been accepted that Congressional members no longer needed to make a case for abolition based on those grounds. Given that Charleston's newspapers were including articles against the slave trade in 1806–7, which was not the case in the 1790s, it appears that a moral case against the slave trade was no longer needed. Instead of reiterating humanitarian concerns, the US abolition act focussed on the technicalities of the legislation in relation to the fines and penalties to be enacted for those who transgressed the new federal law. Thus, as has been noted above, slave importations to the United States were banned at the first moment constitutionally that action on this matter could be taken. Though reservations were expressed about the details of the US abolition law, it was hoped that it would 'answer the purpose of restraining the unprincipled rapacity of the Dealers in human flesh'.[191]

[191] LCP, Samuel Emlen to William Dillwyn, 8 Feb. 1807, Dillwyn and Emlen Family Correspondence, box 6.

Epilogue

The abolition of the transatlantic slave trade to the United States was the result of proscribing the traffic step by step. It was determined by complex contingent factors and not by a wave of anti-slave trade campaigning. This was partly because the attack on the slave trade moved at different paces in various parts of North America; partly because of the location of political sovereignty; and partly because the issue of the slave trade was bound up with broader concerns over slavery and politics in the transition from the thirteen British colonies in North America to the new federal nation. Quakers, emphasising moral and humanitarian arguments against the slave trade, made significant inroads into banning the slave trade in Pennsylvania and New Jersey in the generation before the American Revolution, and their influence later spread throughout the northern colonies and states and into the Chesapeake by the 1780s. But the Quaker anti-slave trade stance did not spread sufficiently among other groups in North America to produce widespread disapprobation of the Guinea traffic by the time of the American revolutionary war. Thus, there was no national consensus against the slave trade when the United States was created.

Numerous colonies tried to restrict slave imports by imposing import duties on Africans for varied purposes. Virginia was the most active colony in this regard, but several others, such as Pennsylvania and South Carolina, passed regular laws to raise import duties on slaves. The restrictions were rarely based on humanitarian motives but on pragmatic economic calculations. However, these moves were always subject to the vetoes of the British Board of Trade and Privy Council and to the political sovereignty held by Britain before 1776. And in no case was there any colonial attempt to ban the slave trade altogether. During the revolutionary era, from the Declaration of Independence to the ratification of the Constitution, lack of a central government meant that the United States as a whole had no political authority to ban slave imports. The Continental Congresses favoured restricting slave imports but had no political mechanism through which they could act. Anti-slave trade action nevertheless had an important effect on state legislation over the slave trade in this period, with Massachusetts, Pennsylvania and Virginia ending their slave trades within a few years of one another.

The slave trade was debated vigorously at the Constitutional Convention of 1787 and Article 1, Section 9 of the Constitution forbade any interference by Congress over the slave trade until 1808. Debates over the ratification of the Constitution revealed that the slave trade was a contentious issue. The congressional ruling on the slave trade stalled any federal action on this matter for twenty years, but in that period, Congress implemented various other restrictions on the traffic in slaves, especially in relation to US participation in the foreign slave trade. The issue of the slave trade was raised and debated in the first federal Congress in 1790 and in subsequent years in the 1790s. Quaker groups lay behind the presentation of petitions to Congress at that time. The contentious views put forward in debates indicated that diverse views existed among politicians on the slave trade but that any attempt to interfere politically with the Guinea traffic would be robustly rebuffed by Lower South representatives, especially the delegation from South Carolina. By 1800, South Carolina, whose state politicians had closed the slave trade in 1787, still clung tenaciously to the view that she could decide whether she wanted to open or close Charleston to African imports. Debates over whether to open or close the slave trade were prominent features of South Carolina's political debates after the US purchase of the Louisiana Territory in 1803 – Charleston being an obvious entry port for any slaves imported for sale to planters in that territory.

When the federal legislature, at Jefferson's behest, debated the slave trade clause of the Constitution in 1806–7, very few delegates, even from the Lower South, supported the slave trade: South Carolina and Georgia had had twenty years since the constitutional clause in which to stock up slaves, and there was a widely held belief that Congress could, and would, act according to the Constitution and ban slave imports at the earliest opportunity. The resulting act of 1807 ending the slave trade to the United States concluded a battle that had proceeded as proscription by degrees rather than as the climax of successful anti-slave trade campaigning. It occurred when the demand for slave labour was expanding in the cotton and sugar belts of the deep South and when it was not crystal clear that reproduction of the existing US slave population would meet this demand.[1] Proscribing the slave trade can be seen as a delayed outcome of the American Revolution and as the first national success for antislavery forces in the United States even though, as noted, it was not mainly the result of antislavery rhetoric or activities.[2]

On 13 February 1807, the House of Representatives passed a bill for the abolition of the slave trade to the United States by 113 votes to 5. The vote suggests there was unanimity on the issue in Congress, but the act was hardly a major endorsement of antislavery for slaveholder power in the United States remained intact.[3] Nevertheless, abolishing the African slave trade to the United States was achieved by passing a significant statute. The act has been characterised by William W. Freehling as 'the most important slavery legislation that Congress ever passed'.[4] Joyce Appleby has also summed up the broad implications of the legislation: 'Jefferson's foreign policy in this one act did more to extend the realm of freedom than any deed of his contemporaries in the age of democratic revolutions'. It was Jefferson's last public act against slavery.[5] In 1813, George Logan praised Jefferson for achieving the proscription of the slave trade to the United States, stating that his 'prompt attention to the abolition of the slave trade' would 'be recorded by the faithful pen of the historian, to your immortal honor'.[6]

The nineteenth-century lawyer and historian George Ticknor Curtis was an early commentator who underscored the importance of slave trade proscription on a national basis. He perceptively explained the achievement of the congressional act against the slave trade, effective from 1 January 1808: 'the separate authority of the states would have been wholly unequal to the suppression of the slave-trade; for even if they had

---

[1] Adam Rothman, 'The Domestication of the Slave Trade in the United States' in Walter Johnson, ed., *The Chattel Principle: Internal Slave Trades in the Americas* (New Haven, CT, 2004), 35.
[2] James Sidbury, *Becoming African in America: Race and Nation in the Early Black Atlantic* (New York, 2007), 135.
[3] Padraig Riley, *Slavery and the Democratic Conscience: Political Life in Jeffersonian America* (Philadelphia, 2016), 120, 124.
[4] William W. Freehling, *The Road to Disunion. Volume 1. Secessionists at Bay, 1776–1854* (New York, 1990), 136.
[5] Joyce Appleby, *Thomas Jefferson* (New York, 2003), 131 (quotation), 138.
[6] HSP, George Logan to Thomas Jefferson, 18 Sept. 1813, Logan and Dickinson Family Papers, box 6.

all finally adopted the policy of a stringent prohibition, without a navy, and without treaties, they could never have contended against the bold artifice and desperate cunning of avarice, stimulated by the enormous gains which have always been reaped in this inhuman trade'.[7]

Though action over the slave trade had been delayed by contentious debates over slavery in the United States and by political divisions between South Carolina and the federal government, the end of the slave trade to the United States was only possible because a brief constitutional clause had separated congressional jurisdiction over its fate from other aspects of slavery. Paradoxically the proscription by degrees that characterised the American struggle to prohibit the slave trade was made necessary by the limits on congressional action for twenty years after 1788 but then was made possible on a federal level, and taken up with alacrity, precisely because it dealt with an aspect of US slavery that could be politically siphoned off from other features of slavery. Jefferson realised the discrete political status of the African slave trade when he gave his presidential address to Congress in late 1806. Thus, the American end of the slave trade, though achieved by degrees, succeeded because it compartmentalised a specific part of the problem of slavery that could, in 1808, lead to federal political action on constitutional grounds. As John Oldfield has put it, 'slaveholders – including figures such as Jefferson – could support abolition of the slave trade, safe in the knowledge that the institution of slavery itself remained intact and, to all intents and purposes, unassailable'.[8]

The Virginian slaveholder James Monroe, as United States minister to the United Kingdom, congratulated William Wilberforce on the British parliamentary abolition of the slave trade and bracketed its success with the virtually simultaneous American ending of the transatlantic slave trade. 'It is a very honourable trait in the character of both countries', Monroe wrote, 'to have combined their efforts for the accomplishment of so benevolent and humane an object. It does them more credit than the combinations which usually take place among nations, which are for the

---

[7] George Ticknor Curtis, *History of the Origin, Formation, and Adoption of the Constitution, of the United States; with Notices of Its Principal Framers*, 2 vols. (New York, 1861), II, 306.

[8] J. R. Oldfield, *Transatlantic Abolitionism in the Age of Revolution: An International History of Anti-slavery, c. 1787–1820* (Cambridge, 2013), 185.

destruction not the preservation of the human race'.[9] Nevertheless there was a crucial difference between the two abolitions. The demise of the slave trade to the United States did not depend, as in the British case, on getting humanitarian arguments accepted by legislators, for the various reasons already explained. Rather, it was a process that proceeded slowly, step by step, with prohibitions of the slave trade into individual states at different points in time and a congressional stalling of action on the slave trade for twenty-one years after the drafting of the US Constitution in 1788. The protection given to slavery in the Constitution was a much more intractable matter to resolve, and in the case of the United States it took the bloodiest war on its own soil to lead to slave emancipation more than half a century after Americans had legally stopped importing enslaved Africans.

Black Americans played little role in the various stages through which the transatlantic slave trade to the United States was ended. But they were often connected to abolitionist groups in cities such as New York and Philadelphia. Beginning on 1 January 1808, when the US act to abolish the slave trade went into effect, black leaders in the northern states gave annual sermons of thanks to mark the official end of the traffic in African captives to the United States.[10] Free black speakers such as Henry Sipkins, Peter Williams, Jr, Absalom Jones and George Lawrence gave orations that supported American republicanism and argued that ending the slave trade was one step towards achieving the main principles of the American Revolution, liberty and equality, for all people. Their collective message was one of hope for a better situation in relation to racial divisions in the United States.[11] Thus, the sermon by Absalom Jones, a free black and lay Methodist preacher, at St Thomas's church, Philadelphia, on 1 January

---

[9] James Monroe to William Wilberforce, 13 Feb. 1807, in Daniel Preston, ed., *The Papers of James Monroe. Volume 5. Selected Correspondence and Papers January 1803–April 1811* (Santa Barbara, CA, 2014), 583–4.

[10] Gary B. Nash, *Race and Revolution* (Madison, WI, 1990), 199.

[11] Paul J. Polgar, *Standard-Bearers of Equality: America's First Abolition Movement* (Chapel Hill, NC, 2019), 148; Henry Sipkins, *Oration on the Abolition of the Slave Trade; Delivered in the African Church, in the City of New-York, January 2, 1809* (New York, 1809); Peter Williams, Jr, *An Oration on the Abolition of the Slave Trade; Delivered in the African Church, in the City of New-York, January 1, 1808* (New York, 1808); Henry Johnson, *An Oration on the Abolition of the Slave Trade, by Henry Johnson; with an Introductory Address, by Adam Carman; Delivered in the African Church in New-York, January 1, 1810* (New York, 1810); Absalom Jones, *A Thanksgiving Sermon, Preached January 1, 1808, in St Thomas's, or the African Episcopal, Church, Philadelphia; On Account of the Abolition of the African Slave Trade, on That Day, by the Congress of the United States* (Philadelphia, 1808); George

1808, expressed hope that the abolition of slave importation to the United States was the first step leading towards full slave emancipation.[12] From 1808 until the 1820s, blacks in New York, Philadelphia and Baltimore celebrated 'Abolition Day', usually on 1 January, in churches and meeting rooms through Bible readings, orations, sermons and prayers.[13] However, by the end of the 1820s these celebrations had largely disappeared in northern cities as it became clear that ending of the African slave trade to the United States was not going to eradicate slavery from the nation.[14]

In the Lower South, slaveholders welcomed the fact that their slave population in future would mainly consist of acculturated creoles rather than Africans or potentially rebellious slaves imported via the Caribbean.[15] For the most part, however, there was a subdued response in the United States to the 1807 act, with few public celebrations, though a few congressmen nevertheless compiled circular letters for their constituents to comment on the passing of the law.[16] The Baltimore Yearly Meeting of the Society of Friends wrote a letter of praise and appreciation to Jefferson. In his reply, he stated that it is 'honourable to the nation at large that their legislature availed themselves of the first practicable moment for arresting the progress of this great moral and political error'.[17]

Lawrence, *An Oration on the Abolition of the Slave Trade, Delivered on the First Day of January, 1813, in the African Methodist Episcopal Church* (New York, 1813).

[12] Leonardo Marques, *The United States and the Transatlantic Slave Trade to the Americas, 1776-1867* (New Haven, CT, 2016), 52. St Thomas church was the first black Episcopal church in the United States.

[13] Mitch Kachun, *Festivals of Freedom: Memory and Meaning in African American Emancipation Celebrations, 1808-1915* (Amherst, MA, 2003), 16-53.

[14] Steven Deyle, 'An Ambiguous Legacy: The Closing of the African Slave Trade and America's Own Middle Passage' in David T. Gleeson and Simon Lewis, eds., *Ambiguous Anniversary: The Bicentennial of the International Slave Trade Bans* (Columbia, SC, 2012), 139.

[15] Lacy K. Ford, *Deliver Us from Evil: The Slavery Question in the Old South* (Oxford, 2009), 149.

[16] Howard A. Ohline, 'Politics and Slavery: The Issue of Slavery in National Politics, 1787–1815' (University of Missouri, Columbia, PhD dissertation, 1969), 429; University of North Carolina, Chapel Hill, Joseph Winston, Circular letter, 26 Feb. 1807; Virginia Historical Society, Richmond, John Rhea, Circular letter, 9 Feb. 1807.

[17] Ohline, 'Politics and Slavery', 430; *An Address of the Yearly Meeting of Friends, held at Baltimore to Thomas Jefferson, Pres. Of the United States, and His Reply* (Baltimore, 1807), n.p. (quotation).

The proscription of the transatlantic slave trade to the United States from 1 January 1808 did not end American involvement in the slave trade. Between 1808 and 1815, numerous individuals complained to the federal government that they were prevented from importing slaves. Captains who had set out on voyages before the 1807 act was passed or who had been prevented, in one way or another, from entering a US port by 1 January 1808 were particularly aggrieved about the way they were treated. In June 1809, one thousand slaves on ships from Cuba were forced to stay in the harbour at New Orleans without being allowed to unload their slaves.[18] In December 1810, James Madison, now President of the United States, spoke before Congress about violations occurring against the proscription of slave importation to the American nation, but this appears to have had little influence on antislavery activists to pursue the matter.[19]

The regulatory framework of the 1807 act against slave importation had a number of omissions. It did not indicate who would enforce the act; this was left to a combination of customs and state officials, the Treasury Department and the small US navy. Moreover, the act provided no funds to facilitate enforcement.[20] The 1807 measure was extended in further acts of 1818, 1819 and 1820. But, as might be expected, none of this legislation fully stopped the slave trade. Some Americans with a continuing interest in the slave trade moved their bases to Cuba and to the small Caribbean islands of St Thomas and St Eustatius, but North Americans generally reduced their participation in this trade in the second decade of the nineteenth century.[21] The end of the legal slave trade to the United States did not solve the problem of smuggling Africans into the nation, however, for it continued for many years thereafter.[22] An illegal slave trade by foreign privateers continued after the 1807 act. It was especially found in the Spanish borderlands, which were difficult to patrol.[23]

[18] Ohline, 'Politics and Slavery', 435–7.
[19] Oldfield, *Transatlantic Abolitionism*, 198–9.
[20] Randy J. Sparks, 'Blind Justice: The United States's Failure to Curb the Illegal Slave Trade', *Law and History Review*, 35/1 (2017), 55.
[21] David Eltis, *Economic Growth and the Ending of the Transatlantic Slave Trade* (New York, 1987), 55–6.
[22] This is a major theme in W. E. B. Du Bois, *Suppression of the African Slave-Trade to the United States of America, 1638–1870* (Cambridge, MA, 1896). See also Ernest Obadele-Starks, *Freebooters and Smugglers: The Foreign Slave Trade to the United States after 1808* (Fayetteville, AK, 2007).
[23] David Head, 'Slave Smuggling by Foreign Privateers: The Illegal Slave Trade and the Geopolitics of the Early Republic', *Journal of the Early Republic*, 33/3 (2013), 433–62.

Spanish Florida and Texas were among the areas favoured by smugglers.[24]

Many slaves brought illegally to the United States had been taken from ships in the Spanish slave trade, which was still legal. Smugglers frequently bribed officials to smuggle slaves into the United States and those dealing with the illicit trade often arrived too late to capture the Africans brought in by this means. It proved difficult for the US authorities to prevent the illegal importation of slaves in East Florida and the Gulf of Mexico.[25] To counter freebooters smuggling slaves into US territory, the federal government invaded Spanish-owned East Florida in 1817, to curtail the traffic and protect its borders. East Florida had been a base for smuggling slaves and contraband into Georgia. Smuggling via this route diminished after Spain ceded Florida to the United States in 1819. US naval action against slave ships had reduced smuggling of Africans into the Gulf states by 1822.[26]

Various estimates have been produced for the scale of this illegal trade. Du Bois's estimate of 250,000 slaves brought illegally into the United States between 1807 and 1862 has been discarded as being based on inadequate evidence.[27] David Eltis has argued that a much lower figure of 46,000 smuggled slaves were landed in the United States between 1808 and 1860.[28] This figure, however, is not supported by data: Eltis arrives at his estimate by generously accepting Philip D. Curtin's suggestion of 1,000 captives imported per year, which would give a total of 54,000 for the years between 1808 and 1861.[29] It is likely that the actual figure was much lower. Imports from transatlantic vessels provided only a total of 504 captives between 1821 and 1865.[30] Captives arrived in the United States from the intra-American trade after 1821. The total is

---

For a detailed analysis of the evasion of the US slave trade proscription, see Sean M. Kelley, *American Slavers: Merchants, Mariners, and the Transatlantic Commerce in Captives, 1644–1865* (New Haven, CT, 2023), 309–37.

[24] Sparks, 'Blind Justice', 56–7.
[25] Sarah A. Batterson, 'A Horde of Foreign Freebooters: The U.S. and the Suppression of the Slave Trade', *Diacronie*, 13/1 (2013), 1–2, 8–9, 13; Richard G. Lowe, 'American Seizure of Amelia Island,' *Florida Historical Quarterly*, 45/1 (1966), 18–30.
[26] Fehrenbacher with McAfee, *The Slaveholding Republic*, 149, 155.
[27] Du Bois, *Suppression of the African Slave-Trade*, 117–18, 124–5, 165–6.
[28] Eltis, 'The U.S. Transatlantic Slave Trade', 353. For arguments against a large Cuba–Florida slave trade after 1807, see Kenneth F. Kiple, 'The Case against a Nineteenth-Century Cuba–Florida Slave Trade', *Florida Historical Quarterly*, 49/4 (1971), 346–55.
[29] Philip D. Curtin, *The Atlantic Slave Trade: A Census* (Madison, WI, 1969), 74–5.
[30] www.slavevoyages.org.

unknown but it probably amounted only to small numbers of confiscations.[31] Slaveholders found that demographic growth gave them a surplus of slaves after 1807 while Americans wanting to continue their participation in slave trading turned their attention to involvement in the foreign slave trade to other countries.[32]

The United States passed a series of supplementary slave trade acts between 1818 and 1820 intended to take a moral stand against slave trading and as a protective measure against piratical strongholds at Galveston, in the Gulf of Mexico and Amelia Island in East Florida. The act of 1818 revised the act of 1807. It increased penalties for buying and selling slaves illegally. A further act of 1819 brought in additional changes to strengthen the anti-slave trade posture. It enabled American naval vessels to cruise along the west African coast and rewarded naval officers with bounties and prize money for capturing slave ships. It also placed confiscated slaves under the jurisdiction of a local federal marshal, who was instructed to arrange for their return to Africa, rather than handing them over to state authorities, which, in the case of southern states, might have condemned them to a life of slavery. An act of 1820, made permanent three years later, defined slave trading as piracy and imposed capital punishment as the penalty. This was the last legislation in the United States concerning the slave trade before the American Civil War.[33] Sean M. Kelley has referred to it as 'the high-watermark of the legislative assault on the slave trade'.[34]

An extensive internal slave trade continued within the United States (amounting to around 700,000 people) in the period from Jefferson's presidency through the Civil War. More black people were moved along this internal middle passage from one state to another than were ever brought across the Atlantic to North America before 1808.[35] This traffic reflected the demographic increase in slavery through fertility, the deployment of surplus slaves to westward areas away from the southeast states, and the unceasing demand for enslaved labour in relation to the cotton boom. Some of the domestic slave trade was an overland affair to western lands, but it was also a seaborne commerce, with New Orleans serving as its major entrepôt.[36] The seaborne shipment of slaves from the

---

[31] Sean M. Kelley has advised me on this point.
[32] Fehrenbacher with McAfee, *The Slaveholding Republic*, 201–2.
[33] Ibid., 150–2, 191; Sparks, 'Blind Justice', 57–8. [34] Kelley, *American Slavers*, 316–17.
[35] Deyle, 'An Ambiguous Legacy', 139.
[36] For the scale and characteristics of this form of slave trading, see Michael Tadman, *Speculators and Slaves: Masters, Traders, and Slaves in the Old South* (Madison, WI,

Chesapeake to the lower Mississippi Valley continued between the 1810s and the 1850s.[37] Other branches of the coastwise slave trade included that operating between New Orleans and Natchez.[38] By the 1850s more than 250,000 slaves were transferred from the South Atlantic states, Kentucky and Tennessee to the Gulf states and Arkansas.[39]

The federal government did little to curtail American participation in the slave trade to other nations. Its actions in this regard were notably weak. Such traffic was illegal in the United States, but it attracted much US participation via ships and crew after 1808.[40] Even at the time of the American Civil War, many slave ships taking captives to Brazil and Cuba were financed in New York City.[41] The federal government experienced difficulties in dealing with US participation in the slave trade. In Spring of 1824, a group of Republican senators attempted to weaken the federal government's ability to suppress the slave trade as a political tactic in an upcoming presidential election. The re-emergence of political parties during that election year helped to push suppression of the slave trade to the background as worries about party politics came to the fore on the federal agenda.[42]

The United States had a small African squadron that sent out occasional cruisers in the 1820s and 1830s.[43] Under the Webster-Ashburton Treaty of 1842 the United States, among several other important issues,

---

1996); Steven Deyle, *Carry Me Back: The Domestic Slave Trade in American Life* (New York, 2006); Robert H. Gudmestad, *A Troublesome Commerce: The Transformation of the Interstate Slave Trade* (Baton Rouge, LA, 2003); and Walter Johnson, ed., *The Chattel Principle: Internal Slave Trades in the Americas* (New Haven, CT, 2004).

[37] See two studies by Calvin Schermerhorn: 'Capitalism's Captives: The Maritime United States Slave Trade, 1807-1850', *Journal of Social History*, 47/4 (2014), 897–921, and 'The Coastwise Slave Trade and a Mercantile Community of Interest' in Sven Beckert and Seth Rockman, eds., *Slavery's Capitalism: A New History of American Economic Development* (Philadelphia, 2016), 209-23.

[38] Richard MacMillan, 'A Journey of Lost Souls: New Orleans to Natchez Slave Trade of 1840', *Gulf Coast Historical Review*, 13 (1998), 49-59.

[39] Richard Sutch, 'The Breeding of Slaves for Sale and the Westward Expansion of Slavery, 1850–1860' in Stanley L. Engerman and Eugene D. Genovese, eds., *Race and Slavery in the Western Hemisphere: Quantitative Studies* (Princeton, NJ, 1975), 179–80.

[40] Riley, *Slavery and the Democratic Conscience*, 119; Fehrenbacher with McAfee, *The Slaveholding Republic*, 135–204.

[41] John Harris, *The Last Slave Ships: New York and the End of the Middle Passage* (New Haven, CT, 2022).

[42] Craig B. Hollander, 'Corrupt Bargaining: Partisan Politics, the Election of 1824, and the Suppression of the African Slave Trade', *Journal of the Early Republic*, 42/3 (2022), 359–87.

[43] Eltis, *Economic Growth and the Ending of the Transatlantic Slave Trade*, 94.

agreed to maintain US warships off the west African coast to search suspected slaving vessels flying the American flag. This was only implemented, however, in a lukewarm manner. Between 1843 and 1861, the United States' Africa Squadron patrolled the West African coast to intercept American ships or those flying the American flag that were participating in slave trading, but this effort was rendered ineffectual by the squadron only having half a dozen ships and also by the fact that American cruisers were often too large and easily seen by illicit traders.[44]

Some American merchants continued to provide ships, equipment and supplies for foreign slave ships in the first half of the nineteenth century. They tried to evade capture by sailing under foreign flags and keeping several sets of papers on board in different languages.[45] It was difficult to ascertain the extent of US involvement in the foreign slave trade for several reasons: some were joint ventures between American, Spanish and British merchants, while some were Spanish voyages using US-built ships and American crew. Americans could act as intermediaries in some aspect of the foreign slave trade, but documentary evidence was often falsified or absent.[46] The United States was often delinquent in intercepting US slave trading vessels and British ships could not capture American ships sailing under the American flag with American papers.[47]

Immediately after the passing of the 1807 act, Americans were significant participants in the slave trade to Cuba. Between 1808 and 1811, for example, slave ships owned by US citizens carried 30 per cent of the Africans taken to that Spanish colony. This share plummeted, however, between 1812 and 1820.[48] The use of the American flag in the Cuban slave trade increased significantly after 1835, but British interception of these vessels appears to have been more vigorous in terms of stop-and-search than American interventions.[49] Certainly, there were only a modest number of captures of slaving vessels or ships fitted out to contain slaves by the US navy. That navy's Brazil squadron, for example, did not take a ship into custody before 1845 even though American involvement occurred in landing more than 350,000 slaves in Brazil during the 1840s and US-built ships were used in 58 per cent of the slaving voyages

---

[44] Ibid., 95; Sparks, 'Blind Justice', 76.
[45] Fehrenbacher with McAfee, *The Slaveholding Republic*, 156–7.
[46] Marques, *The United States and the Transatlantic Slave Trade*, 61–2, 65.
[47] Sparks, 'Blind Justice', 64.
[48] Marques, *The United States and the Transatlantic Slave Trade*, 63.
[49] Fehrenbacher with McAfee, *The Slaveholding Republic*, 162.

connected to Brazil between 1831 and 1850. Americans were heavily involved, in particular, in the contraband slave trade to Rio de Janeiro.[50]

The 1807 act to proscribe slave imports to the United States was not opposed to any significant degree and, as indicated above, it was supplemented by various other acts, notably between 1818 and 1820, that sought to strengthen and extend its penalties for Americans caught in what was now illegal activity. Smuggling of slaves still continued after 1808 but there were attempts to close the loopholes by naval intervention and, in terms of numbers, the level of illegal slave trading into the United States was never really extensive. It proved more difficult to stamp out US participation in the foreign slave trade in the first half of the nineteenth century despite naval patrols and stiff legal penalties. Moreover, US participation in slave trading continued via a substantial internal slave trade from east to west, both overland and coastwise, down to the Civil War. Though the 1807 act was important in ending the legal import of Africans to the United States, these other forms of slave trading proved more intractable to stop.

---

[50] Ibid., 175, 179; Marques, *The United States and the Transatlantic Slave Trade*, 143, 149; Leonardo Marques, 'The Contraband Slave Trade to Brazil and the Dynamics of U.S. Participation, 1831–1856', *Journal of Latin American Studies*, 47 (2015), 659–84.

Bibliography

Manuscripts

Massachusetts Historical Society, Boston

Jeremy Belknap Papers
Dwight Foster Papers
John Adams Papers

Peabody Essex Institute, Salem

Essex County Court of Common Pleas, volume 14

Connecticut Historical Society, Hartford

Oliver Wolcott, Jr Papers
Jonathan Trumbull, Jr Papers
John Treadwell Papers

Rhode Island Historical Society, Providence

Quaker Collection: Providence Society for Abolishing the Slave Trade Minute Book (1789–1827)
Moses Brown Papers (partly available at the Brown University Library Digital Repository, https://repository.library.brown.edu)

New York Public Library

Digital Collections

New York Historical Society

Copies of letters to Granville Sharp
Gilder Lehrman Collection: Benjamin Franklin to Samuel Huntington, 12 January 1788, James Pemberton to Moses Brown, 17 May 1788

New Jersey Historical Society, Newark

Jonathan Dayton Papers

Historical Society of Pennsylvania, Philadelphia

Parrish and Pemberton Families Papers
Pemberton Papers
Pennsylvania Abolition Society Papers (A digital edition of these papers was published by Adam Matthew in 2013.)
    Series 2.1 Loose correspondence outgoing, 1783–1914
    Series 2.1 Committee of Correspondence letterbook, 1789–94
    Series 2.2 Loose correspondence incoming, 1784–95
Cox-Parrish-Wharton Papers, box 1
Wilson MSS: James Wilson's notes
Wallace Papers
George Logan Papers
Simon Gratz Autograph Collection

Library Company of Philadelphia

Benjamin Rush Papers
Dillwyn and Emlen Family Correspondence

Haverford College Library, Quaker Collection

Anthony Benezet correspondence
Richard T. Cadbury Collection
Robert Pleasants letterbook (1754–97), https://digitalcollectons.tricolib.brynmawr.edu
Vaux Family Papers
Allinson Papers
Philadelphia Yearly Meeting of Friends Minutes

Friends' Historical Library, Swarthmore College

Parrish Family Papers, 1780–1866 (Record Group 5 229)
Wood Manuscripts (Record Group 5 192)

Maryland Center for History and Culture, Baltimore

Briggs-Stabler Papers

Library of Congress, Washington, DC

Robert Pleasants letterbook (1771–81)
Pinckney Family Papers
Edward Rutledge Papers
Neil Jamieson Papers

National Archives and Records Administration, Washington, DC

Petitions and Memorials: Various Subjects, Senate Records, Record Group 46

Swem Library, College of William and Mary, Williamsburg, Virginia

Robert Pleasants letterbook (1772–81), https://digitalarchive.wm.edu

Virginia Historical Society, Richmond

John Rhea circular letter, 1807

Library of Virginia, Richmond

William Allason letterbook (1757–70)

University of Virginia Library, Charlottesville

Harry Piper letterbook (1767–76)

William R. Perkins Library, Duke University

Charles Pinckney Papers
Thomas Pinckney Papers
John Rutledge, Jr Papers

University of North Carolina, Chapel Hill

Randolph Collection (available on microfilm at the University of Virginia library)
Joseph Winston circular letter, 1807

South Caroliniana Library, University of South Carolina, Columbia

Manigault Family Papers
Ralph Izard Papers
C. C. Pinckney Papers
Thomas Pinckney Papers

South Carolina Department of Archives and History, Columbia

Clerk's notes filed under Journals of the House of Representatives, rough copy, 1792, House Proceedings, 11, 12, 15 December 1792
South Carolina General Assembly, House Journal, 1803
South Carolina Senate Journal

South Carolina Historical Society

Miscellaneous Manuscripts Collection

Henry E. Huntington Library, San Marino, California

Collection and Papers of R. A. Brock
 Robert Pleasants Papers

Library of the Society of Friends, London

Miscellaneous MSS
Letters to and from Philadelphia

The National Archives, Kew

CO 5/420, 1319, 1321, 1322, 1332, 1349, 1351, 1396, 1404

Newspapers and Magazines

Alexandria Expositor
American Minerva (New York)
American Museum
Aurora General Advertiser
Boston Evening-Post
Boston Gazette
Brunswick Gazette
Charleston City Gazette
Charleston Courier
Charleston Evening Gazette
Chronicle (Augusta, Georgia)
Columbian Centinel
Gazette of the United States
Haverhill Observer
Independent Chronicle (Boston)
Independent Gazetteer (Philadelphia)
Kline's Carlisle Weekly Gazette (Carlisle, Pennsylvania)
Maryland Herald and Hager's Town Weekly Advertiser

National Intelligencer and Washington (DC) Advertiser
New Haven Gazette
New-York Commercial Advertiser
New York Daily Advertiser
New York Daily Gazette
New York Journal
New York Morning Post
Newport Herald
Newport Mercury
Norfolk and Portsmouth Journal
Pennsylvania Chronicle
Pennsylvania Gazette
Pennsylvania Packet
Philadelphia Freemen's Journal
Philadelphia Independent Gazetteer
Pittsfield Sun
Poulson's Daily American Advertiser (Philadelphia)
Providence Gazette
Republican Farmer (Danbury, Connecticut)
Republican Star or Eastern Shore Advertiser
Richmond Enquirer
Salem Gazette
Spooner's Vermont Journal
The Albany Register
The Boston-Gazette, and Country Journal
The Connecticut Courant, and Hartford Weekly Intelligencer
The Connecticut Gazette; and the Universal Intelligencer
The Connecticut Journal
The Democratic Press
The Essex Journal and Merrimack Packet: OR The Massachusetts and New Hampshire General Advertiser
The New Hampshire Gazette
The New-London Gazette
The North Carolina Gazette
The Providence Gazette; and Country Journal
The Sun (Pittsfield, Massachusetts)
The United States Chronicle: Political, Commercial and Historical
Worcester Magazine

Published Primary Sources

A Report of the Records Commissioners of the City of Boston Containing the Boston Town Records, 1758–1769 (Boston: Rockwell and Churchill, 1886). https://onlinebooks.library.upenn.edu

Acts and Resolves, Public and Private, of the Massachusetts Bay Colony, 21 vols. (Boston: State Printers, 1869–1919).

Acts of Assembly passed in the Province of New-York. From 1691, to 1718 (London: John Baskett, 1719).
Acts of the General Assembly of the Province of New Jersey (Burlington, NJ: Isaac Collins, 1776).
Acts of the General Assembly of the State of South Carolina, from February, 1791, to December, 1794, Both Inclusive. Volume I (Columbia, SC: D. & J. J. Faust, State Printers, 1808).
Acts of the General Assembly of the State of South Carolina, from December, 1795, to December, 1804, Both Inclusive. Volume II (Columbia, SC: D. & J. J. Faust, State Printers, 1808).
Adams, Lark Emerson and Rosa Stoney Lumpkin, eds., *The State Records of South Carolina: Journals of the House of Representatives, 1785–1786* (Columbia, SC: University of South Carolina Press, 1979).
An Address of the Yearly Meeting of Friends, Held at Baltimore to Thomas Jefferson, Pres. of the United States, and His Reply (Baltimore: Samuel Wood, 1807).
An Epistle of Caution and Advice Concerning the Buying and Keeping of Slaves (Philadelphia: Philadelphia Yearly Meeting, 1754).
Alexander, Ann, *An Address to the Inhabitants of Charleston, South Carolina* (Philadelphia: by the author, 1805).
Ames, Seth, ed., *Works of Fisher Ames*, 2 vols. (Boston: Little, Brown and Company, 1854).
Annals of Congress of the United States (Washington, DC: Gales and Seaton, 1834–56). https://memory.loc.gov
[Appleton, Nathaniel], *Considerations on Slavery. In a Letter to a Friend* (Boston: Edes and Gill, 1767).
Bartlett, John R., ed., *Records of the Colony of Rhode Island and Providence Plantations in New England, 1636–1792* (Providence: A. C. Green, 1856–65).
Basker, James G., ed., *Early American Abolitionists: A Collection of Anti-slavery Writings 1760–1820* (New York: The Gilder Lehrman Institute of American History, 2005).
Benezet, Anthony, *Observations on the Inslaving, Importing and Purchasing of Negroes with Some Advice Thereon Extracted from the Yearly Meeting Epistle of London for the Present Year Also Some Remarks on the Absolute Necessity of Self-Denial, Renouncing the World, and True Charity for All Such As Sincerely Desire To Be Our Blessed Saviour's Disciples* (Germantown, PA: Christopher Sower, 1759).
Bickford, Charlene Bangs, ed., *Documentary History of the First Federal Congress. Volume 18: October 1789–March 14, 1790* (Baltimore: Johns Hopkins University Press, 2011).
Bickford, Charlene Bangs, Kenneth R. Bowling, William Charles diGiacomantonio and Helen E. Veit, eds., *Documentary History of the First Federal Congress of the United States of America. Volume 16. Correspondence. First Session, June–August 1789* (Baltimore: Johns Hopkins University Press, 2004).
Bickford, Charlene Bangs, Kenneth R. Bowling, Helen E. Veit and William Charles diGiacomantonio, eds., *Documentary History of the First Federal*

Congress of the United States of America. Volume 19. Correspondence: Second Session: 15 March–June 1790 (Baltimore: Johns Hopkins University Press, 2011).

Bowling, Kenneth R., William Charles diGiacomantonio and Charlene Bangs Bickford, eds., Documentary History of the First Federal Congress of the United States of America. Volume 8. Petition Histories and Nonlegislative Official Documents (Baltimore: Johns Hopkins University Press, 1998).

Bowling, Kenneth R. and Helen E. Veit, eds., Documentary History of the First Federal Congress of the United States of America. Volume 9. The Diary of William Maclay and Other Notes on Senate Debates (Baltimore: The Johns Hopkins University Press, 1988).

Boyd, Julian P. et al., eds., The Papers of Thomas Jefferson, 49 vols. to date (Princeton, NJ: Princeton University Press, 1950–).

Branagan, Thomas, Serious Remonstrances Addressed to the Citizens of the Northern States, and Their Representatives, Being an Appeal to Their Natural Feelings & Common Sense, Consisting of Speculations and Animadversions, the Recent Revival of the Slave Trade, in the American Republic (Philadelphia: Thomas T. Stiles, 1805).

Brissot de Warville, J. P., New Travels in the United States of America. Performed in 1788 (London: J. S. Jordan, 1788).

Brock, R. A., ed., The Official Letters of Alexander Spotswood, Lieutenant-Governor of the Colony of Virginia, 1710–1722, 2 vols. (Richmond, VA: Virginia Historical Society, 1882–85).

Brown, Everett S., ed., 'The Senate Debate on the Breckinridge Bill for the Government of Louisiana, 1804', American Historical Review, 22/2 (1917): 345–50.

Brown, Everett Somerville, ed., William Plumer's Memorandum of Proceedings in the United States Senate 1803–1807 (New York: Da Capo Press, 1923).

Brunhouse, Robert L., 'David Ramsay, 1749–1815: Selections from His Writings', Transactions of the American Philosophical Society, new series, 55/4 (Philadelphia: American Philosophical Society, 1965).

Bruns, Roger A., ed., Am I Not a Man and a Brother? The Antislavery Crusade of Revolutionary America, 1688–1788 (New York: Chelsea House, 1977).

Bushman, Claudia L. et al., eds., Proceedings of the Assembly of the Lower Counties on Delaware, 1770–1776, of the Constitutional Convention of 1776, and of the House of Assembly of the Delaware State, 1776–1781, 2 vols. (Newark: University of Delaware Press, 1986–8).

Butterfield, L. H., ed., Letters of Benjamin Rush, 2 vols. (Princeton, NJ: Princeton University Press, 1951).

Carter, Clarence Edwin, ed., The Territorial Papers of the United States. Volume 9. The Territory of Orleans 1803–1812 (Washington, DC: United States Government Printing Office, 1940).

Chesnutt, David R. and C. James Taylor, eds., The Papers of Henry Laurens, vol. 16: September 1, 1782–December 17, 1792 (Columbia: University of South Carolina Press, 2003).

Cohn, Ellen R., ed., The Papers of Benjamin Franklin. Volume 39. January 21 through May 15, 1783 (New Haven, CT: Yale University Press, 2008).

Collections of the Massachusetts Historical Society: The Belknap Papers, fifth series, volume 3 (Boston: The Massachusetts Historical Society, 1877).

Cooke, Jacob E., ed., *The Federalist* (Middletown, CT: Wesleyan University Press, 1961).

Cooper, Thomas and David J. McCord, eds., *The Statutes at Large of South Carolina*, 10 vols. (Columbia, SC: Printed by A. S. Johnston, 1836–41).

Corner, George W., ed., *The Autobiography of Benjamin Rush. His "Travels through Life" Together with His Commonplace Book for 1789–1813* (Princeton, NJ: Princeton University Press for the American Philosophical Society, 1948).

Crosby, David L., ed., *The Complete Antislavery Writings of Anthony Benezet, 1754–1783: An Annotated Critical Edition* (Baton Rouge: Louisiana State University Press, 2014).

Dana, James, *The African Slave Trade. A Discourse Delivered in the City of New-Haven, September 9, 1790, before the Connecticut Society for the Promotion of Freedom* (New Haven, CT: Thomas and Samuel Green, 1790).

De Pauw, Linda Grant, Charlene Bangs Bickford and LaVonne Siegel Hauptman, eds., *Documentary History of the First Federal Congress of the United States of America. Volume 3. House of Representatives Journal* (Baltimore: The Johns Hopkins University Press, 1977).

Deane, Charles, ed., *Letters and Documents Relating to Slavery in Massachusetts* (Cambridge, MA: John Wilson and Son, 1877).

Donnan, Elizabeth, ed., *Documents Illustrative of the History of the Slave Trade to America*, 4 vols. (Washington, DC: Carnegie Institution of Washington, 1930–5).

Drayton, John, *A View of South-Carolina, as Respects Her Natural and Civil Concerns* (Charleston, SC: W. P. Young, 1802).

Edgar, Walter B., ed., *The Letterbook of Robert Pringle, 1737–1745*, 2 vols. (Columbia: University of South Carolina Press, 1972).

Edwards, Adele Stanton, ed., *Journals of the Privy Council 1783–1789*, The State Records of South Carolina (Columbia, SC: University of South Carolina Press, 1971).

Edwards, Jonathan, *The Injustice and Impolicy of the Slave Trade, and of the Slavery of the Africans: Illustrated in a Sermon Preached before the Connecticut Society for the Promotion of Freedom, and for the Relief of Persons Unlawfully Holden in Bondage, at Their Annual Meeting in New-Haven, September 15, 1791* (New Haven, CT: Thomas and Samuel Green, 1791).

Elliot, Jonathan, ed., *The Debates in the Several State Conventions on the Adoption of the Federal Constitution; As Recommended by the General Convention at Philadelphia in 1787*, 5 vols. (Washington, DC: printed for the editor, 1836–45).

Farrand, Max, ed., *The Records of the Federal Convention of 1787*, 4 vols. (New Haven, CT: Yale University Press, 1937).

Force, Peter, ed., *American Archives, Fourth Series: Containing a Documentary History of the English Colonies in North America, from the King's Message to Parliament, of March 7, 1774, to the Declaration of Independence by the*

United States, 6 vols. (Washington, DC: M. St Clair Clarke and Peter Force, 1837–56).
Ford, Worthington C., ed., *Journals of the Continental Congress, 1774–1789*, 34 vols. (Washington, DC: Government Printing Office, 1904–37).
Writings of John Quincy Adams, 7 vols. (New York: The Macmillan Company, 1913–17).
Frost, J. William, ed., *The Quaker Origins of Antislavery* (Norwood, PA: Norwood Editions, 1980).
Georgini, Sara, Sara Martin, R. M. Barlow, Gwen Fries, Amanda M. Norton and Hobson Woodward, eds., *The Adams Papers: Papers of John Adams. Volume 21. March 1791–January 1797* (Cambridge, MA: Belknap Press, 2022).
Hackett, Mary A., J. C. A. Stagg, Ellen J. Barber, Anne Mandeville Colony and Angela Krieder, eds., *The Papers of James Madison, Secretary of State Series. Volume 6. 1 November 1803–31 March 1804* (Charlottesville: University of Virginia Press, 2002).
Hall, Clayton Colman, ed., *Archives of Maryland. Proceedings and Acts of the General Assembly of Maryland. May 1717–April 1720. Volume XXXIII* (Baltimore: Maryland Historical Society, 1913).
Hazard, Samuel et al., eds., *Pennsylvania Archives*, 16 vols. (Harrisburg, PA: T. Fenn & Co., 1831–53).
Henry, William Wirt, ed., *Patrick Henry: Life, Correspondence, and Speeches*, 3 vols. (New York: Scribner, 1891).
Hillman, Benjamin J., ed., *Executive Journals of the Council of Colonial Virginia. Volume VI (June 20, 1754–May 3, 1775)* (Richmond, VA: Virginia State Library, 1966).
Hoadly, Charles J., ed., *The Public Records of the Colony of Connecticut, from October, 1772 to April, 1775 inclusive* (Hartford, CT: Case, Lockwood & Brainard Co., 1887).
Hoare, Prince, *Memoirs of Granville Sharp, Esq. Composed from his own Manuscripts and other Authentic Documents in the Possession of his Family and of the African Institution* (London: Henry Colburn and Co., 1820).
Hobson, Charles F. and Robert A. Rutland, eds., *The Papers of James Madison. Volume 13: 20 January 1790–31 March 1791* (Charlottesville: University Press of Virginia, 1981).
Hopkins, Samuel, *A Dialogue Concerning the Slavery of the Africans; Shewing it to Be the Duty and Interest of the American States to Emancipate All Their African Slaves* (Norwich, CT: Judah P. Spooner, 1776).
  A Discourse upon the Slave-Trade, and the Slavery of the Africans. Delivered in the Baptist Meeting-House before the Providence Society for Abolishing the Slave-Trade &c. At Their Annual Meeting on May 17, 1793 (Providence, RI: J. Carter, 1793).
Hutson, James H., ed., *Supplement to Max Farrand's The Records of the Federal Convention of 1787* (New Haven, CT: Yale University Press, 1987).
Jackson, Donald and Dorothy Twohig, eds., *The Diaries of George Washington. Volume 6: 1 January 1790–13 December 1799* (Charlottesville: University Press of Virginia, 1979).

Jameson, J. Franklin, ed., 'Diary of Edward Hooker, 1805–1808', *Report of the Historical Manuscripts Commission of the American Historical Association for 1896*: 842–929.

Janson, Charles William, *The Stranger in America: Containing Observations Made in a Long Residence in that Country, on the Genius, Manners and Customs of the People of the United States; With Biographical Particulars of Public Characters; Hints and Facts relative to the Arts, Sciences, Commerce, Agriculture, Manufactures, Emigration, and the Slave Trade* (London: Albion Press, 1807).

Jefferson, Thomas, *A Summary View of the Rights of British America* (London: Kearsly, 1774).

Jensen, Merrill, ed., *Ratification of the Constitution by the States: Delaware, New Jersey, Georgia, Connecticut* (Madison, WI: State Historical Society of Wisconsin, 1978).

Jensen, Merrill, John P. Kaminski and Gaspare J. Saladino, eds., *Ratification of the Constitution by the States: Pennsylvania* (Madison, WI: State Historical Society of Wisconsin, 1976).

Johnson, Henry, *An Oration on the Abolition of the Slave Trade, by Henry Johnson; With an Introductory Address, by Adam Carman; Delivered in the African Church in New-York, January 1, 1810* (New York: John C. Totten, 1810).

Johnson, Henry P., ed., *The Correspondence and Public Papers of John Jay*, 4 vols. (New York: G. P. Putnam's Sons, 1890–3).

Jones, Absalom, *A Thanksgiving Sermon, Peached January 1, 1808, in St Thomas's, or the African Episcopal, Church, Philadelphia; On Account of the Abolition of the African Slave Trade, on That Day, by the Congress of the United States* (Philadelphia: Fry and Kammerer, 1808).

Journals of the House of Representatives of Massachusetts. Volume 40. 1763–1764 (Boston: Massachusetts Historical Society, 1970). https://memory.loc.gov

Journals of the House of Representatives of Massachusetts. Volume 43. Part 2. 1767 (Boston: Massachusetts Historical Society, 1974). https://memory.loc.gov

Journals of the House of Representatives of Massachusetts. Volume 47. 1770–1771 (Boston: Massachusetts Historical Society, 1978). https://memory.loc.gov

Journals of the House of Representatives of Massachusetts. Volume 49. 1772–1773 (Boston: Massachusetts Historical Society, 1980). https://memory.loc.gov

Kaminski, John P., ed., *A Necessary Evil? Slavery and the Debate over the Constitution* (Madison, WI: Madison House, 1995).

Kaminski, John P., Gaspare J. Saladino and Richard Leffler, eds., *Commentaries on the Constitution, Public and Private. Volume 2: 8 November to 17 December 1787* (Madison, WI: State Historical Society of Wisconsin, 1983).

Commentaries on the Constitution, Public and Private. Volume 3: 18 December 1787 to 31 January 1788 (Madison, WI: State Historical Society of Wisconsin, 1984).

Kaminski, John P. Gaspare J. Saladino, Richard Leffler and Charles H. Schoenleber, eds., *Commentaries on the Constitution, Public and Private. Volume 5: 1 April to 9 May 1788* (Madison, WI: State Historical Society of Wisconsin, 1995).
Commentaries on the Constitution, Public and Private. Volume 6: 10 May to 13 September 1788 (Madison, WI: State Historical Society of Wisconsin, 1995).
Ratification of the Constitution by the States: Massachusetts, volumes 1 and 2 (Madison, WI: State Historical Society of Wisconsin, 1997–8).
Kaminski, John P., Gaspare J. Saladino, Richard Leffler, Charles H. Schoenleber and Marybeth Carlson, eds., *Ratification of the Constitution by the States: Virginia*, volumes 1–3 (Madison, WI: State Historical Society of Wisconsin, 1988, 1990, 1993).
Kaminski, John P., Gaspare J. Saladino, Richard Leffler, Charles H. Schoenleber and Margaret A. Hogan, eds., *Ratification of the Constitution by the States: Massachusetts*, volumes 3 and 4 (Madison, WI: State Historical Society of Wisconsin, 2000–1).
Ratification of the Constitution by the States: New York, vols. 1–4 (Madison, WI: State Historical Society of Wisconsin, 2003–5, 2008).
Kaminski, John P., Gaspare J. Saladino, Richard Leffler, Charles H. Schoenleber, Margaret A. Hogan and Jonathan M. Reid, eds., *Ratification of the Constitution by the States: New York*, vol. 5 (Madison, WI: State Historical Society of Wisconsin, 2009).
Kaminski, John P., Gaspare J. Saladino, Timothy D. Moore, Johanna E. Lannér-Cusin, Charles H. Schoenleber, Jonathan M. Reid, Margaret R. Flamingo and David P. Fields, eds., *Ratification of the Constitution by the States: Maryland*, vols. 1 and 2 (Madison, WI: State Historical Society of Wisconsin, 2015).
Kaminski, John P., Charles H. Schoenleber, Gaspare J. Saladino, Richard Leffler, Jonathan M. Reid, Margaret R. Flamingo, Patrick T. Conley and Timothy D. Moore, eds., *Ratification of the Constitution by the States: Rhode Island*, vol. 1 (Madison, WI: State Historical Society of Wisconsin, 2011).
Kaminski, John P., Charles H. Schoenleber, Gaspare J. Saladino, Richard Leffler, Jonathan M. Reid, Margaret R. Flamingo, Johanna E. Lannér-Cusin, David P. Fields, Patrick T. Conley and Timothy D. Moore, eds., *Ratification of the Constitution by the States: Rhode Island*, vols. 2–3 (Madison, WI: State Historical Society of Wisconsin, 2012–13).
Kaminski, John P., Charles H. Schoenleber, Jonathan M. Reid, David P. Fields, Michael E. Stevens, Gaspare J. Saladino, Margaret R. Flamingo and Timothy D. Moore, eds., *Ratification of the Constitution by the States: South Carolina* (Madison, WI: State Historical Society of Wisconsin, 2016).
Kennedy, John Pendleton and McIlwaine, Henry Read, eds., *Journals of the House of Burgesses, 1770–1772* (Richmond, VA: The Colonial Press, Edward Waddey Co., 1906).
Koch, Adrienne, ed., *Notes of Debates in the Federal Convention of 1787 Reported by James Madison* (Athens, OH: Ohio University Press, 1966).

Kurland, Philip B. and Ralph Lerner, eds., *The Founders' Constitution. Volume Three. Article 1, Section 8, Clause 5, through Article 2, Section 1* (Chicago: University of Chicago Press, 1987).
Lawrence, George, *An Oration on the Abolition of the Slave Trade, Delivered on the First Day of January, 1813, in the African Methodist Episcopal Church* (New York: Hardcastle and Van Pelt, 1813).
Lee, Richard Henry, ed., *Memoir of the Life of Richard Henry Lee, and his Correspondence...*, 2 vols. (Philadelphia: H. C. Carey and I. Lea, 1825).
'Letters of Joseph Clay, Merchant of Savannah, 1776–1793', *Collections of the Georgia Historical Society*, 8 (1913).
Liancourt, Duke de la Rochefoucault, *Travels through the United States of North America, the Country of the Iroquois, and Upper Canada in the Years 1795, 1796, and 1797: With an Authentic Account of Lower Canada* (London: R. Phillips, 1799).
Life of Jeremy Belknap, D. D., the Historian of New Hampshire with Selections from His Correspondence and Other Writings (New York: Harper and Brothers, 1847).
Maclay, Edgar S., *Journal of William Maclay, United States Senator from Pennsylvania 1789–1791* (New York: Appleton and Co., 1890).
Mastromarino, Mark A., ed., *The Papers of George Washington. Presidential Series. Volume 9. 23 September 1791–29 February 1792* (Charlottesville: University of Virginia Press, 2000).
Mattern, David B., J. C. A. Stagg, Ellen J. Barber, Anne Mandeville Colony, Angela Kreider and Jeanne Kerr Cross, eds., *The Papers of James Madison. Secretary of State Series*, vol. 7 (Charlottesville, VA: University Press of Virginia, 2005).
McRee, Griffith J., ed., *Life and Correspondence of James Iredell, One of the Associate Justices of the Supreme Court of the United States*, 2 vols. (New York: Appleton and Co., 1858).
Memorials Presented to the Congress of the United States of America by the Different Societies Instituted for Promoting the Abolition of Slavery, Etc. in the States of Rhode-Island, Connecticut, New-York, Pennsylvania, Maryland, and Virginia. Published by Order of the 'Pennsylvania Society for Promoting the Abolition of Slavery, and the Relief of Free Negroes Unlawfully Held in Bondage, and for Improving the Condition of the African Race' (Philadelphia: Francis Bailey, 1792).
Mifflin, Warner, *A Serious Expostulation with the Members of the House of Representatives of the United States* (Philadelphia: Nicholas Power, 1794).
Minutes Abolition Convention (1804, 1806).
Morris, Richard B., ed., *John Jay: The Winning of the Peace: Unpublished Papers 1780–1784* (New York: Harper & Row, 1980).
Nash, Gary B. and Michael R. McDowell, eds., *Writings of Warner Mifflin: Forgotten Quaker Abolitionist of the Revolutionary Era* (Newark: University of Delaware Press, 2021).
Needles, Edward, *An Historical Memoir of the Pennsylvania Society for Promoting the Abolition of Slavery; the Relief of Free Negroes Unlawfully Held in Bondage; and for Improving the Condition of the African Race* (Philadelphia: Merrihew & Thompson, 1848).

Nuxoll, Elizabeth, ed., *The Selected Papers of John Jay. Volume 3. 1782–1784* (Charlottesville: University of Virginia Press, 2013).

Oberg, Barbara B., ed., *The Papers of Thomas Jefferson. Volume 40. 4 March–1 July 1803* (Princeton, NJ: Princeton University Press, 2013).

O'Callaghan, E. B., ed., John Romayn Brodhead, *Documents Relative to the Colonial History of the State of New York; Procured in Holland, England, and France*, 11 vols. (Albany, NY: Weed, Parsons and company, Printers, 1853–87).

Park, Edwards Amasa, *The Works of Samuel Hopkins, D. D., First Pastor of the Church in Great Barrington, Mass., afterwards Pastor of the First Congregational Church in Newport, R.I., with a Memoir of His Life and Character*, 3 vols. (Boston: Doctrinal Tract and Book Society, 1852).

Patten, William, *On the Inhumanity of the Slave Trade, and the Importance of Correcting It. A Sermon, delivered in the Second Congregational Church, Newport, Rhode Island, August 12, 1792* (Providence, RI: J. Carter, 1793).

Peters, Richard, ed., *The Public Statutes at Large of the United States of America, volume 2 (1799–1813)* (Boston: Charles C. Little and James Brown, 1845).

Peterson, Merrill D., ed., *Thomas Jefferson: Writings* (New York: Library of America, 1984).

Phillips, Ulrich B., ed., 'South Carolina Federalist Correspondence, 1789–1797', *The American Historical Review*, 14/4 (1909): 776–90.

Preston, Daniel, ed., *The Papers of James Monroe. Volume 5. Selected Correspondence and Papers January 1803–April 1811* (Santa Barbara, CA: Greenwood, 2014).

Price, Clement A., ed., *Freedom not far Distant: A Documentary History of Afro-Americans in New Jersey* (Newark, NJ: New Jersey Historical Society, 1980).

Ramsay, David, *The History of South Carolina, from its First Settlement in 1670 to the Year 1808*, (Charleston: Walker, Evans & Co., 1858).

Reed, William Bradford, ed., *Life and Correspondence of Joseph Reed...*, 2 vols. (Philadelphia: Lindsay & Blakiston, 1847).

Reese, George Henkle, ed., *The Official Papers of Francis Fauquier, Lieutenant Governor of Virginia, 1758–1768*, 3 vols. (Charlottesville, VA: University of Virginia Press, 1980–3).

Rogers, George C., Jr, ed., 'The Letters of William Loughton Smith to Edward Rutledge, June 6, 1789 to April 28, 1794', *South Carolina Historical Magazine*, 69/1 (1968): 1–25, 69/2 (1968): 101–38.

Rogers, George C., Jr, and David R. Chesnutt, eds., *The Papers of Henry Laurens. Volume 5. September 1, 1765–July 31, 1768* (Columbia: University of South Carolina Press, 1974).

Rogers, George C., Jr, David R. Chesnutt, Peggy J. Clark, Walter B. Edgar, eds., *The Papers of Henry Laurens. Volume 4. September 1, 1763–August 31, 1765* (Columbia: University of South Carolina Press, 1968).

Rowland, Dunbar, ed., *Official letterbooks of W. C. C. Claiborne, 1801–1816*, 6 vols. (Jackson, MS: State Department of Archives and History, 1917), volume 3.

[Rush, Benjamin], *An Address to the Inhabitants of the British Settlements in America, upon Slave-Keeping* (Philadelphia: John Dunlap, 1773).

Rutland, Robert A., ed., *The Papers of George Mason 1725–1792*, 3 vols. (Chapel Hill: University of North Carolina Press, 1970).
Rutland, Robert A., Charles F. Hobson, William M. E. Rachal and Jeanne K. Sisson, eds., *The Papers of James Madison. Volume 10. 27 May 1787–3 March 1788* (Charlottesville, VA: University of Virginia Press, 1977).
The Papers of James Madison. Volume 11. 7 March 1788–1 March 1789 (Charlottesville, VA: University of Virginia Press, 1977).
Rutland, Robert A. and Thomas A. Mason, eds., *The Papers of James Madison. Volume 14. 6 April 1791–16 March 1793* (Charlottesville, VA: University of Virginia Press, 1983).
Saunders, William Laurence, ed., *The Colonial Records of North Carolina. Volume IX: 1771 to 1775* (Raleigh, NC: Josephus Daniels, 1886).
Schulz, Constance B., ed., *The Papers of the Revolutionary Era: Pinckney Statesmen Digital Edition* (Charlottesville, VA: The Rotunda Press, 2016).
Scribner, Robert L., ed., *Revolutionary Virginia. The Road to Independence. Volume 1: Forming Thunderclouds and the First Convention, 1763–1774* (Charlottesville: University Press of Virginia, 1975).
Sewall, Samuel, *The Selling of Joseph: A Memorial* (Boston: Bartholomew Green and John Allen, 1700).
The Athenian Oracle, 2nd ed. (Boston: Bartholomew Green, 1705).
Sipkins, Henry, *Oration on the Abolition of the Slave Trade, Delivered in the African Church, in the City of New-York, January 2, 1809* (New York: John C. Totten, 1809).
Smith, Paul H., ed., *Letters of Delegates to Congress, 1774–1789*, volume 4 (Washington, DC: Library of Congress, 1979).
Stevens, Michael E., ed., *The State Records of South Carolina: Journals of the House of Representatives 1792–1794* (Columbia, SC: University of South Carolina Press, 1988).
Stevens, Michael E. and Christine M. Allen, eds., *The State Records of South Carolina: Journals of the House of Representatives 1787–1788* (Columbia, SC: University of South Carolina Press, 1981).
The State Records of South Carolina: Journals of the House of Representatives 1791 (Columbia, SC: University of South Carolina Press, 1986).
Storing, Herbert J., ed., *The Complete Anti-Federalist. Volume 5: Maryland and Virginia and the South* (Chicago: University of Chicago Press, 1981).
Swan, James, *A Dissuasion to Great Britain and the Colonies, from the Slave Trade to Africa* (Boston: E. Russell, 1772).
Syrett, Harold C., ed., *The Papers of Alexander Hamilton. Volume 3. 1782–1786* (New York: Columbia University Press, 1962).
Taylor, Robert J., ed., *The Adams Papers. Papers of John Adams. Volume 3. May 1775-January 1776* (Cambridge, MA: Harvard University Press, 1979).
The Adams Papers. Papers of John Adams. Volume 4. February-August 1776 (Cambridge, MA: Harvard University Press, 1979).
The Journal of John Woolman. With an Introduction by John G. Whittier, 8th ed. (Boston: Houghton, Mifflin and Company, 1884).
Twohig, Dorothy et al., eds., *The Papers of George Washington: Presidential Series*, 14 vols. (Charlottesville: University Press of Virginia, 1987–2005).

Van Horne, John C., ed., *The Correspondence of William Nelson as Acting Governor of Virginia 1770–1771* (Charlottesville, VA: University Press of Virginia, 1976).
Vaux, Roberts, *Memoirs of the Life of Anthony Benezet* (Philadelphia: Parke, 1817).
Veit, Helen E., Charlene Bangs Bickford, Kenneth R. Bowling and William Charles diGiacomantonio, eds., *Documentary History of the First Federal Congress of the United States of America. Debates in the House of Representatives. Volume XII. Second Session: January to March 1790* (Baltimore: The Johns Hopkins University Press, 1994).
Williams, Jr, Peter, *An Oration on the Abolition of the Slave Trade, Delivered in the African Church, in the City of New-York, January 1, 1808* (New York: Samuel Wood, 1808).
Wood, Gordon S., ed., *John Adams: Writings from the New Nation* (New York: Library of America, 2016).
Woods, John A., ed., 'The Correspondence of Benjamin Rush and Granville Sharp 1773–1809', *Journal of American Studies*, 1/1 (1967): 1–38.
Woolman, john, 'Notes and Commentaries on A. Benezet's *A Caution and Warning to Great Britain*' in James Proud, ed., *John Woolman and the Affairs of Truth: The Journalist's Essays, Epistles, and Ephemera* (San Francisco: Inner Light Books, 2010).
Wynkoop, Henry and Joseph M. Beatty, Jr, eds., 'The Letters of Judge Henry Wynkoop, Representative from Pennsylvania to the First Congress of the United States', *Pennsylvania Magazine of History and Biography*, 38/2 (1914): 183–205.

Secondary Sources

Allegro, James J., '"Increasing and Strengthening the Country": Law, Politics, and the Antislavery Movement in Early-Eighteenth Century Massachusetts Bay', *New England Quarterly*, LXV (2002): 5–23.
Alpaugh, Micah, *Friends of Freedom: The Rise of Social Movements in the Age of Atlantic Revolutions* (Cambridge: Cambridge University Press, 2021).
Ames, Herman V., *The Proposed Amendments to the Constitution of the United States during the first century of Its History*, 2 vols. (Washington, DC: Government Printing Office, 1897).
Ammerman, David L., *In the Common Cause: American Response to the Coercive Acts of 1774* (Charlottesville: University of Virginia Press, 1974).
Anstey, Roger, *The Atlantic Slave Trade and British Abolition* (London: Macmillan, 1975).
Anstey, Roger, 'The Volume of the North American Slave-Carrying Trade from Africa 1761–1810', *Revue Française d'Histoire d'Outre-Mer*, 62/226–7 (1975): 47–66.
Appleby, Joyce, *Thomas Jefferson* (New York: Times Books, 2003).
Armitage, David, *The Declaration of Independence: A Global History* (Cambridge, MA: Harvard University Press, 2007).

Ames, Herman V., *The Proposed Amendments to the Constitution of the United States during the First Century of Its History*, 2 vols. (Washington, DC: Government Printing Office, 1897).
Bailyn, Bernard, *The Ideological Origins of the American Revolution* (Cambridge, MA: Harvard University Press, 1967).
  The Ordeal of Thomas Hutchinson (Cambridge, MA: Harvard University Press, 1974).
Batterson, Sarah A., '"An Ill-Judged Piece of Business": The Failure of Slave Trade Suppression in a Slaveholding Republic' (University of New Hampshire PhD dissertation, 2013).
  'A Horde of Foreign Freebooters: The U.S. and the Suppression of the Slave Trade', *Diacronie*, 13/1 (2013): 1–15.
Bauman, Richard, *For the Reputation of Truth; Politics, Religion, and Conflict among the Pennsylvania Quakers 1750–1800* (Baltimore: The Johns Hopkins Press, 1971).
Beeman, Richard R., *Plain, Honest Men: The Making of the American Constitution* (New York: Random House, 2009).
  Our Lives, Our Fortunes and our Sacred Honor: The Forging of American Independence, 1774–1776 (New York: Basic Books, 2013).
Behrendt, Stephen D., 'The Transatlantic Slave Trade' in Robert L. Paquette and Mark M. Smith, eds., *The Oxford Handbook of Slavery in the Americas* (New York: Oxford University Press, 2010).
Berlin, Ira, *Many Thousands Gone: The First Two Centuries of Slavery in North America* (Cambridge, MA: The Belknap Press of Harvard University Press, 1998).
Bilder, Mary Sarah, *Madison's Hand: Revising the Constitutional Convention* (Cambridge, MA: Harvard University Press, 2015).
Bjork, Gordon C., 'The Weaning of the American Economy: Independence, Market Changes, and Economic Development', *Journal of Economic History*, 24/4 (1964): 541–60.
Blackburn, Robin, *The Overthrow of Colonial Slavery, 1776–1848* (London: Verso, 1988).
Blanck, Emily, 'Seventeen Eighty-Three: The Turning Point in the Law of Slavery and Freedom in Massachusetts', *New England Quarterly*, LXXV (2002): 24–51.
Boller, Paul F., 'Washington, Quakers, and Slavery', *Journal of Negro History*, XLVI/2 (1961): 83–8.
Bordewich, Fergus M., *The First Congress: How James Madison, George Washington, and a Group of Extraordinary Men Invented the Government* (New York: Simon & Schuster, 2016).
Bradburn, Douglas, *The Citizenship Revolution: Politics and the Creation of the American Union, 1774–1804* (Charlottesville: University of Virginia Press, 2009).
Brady, Patrick S., 'The Slave Trade and Sectionalism in South Carolina, 1787–1808', *Journal of Southern History*, 38/4 (1972): 601–20.
Broadwater, Jeff, *George Mason: Forgotten Founder* (Chapel Hill: University of North Carolina Press, 2006).

James Madison: A Son of Virginia & Founder of the Nation (Chapel Hill: University of North Carolina Press, 2012).
Jefferson, Madison, and the Making of the Constitution (Chapel Hill: University of North Carolina Press, 2019).
Brookes, George S., *Friend Anthony Benezet* (Philadelphia: University of Pennsylvania Press, 1937).
Brown, Carl Harrison, 'The Reopening of the Foreign Slave Trade in South Carolina, 1803–1807' (University of South Carolina MA thesis, 1968).
Brown, Christopher L., *Moral Capital: Foundations of British Abolitionism* (Chapel Hill: University of North Carolina Press, 2006).
  'The Problems of Slavery' in Edward G. Gray and Jane Kamensky, eds., *The Oxford Handbook of the American Revolution* (New York: Oxford University Press, 2012).
Brown, Christopher Leslie, 'Abolition of the Atlantic Slave Trade' in Gad Heuman and Trevor Burnard, eds., *The Routledge History of Slavery* (Abingdon: Routledge, 2011).
Brown, Ira V., 'Pennsylvania's Antislavery Pioneers, 1688–1776', *Pennsylvania History*, 55/2 (1988): 59–77.
Brown, Vincent, *Tacky's Revolt: The Story of an Atlantic Slave War* (Cambridge, MA: Harvard University Press, 2020).
Burnard, Trevor, 'Anthony Benezet: *A Short History of Guinea* and Its Impact on Early British Abolitionism' in Joy Damousi, Trevor Burnard and Alan Lester, eds., *Humanitarianism, Empire and Transnationalism, 1760–1995* (Manchester: Manchester University Press, 2022):.
Cabot, Andy, 'Why May Not Our Country Be Enriched by that Lucrative Traffic? The Slave Trade and the Failed Politics of Federal Proscription in the Early American Republic (1787–1808)', *XVII–XVIII*, 77 (2020), n.p.
Carey, Brycchan, 'Anthony Benezet, Antislavery Rhetoric, and the Age of Sensibility', *Quaker Studies*, 21/2 (2016): 141–58.
  From Peace to Freedom: Quaker Rhetoric and the Birth of American Antislavery, 1657–1761 (New Haven, CT: Yale University Press, 2012).
Chambers, Douglas B., 'The Transatlantic Slave Trade to Virginia in Comparative Historical Perspective, 1698–1778' in John Saillant, ed., *Afro-Virginian History and Culture* (New York: Garland, 1999).
Chase, Jeanne, 'New York Slave Trade, 1698–1741', *Histoire & Mesure*, 18/1-2 (2003): 95–112.
Chitwood, Oliver Perry, *Richard Henry Lee, Statesman of the Revolution* (Morgantown: West Virginia University Library, 1967).
Clow, Richard Brent, 'Edward Rutledge of South Carolina, 1749–1800' (University of Georgia PhD dissertation, 1976).
Coffin, Joshua, *A Sketch of the History of Newbury, Newburyport, and West Newbury* (Boston: S. G. Drake, 1845).
Cogliano, Francis D., *Thomas Jefferson: Reputation and Legacy* (Charlottesville: University of Virginia Press, 2006).
Colley, Linda, 'What Happens When a Written Constitution Is Printed: A History across Boundaries', *Transactions of the Royal Historical Society*, 6th series, XXXI (2021): 75–88.

Collier, Christopher, *All Politics Is Local: Family, Friends, and Provincial Interests in the Creation of the Constitution* (Hanover, NH: University of New England Press, 2003).

Conforti, Joseph, *Samuel Hopkins and the New Divinity Movement: Calvinism, the Congregational Ministry, and Reform in New England between the Great Awakenings* (Grand Rapids, MI: Christian University Press, 1981).

Connolly, James C., 'Slavery in Colonial New Jersey and the Causes Operating against Its Extension', *Proceedings of the New Jersey Historical Society*, XIV (1929): 181–202.

Cooke, Jacob E., *Tench Coxe and the Early Republic* (Chapel Hill: University of North Carolina Press, 1978).

Cooley, Henry Scofield, *A Study of Slavery in New Jersey* (Baltimore: The Johns Hopkins University Press, 1896).

Corrie, David P., *The Constitution in Congres: The Jeffersonians 1801–1829* (Chicago: University of Chicago Press, 2001).

Coughtry, Jay, *The Notorious Triangle: Rhode Island and the African Slave Trade, 1700–1807* (Philadelphia: Temple University Press, 1981).

Crane, Elaine F., '"The First Wheel of Commerce": Newport, Rhode Island and the Slave Trade, 1760–1776', *Slavery and Abolition*, 1/2 (1980): 178–98.

Crothers, A. Glenn, *Quakers Living in the Lion's Mouth: The Society of Friends in Northern Virginia, 1730–1865* (Gainesville: University Press of Florida, 2012).

Curtin, Philip D., *The Atlantic Slave Trade: A Census* (Madison, WI: University of Wisconsin Press, 1969).

Curtis, George Ticknor, *History of the Origin, Formation, and Adoption of the Constitution of the United States*, 2 vols. (New York: Harper and Brothers, 1854).

Davis, David Brion, *The Problem of Slavery in Western Culture* (Ithaca, NY: Cornell University Press, 1966).

The Problem of Slavery in the Age of Revolution, 1770–1823 (Ithaca, NY: Cornell University Press, 1975).

'American Slavery and the American Revolution' in Ira Berlin and Ronald Hoffman, eds., *Slavery and Freedom in the Age of the American Revolution* (Charlottesville: University Press of Virginia for the United States Capitol Historical Society, 1983).

Deaton, Stanley Kenneth, 'Revolutionary Charleston, 1765–1800' (University of Florida PhD, 1997).

D'Elia, Donald J., 'Dr Benjamin Rush and the Negro', *Journal of the History of Ideas*, 30/3 (1969): 413–22.

Deyle, Steven, '"By Farr the Most Profitable Trade": Slave Trading in British Colonial North America', *Slavery and Abolition*, 10/2 (1989): 107–25.

Carry Me Back: The Domestic Slave Trade in American Life (New York: Oxford University Press, 2006).

'An "Abominable" New Trade: The Closing of the African Slave Trade and the Changing Patterns of U.S. Political Power, 1808–60', *William and Mary Quarterly*, LXVI/4 (2009): 832–49.

'An Ambiguous Legacy: The Closing of the African Slave Trade and America's Own Middle Passage' in David T. Gleeson and Simon Lewis, eds.,

Ambiguous Anniversary: The Bicentennial of the International Slave Trade Bans (Columbia: University of South Carolina Press, 2012): 138–52.

Dierksheide, Christa, '"The Great Improvement and Civilization of That Race": Jefferson and the "Amelioration" of Slavery, ca. 1770–1826', *Early American Studies*, 6/1 (2008): 165–97.

'"Taking Root Deeper Than Ever": Jeffersonians and Slavery' in Joanne B. Freeman and Johann N. Neem, eds., *Jeffersonians in Power* (Charlottesville: University of Virginia Press, 2019).

'Slavery in Jefferson's Worlds' in Dustin Gish and Andrew Bibby, eds., *Rival Visions: How Jefferson and His Contemporaries Defined the Early American Republic* (Charlottesville: University of Virginia Press, 2020).

Dierksheide, Christa and Peter S. Onuf, 'Slaveholding Nation, Slaveholding Civilization' in William J. Cooper, Jr and John M. McCardell, Jr, eds., *In the Cause of Liberty: How the Civil War Redefined American Ideas* (Baton Rouge: Louisiana State University Press, 2009).

diGiancomantonio, William C., '"For the Gratification of a Volunteering Society": Antislavery and Pressure Group Politics in the First Federal Congress', *Journal of the Early Republic*, 15/2 (1995): 169–97.

'Petitioners and Their Grievances: A View from the First Federal Congress' in Kenneth R. Bowling and Donald R. Kennon, eds., *The House and Senate in the 1790s: Petitioning, Lobbying, and Institutional Development* (Athens: Ohio University Press, 2002).

Dodson, Leonidas, *Alexander Spotswood, Governor of Colonial Virginia, 1710–1722* (Philadelphia: University of Pennsylvania Press, 1932).

Donnan, Elizabeth, 'The New England Slave Trade after the Revolution', *The New England Quarterly*, 3/2 (1930): 251–78.

'Agitation against the Slave Trade in Rhode Island, 1784–1790' in *Persecution and Liberty: Essays in Honor of George Lincoln Burr* (New York: Century, 1931).

Dorsey, Peter A., *Common Bondage: Slavery as Metaphor in Revolutionary America* (Knoxville: University of Tennessee Press, 2010).

Drake, Thomas E., *Quakers and Slavery in America* (New Haven, CT: Yale University Press, 1950).

Drescher, Seymour, *Abolition: A History of Slavery and Antislavery* (Cambridge: Cambridge University Press, 2009).

'History's Engines: British Mobilization in the Age of Revolution', *William and Mary Quarterly*, 66/4 (2009): 737–56.

'Divergent Paths: The Anglo-American Abolitions of the Atlantic Slave Trade' in Wim Klooster, ed., *Migration, Trade, and Slavery in an Expanding World: Essays in Honor of Pieter Emmer* (Leiden: Brill, 2009): 259–87.

Du Bois, W. E. B., *The Suppression of the African Slave-Trade to the United States of America, 1638–1870* (Cambridge, MA: Harvard University Press, 1896).

Dun, James Alexander, 'Philadelphia Not Philanthropolis: The Limits of Pennsylvanian Antislavery in the Era of the Haitian Revolution', *Pennsylvania Magazine of History and Biography*, 135/1 (2011): 73–102.

'Atlantic Antislavery, American Ambition: The Problem of Slavery in the United States in an Age of Disruption, 1770–1808' in Andrew Shankman, ed., *The*

World of the Revolutionary American Republic: Land, Labor, and the Conflict for a Continent (New York: Routledge, 2014).

Dangerous Neighbours: Making the Haitian Revolution in Early America (Philadelphia: University of Pennsylvania Press, 2016).

Edelson, S. Max, *Plantation Enterprise in Colonial South Carolina* (Cambridge, MA: Harvard University Press, 2006).

Egerton, Douglas R., *Death or Liberty: African Americans and Revolutionary America* (New York: Oxford University Press, 2009).

Einhorn, Robin, 'The Early Impact of Slavery' in Julian E. Zelizer, ed., *The American Congress: The Building of Democracy* (Boston: Houghton Mifflin Company, 2004).

Einhorn, Robin L., *American Taxation, American Slavery* (Chicago: University of Chicago Press, 2006).

Elkins, Stanley and McKitrick, Eric L., *The Age of Federalism* (New York: Oxford University Press, 1993).

Ellis, Joseph J., *Founding Brothers: The Revolutionary Generation* (New York: Knopf, 2001).

The Cause: The American Revolution and Its Discontents, 1773–1783 (New York: Liveright Publishing Corporation, 2021).

Eltis, David, *Economic Growth and the Ending of the Transatlantic Slave Trade* (New York: Oxford University Press, 1987).

'The U.S. Transatlantic Slave Trade, 1644–1867: An Assessment', *Civil War History*, 54/4 (2008): 347–78.

'Was Abolition of the US and British Slave Trade Significant in the Broader Atlantic Context?' *William and Mary Quarterly*, 66/4 (2009): 715–36.

Eltis, David and David Richardson, 'A New Assessment of the Transatlantic Slave Trade' in David Eltis and David Richardson, eds., *Extending the Frontiers: Essays on the New Transatlantic Slave Trade Database* (New Haven, CT: Yale University Press, 2008).

Ericson, David F., 'Slave Smugglers, Slave Catchers, and Slave Rebels: Slavery and American State Development, 1787–1842' in John Craig Hammond and Matthew Mason, eds., *Contesting Slavery: The Politics of Bondage and Freedom in the New American Nation* (Charlottesville: University of Virginia Press, 2011).

Slavery in the American Republic: Developing the Federal Government, 1791–1861 (Lawrence: University Press of Kansas, 2011).

Fehrenbacher, Don E., 'Slavery, the Framers, and the Living Constitution' in Robert A. Goldwin and Art Kaufman, eds., *Slavery and Its Consequences: The Constitution, Equality, and Race* (Washington, DC: American Enterprise for Public Policy Research, 1988).

Fehrenbacher, Don E. with Ward M. McAfee, *The Slaveholding Republic: An Account of the United States Government's Relations to Slavery* (New York: Oxford University Press, 2001).

Finkelman, Paul, 'Slavery and the Constitutional Convention: Making a Covenant with Death' in Richard Beeman, Stephen Botein and Edward C. Carter, II, eds., *Beyond Confederation: Origins of the Constitution and American*

National Identity (Chapel Hill: University of North Carolina Press, 1987): 195–217.
'The Pennsylvania Delegation and the Peculiar Institution: The Two Faces of the Keystone State', *The Pennsylvania Magazine of History and Biography*, 112/1 (1988): 49–71.
'The Founders and Slavery: Little Ventured, Little Gained', *Yale Journal of Law and the Humanities*, 13/2 (2001): 413–49.
'Regulating the African Slave Trade', *Civil War History*, LIV/4 (2008): 379–405.
'The American Suppression of the African Slave Trade: Lessons on Legal Change, Social Policy, and Legislation', *Akron Law Journal*, 42/2 (2009): 431–67.
'Human Liberty, Property in Human Beings, and the Pennsylvania Supreme Court', *Dusquesne Law Review*, 53/2 (2015): 453–82.
Fischer, David Hackett, *African Founders: How Enslaved People Expanded American Ideals* (New York: Simon & Schuster, 2022).
Fladeland, Betty, *Men and Brothers: Anglo-American Antislavery Cooperation* (Champaign-Urbana: University of Illinois Press, 1972).
Ford, Lacy, 'Reconfiguring the Old South: "Solving" the Problem of Slavery, 1787–1838', *Journal of American History*, 95/1 (2008): 95–122.
Ford, Lacy K., *Deliver Us from Evil: The Slavery Question in the Old South* (Oxford: Oxford University Press, 2009).
Foster, Joseph S., 'James Pemberton' in Craig W. Horle, Joseph S. Foster, Laurie M. Wolfe, Jeffrey L. Scheib, Robert E. Wright, David Haugaard, Dianna DiIllio, Jennifer A. Janofsky and Leigh A. McCuen, eds., *Lawmaking and Legislators in Pennsylvania: A Biographical Dictionary. Volume Three: 1757–1775* (Harrisburg, PA: Penn State University Press, 2005): 1034–5.
Foster, William Omer, Sr, *James Jackson: Duelist and Militant Statesman 1757–1806* (Athens: University of Georgia Press, 1960).
Freehling, William W., *The Road to Disunion. Volume 1. Secessionists at Bay, 1776–1854* (New York: Oxford University Press, 1990).
Freeman, Frederick, *The History of Cape Cod: The Annals of the Thirteen Towns of Barnstable County*, 2 vols. (Boston: W. H. Piper, 1862).
Frey, Sylvia R., *Water from the Rock: Black Resistance in a Revolutionary Age* (Princeton, NJ: Princeton University Press, 1991).
Frost, J. William, 'Quaker Antislavery: From Dissidence to Sense of the Meeting', *Quaker History*, 101/1 (2012): 12–33.
'Anthony Benezet: The Emergence of a Weighty Friend', *Quaker History*, 103/2 (2014): 1–17.
Gellman, David N., *Emancipating New York: The Politics of Slavery and Freedom, 1777–1827* (Baton Rouge: Louisiana State University Press, 2006).
Gigantino, James J., II, *The Ragged Road to Abolition: Slavery and Freedom in New Jersey, 1775–1865* (Philadelphia: University of Pennsylvania Press, 2014).
Goldfarb, Stephen J., 'An Inquiry into the Politics of the Prohibition of the International Slave Trade', *Agricultural History*, 68/2 (1994): 20–34.

Gould, Elija H., *Among the Powers of the Earth: The American Revolution and the Making of a New World Empire* (Cambridge, MA: Harvard University Press, 2012).

Gould, Philip, *Barbaric Traffic: Commerce and Antislavery in the Eighteenth-Century Atlantic World* (Cambridge, MA: Harvard University Press, 2003).

Greene, Lorenzo Johnston, *The Negro in Colonial New England, 1620–1776* (New York: Columbia University Press, 1942).

Gudmestad, Robert H., *A Troublesome Commerce: The Transformation of the Interstate Slave Trade* (Baton Rouge: Louisiana State University Press, 2003).

Hammond, John Craig, 'They Are Very Much Interested in Obtaining an Unlimited Slavery', *Journal of the Early Republic*, 23/3 (2003): 353–80.

'"We Are Due to Be Reduced to the Level of Slaves": Planters, Taxes, Aristocrats, and Massachusetts Antifederalists, 1787–1788', *Historical Journal of Massachusetts*, XXXI (2003): 172–98.

Slavery, Freedom, and Expansion in the Early American West (Charlottesville: University Press of Virginia, 2007).

Hardin, William Fernandez, 'Robert Pleasants (1723–1801)', *Encyclopedia Virginia*. https://encyclopediavirginia.org

Harding, Samuel Bannister, *The Contest over the Ratification of the Federal Constitution in the State of Massachusetts* (New York: Longmans, Green, 1896).

Harris, John, *The Last Slave Ships: New York and the End of the Middle Passage* (New Haven, CT: Yale University Press, 2022).

Harrold, Stanley, *American Abolitionism: Its Direct Political Impact from Colonial Times into Reconstruction* (Charlottesville; University of Virginia Press, 2019).

Haw, James, *John and Edward Rutledge of South Carolina* (Athens: University of Georgia Press, 1997).

Head, David, 'Slave Smuggling by Foreign Privateers: The Illegal Slave Trade and the Geopolitics of the Early Republic', *Journal of the Early Republic*, 33/3 (2013): 433–62.

Hedges, James B., *The Browns of Providence Plantations: Colonial Years* (Cambridge, MA: Harvard University Press, 1952).

Hendrickson, David C., *Peace Pact: The Lost World of the American Founding* (Lawrence: University Press of Kansas, 2003).

Higgins, W. Robert, 'Charlestown Merchants and Factors Dealing in the External Negro Trade, 1735–1775', *South Carolina Historical Magazine*, 65/4 (1964): 205–17.

'The South Carolina Negro Duty Law' (University of South Carolina MA thesis, 1967).

'Charleston: Terminus and Entrepôt of the Colonial Slave Trade' in Marvin L. Kilson and Robert I. Rotberg, eds., *The African Diaspora: Interpretive Essays* (Cambridge, MA: Harvard University Press, 1976).

Higginson, Stephen A., 'A Short History of the Right to Petition Government for the Redress of Grievances', *The Yale Law Journal*, 96/1 (1986): 142–66.

Hodges, Graham Russell, *Root and Branch: African Americans in New York and East Jersey, 1613–1863* (Chapel Hill: University of North Carolina Press, 1999).

Holcomb, Julie L., *Moral Commerce: Quakers and the Transatlantic Boycott of the Slave Labor Economy* (Ithaca: Cornell University Press, 2016).

Hollander, Craig B., 'Corrupt Bargaining: Partisan Politics, the Election of 1824, and the Suppression of the African Slave Trade', *Journal of the Early Republic*, 42/3 (2022): 359–87.

Holton, Woody, *Forced Founders: Indians, Debtors, Slaves, and the Making of the American Revolution in Virginia* (Chapel Hill: University of North Carolina Press, 1999).

  Liberty is Sweet: The Hidden History of the American Revolution (New York: Simon & Schuster, 2021).

Horn, James and Philip D. Morgan, 'Settlers and Slaves: European and African Migrations to Early Modern British America' in Elizabeth Mancke and Carole Shammas, eds., *The Creation of the British Atlantic World* (Baltimore: Johns Hopkins University Press, 2005).

Hornick, Nancy S., 'Anthony Benezet: Eighteenth-Century Social Critic, Educator, and Abolitionist' (University of Maryland PhD dissertation, 1975).

Iaccarino, Anthony A., 'Virginia and the National Contest over Slavery in the Early Republic, 1780–1833' (University of California, Los Angeles, PhD dissertation, 1999).

Ireland, Owen S., *Religion, Ethnicity and Politics: Ratifying the Constitution in Pennsylvania* (University Park: Pennsylvania State University Press, 1995).

Jackson, Maurice, 'The Social and Intellectual Origins of Anthony Benezet's Antislavery Radicalism', *Pennsylvania History*, LXVI (1999): 86–112.

  Let This Voice Be Heard: Anthony Benezet, Father of Atlantic Abolitionism (Philadelphia: University of Pennsylvania Press, 2009).

  'Anthony Benezet: Working the Antislavery Cause Inside and Outside of "The Society"' in Brycchan Carey and Geoffrey Plank, eds., *Quakers and Abolition* (Urbana-Champaign: University of Illinois Press, 2014).

  'Anthony Benezet and the Dream of Freedom: Then and Now' in Marie-Jeanne Rossignol and Bertram Van Ruymbeke, eds., *The Atlantic World of Anthony Benezet (1713–1784): From French Reformation to North American Quaker Antislavery Activism* (Leiden: Brill, 2016).

James, Sydney V., *A People among Peoples: Quaker Benevolence in Eighteenth-Century America* (Cambridge, MA: Harvard University Press, 1963).

Jenkins, William S., *Pro-slavery Thought in the Old South* (Chapel Hill: University of North Carolina Press, 1935).

  coll. and ed., *Records of the States of the United States of America: A Microfilm Compilation* (Washington, DC, 1949).

Jervey, Theodore D., *The Slave Trade: Slavery and Color* (Columbia, SC: State Co., 1925).

John, Richard R. and Christopher J. Young, 'Rites of Passage: Postal Petitioning as a Tool of Governance in the Age of Federalism' in Kenneth R. Bowling and Donald R. Kennon, eds., *The House and Senate in the 1790s: Petitioning, Lobbying, and Institutional Development* (Athens: Ohio University Press, 2002).

Johnson, David, *John Randolph of Roanoke* (Baton Rouge: Louisiana State University Press, 2012).

Johnson, Michael P., 'Runaway Slaves and the Slave Communities in South Carolina, 1799–1830', *William and Mary Quarterly*, 38/3 (1981): 418–41.

Jordan, Winthrop D., *White over Black: American Attitudes toward the Negro, 1550–1812* (Chapel Hill: University of North Carolina Press, 1968).

Kachun, Mitch, *Festivals of Freedom: Memory and Meaning in African American Emancipation celebrations, 1808–1915* (Amherst: University of Massachusetts Press, 2003).

Kaplan, Sidney, '"The Selling of Joseph": Samuel Sewall and the Iniquity of Slavery' in Allan D. Austin, ed., *American Studies in Black and White* (Amherst: University of Massachusetts Press, 1991).

Kaplanoff, Mark D., 'Making the South Solid: Politics and the Structure of Society in South Carolina, 1790–1815' (University of Cambridge PhD dissertation, 1979).

'Confederation: Movement for a Stronger Union' in Jack P. Greene and J. R. Pole, eds., *A Companion to the American Revolution* (Oxford: Blackwell, 2000): 458–69.

'The Federal Convention and the Constitution' in Jack P. Greene and J. R. Pole, eds., *A Companion to the American Revolution* (Oxford: Blackwell, 2000): 470–81.

Kelley, Sean M., 'American Rum, African Consumers, and the Transatlantic Slave Trade', *African Economic History*, 46/2 (2018): 1–29.

American Slavers: Merchants, Mariners, and the Transatlantic Commerce in Captives (New Haven, CT: Yale University Press, 2023).

Kershner, Jon R., *John Woolman and the Government of Christ: A Colonial Quaker's Vision for the British Atlantic World* (Oxford: Oxford University Press, 2018).

Kiple, Kenneth F., 'The Case against a large Nineteenth-Century Cuba-Florida Slave Trade', *Florida Historical Quarterly*, 49/4 (1971): 346–55.

Klarman, Michael J., *The Framers' Coup: The Making of the United States Constitution* (New York: Oxford University Press, 2016).

Klein, Rachel N., *Unification of a Slave State: The Rise of the Planter Class in the South Carolina Backcountry, 1760–1808* (Chapel Hill: University of North Carolina Press, 1990).

Knee, Stuart E., 'The Quaker Petition of 1790: A Challenge to Democracy in Early America', *Slavery and Abolition*, 6/3 (1985): 151–9.

Kulikoff, Allan, 'A "Prolifick" People: Black Population Growth in the Chesapeake Colonies, 1700–1790', *Southern Studies*, 16 (1977): 391–428.

Tobacco and Slaves: The Development of Southern Cultures in the Chesapeake, 1680–1900 (Chapel Hill: University of North Carolina Press, 1986).

'Uprooted Peoples: Black Migrants in the Age of the American Revolution, 1790–1820' in Ira Berlin and Ronald Hoffman, eds., *Slavery and Freedom in the Age of the American Revolution* (Charlottesville: University Press of Virginia, 1983).

Lachance, Paul F., 'The Politics of Fear: French Louisianans and the Slave Trade, 1786–1809', *Plantation Society in the Americas*, 1 (1979): 162–97.

Le Glaunec, Jean-Pierre, 'Slave Migrations and Slave Control in Spanish and Early American New Orleans' in Peter J. Kastor and François Weil, eds., *Empires of the Imagination: Transatlantic Histories of the Louisiana Purchase* (Charlottesville: University Press of Virginia, 2009).

'Blackness without Ethnicity: Some Hypotheses on the End of the African Slave Trade in 1808, Race, and the Search for Slave Identity in Early American Louisiana' in David T. Gleeson and Simon Lewis, eds., *Ambiguous Anniversary: The Bicentennial of the International Slave Trade Bans* (Columbia: University of South Carolina Press, 2012).

Lemons, J. Stanley, 'Rhode Island and the Slave Trade', *Rhode Island History*, 60/4 (2002): 95–104.

Lightner, David L., 'The Founders and the Interstate Slave Trade', *Journal of the Early Republic*, 22/1 (2002): 25–51.

Slavery and the Commerce Power: How the Struggle against the Interstate Slave Trade led to the Civil War (New Haven, CT: Yale University Press, 2006).

Lipscomb, Patrick C., III and Edward H. Milligan, 'A Note on the Authorship of *The Case of Our Fellow-Creatures* (1784)', *Quaker History*, 55/1 (1966): 47–51.

Littlefield, Daniel C., *Rice and Slaves: Ethnicity and the Slave Trade in Colonial South Carolina* (Baton Rouge: Louisiana State University Press, 1981).

'Charleston and Internal Slave Redistribution', *South Carolina Historical Magazine*, 87/2 (1986): 93–105.

'The Slave Trade to Colonial South Carolina: A Profile', *South Carolina Historical Magazine*, 91/2 (1990): 68–99.

Locke, Mary Stoughton, *Anti-Slavery in America: From the Introduction of African Slaves to the Prohibition of the Slave Trade (1619–1808)* (Boston: Ginn and Company, 1901).

Lovejoy, David S., 'Samuel Hopkins: Religion, Slavery and Revolution', *New England Quarterly*, 40z/2 (1967): 227–43.

Lowe, Richard G., 'American Seizure of Amelia Island', *Florida Historical Quarterly*, 45/1 (1966): 18–30.

Lydon, James G., 'New York and the Slave Trade, 1700–1774', *William and Mary Quarterly*, 3rd series, 35/2 (1978): 375–94.

Lynd, Staughton, 'The Compromise of 1787', *Political Science Quarterly*, 81/2 (1966): 225–50.

Class Conflict, Slavery, and the United States Constitution (Indianapolis, IN: Bobbs-Merrill, 1967).

MacLeod, Duncan J., *Slavery, Race and the American Revolution* (Cambridge: Cambridge University Press, 1974).

'Toward Caste' in Ira Berlin and Ronald Hoffman, eds., *Slavery and Freedom in the Age of the American Revolution* (Charlottesville: University of Virginia Press, 1983).

MacMaster, Richard K., 'Arthur Lee's "Address on Slavery": An Aspect of Virginia's Struggle to End the Slave Trade, 1765–1774', *Virginia Magazine of History and Biography*, 80 (1972): 141–57.

MacMillan, Richard, 'A Journey of Lost Souls: New Orleans to Natchez Slave Trade of 1840', *Gulf Coast Historical Review*, 13 (1998): 49–59.

Maestri, Melissa A., 'The Atlantic Web of Bondage: Comparing the Slave Trades of New York City and Charleston, South Carolina' (University of Delaware PhD dissertation, 2015).

Maier, Pauline, *American Scripture: Making the Declaration of Independence* (New York: Alfred A. Knopf, 1997).
Mancall, Peter C., Joshua L. Rosenbloom, and Thomas Weiss, 'Slave Prices and the South Carolina Economy, 1722–1809', *Journal of Economic History*, 61/3 (2002): 616–39.
Marietta, Jack D., *The Reformation of American Quakerism, 1748–1783* (Philadelphia: University of Pennsylvania Press, 1984).
Marques, Leonardo, 'Slave Trading in a New World: The Strategies of North American Slave Traders in an Age of Abolition', *Journal of the Early Republic*, 32/2 (2012): 233–60.
  'The Contraband Slave Trade to Brazil and the Dynamics of U.S. Participation, 1831–1856', *Journal of Latin American Studies*, 47 (2015): 659–84.
  The United States and the Transatlantic Slave Trade to the Americas, 1776–1867 (New Haven, CT: Yale University Press, 2016).
Mason, Matthew, 'Slavery and the Founding', *History Compass*, 4/5 (2006): 943–55.
  Slavery and Politics in the Early American Republic (Chapel Hill: University of North Carolina Press, 2006).
  'Keeping up Appearances: The International Politics of Slave Trade Abolition in the Nineteenth-Century Atlantic World', *William and Mary Quarterly*, 66/4 (2009): 809–32.
  'Necessary but not Sufficient: Revolutionary Ideology and Antislavery Action in the Early Republic' in John Craig Hammond and Matthew Mason, eds., *Contesting Slavery: The Politics of Bondage and Freedom in the New American Nation* (Charlottesville: University of Virginia Press, 2011).
Mason, Matthew E., 'Slavery Overshadowed: Congress Debates Prohibiting the Atlantic Slave Trade to the United States, 1806–1807', *Journal of the Early Republic*, 20/1 (2000): 59–81.
Massey, Gregory, 'The Limits of Antislavery Thought in the Revolutionary Lower South: John Laurens and Henry Laurens', *Journal of Southern History*, 63/3 (1997): 495–530.
McBurney, Christian M., 'The First Efforts to Limit the African Slave Trade Arise in the American Revolution: Part 1 of 3, the New England Colonies', *Journal of the American Revolution*. https://allthingsliberty.com
  'The First Efforts to Limit the African Slave Trade Arise in the American Revolution: Part 2 of 3, the Middle and Southern Colonies', *Journal of the American Revolution*. https://allthingsliberty.com
  'The First Efforts to Limit the African Slave Trade Arise in the American Revolution: Part 3 of 3, Congress Bans the African Slave Trade', 15 September 2020, *Journal of the American Revolution*. https://allthingsliberty.com
McColley, Robert, *Slavery and Jeffersonian Virginia*, 2nd ed. (Urbana: University of Illinois Press, 1974).
McCrady, Edward, *The History of South Carolina under the Royal Government 1719–1776* (New York: The Macmillan Company, 1901).
McCree, Griffith J., *Life and Correspondence of James Iredell*, 2 vols. (New York: Appleton and Co., 1857).

McCusker, John J. and Russell R. Menard, *The Economy of British America, 1607–1789* (Chapel Hill: University of North Carolina Press, 1985).
McDonnell, Michael A., *The Politics of War: Race, Class, and Conflict in Revolutionary Virginia* (Chapel Hill: University of North Carolina Press, 2007).
McMillin, James A., *The Final Victims: Foreign Slave Trade to North America, 1783–1810* (Columbia: University of South Carolina Press, 2005).
Meleney, John C., *The Public Life of Aedanus Burke: Revolutionary Republican in Post-Revolutionary South Carolina* (Columbia, SC: University of South Carolina Press, 1989).
Melish, Joane Pope, *Disowning Slavery: Gradual Emancipation and "Race" in New England, 1780–1860* (Ithaca, NY: Cornell University Press, 1998).
Menard, Russell R., 'Slave Demography in the Lowcountry, 1670–1740: From Frontier Society to Plantation Regime', *South Carolina Historical Magazine*, 101/3 (1995): 190–213.
Menschel, David, 'Abolition without Deliverance: The Law of Connecticut Slavery 1784–1848', *The Yale Law Journal*, 111/1 (2001): 183–222.
Mercantini, Jonathan, *Who Shall Rule at Home? The Evolution of South Carolina Political Culture, 1748–1776* (Columbia: University of South Carolina Press, 2007).
'"Most Contemptible in the Union": South Carolina, Slavery, and the Constitution' in David T. Gleeson and Simon Lewis, eds., *Ambiguous Anniversary: The Bicentennial of the International Slave Trade Bans* (Columbia: University of South Carolina Press, 2012): 35–51.
Minardi, Margot, *Making Slavery History: Abolitionism and the Politics of Memory in Massachusetts* (New York: Oxford University Press, 2010).
Minchinton, W. E., 'The Seaborne Slave Trade of North Carolina', *North Carolina Historical Review*, 71/1 (1994): 1–61.
Minkema, Kenneth P., 'Jonathan Edwards on Slavery and the Slave Trade', *William and Mary Quarterly*, 3rd series, 54/4 (1997): 823–34.
Moore, George H., *Notes on the History of Slavery in Massachusetts* (New York: Appleton and Co., 1866).
Morgan, Kenneth, 'Slavery and the Debate over the Ratification of the U.S. Constitution', *Slavery and Abolition*, 22/3 (2001): 40–65.
  'Proscription by Degrees: The Ending of the African Slave Trade to the United States' in David T. Gleeson and Simon Lewis, eds., *Ambiguous Anniversary: The Bicentennial of the International Slave Trade Bans* (Columbia: University of South Carolina Press, 2012): 1–34.
  A Short History of Transatlantic Slavery (London: I. B. Tauris, 2016).
Morgan, Philip D., 'Black Society in the Lowcountry, 1760–1810' in Ira Berlin and Ronald Hoffman, eds., *Slavery and Freedom in the Age of the American Revolution* (Charlottesville: University Press of Virginia for the United States Capitol Historical Society, 1983).
  Slave Counterpoint: Black Culture in the Eighteenth-Century Chesapeake and Lowcountry (Chapel Hill: University of North Carolina Press, 1998).
  'Ending the Slave Trade: A Caribbean and Atlantic Context' in Derek R. Peterson, ed., *Abolition and Imperialism in Britain, Africa, and the Atlantic* (Athens: University of Ohio Press, 2010): 101–28.

Nadelhaft, Jerome J., 'South Carolina and the Slave Trade, 1783-1787' (University of Wisconsin MA thesis, 1961).
The Disorders of War: The Revolution in South Carolina (Orono: University of Maine at Orono Press, 1981).
Nash, Gary B., *The Urban Crucible: Social Change, Political Consciousness, and the Origins of the American Revolution* (Cambridge, MA: Harvard University Press, 1979).
Race and Revolution (Madison, WI: Madison House, 1990).
The Forgotten Fifth: African Americans in the Age of Revolution (Cambridge, MA: Harvard University Press, 2006).
'Franklin and Slavery', *Proceedings of the American Philosophical Society*, 150/4 (2006): 618-35.
'Warner Mifflin (1745-98): The Remarkable Life of an Unflinching Abolitionist' in Maurice Jackson and Susan Kozel, eds., *Quakers and Their Allies in the Abolitionist Cause, 1754-1808* (Abingdon: Routledge, 2015).
Warner Mifflin: Unflinching Quaker Abolitionist (Philadelphia: University of Pennsylvania Press, 2017).
Nash, Gary B. and Jean R. Soderlund, *Freedom by Degrees: Emancipation in Pennsylvania and Its Aftermath* (New York: Oxford University Press, 1991).
Needles, Edward, *A Historical Memoir of the Pennsylvania Society for Promoting the Abolition of Slavery* (Philadelphia: Merrihew and Thompson, 1848).
Nevins, Allan, *The American States during and after the Revolution* (New York: The Macmillan Company, 1924).
Newman, Richard S., 'Prelude to the Gag Rule: Southern Reaction to Antislavery Petitions in the First Federal Congress', *Journal of the Early Republic*, 16/4 (1996): 571-99.
The Transformation of American Abolitionism: Fighting Slavery in the Early Republic (Chapel Hill: University of North Carolina Press, 2002).
Newman, Richard, 'The Pennsylvania Abolition Society and the Struggle for Racial Justice' in Richard Newman and James Mueller, eds., *Antislavery and Abolition in Philadelphia: Emancipation and the Long Struggle for Racial Justice in the City of Brotherly Love* (Baton Rouge: Louisiana State University Press, 2011).
Oakes, James, '"The Compromising Expedient": Justifying a Proslavery Constitution', *Cardozo Law Review*, 17/6 (1996): 2023-56.
'Conflict v. Racial Consensus in the History of Antislavery Politics' in John Craig Hammond and Matthew Mason, eds., *Contesting Slavery: The Politics of Bondage and Freedom in the New American Nation* (Charlottesville: University of Virginia Press, 2011).
Obadele-Starks, Ernest, *Freebooters and Smugglers: The Foreign Slave Trade to the United States after 1808* (Fayetteville: University of Arkansas Press, 2007).
Ohline, Howard A., 'Politics and Slavery: The Issue of Slavery in National Politics, 1787-1815' (University of Missouri, Columbia, PhD dissertation, 1969).
'Slavery, Economics, and Congressional Politics, 1790', *Journal of Southern History*, 46/3 (1980): 335-60.

Oldfield, J. R., *Transatlantic Abolitionism in the Age of Revolution: An International History of Anti-slavery, c.1787–1820* (Cambridge: Cambridge University Press, 2013).

O'Malley, Gregory E., *Final Passages: The Inter-Colonial Slave Trade of British America, 1619–1807* (Chapel Hill: University of North Carolina Press, 2014).

'Slavery's Converging Ground: Charleston's Slave Trade as the Black Heart of the Lowcountry', *William and Mary Quarterly*, 3rd series, 74/2 (2017): 271–302.

Onuf, Peter S., 'Washington and Jefferson: American Nationhood and the Problem of Slavery' in Dustin Gish and Andrew Bibby, eds., *Rival Visions: How Jefferson and His Contemporaries Defined the Early American Republic* (Charlottesville: University of Virginia Press, 2020).

Oshatz, Molly, *Slavery and Sin: The Fight against Slavery and the Rise of Liberal Protestantism* (New York: Oxford University Press, 2011).

Palmer, Colin A., Maggie Steber and Jerry Pinkney, 'The Cruelest Commerce: African Slave Trade', *National Geographic*, 182/3 (1992): 62–91.

Parkinson, Robert G., '"Manifest Signs of Passion": The First Federal Congress, Antislavery, and Legacies of the Revolutionary War' in John Craig Hammond and Matthew Mason, eds., *Contesting Slavery: The Politics of Bondage and Freedom in the New American Nation* (Charlottesville: University of Virginia Press, 2011).

The Common Cause: Creating Race and Nation in the American Revolution (Chapel Hill: University of North Carolina Press, 2019).

Thirteen Clocks: How Race united the Colonies and made the Declaration of Independence (Chapel Hill: University of North Carolina Press, 2021).

Pasley, Jeffrey L., 'Private Access and Public Power: Gentility and Lobbying in the Early Congress' in Kenneth R. Bowling and Donald R. Kennon, eds., *The House and Senate in the 1790s: Petitioning, Lobbying, and Institutional Development* (Athens: Ohio University Press, 2002).

'Democracy, Gentility, and Lobbying in the Early U.S. Congress' in Julian E. Zelizer, ed., *The American Congress: The Building of Democracy* (Boston: Houghton Mifflin Company, 2004).

Peterson, Mark A., 'The Selling of Joseph: Bostonians, Antislavery, and the Protestant Internmational, 1689–1733', *Massachusetts Historical Review*, 4 (2002): 1–22.

Phillips, Ulrich B., 'The South Carolina Federalists, I', *The American Historical Review*, 14/3 (1909): 529–43.

American Negro Slavery: A Study of the Supply, Employment and Control of Negro Labor as Determined by the Plantation Regime (New York: Appleton and Co., 1918).

Plank, Geoffrey, *John Woolman's Path to the Peaceable Kingdom* (Philadelphia: University of Pennsylvania Press, 2012).

Platt, Virginia Bever, '"And Don't Forget the Guinea Voyage: The Slave Trade of Aaron Lopez of Newport', *William and Mary Quarterly*, 3rd series, XXXII (1975); 601–18.

Polgar, Paul J., *Standard-Bearers of Equality: America's First Abolition Movement* (Chapel Hill: University of North Carolina Press, 2019).

Ragsdale, Bruce A., *A Planters' Republic: The Search for Economic Independence in Revolutionary Virginia* (Madison: University of Wisconsin Press, 1996).
  Washington at the Plow: The Founding Farmer and the Question of Slavery (Cambridge, MA: The Belknap Press of Harvard University Press, 2021).
Rakove, Jack N., *Original Meanings: Politics and Ideas in the Making of the Constitution* (New York: Knopf, 1996).
  'The Articles of Confederation, 1775–1783' in Jack P. Greene and J. R. Pole, eds., *A Companion to the American Revolution* (Oxford: Blackwell, 2000): 281–6.
Randazzo, Jennifer, 'A Convention of Delegates from the Abolition Societies' in James G. Basker, ed., *Early American Abolitionists: A Collection of Antislavery Writings 1760–1820* (New York: The Gilder Lehrman Institute of American History, 2005).
Rappleye, Charles, *Sons of Providence: The Brown Brothers, the Slave Trade, and the American Revolution* (New York: Simon & Schuster, 2006).
Rawley, James A., with Stephen D. Behrendt, *The Trans-Atlantic Slave Trade*, revised edition (Lincoln: University of Nebraska Press, 2005).
Rediker, Marcus, *The Fearless Benjamin Lay: the Quaker Dwarf who became the first Revolutionary Abolitionist* (Boston: Beacon Press, 2017).
Reilly, James Francis, 'Moses Brown and the Rhode Island Anti-Slavery Movement' (Brown University MA thesis, 1951).
Richardson, David, 'The British Slave Trade to Colonial South Carolina', *Slavery and Abolition*, 12/3 (1991): 125–72.
  'Slavery, Trade, and Economic Growth in Eighteenth-Century New England' in Barbara L. Solow, ed., *Slavery and the Rise of the Atlantic System* (Cambridge: Cambridge University Press, 1991).
Riddell, William Renwick, 'Pre-revolutionary Pennsylvania and the Slave Trade', *Pennsylvania Magazine of History and Biography*, 52/1 (1928): 1–28.
Riley, Padraig, 'Slavery and the Problem of Democracy in Jeffersonian America' in John Craig Hammond and Matthew Mason, eds., *Contesting Slavery: The Politics of Bondage and Freedom in the New American Nation* (Charlottesville: University of Virginia Press, 2011).
  Slavery and the Democratic Conscience: Political Life in Jeffersonian America (Philadelphia: University of Pennsylvania Press, 2016).
Roberts, Justin, 'The Development of Slavery in the British Americas' in Ignacio Gallup Diaz, ed., *The World of Colonial America: An Atlantic Handbook* (New York, 2017).
Robinson, Donald L. *Slavery in the Structure of American Politics, 1765–1820* (New York: Harcourt Brace Jovanovich, 1971).
Robinson, Stewart M., *Political Thought of the Colonial Clergy. Words of the Declaration of Independence Foreseen in the Writings of Clergymen prior to July 1776* (n.p., 1956).
Rogers, George C., Jr, *Evolution of a Federalist: William Loughton Smith of Charleston (1758–1812)* (Columbia: University of South Carolina Press, 1962).
Rothman, Adam, 'The Domestication of the Slave Trade in the United States' in Walter Johnson, ed., *The Chattel Principle: Internal Slave Trades in the Americas* (New Haven, CT: Yale University Press, 2004).

Slave Country: American Expansion and the Origins of the Deep South (Cambridge, MA: Harvard University Press, 2005).

Rugemer, Edward B., *Slave Law and the Politics of Resistance in the Early Atlantic World* (Cambridge, MA: Harvard University Press, 2018).

Sassi, Jonathan D., 'Africans in the Quaker Image: Anthony Benezet, African Travel Narratives, and Revolutionary-Era Anti-Slavery', *Journal of Early Modern History*, 10/1–2 (2006): 95–130.

'With a Little Help from the Friends: The Quaker and Tactical Contexts of Anthony Benezet's Abolitionist Publishing', *Pennsylvania Magazine of History and Biography*, 135/1 (2011): 33–71.

'Anthony Benezet as Intermediary between the Transatlantic and Provincial: New Jersey's Anti-slavery Campaign on the Eve of the American Revolution' in Marie-Jeanne Rossignol and Bertram Van Ruymbeke, eds., *The Atlantic World of Anthony Benezet (1713–1784): From French Reformation to North American Quaker Antislavery Activism* (Leiden: Brill, 2017).

Sawula, Christopher P., '"The Hidden Springs of Prejudice and Oppression": Slavery and Abolitionism in Connecticut' (Boston College BA thesis, 2008).

Scanlon, James E., 'A Sudden Conceit: Jefferson and the Louisiana Bill of 1804', *Louisiana History*, 9/2 (1968): 139–62.

Scarborough, Ruth, *The Opposition to Slavery in Georgia prior to 1860* (Nashville, TN: George Peabody College for Teachers, 1933).

Schaffer, Arthur H., *To be an American: David Ramsay and the Making of the American Consciousness* (Columbia: University of South Carolina Press, 1991).

Schermerhorn, Calvin, 'Capitalism's Captives: The Maritime United States Slave Trade, 1807–1850', *Journal of Social History*, 47/4 (2014): 897–921.

'The Coastwise Slave Trade and a Mercantile Community of Interest' in Sven Beckert and Seth Rockman, eds., *Slavery's Capitalism: A New History of American Economic Development* (Philadelphia: University of Pennsylvania Press, 2016): 209–23.

Schoen, Brian, 'Positive Goods and Necessary Evils: Commerce, Security, and Slavery in the Lower South, 1787–1837' in John Craig Hammond and Matthew Mason, eds., *Contesting Slavery: The Politics of Bondage and Freedom in the new American Nation* (Charlottesville: University of Virginia Press, 2011).

Schultz, Stanley K., 'The Making of a Reformer: The Reverend Samuel Hopkins as an Eighteenth-Century Abolitionist', *Proceedings of the American Philosophical Society*, 115/5 (1971): 150–75.

Seed, Geoffrey, *James Wilson* (Millwood, NY: KYO Press, 1978).

Selby, John E., *The Revolution in Virginia, 1775–1783* (Charlottesville: University of Virginia Press, 2007).

Shugerman, Jed Handelsman, 'The Louisiana Purchase and South Carolina's Reopening of the Slave Trade in 1803', *Journal of the Early Republic*, 22 (2002): 263–90.

Sidbury, James, 'Thomas Jefferson in Gabriel's Virginia' in James Horn, Jan Ellen Lewis, and Peter S. Onuf, eds., *The Revolution of 1800: Democracy, Race, and the New Republic* (Charlottesville: University of Virginia Press, 2002).

Becoming African in America: Race and Nation in the Early Black Atlantic (New York: Oxford University Press, 2007).

Sinha, Manisha, *The Slave's Cause: A History of Abolition* (New Haven, CT: Yale University Press, 2016).
Slaughter, Thomas P., *The Beautiful Soul of John Woolman, Apostle of Abolition* (New York: Hill and Wang, 2008).
Soderlund, Jean R., *Quakers and Slavery: A Divided Spirit* (Princeton: Princeton University Press, 1985).
Spalding, Phinizy, 'James Oglethorpe's Quest for an American Zion' in Harvey H. Jackson and Phinizy Spalding, eds., *Forty Years of Diversity: Essays on Colonial Georgia* (Athens: University of Georgia Press, 1984).
Sparks, Randy J., 'Blind Justice: The United States's Failure to Curb the Illegal Slave Trade', *Law and History Review*, 35/1 (2017): 53–79.
Spear, Jennifer, 'Liberty, Slavery, and the Louisiana Purchase of 1803: The Incorporation of the Territory of Orleans' in *Oxford Research Encyclopedia of American History* (New York: Oxford University Press, 2018). https://oxfordre.com/americanhistory/
Stamatov, Peter, *The Origins of Global Humanitarianism: Religion, Empires, and Advocacy* (New York: Cambridge University Press, 2013).
Staples, William Read, *Annals of the Town of Providence: From its First Settlement to the Organization of City Government in June, 1832* (Providence, RI: Knowles & Goff, 1843).
Starr, Rebecca K., *A School for Politics: Commercial Lobbying and Political Culture in Early South Carolina* (Baltimore: The Johns Hopkins University Press, 1998).
Steiner, Bernard C., *History of Slavery in Connecticut* (Baltimore: The Johns Hopkins University Press, 1893).
Sutch, Richard, 'The Breeding of Slaves for Sale and the Westward Expansion of Slavery, 1850–1860' in Stanley L. Engerman and Eugene D. Genovese, eds., *Race and Slavery in the Westward Hemisphere: Quantitative Studies* (Princeton, NJ: Princeton University Press, 1975).
Suttell, Elizabeth I., 'The British Slave Trade to Virginia, 1698–1728' (College of William and Mary MA dissertation, 1965). https://scholarworks.wm.edu
Sweig, Donald M., 'The Importation of African Slaves to the Potomac River, 1732–1772', *William and Mary Quarterly*, 3rd series, 42/4 (1985): 507–24.
Sword, Kirsten, 'Remembering Dinah Nevil: Strategic Deceptions in Eighteenth-Century Antislavery', *Journal of American History*, 97/2 (2010): 315–43.
Thompson, C. Bradley, *John Adams and the Spirit of Liberty* (Lawrence: University Press of Kansas, 1998).
Thompson, Mack, *Moses Brown: Reluctant Reformer* (Chapel Hill: University of North Carolina Press, 1962).
Tise, Larry E., *Proslavery: A History of the Defense of Slavery in America, 1701–1740* (Athens: University of Georgia Press, 1987).
Tomek, Beverly C., *Slavery and Abolition in Pennsylvania* (Philadelphia: Temple University Press, 2021).
Trenholme, Louise Ivory, *The Ratification of the Federal Constitution in North Carolina* (New York: Columbia University Press, 1932).
Turner, Edward Raymond, 'The First Abolition Society in the United States', *Pennsylvania Magazine of History and Biography*, 36/1 (1912): 92–109.

Ulmer, Shirley Sidney, 'The South Carolina Delegates to the Constitutional Convention: An Analytical Study' (Duke University PhD dissertation, 1956).
Vipperman, Carl J., *The Rise of Rawlins Lowndes, 1721–1800* (Columbia; University of South Carolina Press, 1978).
Waldstreicher, David, *Runaway America: Benjamin Franklin, Slavery, and the American Revolution* (New York: Hill and Wang, 2004).
  Slavery's Constitution: From Revolution to Ratification (New York: Hill and Wang, 2009).
Walker, Joseph B., *A History of the New Hampshire Convention for the Investigation, Discussion, and Decision of the Federal Constitution: And of the Old North Meeting House of Concord, in which It Was Ratified by the Ninth State, and thus Rendered Operative, at One O'clock p.m., on Saturday, the 21st Day of June 1788* (Boston: Cupples & Hurd, 1888).
Wallenstein, Peter, 'Flawed keepers of the Flame', *Virginia Magazine of History and Biography*, 102/2 (1994): 229–60.
Walsh, Lorena S., 'The Chesapeake Slave Trade: Regional Patterns, African Origins, and Some Implications', *William and Mary Quarterly*, 58/1 (2001): 139–70.
Washburn, Emory, *Historical Sketches of the Town of Leicester, Massachusetts, during the First Century from Its Settlement* (Boston: John Wilson and Son, 1860).
Wax, Darold D., 'Quaker Merchants and the Slave Trade in Colonial Pennsylvania', *Pennsylvania Magazine of History and Biography*, 86/2 (1962): 143–59.
  'Negro Imports into Pennsylvania, 1720–1766' *Pennsylvania History*, 32/3 (1965): 254–87.
  'Negro Import Duties in Colonial Virginia: A Study of British Commercial Policy and Local Public Policy', *Virginia Magazine of History and Biography*, 79/1 (1971): 29–44.
  'Negro Import Duties in Colonial Pennsylvania', *Pennsylvania Magazine of History and Biography*, 97/1 (1973): 22–44.
  'Reform and Revolution: The Movement against Slavery and the Slave Trade in Revolutionary Pennsylvania', *Western Pennsylvania Historical Magazine*, LVII (1974): 416–29.
  'Black Immigrants: The Slave Trade in Colonial Maryland', *Maryland Historical Magazine*, 73/1 (1978): 30–45.
  'Africans on the Delaware: The Pennsylvania Slave Trade, 1759–1765', *Pennsylvania History*, 50/1 (1983): 38–49.
  '"New Negroes are always in Demand": The Slave Trade in Eighteenth-Century Georgia', *Georgia Historical Quarterly*, LXVIII/2 (1984): 193–220.
Weir, Robert M., *Colonial South Carolina: A History* (Columbia: University of South Carolina Press, 1997).
Westbury, Susan, 'Slaves of Colonial Virginia: Where They Came from', *William and Mary Quarterly*, 42/2 (1985): 228–37.
Westbury, Susan Alice, 'Colonial Virginia and the Atlantic Slave Trade' (University of Illinois, Urbana-Champaign, PhD dissertation, 1981).
Whichard, Willis P., *Justice James Iredell* (Durham, NC: Carolina Academic Press, 2000).

White, Shane, *Somewhat More Independent: The End of Slavery in New York City, 1770–1810* (Athens: University of Georgia Press, 1991).

Whitfield, Harvey Amani, *The Problem of Slavery in Early Vermont, 1777–1810* (Barre: Vermont Historical Society, 2014).

Wiecek, William M., 'The Witch at the Christening: Slavery and the Constitution's Origins' in Leonard W. Levy and Dennis J. Mahoney, eds., *The Framing and Ratification of the Constitution* (New York: Macmillan, 1987).

Wilentz, Sean, *No Property in Man: Slavery and Antislavery at the Nation's Founding* (Cambridge, MA: Harvard University Press, 2018).

Wolf, Eva Sheppard, *Race and Liberty in the New Nation: Emancipation in Virginia from the Revolution to Nat Turner's Rebellion* (Baton Rouge: Louisiana State University Press, 2006).

Wolfe, John Harold, *Jeffersonian Democracy in South Carolina*, James Sprunt Studies in History and Political Science, 24 (Chapel Hill: University of North Carolina Press, 1940).

Wood, Betty, *Slavery in Colonial Georgia, 1730–1775* (Athens: University of Georgia Press, 1985).

'James Oglethorpe, Race, and Slavery: A Reassessment' in Phinizy Spalding and Harvey H. Jackson, eds., *Oglethorpe in Perspective: Georgia's Founder after Two Hundred Years* (Tuscaloosa: University of Alabama Press, 1989).

Wood, Gordon S., *Power and Liberty: Constitutionalism in the American Revolution* (New York: Oxford University Press, 2021).

Wood, Nicholas P., 'John Randolph of Roanoke and the Politics of Slavery in the Early Republic', *Virginia Magazine of History and Biography*, 120/2 (2012): 107–43.

'Considerations of Humanity and Expediency: The Slave Trades and African Colonization in the Early National Antislavery Movement' (University of Virginia PhD dissertation, 2013).

'Abolitionists, Congress, and the Atlantic Slave Trade: Before and after Ratification' in Douglas Bradburn and Christopher R. Pearl, eds., *From Independence to the U.S. Constitution: Reconsidering the Critical Period of American History* (Charlottesville: University of Virginia Press, 2022).

Wood, Nicholas P. and Jean R. Soderlund, '"To Friends and All Whom It May Concerne": William Southeby's Rediscovered 1696 Antislavery Protest', *Pennsylvania Magazine of History and Biography*, 141/2 (2017): 177–98.

Yarbrough, Jean, 'New Hampshire Puritanism and the Moral Foundations of America' in Michael Allen Gillespie and Michael Lienesch, eds., *Ratifying the Constitution* (Lawrence: University Press of Kansas, 1989).

Zahniser, Marvin R., *Charles Cotesworth Pinckney: Founding Father* (Chapel Hill: University of North Carolina Press, 1967).

Zilversmit, Arthur, *The First Emancipation: The Abolition of Slavery in the North* (Chicago: University of Chicago Press, 1967).

Index

A Caution and Warning to Great Britain and her Colonies, in a Short Representation of the Calamitous State of the Enslaved Negroes in the British Dominions..., 54
A Dialogue concerning the Slavery of Africans, 57
A Short Account of Africa and *A Caution and Warning to Great Britain*, 20
A Summary View of the Rights of British America, 61
Adams, John, 17, 58, 63, 69, 105, 115, 144, 155, 167, 177, 179, 181, 221
Africa Squadron, 237
Alexander, Ann, 197
Allen, John, 55
Alston, Joseph, 212
Alston, Jr, Willis, 219
American Convention of Abolition Societies, 172–4, 187
American Museum, 139
An Address to the Inhabitants of the British Settlements in America, upon Slave-Keeping, 31
An Epistle of Caution and Advice concerning the Buying and Keeping of Slaves, 21
An Oration on the Beauties of Liberty, 55
Annals of Congress, 137, 160
Annapolis, 66
antifederalists, 118, 120, 123
antislavery, 15, 19, 21–3, 28, 31, 38, 40, 53, 57, 65, 68, 74–5, 93–4, 108, 114, 136, 138, 148, 156, 168–9, 172, 205, 223–4, 229, 233
Appleby, Joyce, 229
Articles of Confederation, 64, 74, 89, 92, 97, 116
Atherton, Joshua, 117
Aurora General Advertiser, 196, 198

Backus, Isaac, 129
Baldwin, Abraham, 149, 151–2
Baldwin, Ebenezer, 16
Baltimore, 232
Bard, David, 201, 203, 205
Barnwell, John, 127
Bayard, James A., 180
Bee, Thomas, 80
Belknap, Jeremy, 90, 113, 164, 167
Benezet, Anthony, 16, 19–20, 22, 31–2, 40, 52–3, 55–6, 58–9, 65–6, 70, 73, 75, 90
Biddle, Owen, 141
Bight of Benin, 6
Bight of Biafra, 6
Bill of Rights, 142
Blackburn, Robin, 201
Board of Trade, 29, 36, 39–40, 49
Boston, 4, 24
Boston Gazette, 25
Boudinot, Elias, 66, 158, 160, 163
Bradley, Stephen R., 207, 216
Branagan, Thomas, 195, 197
Brazil, 236–7
Breckenridge, John, 206
Brion Davis, David, 108

Brissot de Warville, J. P., 56, 104–5, 150
Brooks, 139
Brown, Carl Harrison, 194
Brown, Christopher L., 60, 89
Brown, John, 60, 85, 178
Brown, Moses, 26, 28, 40, 53, 55, 59, 71–2, 85–7, 90, 103–4, 106, 109, 113–14, 120, 123, 127, 141, 146, 175, 177, 179
Bryan, George, 70
Burke, Aedanus, 149, 151
Butler, Pierce, 97, 157, 182
Byrd, William, 7

Carey, Matthew, 139
Charleston, xi, 4–5, 8, 11, 44–5, 76, 78–9, 81–4, 90, 116, 125, 151, 159, 184, 186, 189, 191, 194, 197–201, 203, 209, 212, 214–16, 225, 228
Charleston Courier, 200, 214–16
Chase, Jeremiah T., 66
Chesapeake, 4, 6–7, 14
Chester Monthly Meeting, 18
Claiborne, William C. C., 202, 209–10
Clark, Daniel, 210
Clarkson, Thomas, 53, 88, 96
Clay, Joseph, 81
Clinton, George, 215
Clymer, George, 163
Coercive Acts, 11, 50
Colman, Benjamin, 56
Confederation Congress, 74, 89, 143
Congress, 10, 12–13, 42, 45, 47, 50, 52, 56–63, 65–6, 73–4, 77, 80, 82, 86–8, 92, 95–6, 98, 100, 103–8, 110–12, 115, 117, 119–20, 123, 127–30, 134, 137, 140, 142–6, 148, 150–2, 154, 156–9, 162–4, 166–9, 171–2, 175–6, 178, 180, 184–6, 190–3, 195–9, 201–5, 208–11, 213–15, 217–25, 228, 230–1, 233
Connecticut, 16, 23, 27, 48, 55, 71–2, 97, 100, 107, 115, 125, 133, 136, 139, 158, 169–70, 177, 180, 206–7, 220, 222
  gradual abolition law, 1784, 71
Connecticut Journal, 16
Constitutional Convention, 11–12, 51–2, 67–8, 70, 76, 83, 86, 88, 90, 92–8, 100, 102, 104, 106, 109, 111–14, 120, 122, 124, 126–7, 131, 133, 135, 140, 204, 216, 228

Continental Congress, 11, 15, 41, 49, 51, 57–9, 61, 64, 66–7, 71, 75, 123
Cooper, David, 73, 87
Coxe, Tench, 96, 113, 132, 144, 165
Cuba, 9, 140, 177, 233, 236
Curtin, Philip D., 234
Curtis, George Ticknor, 100, 229

Daily Advertiser, 148
Dalton, Tristram, 129, 139
Dana, Francis, 105
Danbury, 27
Danish West Indies, 9, 140
Daws, Thomas, 129
Dayton, Jonathan, 207
Declaration of Independence, 63, 97
Delaware, 5–6, 18, 23, 65, 67, 90, 102, 107, 115, 133, 136, 138, 142, 180, 195
  law on the slave trade, 1789, 133
  state constitution of 1776, 67
Denmark, 1
Dickinson, John, 102, 124
Drayton, John, 183
Drescher, Seymour, 108
Drinker, Henry, 143
Drinker, John, 87
Du Bois, W. E. B., 43, 52, 234
Duane, James, 87
Dutch Americas, 9
Dwight, Theodore, 220

Early, Peter, 221
East Florida, 234
Edwards, Jr, Jonathan, 16, 27
Eltis, David, 234
Emlen, Jr, Samuel, 150
Emlen, Samuel, 143
Essay on the Commerce and Slavery of the Human Species, 88
Exeter Freemen's Oracle, 117

Fairfax County Resolves, 41
Finkelman, Paul, 100, 110
First Federal Congress, 12, 28, 57, 74, 132, 137, 140–4, 146, 148, 150–1, 156–9, 161–2, 168, 186
Fitzsimons, Thomas, 146, 163
Florida, 151, 185, 212, 234
Ford, Lacy K., 194, 223
Franklin, Benjamin, 40, 53, 66, 74, 88, 90, 92, 106, 144, 153, 156–7

Index

Freehling, William W., 229
Frost, J. William, 20

Gage, Thomas, 26
George III, 40, 62
Georgia, 4–5, 8, 45, 47, 58–9, 63, 67–8, 77,
    80–1, 88, 95, 98–101, 104, 107, 111,
    121, 127–8, 130, 134, 137, 140–1,
    147, 149, 151, 153–4, 156, 158, 165,
    174, 180, 185, 191, 194, 206, 209,
    218, 221, 228, 234
  legislature of, 82
  state constitution of 1777, 67
Germantown, 18
Gerry, Elbridge, 150
Gillon, Alexander, 84
Gold Coast, 9
Gorham, Nathaniel, 87
Gregg, Andrew, 204

Hamilton, Alexander, 72, 167
Hampshire Gazette, 118
Hardy, Josiah, 29
Hart, Levi, 27, 55
Hazard, Ebenezer, 164
Henry, Patrick, 41
Hepburn, John, 17
Hilhouse, James, 207
Hooker, Edward, 213
Hopkins, Samuel, 16, 56–8, 86, 112, 123
Hopkins, Samuel, 57
Hopkins, Stephen, 60
Howell, David, 66
Hunt, James Green, 182
Hutchinson, Thomas, 25

Independent Gazetteer, 122
Iredell, James, 103, 108, 121, 127
Izard, Ralph, 79, 81, 157, 182, 213

Jackson, 151
Jackson, James, 81, 141, 149, 185, 206–7
Jay, John, 72, 110
Jean Soderlund, 17
Jefferson, Thomas, 10, 13, 39–40, 52, 61–3,
    66, 74, 84, 92, 102, 104, 141, 192,
    211, 216, 218, 229, 232
Jones, Absalom, 231
Jordan, Winthrop D., 200

Keith, George, 17
Kelley, Sean M., 235

Kent, James, 112
Kentucke Gazette, 121
Kentucky, 206, 208
Kerr, Lewis, 208–9

Langdon, John, 102, 205
Laurens, Henry, 76, 83
Laurens, Jr, Henry, 183
Lawrence, George, 231
Lawrence, John, 149
Lay, Benjamin, 18
Lee, Arthur, 38
Lee, Richard Henry, 38, 58, 66
Leicester, 25
Letters from a Farmer in Pennsylvania,
    124
Liancourt, Duke de la Rochefoucault, 183
Lightfoot, Thomas, 87
Lindley, Jacob, 87
Livingston, William, 73
Logan, George, 229
Loughton Smith, William, 111, 133, 148,
    151, 153–4, 158–60, 163
Louisiana, 12–13, 115, 185, 190–4, 199,
    201–2, 205–7, 209–13, 225, 228
Louisiana Purchase, 12–13, 115, 185, 190,
    193, 206, 208, 212, 225
Louisiana Territory, 194, 201–2, 205–9,
    225, 228
Lowndes, Rawlins, 124–6
Lowndes, Thomas, 202–3, 205
Lowndes, William, 191

Macon, Nathaniel, 169
Madison, James, 12, 62, 82, 93, 99, 104,
    111, 128–9, 134, 140–1, 144, 147, 154,
    161–2, 165, 168, 187, 209–10, 233
Manigault, Gabriel, 164, 182
Marques, Leonardo, 3
Martin, Luther, 103, 122
Maryland, 3, 5–7, 11, 16, 20, 33, 37, 65–6,
    71, 76, 88, 96, 98–9, 101, 103, 107,
    109, 115, 122, 124–5, 136–7, 142,
    153, 155, 158, 169–71, 175, 180, 196,
    204, 207, 209, 214
Mason, George, 39, 41, 47, 102, 107,
    124–5, 128
Massachusetts, 11, 16–17, 24–6, 29, 48–9,
    52, 55–6, 69–70, 72, 88, 90, 105, 107,
    113–18, 121, 124–5, 128–9, 131–2,
    139, 150, 156, 158, 164, 177, 179,
    196, 204, 214, 216, 219, 228

Massachusetts Centinel, 117, 129, 164
Massachusetts Constitution, 90
Mather, Cotton, 48
McHenry, James, 99
Medford, 25
Meeting for Sufferings, 53, 65, 86
Meleney, John C., 145
Mifflin, Warner, 19, 66, 74, 90, 139, 142–3, 145, 150, 154, 157, 167–9, 171, 176, 186
Miles, James, 212
Mississippi Territory, 184
Monroe, James, 177, 198, 230
Moore, Thomas, 205
Morris, Gouverneur, 101
Morris, Robert, 107
Moultrie, William, 79

Nash, Gary B., 100, 145
Natchez, 199
National Intelligencer, 195
Neal, James, 116
Nesbit, Richard, 32
New England, 6, 9, 14, 16–17, 23, 25–7, 48, 50, 52, 55, 60, 69, 90, 106, 108, 116, 118, 121, 123, 129, 131, 133, 139, 143, 173, 175, 177, 221
New Hampshire, 23, 67, 70–1, 90, 102, 115, 117–19, 122, 169, 196, 204, 214
  state constitution of 1783, 70
New Jersey, 17–18, 28–9, 32, 65, 73, 107, 115, 125, 136, 142, 158, 203, 206–7, 210, 227
  law banning slave trade, 1786, 73
New Orleans, 4, 191, 199, 208, 212, 225, 233, 235
New York, xv, 2–6, 16–17, 19, 21, 23, 26, 29–32, 36, 41–3, 54, 56, 59–64, 66, 68, 70–4, 77, 81, 83–4, 87–8, 92–4, 97, 103, 113, 115–16, 119, 122, 124, 128, 130–3, 135, 140, 142–3, 145, 148, 150, 153, 156, 162, 165, 169–70, 172–3, 177, 181, 191, 201, 204, 221, 223, 229, 231, 233, 236
  ban on slave imports, 1785, 72
New York Journal, 122
New York Morning Post, 113
Newbury, 56
Newport, 4, 19, 26, 56, 178
non-importation, 23, 26, 39, 47, 50, 58, 61
non-importation agreements, 42, 46

North Carolina, 8, 23, 37, 42–3, 52, 57, 80, 82, 88, 95, 99–100, 103, 107, 111, 115, 127, 169, 180, 184, 197, 201, 204, 219, 232

Observations on the Inslaving, importing and purchasing of Negroes..., 54–5
Oglethorpe, James, 46, 80
Ohline, Howard A., 173, 175
Oldfield, J. R., 155, 217
Orleans Territory, 185, 191

Page, John, 150, 158
Parker, Josiah, 141, 146, 201
Parkinson, Robert G., 57
Parrish, John, 75, 87, 165
Parrish, Jr, John, 150
Parsons, Theophilus, 117
Pemberton, James, 53, 65, 75–6, 83, 86–8, 90, 104, 109, 114–15, 120, 136, 139, 143–4, 146, 148, 151, 155, 157, 161–2, 168, 170, 177–8, 186
Pemberton, John, 143, 146, 150, 157
Pendleton, 81
Pendleton, Henry, 80
Penn, John, 67
Pennsylvania, xv, 6–7, 11, 13, 16–20, 29–31, 47, 52, 55, 65, 69–70, 74–5, 85, 87–8, 90, 96, 101, 107, 109, 111–12, 114–15, 120, 122, 124–5, 127, 129–31, 136, 138, 142–4, 146, 148–9, 151–3, 155–6, 158, 163, 166, 168–72, 174, 177, 185–6, 201, 203–4, 210, 227
  gradual abolition law of 1780, 70
Pennsylvania Abolition Society, 70, 76, 85, 88, 90, 120, 136, 138, 144, 148–9, 151–3, 155, 157, 160, 166, 168, 170, 172, 177–8, 186, 210
Pennsylvania Chronicle, 47
Pennsylvania Gazette, 112, 130
Pennsylvania Society for Promoting the Abolition of Slavery, 121, 132, 169
petitions, 20, 28, 30–2, 35, 38, 40, 50, 65–6, 71–5, 96, 113, 121, 133, 142–4, 147–53, 155–7, 161–2, 164, 166, 168–9, 173–5, 182, 185, 205, 210
Philadelphia, 6, 18, 31, 86
Philadelphia Gazette, 202
Philadelphia Meeting for Sufferings, 20, 171
Philadelphia Yearly Meeting, 17–18, 21, 66, 73, 75, 87, 171

Phillips, James, 88
Pinckney, Charles, 97, 184, 214
Pinckney, Charles Cotesworth, 79–80, 98, 100–1, 107, 125–6, 152
Pinckney, Thomas, 181
Pitkin, Timothy, 222
planters, 69
Pleasants, Robert, 20, 22, 28–9, 32, 40–1, 49–50, 139, 143, 166, 168, 185
Plumer, William, 205
population, 14
Princeton, 66, 87
Privy Council, 23, 34, 36, 39, 49
Providence, 90
Providence Gazette, 196
Puerto Rico, 9

Quakers, 11, 15, 17–19, 21, 26, 28, 30, 41, 50, 52, 54–6, 65–6, 71, 73, 75, 86, 88–90, 113, 116, 120, 127, 130, 132, 136, 141, 143–4, 146–8, 150–1, 153–5, 157–60, 163–4, 167, 169, 173, 176, 186, 205, 227
Queen Charlotte, 55
Quincy Adams, John, 207

Ramsay, David, 76, 79
Randolph, Edmund, 141
Randolph, John, 197
ratification, 12, 94, 96, 114–16, 119–20, 124, 127–9, 131, 133–4, 136, 140–1, 225, 228
Raynal, Abbé, 55
Rhode Island, xv, 4, 16, 19, 26, 53, 56–7, 60, 66, 70, 85, 88, 90, 92, 103, 107, 112, 114–15, 123, 131–3, 136, 139, 144, 165, 168, 170, 176–80, 197, 204
  law against slave trade, 1784, 71
Richardson, James B., 191
Riley, Padraig, 223
Rio de la Plata, 9, 140
Rowan County, 42
Rush, Benjamin, 31–2, 52–3, 59, 72, 76, 79, 90, 96, 109, 111, 113, 117, 121–2, 125, 129, 147, 165, 173
Rutledge, Edward, 77–8, 81, 83, 183
Rutledge, John, 79, 97, 99–100, 106
Rutledge, Jr, John, 157, 183

Saint-Domingue, 181–2, 185–6, 190, 194, 208
Salem, 25

Sandwich, 25
Savannah, 8, 81
Savery, Jr, William, 87
Scott, Thomas, 158
Senegambia, 9
Seney, Joshua, 158
sermons, 55
Sewall, Samuel, 15
Sharp, Granville, 32, 53, 59, 106
Sherman, Roger, 97, 106, 158
Sierra Leone, 9
Simons, Keating Lewis, 212
Sipkins, Henry, 231
slave trade
  bans on, 58
  and Declaration of Independence, 62–3
  disembarkations, 4, 9, 14
  import duties, 11, 24, 26, 28–40, 43–6
  inhumanity of, 17, 27, 40, 42, 47, 54, 56
  laws on, 24–6, 28, 34, 36, 45
  South Carolina, 8
  Virginia, 7
Sloan, James, 203
Smith, Melancton, 87
Smith, Samuel, 207
Society for Establishing the Abolition of the Slave Trade, 88
Some Considerations on the Keeping of Negroes, 19
South Carolina, xi, xv, 4–7, 9–13, 43–6, 49, 53, 58, 61, 63, 68, 76–84, 88, 90, 95, 97–8, 100–1, 103–4, 106–7, 110–11, 121–2, 124–6, 128, 130–1, 134, 137, 141, 145, 147, 149, 151, 153–4, 156–8, 164–5, 174, 180–3, 185–7, 189–94, 196–8, 200–7, 209, 212–13, 215–16, 218, 221, 223–5, 227–8, 230
  Assembly votes on the slave trade, 83
  ban on slave imports, 1787, 84
  House of Representatives, 82, 193, 199
  law on slave trade, 1788, 85
  Senate, 82, 193–4, 198–9
  slave population, 189
Southard, Henry, 203
Stanton Jr, Joseph, 204
Stanton, Joseph, 197, 205
Stiles, Ezra, 16
Stono rebellion, 8, 49

Index

Tallmadge, Benjamin, 222
Taylor, John, 212
Tennessee, 197, 209
The Case of our Fellow Creatures, the Oppressed Africans, 75
The Charleston Daily Courier, 197
The Democratic Press, 217
The Federalist, 128
The Reigning Abominations, Especially the Slave Trade, 48
The Suppression of the African Slave-Trade to the United States of America, 1638–1870, 2
The United States and the Transatlantic Slave Trade to the Americas, 1776–1867, 3
Thornton, James, 87
Townshend duties, 47
Trans-Atlantic Slave Trade Database, 3
Tucker, Thomas Tudor, 147, 149, 151–2

US Constitution, 10, 12, 74, 92, 94–5, 101, 111, 114, 136, 145, 231
    Article 1, Section 9, 95, 110, 112, 116, 120–1, 128, 130, 133, 146, 149, 154, 215, 220
    Article 5, 134, 168
Upper Guinea, 6

Vermont, 69, 90, 214
Virginia, xii, xv, 4–7, 11, 22, 34–42, 47–8, 50, 52, 58, 60–2, 64–5, 68, 74, 76, 86, 90, 96, 98, 100–1, 104–5, 107, 111, 115, 119, 124–8, 130–1, 136–9, 141–2, 145, 150, 153–5, 169–71, 175, 177, 182, 197, 200, 209, 216–18, 221, 227, 232
    import duties on slaves, 37
    law banning slave trade, 69
    law on slave trade, 1786, 86
Virginia Convention, 41
Virginia Gazette, 39, 48

W. E. B. Du Bois, 2
Walker, Quock, 69
Waln, Nicholas, 143–4
Waln, Richard, 76
Waln, Robert, 130, 185
Ward, Samuel, 60
Washington, George, 41, 62, 93, 119, 140, 167, 175
Wayne, Anthony, 129
Webster-Ashburton Treaty, 236
West Central Africa, 9
Wilberforce, William, 198
Wilentz, Sean, 224
Williams, Jr, Peter, 231
Williamsburg, 41
Williamson, Hugh, 100
Wilmington, 43
Wilson, James, 101, 120, 129
Winchester, Elhanan, 48
Wood, Nicholas P., 161, 176
Woolman, John, 19
Wright, John Izard, 212
Wynkoop, Henry, 163

Zane, Isaac, 87

For EU product safety concerns, contact us at Calle de José Abascal, 56–1°,
28003 Madrid, Spain or eugpsr@cambridge.org.

www.ingramcontent.com/pod-product-compliance
Lightning Source LLC
LaVergne TN
LVHW040613250326
834688LV00035B/544